ALSO BY ROBERT W. MERRY

President McKinley:
Architect of the American Century

Where They Stand:
The American Presidents in the
Eyes of Voters and Historians

A Country of Vast Designs:
James K. Polk, the Mexican War,
and the Conquest of the
American Continent

Sands of Empire:
Missionary Zeal, American Foreign Policy,
and the Hazards of Global Ambition

Taking on the World:
Joseph and Stewart Alsop—
Guardians of the American Century

How

Massachusetts

and

South Carolina

Led the Way

to

Civil War,

1849–1861

DECADE
OF
DISUNION

||||||||||||||||||||||||||||||||||||||||||||||||||||||||||||||||||||||||

ROBERT W. MERRY

SIMON & SCHUSTER

New York   London   Toronto   Sydney   New Delhi

100 YEARS
SIMON &
SCHUSTER

1230 Avenue of the Americas
New York, NY 10020

Copyright © 2024 by Robert W. Merry

All rights reserved, including the right to reproduce this book
or portions thereof in any form whatsoever. For information,
address Simon & Schuster Subsidiary Rights Department,
1230 Avenue of the Americas, New York, NY 10020.

First Simon & Schuster hardcover edition July 2024

SIMON & SCHUSTER and colophon are registered
trademarks of Simon & Schuster, LLC

Simon & Schuster: Celebrating 100 Years of Publishing in 2024

For information about special discounts for bulk purchases,
please contact Simon & Schuster Special Sales at
1-866-506-1949 or business@simonandschuster.com.

The Simon & Schuster Speakers Bureau can bring authors to
your live event. For more information or to book an event,
contact the Simon & Schuster Speakers Bureau at
1-866-248-3049 or visit our website at www.simonspeakers.com.

Interior design by Lewelin Polanco

Manufactured in the United States of America

1 3 5 7 9 10 8 6 4 2

Library of Congress Cataloging-in-Publication Data has been applied for.

ISBN 978-1-9821-7649-5
ISBN 978-1-9821-7651-8 (ebook)

*To the memory of two exemplary
mentor-editors who changed my life:*

Al Silverman and Alice Mayhew

Contents

x ‖ *Contents*

DECADE
OF
DISUNION

Introduction

TWO FUNERALS

||||||||||||||||||||||||||||||||||||||||||||||||||||||||||||||||||||||||||||||||||||||||

THE PASSING OF AN ERA

O
n March 27, 1850, as a late-season cold snap encased Washington, D.C., in a sheaf of snow, Senator John C. Calhoun lay abed in his spacious first-floor room a block east of the Capitol, inside Mrs. Hill's austere-looking but congenial boardinghouse. Wracked by fever and persistent coughing, the famous statesman nevertheless had his attendants prop him up against pillows so he could receive visitors or write letters to family members back home in South Carolina, assuring them that he would soon be fine and that they needn't rush to Washington. But more and more now he found himself slipping into the restless sleep of a dying man.

He knew he was dying. But he wished to spare his wife, Floride, and other faraway relatives of the spectacle of his deterioration. And he felt no need of spiritual assurance. When Senate chaplain C. M. Butler rushed to Mrs. Hill's to offer Calhoun a pathway to God, the senator sent him away. "I won't be told what to think," he declared to those around him. Religion, he added, was a "subject I've thought about all my life." Indeed, the sixty-eight-year-old senator responded matter-of-factly when a friend, North Carolina representative Abraham Venable, asked what he considered the best time and manner of death. "I have but little concern about either," he said. "I desire to die in the discharge of my duty; I have an unshaken reliance upon the providence of God."

By Saturday, March 30, with the snow gone and spring reasserting itself, Calhoun had weakened considerably. Toward evening he managed to sit up for a couple hours and discuss, "with fervent interest," the country's state of affairs. Later he asked his secretary, Joseph Scoville, to read from a manuscript he had been preparing, as he felt too "feeble" to read it himself. But soon he waved Scoville off the project. "Very well," he said. "You can read the rest tomorrow."

After midnight, Calhoun's son John, a physician, became concerned about his father's labored breathing. The elder Calhoun, with his pulse faint and sleep elusive, refused any stimulants and urged John to get some sleep. But within an hour, he called out, "John, come to me. I have no pulse." When the younger man reached the bedside, Calhoun asked him to lock up his watch and the manuscript.

"I have never had such facility in arranging my thoughts," he revealed.

"You are overtaxing your mind with thinking," warned his son.

"I cannot help from thinking about the country."

After a period of silent reflection, the senator mused: "If I had my health and my strength to give one hour in the Senate, I could do more for my country than at any previous time in my life."

It wasn't difficult to foresee what he would do with that hour. For weeks Congress had grappled with the seemingly intractable slavery issue and the specter of a national dissolution over the North-South conflict. Kentucky's redoubtable Henry Clay, known throughout the land as the Great Pacificator for his striking adroitness in shaping disparate viewpoints into compromise agreements, had returned to the Senate from retirement the previous December to seek a replay of his political wizardry. At stake, many believed, was nothing less than survival of the Union.

Calhoun had entered the fray on March 4 with a Senate speech trotting out his well-known views on the subject. But he could barely climb the stairs and shuffle to his Senate seat, even clutching the sturdy arm of his friend James Hamilton. By the time he got there he was so exhausted that he had to ask Senator James Mason of Virginia to read the address. The central problem facing America, the speech argued, was the "long continued agitation of the slave question on the part of the North." Calhoun pressed his oft-expressed view that the United States was not a union of citizens but rather a compact of sovereign states whose rights needed protection from the "encroachment and oppression" of any combination of other states or the federal government. He decried the "consolidationist" impulse within the country bent on concentrating power in Washington at the expense of state sovereignty.

Calhoun knew he was on the losing side of the issue, which had in turn sealed his political fate. In explaining to a friend why he had never attained the presidency, he said, "I did not suit the times, nor the times suit me." It didn't always seem that way. His was a storied career that, early on, many thought would lead inevitably to the White House: elected to the House in 1810 at twenty-nine; leader of the young firebrands agitating for war with Great Britain; eight years as war secretary under James Monroe; elected vice president under both John Quincy Adams and Andrew Jackson (themselves bitter rivals); nearly sixteen years in the U.S. Senate; secretary of state under President John Tyler; widely considered among the two or three greatest orators of his generation.

Then there was the magnetic persona—the chiseled face with fervent yellow-brown eyes set into deep sockets and accentuated by coal-black hair; the powerfully crisp and unadorned speech delivered always with syllogistic precision. Brilliant but erratic, mesmerizing but polarizing, impetuous but always courteous, he was the unchallenged leader of his region—and much taken with his own manifest talents. John Tyler called him "the great 'I am,'" and one South Carolina historian observed that he "believed firmly in himself, nor did his greatness ever exceed the estimate he entertained of it."

On Sunday morning, after his restless night, Calhoun stirred as the dawn's first light peeked through the window. When son John entered to inquire after his father's condition, Calhoun replied, "I am perfectly comfortable." Then he fell silent as the sounds of morning activity outside pierced the room—the singing of birds, the clomping of horses. The room inside was entirely silent save for the increasingly audible and extended breaths of the dying man, fully conscious to the end. The breathing ceased at seven fifteen.

The next day Calhoun's South Carolina colleague, Andrew Pickens Butler, rose in the Senate to announce the senator's death "in a very tremulous and sorrowful voice." He had died, said Butler, from an "affection of the heart" following years of a "pulmonary complaint" that had presaged a "short existence." Though a congressional memorial service was hastily scheduled for the next day and black crepe began appearing on buildings throughout Washington, Butler took the early occasion to praise his departed colleague. "His private character," said the senator, "was . . . the exemplification of truth, justice, temperance, and fidelity to all his engagements."

Then Henry Clay rose to honor his friend of thirty-eight years, sometimes a political ally but more often an adversary. "No more," lamented Clay, "shall we be thrilled by that torrent of clear, concise, compact logic."

Next spoke Daniel Webster of Massachusetts, who rivaled Calhoun as a statesman of rare distinction: four years a congressman from New Hampshire and another four representing a Massachusetts district; nineteen years as a U.S. senator; secretary of state under two presidents (later three); orator of nearly unsurpassed majesty. As a legislator he lacked the sly tactical skill and witty rhetorical flair of Clay or the rocklike conviction and tight argumentation of Calhoun. But no one could challenge Webster's nuanced mastery of constitutional law or his eloquence in glorifying the hallowed American system. And no one could match his sheer force of presence, with his oval, crag-filled face, piercing dark eyes under dense black brows, and the expressive lips, purposeful gait, and powerful deep voice.

Over the years, however, he had demonstrated a "love of ease and luxury," as a foreign journalist put it, that led him to accept questionable financial largesse from political supporters anxious for his influence on crucial matters. "If it had been otherwise," wrote the journalist, Harriet Martineau, "if his moral had equalled his intellectual supremacy . . . , he would long ago have carried all before him, and been the virtual monarch of the United States." It wasn't to be.

Now, on the Senate floor on this April morning of 1850, Webster spoke of Calhoun's "genius and character, his honor and integrity . . . and the purity of his exalted patriotism." These attributes, he added, would remain in the consciousness of his contemporaries until "we ourselves shall go, one after another, in succession, to our graves."

It was fitting that Webster would note his own mortality. He and Calhoun were born the same year and entered Congress just two years apart. And, like Calhoun, Webster experienced serious health challenges as the 1850s commenced. Indeed, just thirty-one months after Calhoun's demise and some 420 miles to the north, Daniel Webster would be lying on his own deathbed.

He had resigned his Senate seat in July 1850 to become secretary of state under Millard Fillmore, who succeeded to the presidency that month upon the death of Zachary Taylor. But by 1852 Webster was suffering from a series of unexplained maladies, including severe intestinal discomfort, swelling of his stomach and abdomen, "great pain," and fatigue. His doctors reported that he had "the aspect of a very sick man," though they couldn't precisely identify the problem. By autumn, after his annual sojourn to his expansive estate at Marshfield, some twenty-six miles from Boston on the Massachusetts South Shore, he was often bedridden and sometimes unable to sit up for any appreciable time. "I am in the hands of God," he told his doctors.

He instructed estate workers to move one of his small sailboats to a nearby lake so he could behold its soothing presence from his sprawling, architecturally eclectic mansion. To enhance the impact, he ordered a flag and lantern to be placed near the top of the mast, with the lantern lit each night. "My light shall burn & my flag shall fly as long as my life lasts," he said. He also directed estate staff to drive his cattle past the front of the house so he could make a final inspection.

At one point in the fall, as Webster was having his hair washed by his sister-in-law while family members looked on, he picked up an errant strand, contemplated it for a moment, then said in a low voice, "See how the thread of my life is spinning out." To the assembled he added, "My heart is full, I have many things to say to you all, but I cannot." Then he lost his composure in a flood of tears. Apparently embarrassed, he vowed, "I will be brave & manly, I will die firm."

On October 21, he turned his attention to his will. Upon completion of that task, he summoned his children and wife, Caroline, to inquire whether they approved the document. All approved.

"Now raise me up," he commanded, and upon being propped up in bed, he signed the document in a bold hand, then lay back. "Thank God, for strength to [do] a sensible act," he declared, then exclaimed, "Oh God! I thank Thee for all Thy mercies."

Turning to those assembled, he asked, "Have I, on this occasion, said any thing unworthy of Daniel Webster?" All assured him that he had not.

Two days later he summoned his female relatives to his bedside for a final farewell, then his male relatives. Upon completing that task, he mused, "On the 24th of October all that is mortal of Daniel Webster will be no more."

At one point, in a semiconscious state, he muttered the words "Poet, poetry; Gray, Gray." From one of those assembled came the first line of Thomas Gray's famous "Elegy": "The curfew tolls the knell of parting day."

"That's it, that's it," the dying man cried.

The poem was retrieved, and several stanzas were read aloud as Webster smiled.

He stirred later when an attending doctor read from the Bible: "Though I walk through the valley of the shadow of death, I will fear no evil, for thou art with me; thy rod and thy staff they comfort me."

"Yes!" he declared. "Thy rod, thy staff—but the *fact*, the fact I want."

He slipped into a semi-stupor, reviving just a bit at one point to announce, "I still live!"

An hour and a half later, early on the morning of Sunday, October 24, 1852, Daniel Webster, age seventy, died.

Each in turn, the two second-generation giants of American politics received extensive ceremonial outpourings of grief, respect, and adulation (inevitably mixed with a few denunciations). For Calhoun the ceremonies began at noon on Tuesday, April 2, 1850, in the Senate chamber, with its classical white columns and rich red carpets. The normal scattered desks had been replaced with tightly positioned chairs, and the chamber was jammed with members of Congress, cabinet officials, foreign ambassadors, and Supreme Court jurists. President Zachary Taylor was seated behind the rostrum, to the right of the vice president, while the circular gallery above was "filled with ladies," as Washington's *Weekly Union* noted. At twelve thirty, the deceased was brought in, reposed in a temporary metal coffin that was placed directly in front of the vice president's desk. It was covered with a black velvet pall.

The sermon by Senate chaplain Butler—"brief and impressive," according to the *Charleston Courier*—offered appropriate praise for Calhoun's earthly deeds, while also emphasizing, said the *Weekly Union*, "the never-to-be-forgotten moral that no qualifications, however eminent, can save man from the power of death." Afterward, attendees departed the chamber based on a protocol sequence called out by a Senate officer. They moved to carriages positioned to follow the casket to the congressional burial ground. There the deceased senator was to be claimed by a "Committee of Twenty-Five" selected by South Carolina's governor to escort the body back to Charleston for burial.

Members of the Committee of Twenty-Five arrived in Washington on April 20, and two days later they were waiting at eight o'clock in the morning when Calhoun's casket arrived by congressional escort at the Capitol. Waiting there also was a large contingent of dignitaries. They formed a long train of carriages to follow the hearse, pulled by twelve black horses, as it moved in slow procession from the Capitol steps, along the south side of Capitol Hill, down Maryland Avenue, and then to a Potomac wharf. There the casket was placed in the upper saloon of the waiting steamer *Baltimore*, shrouded in "appropriate insignia of the melancholy service she was to perform," said an official report of the day's events.

Church bells tolled and solemn music filled the air as the *Baltimore* pulled away from the dock and steamed downriver. At numerous stops along the nearly six-hundred-mile journey, *Baltimore* passengers encountered the peel of church bells, the roar of cannons, dirgelike music, flags flying at mid-staff, and buildings covered in black crepe.

In Fredericksburg they stopped for lunch, passing through streets lined with silent mourners. In Virginia's capital of Richmond, a large crowd gathered as Calhoun's body was placed for the night in the Capitol. "Virginia will mingle freely her tears with those of Carolina," said the governor the next morning, in releasing the remains back to the Committee of Twenty-Five. Large crowds formed wherever the coffin went. Similar scenes emerged at Petersburg, Virginia, and Wilmington, North Carolina, before the *Baltimore* finally entered Charleston Harbor on Thursday morning.

The city was waiting, "clad in habiliments of woe," said the *Charleston Courier*, adding that the subsequent procession was "the largest of the kind ever known in our city." Along the way muffled drums set a solemn cadence as church bells tolled and artillery guns announced their grief. At the Citadel square, in a brief ceremony, Governor Whitemarsh Seabrook received the mortal remains "with the deepest emotions."

The procession moved on to city hall, where the Calhoun casket, draped in a black velvet pall edged with a heavy silk fringe and enflounced in silver, lay in state for the rest of the day and through the night. There commenced an "incessant stream of visitors," thousands of citizens from near and far, moving in single file, into the building, past the elaborate catafalque, and back into the street. The *Courier* observed "young and old, the intellectual and the beautiful, the public dignitary and the private citizen, rich and poor, bond and free, all united in paying a heartfelt tribute of mingled honor and sorrow." Many of the ladies tossed flowers toward the casket, brightening the room with a multicolored floral carpet.

The next day at dawn the bells resumed their tolling, and at ten the body was borne on a bier by a guard of honor to St. Philip's Church, where John Wesley had preached and George Washington had worshipped. There a simple ceremony unfolded, with an anthem sung by a full choir, a burial service read by the state's Episcopal bishop, and a funeral discourse. The body was placed in a temporary vault in the St. Philip's churchyard, protected by a block of white marble marked by the eloquence of a single word: CALHOUN.

The ceremonies that followed Daniel Webster's death in 1852 were more confined in time and space. Congress was not in session, and thus no elaborate ceremony ensued at the Capitol. And there was no sojourn of the deceased from city to city for multiple mournful observances. Webster was buried where he died, at his Marshfield estate, following a display of the body under a spreading tree and a simple funeral at the home in which he had lived for twenty years.

But the outpouring was sincere and vast. Spontaneous gatherings materialized throughout the region, at Massachusetts locations such as Groton, Lynn, Leicester, and the Bunker Hill Monument, as well as other locations in the state and beyond. A mass audience appeared at Boston's famous Faneuil Hall at noon on Wednesday, October 27, at the call of the state's other great statesman of the time, Edward Everett, a longtime politician, teacher, diplomat, and writer. Everett stated that Webster's "greatest moment must be found in his works. There he will live and speak to us and our children when brass and marble have crumbled into dust."

On the day of the funeral, Wednesday, October 27, some ten thousand mourners from all over the Northeast arrived at Marshfield—friends, admirers, dignitaries, neighbors, strangers. The day was clear and crisp, "as if Nature herself were sympathizing with the august occasion," said the *Boston Evening Transcript*. Boston and many neighboring cities, meanwhile, seemed almost empty, closed in observance of the occasion and almost thoroughly draped in black.

At nine that morning the Webster casket was taken from the house and placed on a bier on the front lawn, then opened to reveal the senator in silent glory, attired in his signature blue coat with brass buttons. Lines of two were formed for viewing on each side of the casket, and the procession continued for nearly four hours. Then the service commenced, with the Reverend Ebenezer Alden positioned at the front door so he could be heard by the multitudes on the lawn as well as by the dignitaries inside.

An hour later, at the conclusion of the service, a new procession was formed, composed entirely of men moving on foot. It followed the coffin, "at slow and solemn pace," to the burial site, about a mile away on a low rise. The coffin was then placed in the Webster family vault, where rested Webster's first wife and two of his children. "The last scene concluded," reported the *Evening Transcript*, "the throng of people assembled about the enclosure quietly and sadly dispersed."

These two deaths marked the end of an era. It was an era defined by issues and clashes in which Calhoun and Webster were almost always on opposing sides, placed there by the regional influences that had shaped their political, social, and cultural sensibilities. Calhoun agitated for war with Britain in 1812; Webster opposed the war (though he never joined others of his region who threatened secession over the issue). Calhoun, though an early protectionist, became a free trader; Webster, though an early free trader, ultimately embraced protectionism. Calhoun advocated the "nullification" right of states to declare federal laws null and void as applied to those states; Webster steadfastly rejected that doctrine. To Calhoun's view of America as a compact of sovereign states, Webster replied that, no, it was a national confederation of citizens. The two men did join in supporting the Second Bank of the U.S. from attacks by President Andrew Jackson, but only because Calhoun hated Jackson more than he did the bank. And they both opposed the Mexican War of 1846 to 1848, though for different reasons.

These were the political conflicts that roiled the country from James Madison's presidency to that of James Polk, from around 1812 to 1849. But now these controversies were receding into the background as America struggled increasingly with a single issue containing enough explosive power to rend the nation. Slavery, long a portentous dilemma simmering over the flames of politics, now was erupting into a seemingly hopeless conflagration of civic passions. Calhoun, true to his sectional heritage, had always defended slavery as a fundamental element of the southern way of life. Webster, like most New Englanders, had always abhorred it. Webster never put himself at the vanguard of the antislavery movement, though, and the issue therefore had never created a deep divide between the two men.

But, even before their respective funerals, the nation struggled with slavery in ominous new ways, brought on by recent American territorial acquisitions and polarizing questions over whether those lands would enter the Union as free or slave states. This dawning new era of agitation was evident in a strange episode in the House of Representatives in December 1849, when the chamber failed to elect a Speaker by majority vote. It was evident also a few weeks later with the congressional efforts of Henry Clay and others to fashion a compromise on the issue that, they hoped, might neutralize the passions surrounding it.

Calhoun died in the middle of that compromise initiative, while Webster's commitment to some compromise elements severely attenuated his political standing in many quarters of the country, including his home state. He escaped the wrath of his constituents only by accepting Fillmore's offer of the State Department portfolio.

For decades these men had dominated the politics of their respective states. Now they were gone, and South Carolina and Massachusetts, each guided by its own intensifying passions, would map out their paths into the future without these commanding figures leading the way. Those paths, as it turned out, would take the two disparate states to opposite poles of fervor on the issue of slavery in America.

1

NEW WORLD BEGINNINGS

||||||||||||||||||||||||||||||||||||||||||||||||||||||||||||||||||||||||||||||||||||||||

TWO COLONIES, TWO CULTURES

O n a June day in 1630, a great English ship called the *Arbella* completed a two-month journey across the Atlantic Ocean and entered Massachusetts Bay with a contingent of English families and all their worldly possessions. It transported also the farm animals and equipment needed to carve a slice of the New World wilderness into a fledgling society. Thus began a harrowing adventure that would be a milestone in the history of Anglo-Saxon America.

The *Arbella* was the first of seventeen ships that deposited a thousand or so men, women, and children onto the distant American shore that summer. Nearly two hundred perished during the first winter, and another hundred fled back to England as soon as favorable weather returned. But the human flow that began with the *Arbella* continued through the 1630s, transporting some twenty-one thousand English folk to the emerging Massachusetts Bay Colony, along with the distinctive mores, folkways, and spiritual sensibilities they carried with them in their minds and hearts.

They were Puritans, as manifest in their austerity of dress, seriousness of manner, and intensity of religion. They acquired these traits and lifestyles from the area where most of them had lived in eastern England, a small enclave of nine counties centered geographically on the market town of Haverhill, near the convergence of Suffolk, Essex, and Cambridge counties. A historian of that region described these people, whether gentle or simple, as "dour, stubborn, fond of argument and litigation, strongly Puritan."

This East Anglian region generated the English realm's most concentrated opposition to King Charles I and his increasingly oppressive rule. For more than a decade, known as the "eleven years' tyranny" (1629 to 1640), Charles sought to govern without Parliament and installed as head of the once-tolerant Anglican Church a severe prelate named William Laud. Laud stamped the realm's Puritans as subversives, sought to purge them from the established Church, and burdened them with all manner of harassment, fines, and banishment from university and Church vocation. He considered the East Anglians to be the "throbbing heart of heresy in England," as one historian put it.

This was as intolerable to the Puritans as the economic stagnation and epidemic diseases also ravaging England at the time. In the view of John Winthrop, a leading Puritan lawyer and advocate of the American migration, the lands of England had become "weary of her Inhabitants, so as man which is most precious of all the Creatures, is here more vile and base than the earth they tread upon." As the migration plan took shape, participants turned for leadership to Winthrop, who proved himself a gifted governor for the transatlantic voyage and later for the Massachusetts challenge. He also sheathed the enterprise in inspiring language, as when, during the passage, he talked of creating a new "Citty upon a Hill" that would become "a story and a byword throughout the world."

But most Puritans on that voyage held a more rustic sense of their adventure. Religion dominated their lives, and they wanted the freedom to embrace it in their own way. As the noted historian David Hackett Fischer wrote, when they described their motivations for crossing the Atlantic, "religion was mentioned not merely as their leading purpose. It was their only purpose."

Then, in 1641, a decade after the remarkable Puritan migration began, it ceased, as events in England presaged an end to the king's "personal government" and his trespasses upon religious freedom—and an end also, eventually, to his life.

By then the colony was in full bloom, spreading across the landscape of New England in the form largely of small, efficiently run farms and tidy villages. Nearly all of the Massachusetts communities were farm towns, and most citizens were yeoman farmers who soon generated agricultural surpluses—in grain, meat, fish, butter, cheese, timber—shipped to markets in Virginia, the West Indies, and Great Britain. A merchant class soon emerged along with a hearty presence of religious leaders. By 1640 the colony boasted some three hundred university-trained clergymen, and the population was doubling every generation, almost entirely from robust internal birth rates. The population reached one hundred thousand by 1700 and more than a million a century later.

These people, as historian Fischer has noted, "became the breeding stock for America's Yankee population"—nearly all descended, he adds, from those initial twenty-one thousand English migrants. In time, Massachusetts Bay descendants built communities in eastern New Jersey, northern New York, Maine, New Hampshire, Canada, and eventually westward in a band stretching to the Pacific Northwest, where many place-names echoed those of New England cities and towns—Portland, Salem, Albany, Quincy, Everett. The Puritan culture shaped much of the societal ethos of the U.S. northern tier, even as the populace became more secular and the focus shifted from individual salvation to the cause of human betterment.

In April 1670, three decades after the Puritan migration ended, another ship entered another New World harbor a thousand miles to the south. Called the *Carolina*, it carried ninety-two English emigrants along with fifteen tons of beer, thirty gallons of brandy, fifty-nine bushels of flour, twelve suits of armor, a hundred beds, 1,200 grubbing hoes, and 756 fishhooks. The destination was a place later known as Charleston, in South Carolina, and the aim was to establish a colony dedicated to the creation of wealth.

This wasn't a crown colony overseen by the king's ministers, but a proprietary one for which King Charles II granted a huge tract of territory to a group of London investors, who then sought to lure settlers with the promise of land and the dream of prosperity. A few of the early migrants were from the landed gentry, but most were simple folk, including many indentured servants tied to their owners for two to seven years. The proprietors promised 150 acres to free settlers over age sixteen, with another hundred for each able-bodied servant brought along.

People arrived from England, a few from New York, and a growing number began showing up from Barbados and other West Indian islands, where lucrative sugar plantations already had emerged, generating substantial wealth for enterprising Englishmen and their families. Many of the prosperous islanders considered South Carolina an ideal destination for their younger sons, barred from significant inheritance by the prevailing "primogenitor" practice of favoring oldest sons. These were swashbucklers, men of swagger who loved their dogs and horses, fancied tavern life, ate and drank with abandon, and displayed their social position ostentatiously in dress and manner. They came to South Carolina with just two things in mind: to get rich and then to get richer.

Though fervent in their attachment to the Anglican Church, they evinced no particular piety. Though profoundly loyal to the English monarchy and proud of their Cavalier heritage, they harbored little respect for the king's proprietors back in London, bent on protecting their investment from afar. The independent-minded "Barbadians"—or "Anglicans," as they later were called—viewed the proprietors as a meddlesome lot impeding their moneymaking efforts.

The Anglican influx included large and small sugar producers, artisans, merchants—and slaves. Slavery had become an integral part of the Caribbean sugar culture, as reflected in its magnitude before and after the introduction of sugarcane. In 1638, before sugar, there were two hundred slaves on Barbados; fourteen years later, there were twenty thousand, more than the white population. When the Anglicans arrived in Carolina, they brought with them their slaves and their slave culture.

They arrived in sufficient numbers to give them dominance over the fledgling governmental structures established for Charleston and the surrounding "low country," where most of the Anglicans settled into large tracts of land. That precipitated tensions between the self-seeking Anglicans and the London proprietors and also between the Anglicans and other British emigrants, called "dissenters" (mostly Presbyterians of Scottish or Scots-Irish extraction), who esteemed the proprietors and chafed under the emerging Anglican ascendancy.

The issues that emerged among the Anglicans, proprietors, and Presbyterians were real, but religion was not one of them. Always alert to financial opportunities, the Anglicans struck up a lucrative trade with nearby native Indians, which was fine. But then they engaged in an Indian slave trade, which disturbed the proprietors and their dissenter loyalists, who also opposed the Anglican practice of trading with ruthless Caribbean pirates. Tensions eased when the Anglicans turned to cattle and hog farming and then entered a lucrative trade in deerskins, obtained through treaty arrangements with local Indian tribes and sold mostly to avid European buyers.

With the money generated through their high-margin deerskin enterprises, Anglican traders bought more and more low-country land as an extravagant emblem of their success. Then they developed two staple crops—rice and indigo—that would transform their lives and their colony. Rice production shot up sixfold in the first decade of the new century, then tripled in the 1720s. In one three-year period, meanwhile, annual production of indigo, used to make dyes for the burgeoning English textile industry, went from just 17 pounds to 137,000 pounds. Added to this cash infusion was money generated from an expanding production of "naval stores"—tar, pitch, turpentine, masts—sold to the Royal Navy for maintenance of its far-flung warships. In six years, naval store sales increased eightfold.

Soon Charleston was one of the largest cities in America, behind only Philadelphia, New York, and Boston, and probably the richest. The surrounding colony also prospered—"in as thriving circumstances as any colony on the continent of English America," as one observer of the time noted. Money was changing hands with increasing velocity for all kinds of transactions, and this tidal wave of consumerism and entrepreneurship was generating wealth and creating a nouveau aristocracy of both planters and merchants, who formed a close alliance through extensive business dealings and well-conceived marriages. More than eighty commercial ships a year cleared Charleston Harbor in the early eighteenth century, and nearly five hundred adult males were making money one way or another in the export-import trade.

In short, Carolina was developing into a distinct North American culture. Historian Walter J. Fraser writes that the Southern climate, the evolving agricultural society, the institution of slavery, and the colony's particular brand of Anglicanism "were shaping in the hearts and minds of Charlestonians a worldview different from that of Bostonians, New Yorkers, and Philadelphians." Walter Edgar, a leading authority on the region, adds that the "unashamed pursuit of wealth and the open enjoyment of the pleasures it could buy" set South Carolinians apart from other English-speaking colonies. "They may well have been the only colonial society to produce a new cultural identity," he writes.

Of all the New World colonies established in the seventeenth century, no two were as disparate in outlook, religion, moral precepts, or cultural sensibility as Massachusetts and South Carolina. The two peoples came from different parts of England, departed the motherland for different reasons, pursued different approaches to creating a wilderness society, and embraced far different views of life on earth. Had they remained in England through the 1600s, most of them likely would have been fighting each other in the English Civil War.

The disparity is starkly seen in the regions' religious attitudes. The Puritans lived under the sway of an austere form of Calvinism that conveyed a strong sense of pervasive human depravity. For them life was a constant strife between good and evil in which most people would falter. That's why, in their view, Christ died for just a special elect and not for all humanity. Joining the chosen few required an arduous struggle.

These Calvinists also embraced a strong sense of love, based on the idea that mankind was so flawed and tainted that salvation was possible only through the miraculous love and mercy of God. Humans, by extension, must strive to honor this spiritual gift by loving their own fellow men and women in a godly way.

These and other precepts were strongly felt and resolutely observed throughout most of Massachusetts and surrounding areas. As Fischer writes, "The spiritual purposes of the colony were fully shared by most men and women. . . . Here was a fact of high importance for the history of their region."

No such ardent religiosity emerged in South Carolina, though Charleston was known as a "city of churches" whose many spires accentuated the urban skyline. The colony's Calvinists, both Anglican and Presbyterian, focused on the general concepts of salvation and redemption, while avoiding the emotionalism often generated by intricate doctrinal preoccupations. Though the Anglicans held political sway over the low country, they soon were outnumbered by other Calvinist worshippers, including the Presbyterians as well as Congregationalists and a contingent of French Huguenots who arrived beginning around 1680 to escape the latest wave of persecution from the Bourbon monarchy. But not even the Carolina Calvinists embraced Christianity with anything approaching the ardor of Massachusetts Puritans.

Anglican officials at one point passed laws that prohibited non-Anglicans from serving in certain key governmental positions and denoted the Church of England as the colony's established religion. But this so-called Exclusion Act was often ignored in practice, and despite the establishment legislation no serious efforts were made to convert non-Anglicans to the faith of the low country's predominant Anglicans. Eventually England's Queen Anne and the House of Lords disallowed both acts. In any event, those initiatives were efforts at political leverage more than of religious orthodoxy. And, as Walter Edgar points out, Carolinians didn't go to church to get stirred up; thus the "dominant middle way of the Church of England was well suited to the harmony of the prosperous colony." Carolinians were happy to live cordially alongside others of different denominational convictions.

A similar casualness guided the Carolinian attitude toward social status. With so much money being made, the prevailing Anglicans didn't much care how people accumulated their wealth or when they had done so. The newly rich, even those who had obtained wealth through grubby means—by selling captured Indians into bondage, for example, or engaging in the brutal African slave trade—were welcomed into the upper echelons of society so long as they could entertain their well-established neighbors with flair and elegance. And Carolina's upper crust, whether of the old or new stock, certainly didn't view their frenzied pursuit of wealth as reflecting moral decline, notwithstanding the hedonism that accompanied the money chase. Indeed, the colony generally abhorred moral snobbery of any sort and observed an attitude of "live and let live."

Live and let live was certainly not in the thinking of New England Puritans. Their driving civic imperative was protecting the unity and order of society from errant personal behavior such as violating Sabbath laws (including a prohibition on Sunday sex), disturbing the peace, straying from strict sexual norms, and ignoring strictures against idleness, lying, and drunkenness. The Puritans practiced what Fischer calls "institutional savagery" in enforcing individual order. They burned rebellious servants, maimed political dissenters, flogged Quakers, and executed suspected witches. At one point the colony had thirteen designated capital crimes, including blasphemy.

Further, the Puritans wanted a social harmony that they considered impossible in a highly stratified society. They opposed the emergence of an aristocracy of large landowners or the rise of a hugely rich merchant class. By the same token, they didn't want poor immigrants who, they suspected, couldn't contribute to the new society. Social distinctions were acknowledged and gently maintained among gentry, yeomen, and laborers, but they existed within a relatively narrow range of social status, generally the middling strata of traditional English society. People of these classes mingled with relative ease in work, play, and worship.

Carolinians, by contrast, believed that the best form of government was an "aristocratic republic" guided by those who had demonstrated their worth through financial success and whose wealth gave them a valuable independence of mind. Notably, the descendants of the early Anglican founders still maintained their social and political dominance up to the American Revolution. There was in the colony, and later the state, an intricately balanced system of power distribution, with nearly universal white manhood suffrage. But the power center remained Charleston and the surrounding low country, and that power distribution was closely guarded and protected by the aristocrats of the bustling port city and, later, the new capital city of Columbia.

Carolinians also welcomed newcomers of different backgrounds more openly than did the Massachusetts Puritans. Though the French Huguenots encountered some social discrimination upon arriving in the mid-seventeenth century, and colonial leaders at one point combined counties to thwart the emergence of a local Huguenot voting majority, the newcomers generally were left alone to pursue their destiny. Many thrived. As one wrote to a London friend, "Carolina is a good country for anyone who is not lazy."

More numerous were the Scots and Scots-Irish who moved into the South Carolina backcountry beginning around 1750, part of a vast New World migration from the borderlands of northern England, northern Ireland, and the Scottish Highlands. They arrived initially in Pennsylvania beginning in 1717 but soon gravitated south and west, through Virginia and the Carolinas, then into Kentucky and Tennessee. These were rustic folk, largely Presbyterian, mostly from the bottom rungs of Old World wealth and status (though a few hailed from established borderland families). The vast majority were small farmers, farm laborers, and mechanics. They weren't looking for religious freedom or cities upon hills, but for economic betterment, and they went after it with zeal.

Fully aware of their humble origins, they nevertheless demanded social respect, often with an insolence that startled and irritated those of higher station. Some in South Carolina, upon seeing the Scots' prideful ways and the frolicsome manner of their womenfolk, took a dim view, complaining that these upstarts seemed to pursue a rather loose backwoods morality. One cleric, perhaps mixing a touch of prurience with his moral outrage, complained of the women's tight-fitting dresses showing "the roundness of their Breasts and slender Waists" and their short petticoats that tended "to shew the fineness of their Limbs."

But the backcountry Scotsmen and their women prospered in the western wilderness through hard toil and much resourcefulness. Soon they melded into the prevailing Carolina culture, their story personified by the life and career of John C. Calhoun, whose family arrived in the forbidding backcountry wilderness in 1760 (Calhoun's grandmother was killed by Cherokee Indians upon arrival) and who became Carolina's leading politician of all time. Political tensions emerged occasionally between the low-country and backcountry people, but the interaction remained equable and manageable.

As the colonies of Massachusetts and South Carolina became states and moved into the nineteenth century under the auspices of the new American government, major changes washed over both. Massachusetts absorbed two central developments.

One was the emergence of industrial vigor wrought by steam power and the necessity for innovative acuity as a growing population pushed agricultural production to its capacity. The new century witnessed more and more people starting commercial enterprises, creating cottage industries, pursuing investment opportunities, and joining an expanding Boston merchant class. Then in 1812 Francis Cabot Lowell devised a plan to establish a manufacturing plant that could handle all aspects of producing cloth from raw cotton, including spinning, weaving, and fiber processing. By 1822 the company's sales had shot up to $345,000 from just $3,000 in 1815, and Lowell's associates were expanding their enterprise into a mammoth complex of manufacturing capacity.

The concept was adapted to other industries, and Massachusetts soon excelled in the manufacture of textiles, leather goods, and numerous other consumer products. By 1860, textile and shoe manufacturers together employed 110,000 workers, about 53 percent of the state's industrial employment.

Another major change came in the form of new modes of thinking about life in the here and now and in the hereafter. Many of the new industrial workers brought with them a greater diversity of religion, a more secular outlook, greater optimism about humanity, and a reluctance to embrace the conformity of thought and action that New England civic leaders and the clergy had sought to enforce. By this same time, Unitarianism was the predominant religion of Massachusetts, and intellectual leaders, responding to German and English Romanticism, were exploring new and disruptive modes of thought. Transcendentalism, developed and pressed by such powerful Massachusetts figures as

Ralph Waldo Emerson and Henry David Thoreau, emerged to further shake up New England sensibilities.

It taught that mankind is essentially pure, but corrupted by societal institutions, including organized religion. Freed of these vulgar influences, the individual would find his way to human goodness and bring about, in alliance with other seekers of virtue, a unity of humankind. At its foundation, this was a far cry from the essential Puritan preoccupation with human depravity and the metaphysical struggle between good and evil. Massachusetts intellectuals and activists were abandoning the idea of providence in favor of the idea of human progress.

And yet some elements of the Puritan ethos survived this profound transformation. Puritanism was fervent, moralistic, universalist, exhortatory; so was the secular humanitarianism of eighteenth-century Massachusetts. Historians Richard D. Brown and Jack Tager write that the state "emerged as a nursery for the missionaries of a hundred causes." Reform movements sprang up for societal improvement in a host of areas—temperance, women's rights, education, public health, personal hygiene, prison policy, the care of the physically and mentally impaired. And, of course, the moral imperative of abolishing chattel slavery throughout America. Brown and Tager report that Massachusetts emerged as an acknowledged "hotbed of abolitionism and as the leading opponent of returning fugitive slaves."

That was not a stance likely to endear Puritan descendants to the folks down in South Carolina, roiled by new challenges and fears even as the aristocracy there generated ever greater wealth and displayed it more and more ostentatiously in Charleston drawing rooms and huge manor houses springing up on low-country plantations. These challenges and fears centered primarily on one thing, the institution of slavery, though Carolinians often were loath to acknowledge as much. But a century and a half of expanding and defending the institution had placed South Carolinians in a precarious existence from which they couldn't escape. For generations they had pursued their favored business model because it generated the greatest returns: a plantation economy producing staple crops with slave labor for world markets. The more successful they were in pursuing this model, the more slaves they needed.

Financial considerations proved powerful, too. Rice planters figured that a slave would pay for him- or herself in four or five years, then generate an ongoing annual return of between 16 and 25 percent, depending on the price of rice. The greed of slave merchants also figured in the equation: the importation of slaves generated higher profits than any other imports.

Between 1703 and 1708, South Carolina's white population increased 7 percent, to 4,080, while the slave population increased 37 percent, to 4,100. For the first time, blacks outnumbered whites in the colony. Then, in the 1720s, some ten thousand West Africans arrived, pushing the proportion of blacks in South Carolina past 60 percent (though the backcountry influx of Scots and Scots-Irish put whites back into the majority for a time).

The large numbers of slaves generated anxiety as vague visions of slave rebellions seeped into the consciousness of the planter class. What didn't seep into their consciousness, it seems, was any sense of just how unnatural it was to hold other human beings in ownership bondage, thus generating a longing for escape and gnawing desires among some for retributive violence. The greed factor was too strong for any such contemplation. Remove slavery from the Carolina business model, and the whole system would come crashing down.

The anxiety over possible slave revolts wasn't unfounded. In June 1722, South Carolina officials uncovered "a wicked and barbarous plott . . . to destroy all the white people in the country and then to take the town." The alleged plotters, led by a freed black man named Denmark Vesey, were dealt with brutally—"burnt . . . hang'd [or] banish'd," according to a contemporary report. The town watch in Charleston received extra resources to augment night patrols, and new slave laws were enacted to bolster control over those in bondage.

Two decades later, in 1739, the white population's worst fears came to pass with the so-called Stono River Rebellion, which began with the killing of store owners about twenty miles southwest of Charleston. The rebels then moved south, killing whites as they proceeded on a route toward Spanish Florida and freedom. Scores of slaves, beckoned by rumor and drum calls, joined the rebellion, swelling the insurgent force to nearly a hundred before a counterforce arrived to suppress the uprising. When it was over, some seventy-five South Carolinians, blacks and whites, had been killed.

The people of South Carolina were in a cyclical trap. To maintain economic growth, they needed to cultivate more and more acreage for their staple crops (including the new money generator of cotton); to do that they needed more slaves; but, as the slave population grew, so did anxieties about the threat of insurrection; as anxieties grew, institutional controls over those in bondage tightened; as they tightened, the prospect of rebellion increased; and the cycle continued. This iron grip was reflected in what happened after efforts by government officials to curtail the influx of slaves by imposing import taxes and quotas. Political pressures always ensued that led to legislative retreat. By 1820, South Carolina's white population was once again in the minority—and declining quickly relative to the state's blacks.

Meanwhile, over the decades, various slave rebellions and conspiracies in North America and the West Indies kept alive the sense of vulnerability. Perhaps as alarming as the killings from such insurrections was the fact that two of them, in British Jamaica and French St. Dominique (later Haiti), had led Britain and France to abolish slavery in their territories. Any groundswell of such abolitionist sentiment in America could be a disaster for South Carolina and the rest of the U.S. slave empire.

By the early 1830s many South Carolina leaders felt they could build a protective barrier against federal intrusions with the "nullification" doctrine, giving states the power to negate federal laws within their borders if they considered those laws unconstitutional. The immediate issue was a tariff enacted in 1828—the so-called Tariff of Abominations—that had devastated much of the South Carolina economy. But the tariff issue also was seen by many as a stand-in for slavery, for if southern states could nullify a tariff law they could do it also to any federal encroachments upon southern slavery.

John Calhoun, then vice president under Andrew Jackson, took the lead on the issue with a firm belief that Jackson, a rustic backwoods populist, would go along. Calhoun miscalculated. In a famous toast Jackson made clear he viewed nullification as an assault on the Constitution. He didn't mince words in backing up his position. "[P]lease give my compliments to my friends in your state," he told a South Carolina visitor at one point, "and say to them, that if a single drop of blood shall be shed there in opposition to the laws of the United States, I will hang the first man I can lay my hand upon engaged in such treasonable conduct, upon the first tree I can reach."

With nullification dead, South Carolinians felt more and more vulnerable to Northern agitations against slavery. But they were on the defensive now. "A people owning slaves are mad, or worse than mad," declared the prominent South Carolina politician, planter, and newspaper publisher Robert Barnwell Rhett, "if they do not hold their destinies in their own hands." It wasn't clear, though, that South Carolinians could control their destinies at all. They were reduced to meddling with the post office in efforts to thwart delivery of antislavery propaganda in the state and seeking to ensure that abolitionist petitions sent to Congress were set aside without consideration or discussion. Beyond that, South Carolina politicians and intellectuals became obsessed with crafting elaborate arguments on behalf of human bondage as a positive good, making possible higher levels of civilization—such as, for example, their own.

Much of the swagger was gone now from the descendants of those "Barbadians" who had arrived with such élan nearly two centuries before and set South Carolina upon its historical preoccupation with wealth creation based on human bondage. In the place of the swagger was a growing attitude of defiance.

2

CRISIS IN MINIATURE

||||||||||||||||||||||||||||||||||||||||||||||||||||||||||||||||||||||||||||||||||||||||||||||||

THE HOUSE SEIZES UP OVER SLAVERY

Whit hen America's lawmakers filtered into Washington, D.C., in late 1849 for the start of the 31st Congress, nearly everyone knew they faced a maelstrom of political peril. "A crisis in our affairs is rapidly approaching, and great events are near at hand," warned the city's leading Democratic newspaper, the *Daily Union*. It referred to the gathering crisis over whether the emotion-charged institution of slavery would be allowed to spread into the vast new southwestern and coastal territories—designated at the time as New Mexico and California—secured for the United States through President James Polk's recent bloody and controversial war with Mexico.

Though most citizens cherished Polk's vision of a transcontinental America, facing two oceans and stitched together by ribbons of railroad track, the growing chasm between the North and South marred that heady concept. Some people desperately seized upon the notion that if the North would just stop its antislavery agitations and the South would cease threatening to leave the Union, some kind of mutual accommodation might be possible. Washington's *National Intelligencer*, a Whig newspaper, gave expression to this hopeful concept on Congress's first day of deliberations.

"Having regarded this topic as one on which . . . the popular sentiments in the two opposite quarters of the country can never harmonize," said the paper, "and been entirely convinced that the discussion of so hopeless a matter could do no possible good, we have always, as far as depended upon our voluntary action, kept it out of our columns." The paper deplored those "partisans" on both sides who had exploited the issue "as a bugbear to frighten weak minds and drive them into the party nets."

But such well-intentioned attitudes didn't accurately capture the relentless force of emotion welling up from within the country and distilled now with ever-greater potency in Washington. "Slavery here is the all engrossing theme," Henry Clay wrote to a friend upon arriving for the new congressional session. "My hopes and my fears alternately prevail as to any satisfactory settlement of the vexed question." When Daniel Webster arrived, he saw the same thing. "There is so much excitement & inflammation on the subject of Slavery, Dissolution, &," he observed, "as that it overwhelms, or threatens to overwhelm, all really important measures."

While discerning political observers understood the depth of the gathering crisis, hardly anyone anticipated just how it would tie the House of Representatives into snarls of dysfunction and confusion as the body sought to organize itself for the new congressional term. For three weeks, the chamber tried and failed to elect a Speaker. Without a Speaker, the House couldn't function. Without a functioning House, the Senate couldn't accomplish any serious business. Zachary Taylor, the Mexican War hero who had become president the previous March, couldn't send up his Annual Message or set the national agenda. Congress couldn't appropriate money. The government froze. The country looked on in bewilderment bordering on disgust. It was a crisis in miniature reflecting the larger emergency at hand.

During the ordeal, three party candidates vied for the speakership, along with a shifting collection of others who emerged and then faded during the sixty-three ballots that consumed House members through most of December. One of the three was a Boston patrician named

Robert C. Winthrop, a direct descendant of that Massachusetts founder John Winthrop. He was a forty-year-old Whig and Webster protégé who had been Speaker in the previous Congress and wanted the job again. Tall, lean, sonorous of tongue, and scholarly in appearance, with a triangular face framed by long sideburns, Winthrop was known for his intellectual bent and high-mindedness. He kept himself "above the tricks of intrigue," said one Pennsylvania newspaper, which wondered, though, if he wasn't perhaps "a little too refined and dignified" for the political rough-and-tumble of crisis times. Most Whigs brushed aside such concerns. "The nomination is due to Mr. Winthrop by every consideration of propriety," argued the *New York Courier*. "If he fails of an election, no other whig can succeed."

The party's House caucus, meeting late into the evening of December 1, selected Winthrop as its candidate in part because Whig leaders thought he could bridge the North-South gap. Though fervent in his antislavery views, in keeping with the prevailing sentiment of his native New England, he nevertheless hewed to a moderate course. As he told colleagues upon looking back on his nearly ten-year congressional career, he always promised that he wouldn't "agitate the subject of slavery." He added: "I have adhered to that declaration. . . . I have sympathized with no fanatics. . . . I have enlisted in no crusade upon the institutions of the South."

But this attitude rankled the North's antislavery forces gaining ground under the Free Soil Party, which had emerged during the previous year's presidential campaign. These were the people, after all, that Winthrop called fanatics. One abolitionist newspaper dismissed the Massachusetts politician as a "lickspittle of slavery . . . —a doughface of showy but mediocre ability." But most caucus members figured that, while Winthrop wouldn't get the votes of fiery abolitionists such as Ohio's pietistic Joshua Giddings, he would capture most of his northern Whig brethren. And the attacks from antislavery provocateurs, it was assumed, would help cement southern Whig support.

The Democrats took an opposite tack, choosing a southern slaveholder who was nonetheless deemed acceptable to northern Democrats. He was Georgia's mountainous Howell Cobb, thirty-four, with thick auburn hair, lively blue eyes, and a hearty laugh. His southern heritage didn't induce in him the angry proslavery passion increasingly evident in the rhetoric of many southern politicians. Among colleagues he was "a general favorite," as one historian later reported.

Finally, there was thirty-five-year-old David Wilmot of Pennsylvania—a big fellow, outspoken and impetuous, often slovenly in dress and manner, with a chaw of tobacco ever-present in his mouth. When he set himself upon a course, he did so with fearless grit, as he did in 1846, in the midst of a congressional debate on Polk's Mexican War, when he attached to a funding bill his famous "proviso" designed to prohibit slavery in any lands acquired from Mexico as a result of the war. Instantly the war debate became intertwined with the slavery issue, which then gained ominous force after the United States actually acquired those vast western tracts. Immediately, southerners chafed at the prospect of being excluded from lands acquired through the expenditure of southern as well as northern blood. Wilmot's proviso never cleared Congress, but it hovered over official Washington like a dark and menacing thundercloud.

The Pennsylvanian was the chosen speakership candidate of the fledgling Free Soilers, an amalgam of antislavery northerners that included a contingent of New York Democrats, called "Barnburners," under the leadership of former president Martin Van Buren; the so-called Conscience Whigs of Massachusetts, long animated by the horrors of slavery; strong midwestern abolitionists in the vein of the irascible Giddings; a smattering of Wilmot Proviso Democrats throughout the North; and adherents of the old antislavery Liberty Party. With Van Buren at the head of the ticket in the 1848 presidential canvass, the Free Soilers collected 291,501 votes, compared to 1,361,393 for Taylor and 1,223,460 for Democrat Lewis Cass of Michigan.

The new party also sent thirteen Free Soilers to the U.S. House. And with the major parties at near parity in the chamber—112 Democrats to 105 Whigs—this meant the Free Soilers held the balance of power in the speakership balloting, *if* they wanted to employ their small but crucial leverage; and *if* sectional divisions within the Democratic and Whig parties didn't throw the whole thing into chaos.

Everyone knew the stakes when the House convened for its first session of the new Congress on Monday, December 3. The Speaker held the power to set the agenda for floor action and to appoint all committees—hence the power to control the chamber. That represented a huge advantage in the coming debates and maneuvers over slavery in the territories.

With 111 votes needed for a majority (not all members having yet arrived in Washington), the first-ballot results were: Cobb, 103; Winthrop, ninety-six; Wilmot, eight. Some thirteen votes went to a smattering of other candidates. The chamber moved quickly through three more votes, with largely the same result. The highly partisan *Union* rejoiced at what appeared to be Cobb's solid prospects—"decidedly the most favorable," as the paper said.

But the next day, after the House went through six more votes, Cobb had slipped to ninety-nine tallies, with ninety-seven for Winthrop and nine for Wilmot. On December 5, with the thirteenth ballot, Cobb dropped to ninety-three, with Winthrop ahead at ninety-eight and Wilmot getting no votes at all. The following day, with House members discerning signs of futility, Andrew Johnson of Tennessee offered a resolution: if the next vote didn't yield a speaker, he suggested, the House should waive the requirement for a majority tally in the following vote and accept a plurality outcome. Johnson, a Democrat, said he would rather have any competent Whig or Democrat in the Speaker's chair than to have the current embarrassment continue.

North Carolina's Abraham Venable disagreed. The problem, he said, was that too many members were clinging to candidates who had no chance of victory, thus foreclosing any pathway to a majority conclusion. He said these men would soon learn just how "preposterous" their behavior was when they went home "to settle with their constituents." The House rejected the Johnson motion and proceeded to the fourteenth ballot, which brought Winthrop up to ninety-nine votes to Cobb's eighty-nine. The deadlock looked hopeless, as did Cobb's prospects.

Then on December 9 the *Intelligencer* reprinted a story from the *New York Express* that, said the *Intelligencer,* could "shed light upon the predicament in which the House of Representatives now finds itself."

The *Express* presented a detailed description of the December 1 Whig caucus that had voted to nominate Winthrop for Speaker. As it turned out, a lot more happened at that closed-door session than any newspapers had revealed. A fiery slavery debate had erupted, and six southern Whigs had stormed out of the caucus. The episode looked like "an evil omen," the *Express* reported.

At the center of the controversy was a congressman named Robert A. Toombs, a broad-faced, barrel-chested Georgia planter once described by a contemporary as "the stormy petrel . . . always intolerant, dogmatic and extreme." Toombs feared that the Wilmot Proviso would become law for the entire Mexican cession. And it didn't help that a slavery exclusion had been added to legislation, signed by Polk earlier in the year before his term ended, that established a territorial government in the Oregon region acquired by Polk in 1846 through tough negotiations with Britain.

Toombs's agitation centered on President Taylor and Toombs's suspicion, shared by growing numbers of southern politicians, that the president had snookered his native South during the late campaign and now had fallen under the sway of northern abolitionists. Taylor often seemed to be a captive of his own whims and hence wasn't an easy man to figure out, but Toombs felt he understood the general quite well. He didn't like what he saw.

Taylor, a rustic-looking, blunt-spoken figure of sixty-five with an air of superiority and a tendency toward peevishness, had served his entire adult life as an army officer. Born into a wealthy family with large landholdings in Virginia and Kentucky, he owned a Louisiana plantation with 145 slaves. Known to his troops as Old Rough and Ready, he had thrived over the years in the military environment. But he was a man of little spark or imagination and showed almost no curiosity about subjects beyond his immediate involvement. In times of peace, he seemed languid, as if merely going through the motions of military life. In war he demonstrated an instinct for action that had served him well in the few combat episodes he had encountered.

Then came the Mexican War, and he quickly became a national luminary based on military victories he engineered in disputed borderlands and on Mexican soil—at Palo Alto, Resaca de la Palma, Monterrey, and, most stunning of all, Buena Vista. But Taylor's superiors in Washington came to view his judgment as spotty. After his Monterrey triumph, he allowed Mexican general Pedro de Ampudia to slink off with his seven thousand troops and weapons, including artillery, to fight another day.

Worse, he defiantly ignored orders to encamp his troops at the easily fortified city of Monterrey and instead ventured south toward Buena Vista, where he became highly vulnerable to a much larger force under Mexican general Antonio López de Santa Anna. The Mexicans nearly crushed Taylor's army, but through brilliant tactical dexterity he managed to outmaneuver Santa Anna, avoid devastation, and withdraw to safer ground. Though the episode brought widespread adulation from the American people, Taylor's victory lacked strategic significance and expended substantial American blood to little purpose. The general's commander in chief, President Polk, wrote to his diary, "The truth is that from the beginning of the War he has been constantly blundering into difficulties, but has fought out of them, but at the cost of many lives."

Later, in a long and bizarre political flirtation with his country, the now-heralded Taylor suggested he would seek the presidency only if assured he could attain the office *"untrammeled with party obligations or interests of any kind"*—in other words, through some sort of immaculate ascension. When informed that that wasn't how American politics worked, he labeled himself a Whig and was instantly embraced by large elements of that party beguiled by his military acclaim and untroubled by his lack of any political identity or civic experience.

Awarded the Whig nomination, he presented himself in fuzzy terms that obscured what he thought about the day's pressing issues, if indeed he had thought much about them at all. He generally projected two separate personas and outlooks for the country's two antagonistic sections. Southerners generally took heart in his regional heritage and slave ownership, while many northerners seized upon wispy expressions suggesting he might oppose slavery expansion and wasn't much of a fan of the presidential veto (and hence, it was surmised, might not veto Wilmot's proviso should it be enacted).

The finesse worked. Taylor became president. Polk, after spending time with the general on Inauguration Day, wrote to his diary: "Gen'l Taylor is, I have no doubt, a well meaning old man. He is, however, uneducated, exceedingly ignorant of public affairs, and, I should judge, of very ordinary capacity."

Once elected, Taylor could no longer temporize on the slavery issue, especially after Toombs sought clarity. Upon his arrival in Washington for the 31st Congress, the Georgian went to the White House and put the question directly to Taylor: Would he veto the Wilmot Proviso? Replied the president: "I have given and will give no pledges to either the opponents or supporters of the proviso, but if Congress sees fit to pass it, I will not veto it."

That's when Taylor lost Toombs. "My course became instantly fixed," he later told a friend, adding he dedicated himself immediately to preventing northern Whigs from gaining control of the House and its critical committee assignments. That meant upending Winthrop's speakership prospects. "I would not hesitate," he said, "to oppose the proviso even to a dissolution of the Union."

Accordingly, at that December 1 Whig caucus meeting, Toombs put forth a resolution designed to grab his colleagues' attention: "Resolved, That Congress ought not to pass any law prohibiting slavery in the territories of California or New Mexico, nor any law abolishing slavery in the District of Columbia." The *Express* reported that in the meeting hall "an intense excitement was aroused."

Edward Stanly of North Carolina promptly opposed the motion, not because he disfavored the intent—he was a southerner, after all—but because this wasn't the time or place to engage in sectional disputes. He moved to lay the Toombs resolution on the table, essentially killing it. William Duer of New York expressed chagrin that anyone at this Whig assembly would posit "an exclusive slavery test, when the Whig party in the North had disclaimed any such test, and repeatedly declared that it considered [itself] a national, not a sectional party."

As the debate ensued, it became clear that Toombs had driven a wedge through his own party. Then Toombs's Georgia colleague, Alexander H. Stephens—small, frail, and often infirm, but a figure of passion and eloquence—widened the rift by declaring slavery in Washington,

D.C., to be inviolable. He warned—"not . . . in threat but in sorrow"—that if those in the country with prevailing numerical power actually abolished slavery there, "the Union must and will be dissolved."

When the caucus voted to reject Toombs's resolution, Toombs and Stephens, along with four southern colleagues, walked out. In the subsequent balloting they cast their votes for Meredith Gentry of Tennessee, who couldn't win. But now it seemed Winthrop couldn't win, either. Though he held steady in subsequent votes at 102, he still needed a dozen additional votes from Free Soil abolitionists or southern Whigs. But the Free Soilers considered him too soft on the South, and Toombs's southern Whigs wouldn't budge.

Meanwhile, Cobb's vote fell as Democrats began looking for a new candidate who could break the logjam. The four ballots on December 7 saw Cobb down to around sixty-five votes, then plummeting to a mere five on the twenty-eighth ballot. Emery Potter of Ohio became a serious contender with seventy-six votes.

Then a new entry emerged. He was Indiana Democrat William J. Brown, forty-four, who had served a single term in the House before taking a high-level postal job under President Polk. Now he was back in the House and anxious to demonstrate leadership prowess. On December 11, through seven votes, Brown's tally went from 88 to 109, just five short of a majority.

At that point Winthrop rose to ask his friends to withdraw their support. Nothing could give him greater pain, he said, "than to feel conscious of standing in such an attitude before the House as to interfere with its organization." Floor chaos ensued as Whigs sought a quick adjournment so they could regroup, while Democrats wanted another vote to put their man Brown over the top. The Whigs prevailed, and the House adjourned "in great confusion."

The next day Brown's vote total climbed to 112, just two shy of victory. He seemed unstoppable. But disturbing rumors began filtering through the House floor, and Stanly, the North Carolina Whig, made an oblique reference to them in a feisty floor speech in which he suggested he could look at his party colleagues without blushing, but wasn't certain the opposition could do the same. This brought to his feet

Thomas Bayly, a Virginia Democrat, who objected to the insinuation "that something improper has taken place between the democratic party and the free-soilers. . . . Sir, it is such an insinuation as the gentleman ought not to make lightly, or to which we ought in silence to submit."

George Ashmun of Massachusetts interjected: "Has not a correspondence taken place between the member from Indiana [Mr. Brown] and some member of the free-soil party, in which he has pledged himself to constitute the committees in a manner satisfactory to them?"

> **Mr. BAYLY:** I know of no such correspondence. Is the gentleman authorized to say that there has been such an one? If so, what is his authority?
>
> **Mr. ASHMUN:** Common rumor.
>
> **Mr. BAYLY:** And does not the gentleman know that common rumor is a common liar? [Turning to Mr. Brown.] Has any such correspondence taken place?
>
> Mr. BROWN shook his head.
>
> **Mr. BAYLY**, continuing: I am authorized to say that no such correspondence has taken place.

But it had. Wilmot had written Brown on December 10, recounting a conversation in which Brown had promised to constitute the three key committees with jurisdiction over slavery in ways satisfactory to the Free Soilers in exchange for Free Soil votes in the speakership race. Brown's reply confirmed the deal. When this exchange became public, Brown promptly withdrew from the race.

That left the House further stymied. "Not only are we without a speaker," declared Albert Gallatin Brown, a Mississippi Democrat, on the floor of the chamber, "but both parties are without a candidate." He proposed a resolution making Howell Cobb the Speaker based on the Democrats' majority status in the body. That was quickly rejected, but it unleashed a torrent of political anger and vitriol. It had been almost possible for several days to forget that this wasn't merely a procedural struggle but rather an effusion of passions over slavery. Richard Meade, a Virginia Democrat, brought the chamber back to reality on December 13.

"We have been acting for eight days a farce," he declared. The crux of the matter, he added, was a concern that House committees would generate legislation "which will produce discussion and agitation on a question which threatens the peace and integrity of the country." Everyone knew precisely which question he was talking about. Then Meade issued his own threat against the peace and integrity of the country, based on his fervent anti-Wilmot sentiments. "But, sir," he intoned, "if the organization of this House is to be followed by the passage of these bills—if these outrages are to be committed upon my people, I trust in God, sir, that my eyes have rested upon the last Speaker of the House of Representatives."

When New York's Duer suggested mildly that Meade's words seemed to stamp him as a "disunionist," the Virginian erupted in anger.

"It is false," he yelled.

"You are a liar," shot back Duer.

These assaults on decorum generated a commotion on the floor so intense that the sergeant at arms had to enter the scene with his mace in order to restore order. Robert Toombs then rose to declare that he himself would gladly accept the disunionist label:

> I do not hesitate . . . to avow before this House and the country, and in the presence of the living God, that if by your legislation you seek to drive us from the territories of California and New Mexico, purchased by the common blood and treasure of the whole people, and to abolish slavery in this District, thereby attempting to fix a national degradation upon half the States of this confederacy, I am for disunion; and if my physical courage be equal to the maintenance of my convictions of right and duty, I will devote all I am and all I have on earth to its consummation.

Edward Baker of Illinois, a Whig and Mexican War veteran, figuratively laughed at such taunts. It was difficult for northerners, he said, to believe their southern brethren were in earnest.

"We will teach you we are in earnest," retorted Democrat Daniel
Wallace of South Carolina.

Mr. BAKER: I should be obliged to the gentlemen if they would
tell me how this knowledge is to be imparted.

Mr. WALLACE: When I said they would teach you, I spoke in
the name of the people of the South; and, in my opinion,
they will have their rights in spite of the North—and it is
that we intend to teach you.

Mr. BAKER: Sir, I profess myself still unable to learn, from the
gentleman's explanation, how we are to be taught. . . . Gentlemen, when you threaten it, we shall doubt—when you
protest, we shall disclaim; but no fervid declarations, no
fiery appeals to southern feelings, no solemn invocations addressed to the Almighty, (as if, indeed, he were a God of discord,) will make us believe that here in this hall there is one
man who chambers in his secret heart a purpose so accursed
and so deadly.

Alexander Stephens couldn't let that go. "I tell you, before that God
that rules the universe," he declared, "that I would rather the southern
country, with all her statesmen and all her great spirits, was offered up
an honorable sacrifice, than that we should submit for one instant to
degradation. [Great applause.]"

And so it went until passions were exhausted for the moment and
members finally got back to voting. The results generated no cheer
for either party or either region. Fully thirty members received votes,
though fourteen got just one and another six received two. Winthrop
and Cobb, back in the game, led the pack with fifty-nine and forty votes,
respectively. Further balloting offered no sign of any breakthrough.

Members put forth various ideas for breaking the deadlock—lopping
off the candidates with the fewest votes after each ballot until a majority emerged; selecting a bipartisan committee to craft some kind of
emergency process; reducing the required number of votes for victory,
ballot by ballot, from the full majority number; going with a plurality

outcome (suggested numerous times). None of these could get majority approval.

By Saturday, December 22, House members had had enough. The previous day's balloting, the fifty-ninth since December 3, had yielded no hope for any kind of resolution within the foreseeable future. Twenty-one members received votes, which in itself precluded the emergence of any majority resolution. When Tennessee Democrat Frederick Stanton dusted off the hoary notion of going with a plurality, members could no longer resist. Stanton suggested three more ballots under majority rule, but if no one emerged, then the next tally would select a Speaker based merely on who got the most votes, even without a majority.

After much debate and disposition of numerous substitute amendments, the Stanton Resolution passed 113 to 106, and the chamber promptly went through the three majority votes. They revealed that Cobb and Winthrop had shot back up to numbers close to where they had been in the early balloting nearly three weeks before. But neither could get a majority. In the subsequent plurality vote, Cobb received 102 tallies to Winthrop's 100. The House avidly passed a resolution, 149 to 33, declaring Cobb the speaker.

"The long agony is over," proclaimed the *Union*. But it wasn't over. In order to get a speaker, the House had abandoned its hallowed principle of majority rule, a haunting lapse for many. Beyond that, the extended drama—at various times frustrating, frightening, and farcical—reflected the broader political realities of the nation. America was split down the middle over slavery. The Free Soilers could exercise leverage from their balance-of-power position, but seemed more inclined to indulge their political fervor. And neither of the major parties could span the North-South divide with speaker candidates considered moderate, such as Winthrop and Cobb. The hopes of party elders for solidarity were dashed when a group of southern Whigs and a few southern Democrats shunned party loyalty in favor of regional sensibilities. And so the festering passions on both sides continued to generate tremors in the body politic. The nation, it now seemed clear, was on a path toward catastrophe.

3

THE CRUCIBLE OF 1850

||||||||||||||||||||||||||||||||||||||||||||||||||||||||||||||||||||||||

CURTAIN CALL FOR THE OLD GUARD

On the evening of January 21, 1850, Henry Clay ventured into a torrential Washington rainfall and appeared unannounced at the Louisiana Avenue home of Daniel Webster, a few blocks northwest of the Capitol. The visitor didn't look well. Aside from being drenched, he appeared weary and coughed incessantly. Although the two powerful Whigs had been friends and rivals (mostly rivals) for nearly four decades, they had hardly spoken with each other for eight years, during Clay's Washington absence. But now he was back, bent on taming the treacherous slavery issue, once and for all, through a comprehensive compromise.

Webster welcomed his unexpected guest and listened as Clay outlined his legislative plan and entreated his colleague to join the effort. The Massachusetts senator embraced the concept in principle, but said he needed to study the details before committing himself. The two men parted with a handshake on what would become their final collaboration.

Eight days later Clay rose in the Senate to put forth eight resolutions designed to advance "the peace, concord, and harmony of the union of these States" by settling "all existing questions of controversy between them arising out of the institution of slavery, upon a fair, equitable, and just basis." Thus began an eight-month clamor of intense political contention that produced, in the end, a compromise much along the lines of Clay's concept. But the drama was fraught with zigs and zags, surprises, and revelations about the state of American politics.

The story comes into focus through the attitudes and ambitions of four central figures. They were President Taylor, slow of thought and politically unschooled, but ironclad in his convictions and intentions; and the so-called Great Triumvirate of Clay, Webster, and Calhoun, battle-scarred old lions of the veld, struggling now to maintain their political might even as the timbre of their roar dissipated.

Taylor knew he had to quell the slavery passions roiling the nation, and he set about to do so in his own way. Characteristically, though, he viewed it narrowly—largely as a product of the incendiary Wilmot Proviso, pushed by aggressive antislavery northerners, but hated and feared by the South. If he could neutralize the proviso, he calculated, he could calm the civic waters. The immediate challenge centered on those vast lands of California and New Mexico, still under military rule because Congress hadn't managed to determine how their status as free or slave states would be settled. They were ready for an interim territorial status leading to statehood, but as territories they would come under the jurisdiction of Congress, where the slavery deadlock remained intractable.

So Taylor hatched a clever plan. He would have both entities organize themselves for immediate statehood, bypassing the territorial phase and determining their own slavery policy in the process. Then Congress wouldn't take jurisdiction, and Wilmot's proviso wouldn't come up. As it happened, Californians already had moved in that direction and had voted unanimously for a constitutional provision outlawing slavery in their state. New Mexico seemed poised to pursue a similar course. The Taylor Plan, as it became known, made sense for California, which had experienced a massive influx of Americans lured there by the exciting gold discoveries near Sutter's Mill and because the people there were clamoring for mature governmental structures. Many in Washington, however, didn't consider New Mexico, sparsely populated and barely organized even as a territory, ready for direct statehood.

But in his annual message to Congress, delivered the previous December, Taylor had recommended congressional approval for both when their statehood applications arrived—and, in the meantime, he wanted no congressional action on the matter. He added that "all causes of uneasiness may be avoided" if lawmakers would stay away from "those exciting topics of a sectional character which have hitherto produced painful apprehensions in the public mind."

To Henry Clay, this was just the kind of inadequacy he had come to expect from Taylor. Yes, the matter of slavery extension into the Mexican cession required immediate attention, Clay believed, and leaving that vexing question to the people of the new states, known as "popular sovereignty," was a good idea. But other emotion-laden issues related to slavery also cried out for resolution, and Taylor had glossed over them. Clay advocated a truly comprehensive solution that would pull all the nettlesome issues surrounding slavery together in a way that could garner enough support from enough lawmakers on enough separate issues to bring about a collective accommodation.

By this time Clay had taken on the appearance of an old man, his hair receding and thinning, his face gaunt, his gait slowed. And the persistent cough presaged a possibly more ominous decline. But he remained trim as ever, his posture still ramrod straight, his demeanor always jaunty, his famous drollery at the ready. Now, at the autumn of his career, he seemed determined to produce a supreme achievement to cap his illustrious political résumé. And his love of country no doubt added urgency to the project.

But other human emotions also came into play. Stung in 1848 at being rejected for the presidential nomination of the Whig Party, which he had founded, Clay felt the sting all the more because of his low opinion of Taylor. He viewed the general's nomination as the triumph of a "mere personal party" over the principled institution of his creation. Later, after Taylor's presidential victory, Clay feared it would mean "the ruin of the Whigs." But not if he could prevent that ruin by outmaneuvering a president he considered fuzzy-headed and inept.

And Clay could mobilize throngs of followers. Upon his Washington arrival, he revealed to a friend, he was urged by members of both parties to "calm the raging elements." Although fear of failure had induced hesitations for a time, he now felt certain that he was the man for the job. After all, with Andrew Jackson's death some five years earlier, Clay clearly was America's most popular man, pursued, applauded, and fawned over by throngs of citizens wherever he went. "Much deference and consideration are shown me by even political opponents," he wrote to a friend after traveling to Washington for the new congressional session. Attending a White House New Year's party, he found himself, as he boasted to his wife, "an object of as much attraction as the President himself."

Clay didn't have much to lose in taking on Taylor, who was friendly enough on the surface but demonstrated no interest whatsoever in Clay's views on politics or policy. As a Washington player, the Kentuckian couldn't be shunned by the president any more thoroughly than he already had been.

Daniel Webster found himself in a similar posture. After giving Taylor's 1848 candidacy merely lukewarm support, he now held little influence over the administration. But his bigger problem was the accretion of influence he was experiencing in his own state.

Webster had gotten himself ill-positioned on the slavery issue. He had always decried the institution, sometimes with passionate eloquence—but always from afar. Like his young protégé, Robert Winthrop, he had never joined the North's antislavery provocateurs or enlisted in crusades upon southern institutions. He favored noninterference in hopes that the evil institution would wither away on its own. Thus, he was known as a New England "Cotton Whig"—uncomfortable with emotional agitations on the issue and bent on maintaining the lucrative flow of southern cotton to burgeoning Massachusetts textile factories.

This Webster ethos generated increasing scorn from the state's rising Conscience Whigs, who viewed slavery as a civic evil and considered its eradication a moral imperative. Some even abandoned their Whig heritage to align with the emergent Free Soil Party. These Massachusetts Whigs and their followers had begun to dismiss Webster as "a relic of a bygone era," as one biographer put it.

They were not entirely wrong. "All this agitation, I think," Webster wrote to a friend, "will subside, without serious result, but still it is mischievous." At the start of the 31st Congress, he predicted that emotions would "cool off" and added: "No bones will be broken." And so it was natural that Webster would sign on to Clay's grand compromise concept designed to prevent broken bones. He knew his state's Conscience Whigs wouldn't like it but considered their antagonism a price worth paying.

As for Calhoun, everyone knew he was dying. Even during the previous congressional session, long before he needed a steady hand just to make his way to his Senate desk for the March 4 reading of his final speech, he had fainted three times in the Senate lobby. "Ah, Mr. Rhett," he sighed to his South Carolina protégé, Robert Barnwell Rhett, following one of his fainting episodes, "my career is nearly done. The great battle must be fought by you younger men." But, with his characteristic ingenuity, he had set in motion a series of events designed to help such younger men carry on the fight.

Peering into the future, Calhoun could see that the North was outflanking the South in population, political power, and economic might. Thus the North eventually would abolish slavery and destroy the southern way of life. The South must therefore unite into a tight entity with enough political muscle to force the North to back off, to cease the antislavery agitations and let southerners live their own lives in their own way. No more southern Whigs vs. southern Democrats, but rather a consolidated southern party confident enough and bold enough to force a northern retreat under threat of a Union breakup.

Back in December 1848, Calhoun had called a meeting of southern senators and congressmen in Washington with the aim of producing an address to the people of the South. It would outline the dire threat of northern encroachment and advocate southern coalescence in response. The resulting document, written largely by Calhoun and ready for signatures in January 1849, reiterated his well-worn expressions of protest and defiance. "If you become united, and prove yourselves in earnest," said the statement, "the North will be brought to a pause . . . ; and that may lead to a change of measures, and the adoption of a course of policy that may quietly and peacefully terminate this long conflict between the two sections."

However realistic or fanciful this concept may have been, it didn't resonate much with southern members of Congress. Only 48 of 121 members from Calhoun's region signed the document, even after it had been toned down through several drafting sessions. And only two of forty-eight southern Whigs signed it, since by this time Zachary Taylor had become president, and southerners expected him to take up their cause. It was a signal defeat for Calhoun.

But these southern politicians in Washington, reluctant to betray their party ties, didn't reflect the rising tide of alarm back in their states as northern lawmakers seemed to be edging toward sufficient unity of their own to outlaw slavery in Washington, D.C., and perhaps even apply Wilmot to California and New Mexico. Throughout 1849, therefore, a percolation of southern agitation ensued, with numerous states—Virginia, Florida, Missouri, South Carolina—passing resolutions calling for the kind of sectional unity and perhaps even collective action for which Calhoun had been advocating.

It resulted in a large, unofficial, bipartisan conference of southern states at Jackson, Mississippi, in October. The delegates called for a larger and more official convention of all slave states to commence at Nashville, Tennessee, on June 3, 1850. Several southern governments promptly announced they would send delegations, while other states seemed headed in that direction. Southern anxiety increased after Taylor's declaration to Robert Toombs, on the eve of the new Congress in December, that he would not veto Wilmot if it reached his desk. Further, Taylor had surrounded himself with northern Wilmot men, particularly New York senator William Seward, a forceful and cagey pol with a powerful hatred of slavery. Finally, Taylor had made clear that, as a strong nationalist, he would employ overwhelming force to protect and preserve the Union.

All this proved incendiary throughout the South and boosted the Calhoun outlook in the region. The *Charleston Courier*'s Washington correspondent quoted Alabama representative Henry Hilliard as declaring that, as the *Courier* writer put it, "the South is fully resolved to resist any measures that shall exclude her people from residence in the territories acquired from Mexico." Alabama senator Jeremiah Clemens, considered a measured and moderate southern spokesman, now was predicting that another three weeks of slavery agitation would render it "impossible to save the Union." He warned: "We do not intend to stand still and have our throats cut." Northern politicians responded in sorrow. "My soul sickens at the threats to dissolve the Union," said Delaware's John M. Clayton, a longtime senator and now Taylor's secretary of state.

S uch was the state of the nation as Clay thrust himself into the fray with his eight resolutions, presented to the Senate on January 29 and outlined in elaborate detail in a two-day floor speech on February 5 to 6. The provisions:

California would join the Union as a free state based on the Californians' own constitution. Congress would not be involved, and Wilmot would not come into play. For the rest of the Mexican cession, territorial governments would be established, "without the adoption of any restriction or condition on the subject of slavery." Popular sovereignty would prevail unless the country somehow accepted the southern view that the Constitution prescribed a right for all Americans to enter all U.S. territories with their property (including slaves).

But, said Clay, slavery had been prohibited by Mexican law in the acquired lands, and that law still applied. Further, those lands simply weren't hospitable to slavery and never would be. "I do believe," intoned Clay, "that not within one foot of the territory acquired by us from Mexico will slavery ever be planted." Americans, he said, should bow to the power of the "two truths—one of law and the other of fact."

Clay next addressed an increasingly fevered boundary dispute between the slave state of Texas and the free territory of New Mexico. Texas, claiming vast lands stretching west into the Mexican cession, threatened military action to assert its claim. Clay largely debunked the Texas demand but proposed that the United States assume a large Texas debt retained when the United States annexed Texas in 1845.

Two of the resolutions dealt with slavery and the slave trade in

Washington, D.C. Since the capital rested on territory donated to the Union by Maryland, a slave state, it would be "inexpedient," argued Clay, for Congress to abolish slavery there without that state's consent. But, on the matter of ending the D.C. slave trade, he considered that "expedient," as large numbers of people, of both North and South, felt severe discomfort with the spectacle of slave auctions in the shadow of hallowed governmental structures.

Finally, Clay's proposal would certify that the interstate slave trade was not subject to congressional interference; and it would bolster federal fugitive slave laws to meet the constitutional requirement that runaway slaves "shall be delivered up on Claim of the party to whom [their] Service or Labour may be due."

Looked at as an accounting ledger, it seemed that the North scored the largest tangible gains—California as a free state by law; New Mexico to be carved up into states that almost assuredly would be free based on terrain and local preference; Texas curtailed in its extensive land grab; the D.C. slave trade abolished. But Clay gave the South a significant intangible concession—an implicit acceptance of slavery where it already existed, even as the South's power in the country declined in relative terms. There would be no Wilmot Proviso; no congressional interference in the interstate slave trade; no assault on D.C. slavery; no more willful actions on the part of northerners to thwart the recovery of runaway slaves.

At one o'clock on the afternoon of February 5, the Senate convened to hear the first installment of Clay's four-and-a-half-hour speech elaborating on his plan. Upon his Capitol arrival, the senator discovered throngs of citizens jammed into the galleries, hallways, Rotunda, and the Senate chamber—"more crowded than we ever saw it," reported the *Union*—all there to experience the flowing eloquence and exacting logic of the Great Pacificator. The man of the hour suffered from a cold, and the nettlesome cough persisted. Indeed, he felt "quite weak and exhausted," as he told a friend on the way into the huge marble building. But when he rose to speak, he straightened to his full height and took command of the chamber as in days of old.

"I have witnessed many periods of great anxiety, of peril, and of danger even to the country," declared Clay, "but I have never before arisen to address any assembly so oppressed, so appalled, so anxious." He ascribed the dark mood to "passion, passion—party, party—and intemperance," and expressed fears that such sentiments would thwart his great effort. Then he presented an elaborate justification for each of his resolutions and assured his audience that he sought no assaults on principle, but merely adjustments in feelings and opinions. In short, Clay had calibrated his program with intricate shrewdness to siphon off the most impassioned political sentiments from around the edges of the slavery issue, to bolster the political standing of the restrained center, and restore discourse to a more sonorous octave.

"What is a compromise?" Clay asked the next day in his peroration. "It is . . . a work in which, for the sake of peace and concord, one party abates his extreme demands in consideration of an abatement of extreme demands by the other party." Beseeching his colleagues to pursue such a course, he intoned, "Let us go to the limpid fountain of unadulterated patriotism, and, performing a solemn lustration, return divested of all selfish, sinister, and sordid impurities, and think alone of our God, our country, our consciences, and our glorious Union."

The Clay speech rocked the nation, setting off a debate that seemed to incorporate a greater sense that perhaps a durable solution could actually be found. Predictably, it garnered plenty of criticism from southern radicals, now increasingly called "fire-eaters," and northern abolitionists. The Democratic *Union* dismissed the plan as containing "nothing of the true spirit of compromise." But the southern-leaning *New York Herald*, while predicting Clay's arguments would be "stoutly resisted" in many quarters, added that they "cannot fail to make a vast impression upon the restless mind of the whole country." The *Charleston Courier* reflected Clay's impact on many southerners by suggesting, "The plan of a withdrawal from the Union by the South is now condemned by southern members as inexpedient."

Following Clay's speech, the Senate debate unfolded through February and into March, taking on some powerful poignancy with the March 4 Calhoun speech read by Senator Mason as the broken South Carolinian looked on, and later with the ceremonial outpouring that followed Calhoun's death.

As for Webster, he had been in the grip of indecision since his session with Clay on that rainy night of January 21. As a staunch Whig, he felt bound to heed the entreaties from party bigwigs that he support the Taylor Plan. Some even dangled promises that they would bolster him up for an 1852 presidential bid if he wished to run. But in the end he could see that he couldn't dodge the secession crisis. He would support Clay in an elaborate Senate speech, which meant he would disregard the most aggressive antislavery arguments of his region and seek to assuage southern concerns in the interest of national unity.

The atmosphere was thick with anticipation on March 7 as throngs arrived for Webster's address in numbers that rivaled Clay's audience of a month before—"multitudes of both sexes," said the *National Intelligencer*. The Massachusetts senator emphasized with breathtaking clarity that he had no intention of embracing either section or any partisan passions. After describing the secular and religious sensibilities of southerners, he added, "And candor obliges me to say, that I believe they are just as conscientious, many of them, and the religious people, all of them, as they are at the North who hold different opinions." In deriding "absolutists," who "think that nothing is good but what is perfect," he studiously avoided any distinction between northern or southern absolutists. In both instances, he said, they have "none too much charity towards others who differ from them." He offered not so much as a nod toward the Conscience Whigs of his state and spoke not at all of slavery as a moral issue.

Even more incendiary was Webster's call for bolstering the nation's fugitive slave laws, thus implicating antislavery northerners in a system they considered a blot of immorality upon the national escutcheon. The constitutional language that requires states to deliver up fugitives from service, declared Webster, "is as binding in honor and conscience as any other article." This from a man who represented a state considered a hotbed of resistance to even mild fugitive slave laws.

Regarding northern abolition societies, Webster decried the "mischiefs their interference with the South has produced." But he also deplored the South's mischievous secession talk. "Peaceful secession!" he thundered. "Sir, your eyes and mine are never destined to see that miracle."

Webster's words swept across the nation in pamphlet form and newspaper reprints, with two hundred thousand pamphlets distributed just from Washington. Early responses were favorable. The *National Intelligencer* said it gave "fresh lustre to the fame of the great orator," and the secessionist-leaning *Charleston Mercury* said the senator "marks his way so clearly, and treads so loyally on the plain track of the constitution . . . that the difficulty is not to agree but to disagree with him."

But antislavery northerners quickly coalesced into a powerful cry of opprobrium. "[U]nequal to the occasion and unworthy of its author," declared Horace Greeley's *New York Tribune*. The *Boston Daily Atlas*, a Whig paper, reported that only six New England newspapers supported Webster's arguments while seventy opposed them. As for politicians, the *Atlas* added, "Throughout the Northern portion of either branch [of Congress], the dissent is almost, if not quite, universal."

Indeed, Horace Mann, a Whig representative, called him a "fallen star," and even Robert Winthrop privately described portions of the speech as "quite atrocious." A prominent Boston merchant named John Murray Forbes complained that Webster had "surrendered to the slave-owners" and predicted the senator couldn't get "the vote of one third of his own party for any office." Recognizing the seriousness of Forbes's observation, Webster rushed back to Massachusetts even before the end of the congressional session to steady up his political standing. With his own political survival threatened, Webster had little time now for Clay's compromise efforts.

As the Senate debate proceeded in both the Senate and the House, events unfolded in quick succession. Clay became chairman of a Senate Select Committee of Thirteen, charged with fine-tuning the compromise elements and meshing them into a coherent concept for Senate consideration. In April, the committee took action, initially opposed by Clay but ultimately embraced by him, to wrap the various compromise proposals into a single bill, called the "omnibus bill." The idea was to force lawmakers to accept provisions they didn't like in exchange for provisions they favored. Breaking the various elements into separate bills, the committee feared, would lead to some of them being rejected, or vetoed by Taylor, which could derail the entire effort.

On May 8, Clay publicly unveiled the select committee's omnibus measure, which by now had incorporated the idea of carving out a separate state of Utah (in the process of being organized by Mormon migrants) from the broader expanse of New Mexico. Tensions flared between Clay and Taylor as the senator increasingly chided the president for his insistence that only the California and New Mexico questions needed immediate attention and were proceeding just fine on their own. Taylor remained the leading impediment to Clay's omnibus approach.

On June 3 the Nashville Convention on southern unity convened amid much southern fanfare. It met for nine days, then adjourned with an agreement to meet again after the current congressional session if events seemed to warrant it. But only five state legislatures sent official representatives, while four others sent delegations without any legislative imprimatur and six slave states stayed away. Calhoun's dream of southern unity didn't materialize, and the South remained divided between a majority of moderates inclined to await the outcome of the congressional compromise effort and a smaller contingent of fire-eaters leaning toward secession to protect what they considered embattled southern rights. It seemed clear that Clay's omnibus bill, which had reached the Senate floor by the time of the convention, had neutralized some of the southern anxiety.

By late June, New Mexico had sent to Congress a constitution and statehood application that claimed nearly all of the land coveted by Texas. This was precisely what Taylor had anticipated and what he now favored with his characteristic stubbornness. But fevers were running high on the territorial question. After the *National Intelligencer* reported on July 3 that U.S. forces and Texas militias were edging close to actual hostilities, a number of southern Whigs implored the president to seek a negotiated outcome of the territorial dispute. Taylor defiantly threatened to throttle any Texas provocations and hang the instigators. His intransigence wasn't helping the cause of congressional compromise.

Then, on July 5, the president became ill, probably with cholera, and four days later he died. The new president was Millard Fillmore, an imposing figure with a pleasant round face, an easy manner, and a taste for stylish attire. Born into an impoverished family of dirt farmers in central New York, Fillmore struggled from early adulthood to better himself intellectually, socially, and financially. He clerked for the law, took up a small-town practice, got elected to the state legislature, and served four terms in Congress. He was New York State comptroller and a relatively obscure figure on the national scene when Taylor tapped him to join the general's presidential ticket in 1848. Discerning acquaintances noted that Fillmore's grit and ambition were mixed with a certain diffidence, a touch of insecurity stemming perhaps from his modest background and lack of formal education.

But now he was president, and he viewed the gathering crisis far differently from Taylor. He favored Clay's comprehensive compromise, viewed popular sovereignty as the best means of settling territorial slavery questions, and brought a spirit of flexibility to the Texas boundary dispute. And he had displayed an impressive independence of mind as vice president when he informed Taylor that, if Clay's omnibus bill came down to a tie vote in the Senate, he would break the tie in Clay's favor. Indeed, Fillmore and Clay had been on friendly terms for years, and the new president quickly established a warm political alliance with the Kentuckian. "My relations with the new chief are intimate and confidential," an elated Clay informed his son.

With Taylor gone, along with the internal Whig split between Clay and his president, prospects brightened for the omnibus compromise. On July 22, with the Senate showdown looming, Clay took the floor for a final impassioned defense of his handiwork. It was a bravura performance. "Mr. President," he intoned, "all the tendencies of the time, I lament to say, are towards disquietude, if not more fatal consequences." But the compromise was designed to "leave nothing in the public mind to fester and agitate the country." The speech was widely hailed, and the omnibus legislation seemed destined for congressional approval.

Then it all went awry. The trouble began with a parliamentary maneuver on the Senate floor by Maryland's James A. Pearce, an omnibus partisan, who merely wanted to clean up a provision related to the Texas–New Mexico dispute. But his approach opened up an opportunity for Texas supporters to nix that section of the bill altogether. With that section gone, the logic of the omnibus approach unraveled, as senators concluded they could pull the measure apart, vote only for favored provisions, and go on record as rejecting others. Compromise opponents promptly seized the initiative with motions to pull out other omnibus sections, starting with California. Soon there was no omnibus, and Congress was back at the beginning.

A stunned and dejected Clay, exhausted from six months of intense legislative labors, fled Washington for an extended respite of sunbathing and recuperation at Newport, Rhode Island. The nation was left to contemplate the reality that the old guard of American politics resided now in the past. Calhoun was dead. Clay languished in defeat. And Webster, his Massachusetts standing in tatters, was safely away from partisan politics. Leadership to address the ominous slavery agitation would have to come now from the next generation.

One possibility was Stephen A. Douglas, the irrepressible senator from Illinois and chairman of the critical Committee on Territories. Just thirty-seven, he had been elected to the Senate three years earlier after a meteoric career that had included stints as rural lawyer, state legislator, Illinois Supreme Court judge, and congressman. Just five feet four, with broad shoulders and stubby legs, he was built like a block of wood, with a smaller block of wood atop serving as his head. But inside that head was a remarkable mind directing an iron will. Those inclined to dismiss the man based on first impressions soon learned that he dominated just about every assemblage in which he found himself, based on his zesty good humor, quick tongue, and wide-ranging intellect. One contemporary compared his political skills to the physical attributes of a prizefighter: "Pluck, quickness and strength; adroitness in shifting his position, avoiding his adversary's blows and hitting him in unexpected places."

Douglas had anticipated the Clay debacle, largely because he didn't think the omnibus approach could ever work. Now, under the authority of his Committee on Territories, he seized the initiative with the intent of molding and shaping the various Clay resolutions in ways that would garner majority support on a piecemeal basis.

He began with the Texas boundary issue and settled it quickly with a compromise that gave the state 33,333 more square miles than Clay's proposal, with a $10 million inducement thrown in to cover Texas debts. The Senate passed the bill on August 9, then approved the California statehood measure four days later. With Fillmore's strong endorsement, the New Mexico territorial bill cleared the floor on August 14, with the fugitive slave measure following a few days later. Within three weeks Douglas had pushed through the Senate the entire Clay package. Propelled by the Senate momentum, the measures all received rapid approval from the House.

What happened? As it turned out, Clay had done his work well in piecing together just the right issues to induce enough members to transcend regional passions and focus on the higher goal of national tranquility. His error had been tactical—pulling them all together into the clunky omnibus. Douglas's timely leadership had overcome that lapse by pulling the disparate measures out of the omnibus and crafting winning coalitions for each in turn. But Webster earned recognition as well for his courageous resolve to rise above the passions of his constituents and focus instead on the imperatives of Union cohesion. And Fillmore had added a final push of presidential leadership that had brought along many northern Whigs who, under Taylor, had been staunch Wilmot Proviso men.

Widespread jubilation greeted passage of the compromise legislation. Throngs of celebrants surrounded Clay wherever he showed up on his trip back to Washington in late August, and crowds filtered through the capital city to serenade compromise leaders and display their elation. On one momentous night, writes historian David M. Potter, an admonition circulated that it was the duty of all patriots to get drunk, whereupon a blitz of fervent patriotism ensued.

Fillmore expressed the sentiment of many when he stated, in his Annual Message of December 1850, that the compromise legislation was "in its character final and irrevocable." Douglas echoed that admonition. "Let us cease agitating," he said, "stop the debate, and drop the subject." Michigan's Lewis Cass, the Democrats' 1848 presidential nominee, agreed. "I think the question is settled . . . ," he said.

But it wasn't clear that the most fervent agitators of both regions and all political parties would accept those admonitions and embrace the idea that they had no further say in the controversy. Amid the celebrations and good feelings about a cataclysm averted, there was good reason to believe that "finality"—a term gaining wide currency among the hopeful—might not be the last word on this grand compromise, as brilliant and encouraging as it was. Clay's underlying aim had been to isolate and marginalize the political forces represented by southern fire-eaters and the North's morality-driven abolitionists, to overwhelm them with a powerful, ongoing flow of unionist patriotism. But would those citizens who harbored the most intense passions on the subject accept that isolation and marginalization? Two places to look for answers to that question turned out to be Massachusetts and South Carolina.

4

BAY STATE TURMOIL

||||||||||||||||||||||||||||||||||||||||||||||||||||||||||||||||||||||||||||||||||

MASSACHUSETTS ENTERS A NEW POLITICAL ERA

I n mid-July 1850, as the congressional machinations over Henry
Clay's compromise concepts progressed, Robert Winthrop received a visit from his longtime friend Joseph Grinnell, a fellow Massachusetts congressman and also a close friend of the new president,
Millard Fillmore. Grinnell said he was acting as a presidential emissary
to explain a delicate quandary facing Fillmore. He revealed that the
president had been consumed with a bout of paralyzing irresolution.

This didn't surprise Winthrop, given the new president's reputation
for having a sometimes diffident and always cautious nature. But Fillmore had begun his presidency a few days earlier with uncharacteristic
audacity when he fired the entire Zachary Taylor cabinet and set about
to replace Taylor's men with his own. Now, though, reported Grinnell,
he was back to his usual hesitancy, agonizing over the crucial hiring
decisions confronting him. In visiting Fillmore recently, Grinnell found
the president "in a pitiable state of indecision," grappling with "many
doubts and difficulties."

One of those difficulties involved Winthrop. It seems Fillmore
was struggling particularly with whether to offer the secretary of state

portfolio to Daniel Webster or to Winthrop. Grinnell said the president wished to discuss his dilemma with Winthrop and determine his interest in the job.

The next day, July 17, Winthrop appeared at Fillmore's suite in Willard's Hotel, where the new president maintained offices pending the White House departure of Taylor's widow, Margaret. As Winthrop later described the scene, he was escorted into a makeshift dressing room, where he sat with the president on a narrow bed. After pleasantries, the plainspoken congressman got straight to the point. He said he understood the president was pondering whether to give the State Department to Webster or himself and wanted his frank opinion on the matter. Fillmore nodded.

After careful consideration, continued Winthrop, he had "come to a very decided conclusion that Webster should have the preference." He described the senator as an "intellectual giant." It was true, he acknowledged, that the man sometimes succumbed to "jealousy and pique," and Winthrop certainly knew full well "the awful nature of Webster's frowns." But, he added, the senator was a "true patriot," whose contentious March 7 address, much as Winthrop disagreed with some of it, "was dictated by a sincere desire to save the country from civil war." As for himself, said Winthrop, he faced multiple political difficulties at home, beset by anti-Whig Democrats, Free Soilers, and "certain Webster Whigs" outraged at the congressman's half-hearted endorsement of Webster's speech. Those adversarial forces, he said, could undermine his standing in the cabinet.

When Webster later heard of his friend's magnanimity, he sought out Winthrop to express gratitude. "Now, if there is anything under the sun that I can do for you, name it," said the great statesman. "Shall I write to Governor Briggs asking him to appoint you as my successor?" Winthrop, ever the political ascetic, replied that any such offer "must come unsought." He would not ask for it nor ask any friends to ask for it in his behalf.

He got it anyway. George Briggs, a wily and resourceful Whig serving his seventh year as Massachusetts governor, appointed Winthrop to fill Webster's unexpired term, and he entered the Senate on July 30. Later it was revealed that Fillmore and Webster had applied "extreme pressure" on Briggs to appoint Winthrop and keep the seat within the control of moderate Whig forces. But if Winthrop wanted a full six-year term, he would have to pass muster with the Massachusetts legislature in January.

That wouldn't be easy, given that Massachusetts politics had become a roiling cauldron of new political crosscurrents, animosities, doctrines, and coalitions. Unfolding events revealed the abhorrence that many state residents held toward the Clay/Douglas Compromise, particularly the Fugitive Slave Act. Yet plenty of political power remained in the hands of old-school politicians who viewed the compromise as the last, best hope for saving the Union. An epic struggle was brewing, and there would be winners and losers.

Nothing in Robert Winthrop's background would lead anyone to peg him as a loser. He was born in 1809 into wealth and position, a circumstance that had been a family birthright since the first Winthrops arrived in 1630. Educated at private schools, he passed the Harvard entrance exam at fourteen. Once there, he became a member of Phi Beta Kappa, commander of the campus military company, orator at the Hasty Pudding Club, speaker at his class commencement. Guests at his graduation soiree included President John Quincy Adams, and, following his marriage to Eliza Blanchard in 1832, his honeymoon trip to Virginia and Washington, D.C., included conversations with former president James Madison and current president Andrew Jackson.

From early adulthood he seemed destined for a notable political career: elected to the state's House of Representatives at twenty-six and chosen Speaker three years later; member of Congress at thirty-one, House Speaker at thirty-eight. Yet he often projected a certain stand-offishness that was unusual for a politician. Webster, seeking to impart some avuncular counsel during Winthrop's early career, wondered whether a man of his "scholarly instincts and fastidious tastes" wouldn't find it a bit "grievous and disheartening" to deal with the underside of Washington, D.C., politics—or, as he elaborated, "whether you will not one day weary of it all, and wish yourself back in your study at home."

Yet that never happened, and Winthrop excelled at the political game while shrouding the zest that propelled him. And his commitment to fair play drew colleagues to his always gracious legislative dealings. After his Senate arrival, Winthrop found himself in a floor exchange with Louisiana senator Pierre Soulé, who incorrectly denied the existence of a Louisiana statute cited by Winthrop. Later, after he had located the statutory language that proved Soulé wrong, Winthrop went to his colleague privately and offered him a chance to correct the record in his own way, rather than issuing the correction himself on the Senate floor and embarrassing the Louisianan.

Contemplating the challenge of retaining his Senate seat, Winthrop could foresee plenty of adversity. First off, it wasn't clear just how valuable the Webster connection was now, given the animosities kicked up by his inflammatory March 7 speech. Meanwhile, the hostility between Cotton Whigs and Conscience Whigs intensified month by month, and the restless Free Soilers had emerged as a disruptive political force, smarting over the Clay/Douglas Compromise and its fugitive slave component. Winthrop had voted against that runaway-slave bill, but his general support for the compromise remained a point of contention for many constituents.

"I am by no means sure Massachusetts Whiggery will survive the shock . . . of the Fugitive Bill," wrote Winthrop to a friend. His pessimism increased with rumors of an emergent "coalition" of Massachusetts Free Soilers and the state's antislavery Democrats, incensed over their national party leaders' solicitude toward the South. How any high-minded man could embrace such an unholy alliance passed his comprehension, mused Winthrop, adding, "but then, high-minded men are scarce in politics."

For Winthrop, high-mindedness meant loyalty to party and party principles. That's why he had supported the Taylor Plan until Taylor's death and then had embraced the Fillmore course as emphatically as possible within the limits of his conscience and political imperatives. But to others, high-mindedness meant shedding old party shibboleths in favor of moral fervor in the antislavery cause. Assessing that moral fervor now, Winthrop figured he likely would be the "principal loser by the transaction" that seemed to be emerging between Free Soilers and Democrats.

I f that budding transaction troubled Winthrop, it must have seriously rattled Abbott Lawrence, the quintessential Cotton Whig. Born in Groton, Massachusetts, in 1792, he arrived in Boston at age eighteen with three dollars in his pocket, an apprenticeship agreement with his older brother, Amos, and a commercial brilliance that soon made him rich and elevated him to a stature described by one contemporary as the region's "most important person."

Abbott and Amos Lawrence developed an import business that became the largest wholesale mercantile house in the country. But their real money came when they ventured into textile manufacturing just as that industry was taking off. They joined other stouthearted Massachusetts entrepreneurs, who introduced the power loom into the manufacture of cotton products and soon dominated the industry nationally.

These men demonstrated political skills that matched their business acumen. Abbott Lawrence, whose thin lips and prominent eyebrows gave him a look of resolute purpose, served two stints in the U.S. House and vied for the vice presidency in 1848. President Taylor later sent Lawrence to London as ambassador to the Court of St. James's.

He excelled at behind-the-scenes maneuvering and at directing events through carefully calculated campaign contributions and even in supplementing the personal finances of favored civic figures. Indeed, it was an open secret that he and his colleagues had augmented Daniel Webster's income for decades. As John Quincy Adams, who served in the U.S. House for seventeen years following his one-term presidency, wrote to his diary, "All Webster's political systems are interwoven with the explorations of a gold-mine for him, and all his confidential intimacies with Lawrence have been devices to screw from [Lawrence] . . . money by the fifty or hundred thousand dollars at a time."

Lawrence was a traditional Whig, dedicated to Henry Clay's famous

"American System" of high tariffs and federally supported internal improvements such as roads, bridges, and canals—all policies considered good for business. Bad for business would be intersectional tensions or a Whig fissure undermining the party's ability to protect and nurture Clay's traditional economic prescriptions. And, of course, the industrialists opposed anything that could interrupt the flow of southern cotton into their lucrative textile factories.

But Texas annexation, the Mexican War, and Wilmot's proviso had ushered in a new political force in Massachusetts: the so-called Young Whigs, mostly from established upper-crust families, who begrudged the rise of industrial new money and the political power that came with it. They set themselves firmly against both Webster and Lawrence, whose old-school rivalry these young activists considered superficial and silly. To them, the central issue, transcending all others, was the moral evil of slavery. Soon the Young Whigs would expand in number and attach themselves to increasingly influential Conscience Whigs. Some would abandon the party altogether and join the Free Soilers.

One of the early Young Whigs was Charles Francis Adams, scion of the famous family, whose intellectual journey through the tangles of the slavery question reflected his state's similar passage. Born in 1807, he grew up in the shadow of his father and grandfather, both U.S. presidents, and struggled with an internal conflict between a propulsive ambition to meet family expectations and persistent fears that he wouldn't measure up.

It didn't help that the boy's father, John Quincy Adams, pushed him relentlessly to excel in all endeavors, which often induced him to retreat to an inner world or even purposely mispronounce words or stumble in his reading—acts of subtle rebellion that the father considered "perverse." Socially awkward, the boy induced in John Quincy a "great concern" about his "antipathy to going into company," while his mother went fishing with him because he lacked childhood friends for such outings. He developed into a man of rectitude, solidity, and self-control, but also of shyness, reserve, and a degree of sanctimony (a trait inherited from his father). Though an attractive young man, he displayed his smile with parsimony, and his eyes gave him a guarded look.

Not surprisingly, Charles Francis developed a dislike for the "distressing vulgarities" of politics. He pursued instead a literary life, writing commentary and criticism for various publications. After an initial failure to make a mark, which further eroded his confidence, he finally got a break with the rise of the anti-Masonic movement, which young Adams and his father embraced. The son's writings on the topic gained notice, and he was invited to participate in a statewide anti-Masonic convention. He had found his niche: writing commentary on topics of the day while venturing warily into the thicket of politics.

In 1840 Whig officials asked him to run for the legislature, and he served in both the state house and senate between 1841 and 1846. Soon his insecurity and professional hesitancy gave way to greater confidence and professional esteem (though the neurotic young man now struggled with questions of whether he deserved his new prestige).

Adams's rise in stature coincided with the evolution of his views on slavery. He always had abhorred the institution, as had his forebears for generations. But he evinced little interest in agitating the issue and wrote in 1834 that "the most expedient course is to leave the matter for those to settle who are most deeply interested in doing so." He frowned upon northern abolitionists bent on tormenting the South and accepted the Constitution's provisions that had embedded southern slavery in the American system. But he didn't see any need to placate southerners beyond the letter of the Constitution. Hence, no slavery expansion.

Then a series of political developments in the 1830s agitated Adams more and more on the issue. Some Cotton Whig friends denounced Boston's abolitionist editor William Lloyd Garrison in terms that Adams found jarring. Garrison later was seized and dragged through the streets of New York City by a gang of proslavery thugs in a display of mob menace that shocked Adams. When proslavery zealots killed abolitionist editor Elijah Lovejoy in Alton, Illinois, Massachusetts attorney general James Austin publicly attacked not the killers but Lovejoy, who, he said, "died as the fool dieth." That was too much for Adams, who now viewed Boston as a city that was "corrupted heart and soul by the principles of slavery."

He joined the issue as never before and found exhilaration not only in the fight but also in the good fellowship with other Young Whigs.

But the Young Whigs found themselves squeezed between two increasingly hostile political forces: the extreme abolitionists, whom these more measured young men considered too radical for mainstream politics, and the increasingly defensive Cotton Whigs such as Winthrop, Edward Everett, and the Lawrence brothers, clinging to a status quo that might collapse at any time. With Massachusetts Whigs now hopelessly split, more and more Young Whigs gravitated to the Free Soil banner. Many, including Charles Francis Adams, ended up at the party's national convention in Buffalo that began on August 9, 1848, and nominated New York's Martin Van Buren as its presidential candidate. As a Democratic president in the late 1830s, Van Buren had been described frequently as "a northern man with southern principles." But now he was a firm Wilmot Proviso man as he sought a return to the White House.

His running mate turned out to be Charles Francis Adams, now a full-throated Free Soil man who also, not coincidentally, possessed a famous name that carried weight in political circles. He was elated at age forty-one to have reached finally a level of success worthy of his family—or nearly so. As he put it to his diary, the honor was "valuable only as it places me somewhat near the level of my fathers."

Over on Boston's Cornhill Street, near Adams Square, where William Lloyd Garrison ran his weekly newspaper, the *Liberator*, the great abolitionist merely harrumphed at the news from Buffalo. The new party, he complained, did not "aim at the life, but only at the growth, of Slavery." But Garrison nonetheless perceived significance in politicians abandoning old party loyalties and taking up with former enemies. "When Martin Van Buren and Charles Adams combine," he conceded, "the Revolution is at least begun."

The revolution he had in mind was the immediate eradication of slavery and full equality for blacks. And, if that revolution meant the dissolution of the Union or the shredding of the Constitution, he was fine with that. God's law supersedes man's law, he believed, and he wouldn't even vote because he didn't want to participate in what he considered a fallen nation. He attacked the Constitution, whose creators had accepted slavery as a reality of their time, as "a covenant with death and an agreement with hell."

He was born in 1805 in Newburyport, Massachusetts, the son of a seaman who abandoned the family when young Lloyd, as he was known, was barely more than a toddler. Alone with five children, his mother, Maria, struggled through life with grit and a strong religious reverence but few financial prospects. Searching for opportunity, she moved to Lynn, Massachusetts, and then to Baltimore, leaving young Lloyd with a succession of Newburyport friends and benefactors. He followed his mother to Baltimore at one point, at age ten, but soon returned to more familiar surroundings in pursuit of a trade. He tried carpentry, but it didn't work out. His prospects looked bleak.

Then, in October 1818, the boy saw a sign in the offices of the *Newburyport Herald*: "Boy Wanted." Young Lloyd Garrison, at thirteen, became a newspaper apprentice under *Herald* editor and co-owner Ephraim Allen. Thus began a career that would bring him extensive fame and endless controversy.

He was a winsome lad, sunny in outlook and full of good cheer despite the childhood adversity. He enjoyed banter, spouting puns, and reciting poetry ("especially his own," as one biographer wrote). His voluble nature amused peers among the city's artisans and shopkeepers, who jocularly called him "M' Lord Garrulus." Slight but imposing, he projected a subdued confidence, dressed with style, displayed a quick mind, and conducted himself with courtesy. Within a few years Allen elevated Garrison to foreman of the company's printing office and its newspaper production shop.

The rising young man never faltered in his devotion to his mother, "a woman of sorrowful spirit," as Maria described herself, but also of an impassioned religious faith. After her death in 1823, Garrison retained a loving memory of her "vigorous, lustrous [mind] sanctified by an ever-glowing piety." Though Garrison wished to live his life in fidelity to her Baptist evangelism, he knew he would have to find his own ever-glowing piety in the secular realm. He found it in antislavery agitation, a calling he could embrace with the same moral zeal displayed by Maria in her religious preoccupations.

But that calling posed risks beyond the episode with the New York mob. Working in Baltimore for a Quaker advocacy sheet called *Genius of Universal Emancipation*, Garrison in 1829 published an item accusing a Massachusetts shipper of engaging in the domestic slave trade by shipping slaves from Baltimore to New Orleans. The shipper sued. More ominously, Garrison was charged with criminal libel and convicted. When he couldn't pay the $50 fine, he was sentenced to a six-month jail term. He served seven weeks before a friend, the wealthy New York entrepreneur Arthur Tappan, paid the fine and extracted him from his Baltimore jail cell. He walked out defiant as ever. "I am willing to be persecuted, imprisoned and bound for advocating African rights," he said, "and I should deserve to be a slave myself, if I shrunk from that duty or danger."

Two years later, on January 1, 1831, Garrison brought out volume one, issue one of the *Liberator* and set the tone that would characterize his fiery sheet for the next thirty-five years. "I will be harsh as truth," he declared, "and as uncompromising as justice. . . . I am in earnest—I will not equivocate—I will not excuse—I will not retreat a single inch— AND I WILL BE HEARD."

The paper didn't generate much money for the impassioned editor, but it gave him a platform that he leveraged brilliantly through the decades. Vehement, pugilistic, often searing in his attacks, he gained notice when other northern papers reprinted his unvarnished commentary and when southern editors inevitably extended his public exposure with further attacks. Soon his name was widely recognized throughout much of the country, as was his defiance. He would withstand his adversities, he declared, "like the oak—like the Alps—unshaken, storm-proof."

Garrison also was instrumental in the formation of the New England Anti-Slavery Society, founded in the same year as the *Liberator* and, like the *Liberator*, dedicated to the immediate abolition of slavery and full civil rights for freed blacks. Two years later he expanded the antislavery movement by cofounding, with Arthur Tappan, the American

Anti-Slavery Society. Both associations thrived on the moral force of their antislavery cause.

It wasn't merely defiant southerners who recoiled at the belligerence of Garrison and other antislavery radicals. Even many northerners lamented the increasingly defensive acrimony of southerners in response to the radicals' incessant provocations. One result was that, whereas numerous antislavery societies had dotted the southern landscape prior to 1837, afterward not one was left. William Ellery Channing, a prominent Unitarian theologian whose abolitionist sentiments were never in doubt, wrote in 1835 that the antislavery crusade of Garrison and others had "stirred up bitter passions, and a fierce fanaticism, which have shut every ear, and every heart." It seemed to many that the radical abolitionists, perhaps Garrison in particular, had contributed to the sectional standoff that roiled the nation by 1850.

One prominent Massachusetts figure who didn't gravitate to Garrison or his fiery rhetoric was a man-about-town named Charles Sumner. This troubled Garrison, as Sumner was a powerful antislavery warrior in his own right and had been a *Liberator* subscriber since 1835. But the more cautious Sumner eschewed what he considered the "vindictive, bitter, and unchristian" tone of the *Liberator*. Besides, while Garrison accepted his modest income as the price of his moral crusade, Sumner aimed at higher targets of prestige and comfort.

Born in 1811, he grew up as one of nine children in a home of austere joylessness. The boy's parents displayed almost no household affection or mirth and seemed seldom satisfied with the attainments of young Charles, who taught himself to read Latin and was accepted into the prestigious Boston Latin School. At Harvard he read prodigiously in history and literature (though he struggled with math and science) and displayed a facility for learned conversation and rousing public speaking. His friends called him "Chatterbox."

After Harvard legal studies, he entered the law and seemed headed for a successful career. Tall, lanky, and ebullient, he cut a hearty presence and made friends easily, often with people of high social rank. He lacked wit, however, and seldom brought levity into his conversations. His friend William Story said he was "almost impervious to a joke," and he suffered from a debilitating shyness toward women. (He was married once, at age fifty-five; the union was unhappy and relatively brief.)

But he cultivated male friendships and connections with verve and determination. During extensive travels through Europe, he connected through friends with European luminaries of the time, including Sir Robert Peel, Lord John Russell, Thomas Carlyle, Thomas B. Macaulay, and Austria's Prince Metternich. His friendship circle, he wrote home, "is truly *prodigious* . . . almost *unmanageable*."

Returning to Boston and what he called "the great grindstone of the law," he revealed a troublesome trait—a lack of constancy. His law practice fizzled as he struggled to summon the mental discipline to master the necessary details. He entered a period of melancholia, feeling stranded professionally and thwarted in his desire to follow his friends into matrimony. He eventually gravitated to literary pursuits and activism in behalf of social causes—prison reform, education, international peace, and, of course, the blight of slavery. He developed an almost religious-like faith in mankind's capacity for human improvement, "the good of the whole human family, its happiness . . . its progress."

Following the trendy Massachusetts transcendentalists, he concluded that, if humans were shaped by their environment, then there could be no limit to the betterment of mankind. Evil could be eradicated. This heady high-mindedness, it seemed, served as a balm for the anxieties and disappointments of his private life. "The darker his own personal prospects became," wrote biographer David Donald, "the greater grew his willingness to recognize a duty to improve society."

Increasingly, Sumner embraced a gauzy idealism expressed in a tone of zealotry—railing against patriotism in Fourth of July speeches, calling for the end of warfare throughout the world, pressing for antislavery agitation beyond what most establishment figures considered prudent. Worse, he became what David Donald called a "master of invective," directing at opponents such venom and cruelty that many Bostonians recoiled in shock and shunned him socially. So vociferously did he attack Robert Winthrop for his House vote authorizing military action against

Mexico that Winthrop terminated their long-standing friendship. "I shall allow no man to cast scandalous imputations on my motives and apply base epithets to my acts in public, and to call me his friend in private," Winthrop wrote to Sumner. "My hand is not at the service of any one who has denounced it with such ferocity as being stained with blood."

A fundamental element of Sumner's persona was gaining notice: self-assured and self-absorbed, he possessed almost no self-awareness. And yet this lack contributed to his irrepressible nature, the impulse to charge ahead with little regard for the reactions of others or the lingering impact of those reactions. When he lost friends over his words and deeds, he merely collected new friends.

Through the 1840s he became more and more embroiled in the clamor of politics and projected himself increasingly under the banner of his fervent antislavery passion. But he resisted entreaties to run for office—until 1848, when he challenged Winthrop as a Free Soil congressional candidate. He lost handily that year and again two years later against Winthrop's successor, but the taste of electoral politics proved savory, and soon the irrepressible Charles Sumner was a force to be reckoned with in his home state.

As these men of Massachusetts, along with other figures of status and influence, sought to position themselves in a fast-fluctuating political environment, the state's three major parties also struggled with the swirl of events. It didn't take much wisdom to see that the Whigs were in trouble—beset by seemingly intractable fissures that threatened to sap the party's strength and its longtime state dominance. It didn't help that Webster, from his Washington cabinet post, inflamed the situation further by pushing the Compromise on resistant party leaders—in part, many suspected, to keep alive his unceasing presidential aspirations.

Meanwhile, Democratic leaders saw an opportunity to end Whig supremacy in the state by amassing enough political clout to enact governmental reforms designed to position democrats more favorably in the state. The aim, as one disgruntled Democrat put it, was to "equalize political power, and teach a class of men . . . that their right to office was not hereditary and perpetual." But as a minority party, the Democrats couldn't do this on their own. They had to align with the Free Soilers, who held the legislative balance of power.

That sounded like a good idea to Henry Wilson, a young shoemaker and president of the Massachusetts Senate, who had helped stitch together the Free Soil Party in 1848 and now served as its Massachusetts leader. This was a chance, he calculated, for his fledgling party to bootstrap itself into greater political prominence. But Charles Francis Adams and some of his political allies objected to such a combine based on pure power considerations rather than on hallowed principles. Wilson backed off.

Still, the prospect of such an alliance constituted an ongoing threat to the Whigs' statewide ascendancy. Through force of will and his potent statewide following, Webster managed to sway some early Whig decision-making, including Winthrop's Senate appointment and the selection of numerous congressional candidates for the 1850 elections. But the statesman's insistence on forcing Whig leaders in a direction they opposed merely widened the party fissures, while increasing Whig defections to the Free Soil Party. Already, the Free Soil emergence had forced Whig office seekers into three-way races that had diminished their prospects for winning elections.

It got worse after Whigs took a beating in the fall canvass. Although the party still maintained a solid legislative plurality, Democrats and Free Soilers together constituted a majority. That provided new impetus for them to combine into that "coalition" they had been talking about. In a series of meetings beginning on January 1, 1851, representatives of the two parties hashed out a distribution of spoils—or, as Winthrop sardonically put it, "an equitable division of the loaves and fishes."

There wasn't much contention on this division. Democrats, focused on their statewide aim of power accumulation, wanted to install their men in key state offices and legislative positions, such as governor, lieutenant governor, and House Speaker. The Free Soilers, preoccupied with the national slavery issue, were fine with that. They wanted one thing in particular: Webster's old Senate seat. With this trade-off easily sealed, the coalition was born.

It scored a big win when Whig governor Briggs failed to get a majority in the popular vote. That sent the decision to the legislature, where the coalition held sway and promptly awarded the governorship to Democrat George Boutwell. The Democrat–Free Soil combine was working nicely (though Boutwell proved more of a Compromise man than many had anticipated).

Attention now turned to the legislative task of filling that U.S. Senate seat for a full six-year term. Winthrop naturally got the Whig nomination, while the coalition had turned its nomination choice over to the Free Soilers. They promptly selected, of all people, Charles Sumner.

The selection sent shock waves through the body politic, particularly among some Democrats and Cotton Whigs. A Democratic caucus at Cambridge, Massachusetts, passed a resolution heralding anti-Sumner Democrats for shunning "so objectionable a politician." The *Boston Statesman* labeled Sumner "a Garrison disunionist" and "an out-and-out one idea slave agitator." Another newspaper castigated the Democrat–Free Soil combine as "one of the most disgraceful bargains ever known in the political annals of this country."

But the Free Soilers knew what they were doing. Since the coalition bargain didn't require individual party members to vote for coalition candidates, they needed a man who could command the largest number of Democratic votes. That clearly was Sumner, who never had been an ardent Whig and had demonstrated over the years a certain receptivity to some elements of Democratic populism.

Sumner, meanwhile, played the game with uncommon finesse for a man considered by many to be often out of control. Early in the flirtation between Henry Wilson and the Democrats, he adopted an uncharacteristic coyness, avoiding public gatherings where he would have to discuss the matter. But he quietly conveyed to Wilson that he favored the idea and was available for the Senate nomination. In the meantime, he maintained his abolitionist profile with his usual astringent language, particularly in castigating Millard Fillmore at a Free Soil convention in October. The president's embrace of the Clay/Douglas Compromise placed him at the "depths of infamy," declared Sumner, adding, "Better far for him had he never been born; better far for his memory, and for the good name of his children, had he never been President!"

When the legislative balloting began in January, Sumner scored a 60.53 percent Senate majority on the sixth ballot. He was halfway to victory. The House proved more troublesome, as a Massachusetts congressman named Caleb Cushing, a Whig-turned-Democrat who despised Sumner, pulled together some thirty House Democrats unwilling under any circumstances to vote for the stern abolitionist. On the first ballot, Sumner fell eight votes short of victory as Cushing's stalwarts scattered their votes on also-ran candidates. On the second ballot, he was five votes shy. After the tenth ballot, with Sumner still stymied just short of election, the *Statesman* hailed the Cushing stalwarts: "All honor to these noble patriots for this devotion to their principles!"

Winthrop, placing second in each ballot, but never near victory, took a philosophical view toward his looming defeat. Still, he couldn't resist some feelings of disgust at the likely outcome. "I confess," he wrote to a friend, "my stomach revolts from Sumner."

Finally, on the twenty-sixth ballot, on April 23, two Whigs switched over to Sumner, giving him just enough votes for a majority—193 to Winthrop's 166. "The long agony is over," wrote Garrison's *Liberator*, adding that Sumner's triumph had been "the occasion of great rejoicing to his friends." The *Boston Evening Transcript* reported that Free Soilers celebrated "with rockets and Bengal lights, and illuminations." A discordant note emerged, though, when Henry Wilson's celebratory speech was interrupted by shouts for Daniel Webster and also for the Union and the Constitution. The coalition rally was cut short, and the *Evening Transcript* suggested that, if it had been intended "to glorify the election of Mr. Sumner as United States Senator, it was an entire abortion."

Clearly the outcome didn't subdue the political passions of the time. But it represented a momentous victory for the antislavery cause and a fearsome blow to the Massachusetts Cotton Whigs. The Boston street protesters could shout Webster's name throughout the night, but Charles Francis Adams probably came closer to the mark when he suggested to his diary that Sumner's rise represented "the downfall of Mr. Webster." Webster pronounced himself "grieved and mortified."

Winthrop, as it turned out, suffered a double defeat. After the Senate race, some friends put him up for the next one-year gubernatorial term. He confided to a friend that the job offered "no charms," though he did acknowledge that to *have been* governor some two hundred years after his great ancestor held the same position "would be a pleasant historical coincidence." So he went for it. But the same dynamic that had ensnared Governor Briggs the previous year also upended Winthrop. Denied a majority in the popular vote, he was crushed in the subsequent legislative balloting by the Democrat–Free Soil coalition. Winthrop's once-promising civic career now lay in tatters as Massachusetts entered a new political era.

5

PALMETTO STATE STRUGGLES

||||||||||||||||||||||||||||||||||||||||||||||||||||||||||||||||||||||||||||||||||||

TRIUMPH OF THE COOPERATIONISTS

John C. Calhoun's death in March 1850 generated two vital questions for South Carolina and the South: Who would take the Senate seat that for decades had been Calhoun's political birthright? And who would fulfill his role as the South's leading spokesman and defender? On the first question, South Carolinians generally identified the two most serious contenders as Robert Barnwell Rhett and James Henry Hammond. On the second, those men both harbored aspirations of becoming the South's defining figure.

They shared similar backgrounds. Born seven years apart, they grew up in modest circumstances that fueled raging fires of ambition. Both gravitated to the law but found greater satisfaction in politics. Both entered the planter class through marriage (augmented, in the case of Rhett, by a highly favorable land purchase). Both entered Congress as articulate and fiery states' rights advocates. Both held statewide political office—attorney general for Rhett, governor for Hammond.

They weren't alone in the upper reaches of South Carolina's yeasty and competitive political environment. Particularly well entrenched was

Calhoun's last Senate colleague, Andrew Pickens Butler of Edgefield County, elected to fill the unexpired tenure of George McDuffie in 1846 and reelected to a full six-year term two years later. The scion of a back-country planter clan with tentacles of familial connection throughout the state, Pickens Butler, as he was known, grew up in privilege and kept his ambition concealed under a veneer of good fellowship. His thirteen years on the state bench gave "Judge Butler" an aura of distinction.

The story of South Carolina's path through the coming decade can be traced in part through the ambitions, triumphs, and travails of these three men, each representing elements of contention that shaped the state's struggles against northern antislavery pressures. A tight consensus had emerged on the state's need to defend its rights and protect slavery at all costs. But political conflict percolated over questions about the best tactical approaches in that defense and how far to go in executing it.

P ickens Butler, born in 1796, was a big man with a massive face, accentuated by dark, thick eyebrows offsetting a flow of milk-white hair that seemed to be "contending with the blasts of winter," as one contemporary political observer described it. His penetrating blue eyes and buoyant smile produced a friendly demeanor, fortified by a ready supply of quips and a hearty laugh. "[G]ive him the stage," wrote James Hammond, Butler's backcountry neighbor, "and [he will] give you an exhibition that will make your sides crack." Butler's humor sometimes became good-natured ridicule directed at social companions. But, as Hammond noted, "he cannot take a retort," occasionally displaying ir-ritation when subjected to his own brand of ribbing.

Similarly, on the bench he was seen as an "honorable and fair judge" who also, however, displayed an occasional peevishness in handing down rulings. Hammond praised Butler's "common sense" and repu-tation for being "highminded and honorable." But he viewed the man as lacking "powers of rhetoric or logic." Still, his was a crafty intellect, and it combined with his family heritage and famous bonhomie to serve him well in Washington, as did his capacity for avoiding interpersonal rancor over partisan or sectional disputes. Though not a man of soaring eloquence, he captivated audiences with a robust expressiveness studded with wry colloquialisms and literary and historical references.

His father, William, had been a general in the Revolutionary War, and young Butler grew up knowing that a grandfather and an uncle had died in the struggle for independence. As a youth he attended the best schools and then entered South Carolina College (later the University of South Carolina), incubator of boisterous manhood for the state's upper crust. He entered the South Carolina bar in 1818 and was elected to the state house of representatives as a Democrat when still in his mid-twenties. He later spent nine years in the state senate and participated in South Carolina's nullification battles against President Andrew Jackson.

A highly successful lawyer, Butler also maintained a thousand-acre plantation called Stonelands, not far from Edgefield, across the Savannah River from Georgia. Married twice and twice widowed, he remained single from age thirty-eight to his death. His only child, a daughter named Eloise from his second marriage, was raised largely by her maternal grandmother.

Butler had grown weary of life on the bench, when McDuffie resigned his Senate seat following a stroke. Seizing the opportunity, he went up against James Hammond for the legislative nod in December 1846. Hammond led in the first balloting but succumbed to Butler's majority tally on the fourth vote. "No man but Butler could have beaten me," said the often self-absorbed Hammond.

In the Senate, Butler demonstrated a facility for congressional politics honed during his days in the South Carolina legislature. Soon he became chairman of the high-profile Judiciary Committee, with jurisdiction over many slavery issues, and from that perch he exercised considerable sway over debates on the subject.

During the 1850 Compromise contention, he rejected Clay's embrace of the Union as his "first allegiance." "I know no other Union," he said, "than what has been recognized by the State of South Carolina." He echoed Calhoun in emphasizing equality of the states, not of citizens, and warning obliquely of national crisis if southern rights were further trampled. He assailed what he considered a doctrine "under which southern institutions must not only crumble, but under which southern men must be made to understand that hereafter they hold their franchises by sufferance." Any such government, he added, "must be under the influence of an irresponsible despotism."

Of the six Compromise votes engineered by Stephen Douglas in 1850, Butler supported only the fugitive slave measure. Although he could be blunt in his rhetoric, he generally avoided fiery threats and projected a moderation of expression that sometimes put him at odds with his younger and more headstrong South Carolina rivals, Barnwell Rhett and James Hammond.

Rhett (christened Robert Barnwell Smith) was born in 1800 in the Carolina low country, the eighth of fifteen children. The father, though an educated man, had failed as a planter, and the son felt compelled to gloss over the recent years of family hardship and hark back to prominent forebears, including Abigail Smith Adams, wife of President John Adams. At age thirty-seven, Barnwell Smith adopted the surname of Rhett, thus honoring a distinguished ancestor while assuming a more distinctive-sounding cognomen with perhaps greater political resonance.

Long before that, though, he demonstrated his drive for success by voracious reading and studying for the law. With his Harvard-educated cousin, Robert W. Barnwell, he established a lucrative law practice at Walterboro and captured a seat in the state house of representatives at twenty-six. A year later he married Elizabeth Washington Burnet, ten years his junior, an orphan who had become the ward of her mother's brother, William DeSaussure, from a prosperous Huguenot family. With the marriage, wrote historian John McCardell, Rhett's "fortunes began to rise."

He bolstered his wealth by exploiting plummeting property values that resulted when Britain outlawed slavery ownership by Britons living outside the empire. From one British subject forced to sell his South Carolina holdings at bargain prices, Rhett purchased several hundred acres of rice land on the Ashepoo River and more than a hundred slaves. Now a planter as well as a rising politician, he became a man of mark.

Tall and trim, with lucent gray-blue eyes and a thin mouth that turned down slightly at the corners, he projected a countenance that could shift rapidly from fun-loving to defiant. "His temperament was nervous and mercurial," said his daughter Elise Rhett Lewis, "he was quick in movement and quick tempered." His mind alighted heavily upon big conclusions, with little regard for nuance or subtlety, and once a conclusion was formed it became instantly impregnable from any troublesome self-doubt or counterarguments.

Yet Rhett maintained a courtly manner and displayed an elaborate kindness toward women and children, as well as compassion for the poor. No one questioned his devotion to family or his moral steadfastness within the context of his time and place.

John Quincy Adams, a distant relation, captured the dichotomy in Rhett's persona by noting "all his fire" and his "energy, industry and elevated private character"; but also in comparing his manner of speech to "that of a howling dog"—"his enunciations . . . so rapid, inarticulate, and vociferous." Rhett's political howls generated plenty of opprobrium among colleagues. George McDuffie described him as "vain, self conceited, impracticable and selfish in the extreme, and by his ridiculous ambition . . . has rendered himself odious in Congress and in the State." Yet Rhett's devoted following among constituents rendered him a man who couldn't be ignored.

He emerged as a significant political figure at home and in Congress through four issues—nullification; the so-called congressional gag rule that allowed the summary quashing of antislavery petitions from citizens; Democratic proposals for an "independent treasury" to give focus to monetary policy; and, ultimately, slavery. Hovering over them was the irrepressible figure of John C. Calhoun, beset by two political obsessions that didn't always align. One was the overarching presidential ambition that still dominated his consciousness. The other was his passionate need to hold sway over South Carolina as his personal political redoubt, in part to advance those presidential aspirations should opportunity knock.

Well before Calhoun pounced on the nullification campaign following the 1828 passage of the Tariff of Abominations, Rhett, as a young state legislator, seized the issue with incendiary audacity. "Washington was a disunionist," he declared. "Adams, Patrick Henry, Jefferson, Rutledge, were all disunionists and traitors. . . . [S]hall we tremble at epithets?" Even after Calhoun's later nullification revolt fizzled in the face of Andrew Jackson's threat of military action, Rhett still embraced the doctrine.

Entering the U.S. House in 1837, Rhett jumped on the gag-rule controversy, calling for a constitutional amendment banning slavery debates in Congress and prohibiting antislavery agitation by northern states. The Constitution needed correction, he argued, because it had "proved inadequate to protect the southern States in the peaceable enjoyment of their rights and property." He called also for a southern convention to air southern grievances. Nothing came of either proposal, but they brought national attention to the fervent young man.

Rhett's actions and clear devotion to the Calhoun agenda caught the Great Man's attention, though he felt a need to caution the rising provocateur on his rhetorical intemperance. But Rhett particularly endeared himself to Calhoun in 1838 by joining him in supporting President Van Buren's call for an independent treasury, designed to protect federal monies and ensure currency stability. Most South Carolina politicians, still smarting from the nasty nullification fight, instinctively opposed major Democratic initiatives. But when Calhoun shocked the state's political establishment with his turnabout on the issue, he found himself in near isolation among delegation colleagues, save for his cousin Francis Pickens and Rhett.

It seemed like a foolhardy move, but Calhoun, true to his reputation for political dexterity, turned the state around and fostered a legislative resolution instructing state representatives in Washington to support the Van Buren initiative (which Congress eventually killed). It was a signal victory for Calhoun, with Rhett riding along as a recognized ally. As the *Charleston Mercury* later reminded readers, "[I]n all times past, no public man in this State has ever pitted himself in direct *hostility* to John C. Calhoun who has not fallen" as a result.

But the independent-minded Rhett defiantly set himself against Calhoun during the 1844 presidential campaign. Calhoun desired, first, to protect his prospects for the Democratic nomination should front-runner

Martin Van Buren falter; and, second, to secure a Democratic presidential victory in any event. He wanted no intraparty strife within South
Carolina and certainly no open hostility to Van Buren or the party leadership. But Rhett, furious at the inability of Van Buren's congressional
allies' to trim Whig tariff rates pushed through Congress during John
Tyler's administration, helped stir up a South Carolina mobilization for
a state convention and "separate state action" to oppose the tariff. The
impetuous politician even skulked behind Calhoun's back to open up a
communications channel with Van Buren (who dismissed Rhett as lacking self-control).

Intent on avoiding a messy party gash, Calhoun worked deftly behind the scenes to isolate the Rhett movement and maintain a semblance
of party peace through the campaign, which elevated to the presidency
the Democratic dark horse from Tennessee, James K. Polk. But Calhoun
also quietly pulled away from his disloyal protégé. Rhett, basking in his
usual self-regard, dismissed the rebuff as an opportunity to increase his
political independence.

Events thereafter moved forward rapidly. Polk, a boldly effective
president, slashed tariff rates, pushed through Congress Van Buren's independent treasury, and completed the process, initiated by President
Tyler, of annexing Texas as a U.S. slave state. He also led America into
war with Mexico, which eventually conferred upon the United States
those vast new lands destined to inflame the slavery issue as never before. Nothing reflected that development more clearly than the growing
southern unity generated by David Wilmot's famous proviso. Even the
Calhoun-Rhett rift began to heal.

That was fortunate for Rhett because he harbored an ambition for
which he likely would need Calhoun's good wishes. He wanted to represent South Carolina in the U.S. Senate. In 1849 he had ended his
twelve-year House tenure following disappointment at not being seriously considered for McDuffie's old slot in 1846. Rhett decided that he
"would serve South Carolina in the Senate or not at all," as one biographer put it. Now his attention turned to Calhoun's seat. If the senator
somehow regained his health and became president or if his infirmities
forced the Great Man to resign, Rhett might be positioned to acquire

that seat, particularly if Calhoun were to endorse him. But, of course, neither of those things happened. Instead, it was Calhoun's death that opened the avenue for a possible senatorial elevation for Rhett. But first he had to get past James Henry Hammond.

Of all the consequential figures of South Carolina and Massachusetts as the slavery crisis enveloped the nation, James Hammond stood out as the most enigmatic, the most troubled, and the most intriguing. Certainly he was a genius, as manifest in the quickness, depth, and broad scope of his frenzied mind. Yet in the shadows of his consciousness lurked demons that threatened to pull him back and knock him down. In a remarkably revealing diary, called "Secret and Sacred," he talks about a mysterious health problem that included attacks of anxiety and bouts of depression, along with debilitating fatigue. Whatever its origin and nature, it haunted him and badgered him intermittently through life.

He was born in 1807 and reared under the stern tutelage of his father, a transplanted Massachusetts native who ran a respected Methodist academy and taught languages and administered food services at South Carolina College. Elisha Hammond, as his son later recounted, instilled in the lad "a 'holy thirst' for knowledge—a noble desire to excel." Yet the father's instruction revealed a nagging anxiety that young James might slacken his steadiness of purpose. "[M]any a sound flogging did he give me on these premises," recalled the son.

The boy grew up fearing that he lived on the cusp of humiliating failure and that the struggle to avoid it raged within him as much as in the world beyond. "I still fear myself," he acknowledged at middle age, concerned that he could never sufficiently maintain a tight self-control. "I often think I should be better," he confessed, "if I had one of those thrashings that my father used to bestow on me."

At South Carolina College, he mingled successfully with his well-born contemporaries and gained attention for his dashing good looks and magnetic persona. The luminance he demonstrated at the campus oratorical society earned him an invitation to give the valedictory address at graduation. State leaders marked his rise. "The Governor notices him," Elisha Hammond wrote proudly to a daughter, "in every company in a very particular manner."

Upon graduation he tried teaching, but considered it beneath him. Turning to the law, he became an effective trial advocate and spoke out forcefully on public policy concerns. Then, during the nullification crisis, a group of influential politicians, bent on creating a newspaper to bolster the cause, asked Hammond to become the editor. Seizing the opportunity, he placed himself at the vanguard of South Carolina's nullification revolt.

He gave the paper, called the *Southern Times*, a rare intellectual depth and journalistic flair. The central issue, he argued, wasn't the despised tariff, which after all could be compromised simply by altering tax levels. No, the problem was northern intrusion and southern vulnerability under a false and dangerous doctrine of unchecked congressional prerogative. Declared Hammond's paper, "We demand an abandonment of the power which Congress has assumed to pass the [tariff] law."

Hammond's efforts generated praise. Governor James Hamilton gave him a commission in the state militia, and McDuffie called the paper "decidedly the ablest journal in the state." Calhoun said Hammond's performance had "met my full approbation." Yet the young striver ached to become a man of greatness, beyond a mere journalist, and far beyond the standing of his peers. For that he needed a platform. In South Carolina, that meant acreage and slaves.

He acquired them by marrying Catherine Fitzsimons from a rich Charleston merchant family. She wasn't much to look at, and in fact her unattractive appearance generated some wicked mirth among Hammond's old college chums. But she was an heiress, and she brought to the union a hundred slaves and vast landholdings, including a plantation called Silver Bluff, across the Savannah River from Augusta, Georgia. At twenty-four, Hammond had arrived at the destination of his dream—a consequential position within the planter aristocracy, with a lavish income and a pathway to political distinction.

Mastering the intricacies of plantation management, he transformed an ill-run enterprise into a relatively smooth operation. In 1834 he parlayed his new status into a successful run for the U.S. House and quickly gained recognition as a leading defender of that controversial House gag rule. His rhetorical pugilism and undisguised warnings of disunion if southern demands were ignored riled Calhoun, who struggled to keep the states' rights fight within the context of Union loyalty. But Hammond gained a devoted following among South Carolinians who hoped his agitations might help establish an explicit congressional shield against antislavery assaults.

Then it happened—his first punishing attack of nervous exhaustion, accompanied by intestinal pain and digestive ailments. Prescribed a mercury compound to sooth his nerves, he ended up with mercury poisoning. He returned to Congress but discovered his anxiety precluded a House floor appearance. Describing himself as "[b]roken down at Twenty-Eight . . . one foot in the grave," he sought medical help in Philadelphia. Doctors there could only suggest a foreign tour, preferably in Europe, to subdue his nerves.

Alarmed by these developments, he resigned his House seat and traveled through Europe with Catherine for two years, returning in the fall of 1838. He still suffered occasional fatigue and depression, perhaps exacerbated by his lack of a political platform and envy of Rhett's seemingly inexorable rise as congressman and political player. But he thrust himself into a program to conquer his internal demons and resume his pursuit of greatness through politics.

He ran for governor in 1840 and lost, largely because of opposition from Rhett's increasingly powerful statewide machine, or "regency." The regency, mindful of Calhoun's interests, wanted a unionist in the job to help assuage those lingering animosities from the nullification battles. Languishing in defeat, Hammond poured mournful musings into his new journal, revealing himself as a man beset by broken dreams, melancholia, self-pity, and occasional physical exhaustion. "I can bear no fatigue and therefore am debarred from being a man of action," he wrote. "I cannot be a man of intellect for an hour's reading knocks me up completely. . . . [W]ith a sound constitution I verily believe I should have been a great man."

His political prospects brightened when the regency decided to endorse him for the next gubernatorial term, beginning in December 1842. He glided into a two-year governorship, which conferred considerable prestige despite being a largely ceremonial office. But his elevation to the lofty sinecure was marred by a simmering scandal so sordid as to justify the concerns of Elisha Hammond about his son's self-control.

During extended visits to Columbia, where he had built a mansion, Hammond frequently interacted with the family of his brother-in-law, Wade Hampton II, husband of Catherine's sister. The Hamptons had four teenage daughters, who harbored particularly affectionate feelings toward their dashing uncle James, expressed in their allowing unseemly flights of intimacy between themselves and their uncle. These included, as described by Hammond in his journal, "lolling on my lap, pressing their bodies almost into mine, wreathing their limbs with mine . . . and permitting my hands to stray unchecked over every part of them and to rest without the slightest shrinking from it." The encounters went on for nearly two years and included, Hammond reveals, "every thing short of direct sexual intercourse."

Wade Hampton caught a hint of his brother-in-law's licentious behavior, but apparently believed the transgression was confined to Hammond's unsuccessful effort to seduce just one of his daughters. Enraged, he sent Hammond a letter severing all ties with him and his family in language so severe that Hammond believed Hampton intended to destroy him socially and perhaps attack him physically or even kill him. In the end Hampton simply let the inevitable rumors gestate and spread through plantation society, with the result that the Hammonds were excluded socially from many salons and manor houses. There wasn't much Hammond could do but hunker down and refuse to discuss the topic with anyone, particularly his poor wife, who initially remained baffled by the family's reduced social standing and the hostility of her Hampton relatives. But those new realities "eventually required explanation and disclosure," as biographer Drew Gilpin Faust explained.

Meanwhile, Hammond wallowed in self-pity. "I am at this moment surrounded by more and bitterer enemies than ever man had," he wrote. "God forgive them and preserve me. And give me patience to endure to the end."

The end didn't come quickly. When Hammond was put up for McDuffie's Senate seat in 1846, the brother-in-law revived his anti-Hammond whisper campaign in an effort to undermine his candidacy (though the rumors he unleashed in his vengeful wrath victimized Hammond far less than they did Hampton's own daughters, none of whom ever received a marriage proposal). But the rumors no doubt contributed to Hammond's loss to Pickens Butler in the 1846 senatorial contest.

Through the years of the ordeal, Hammond projected himself in his journal as a man struggling with his own dark nature. Sometimes he actually acknowledged his turpitude, but nearly always with some kind of qualification. "The event," he wrote early in the drama, "will embarrass me through life. I have been wrong in the matter—the result of impulse, not design." At other times he couldn't bring himself to confront the true nature of his depravity. In discussing the inevitable difficulties that emerged in his marriage, he wrote, "I am wholly to blame, not so much, as I view matters, for what I have done as for what I left undone, for want of caution which led to discoveries."

But mostly he manifested bereavement over the apparent death of his dreams for immortal greatness, in part because of the scandal, but largely, as he saw it, from his precarious health. When Virginia's influential Beverley Tucker wrote to suggest Hammond should aspire to replace Calhoun as the South's states' rights leader, he dismissed the flattering entreaty in a journal entry. "What a mere shell of a man I am," he lamented, adding: "Stricken in the bud . . . when so much of the flower was expanded as to give promise at least of good fruit, that is doomed to decay ere it can be tasted."

For South Carolinians, the convergence of Calhoun's death and the Clay/Douglas Compromise effort posed haunting political questions that went beyond his possible successor as senator and southern statesman. For years Calhoun had pressed his southern-security formula: promoting regional unity as a counterweight to an ascendant North and thus securing institutional protections for the South even in a northern-dominated Union. That's how he remained the South's leading figure, while honoring the hallowed Union—and also, not coincidentally, how he kept alive his presidential hopes.

But, with Calhoun now gone, younger men such as Rhett and Hammond rejected his formula as unrealistic. As Hammond put it, Calhoun was "so unyielding and so unpersuasive, that he never could consolidate sufficient power to accomplish anything great." To Hammond and Rhett, greatness required a recognition that slavery was doomed if the South remained within the United States.

That's why Hammond rejected the Clay Compromise. "It presupposes," he wrote, "a desire on both sides to be at peace, when such is not the fact." South Carolinians generally agreed. Meeting in cities across the state, they decisively rejected the Clay measures, while newspapers unleashed torrents of invective against them. "Clearly," wrote historian Philip May Hamer in a 1918 treatise, "South Carolina did not desire to compromise."

But prevailing sentiment in the rest of the South wasn't so easily ascertained. With new equations introduced into the region's political calculus, it would take time to determine their full impact. Some looked for answers at Nashville's southern convention in June 1850.

South Carolina sent eighteen delegates to the meeting, including Rhett and Hammond. Rhett wrote the convention's final "address," a catalog of complaints about the North's antislavery agitations, while Hammond shepherded it through committee and to a favorable convention floor vote. Addressing the southern people, the document declared that they had been "arraigned as criminals" in a hostile Congress. It added, "Slavery is dragged into every debate, and Congress has become little else, than a grand instrument in the hands of abolitionists to degrade and ruin the South."

For all the angry words, though, the delegates weren't prepared to unite behind any bold action. The most they came up with was a proposal to extend the so-called Missouri Compromise line (latitude 36°30') to the Pacific Ocean, meaning slavery would be permitted south of the line but would be prohibited north of it. Few believed, however, that the North would go for that. The Nashville delegates adjourned with a resolution to convene again in November, after the congressional session, when the Compromise outcome would be known. But few thought a second meeting would actually happen.

During the Nashville conference, the South Carolina delegation had adopted a restrained posture, avoiding appearances of being "a bed of hotheads" bent on dragging other southern states into drastic action. Rhett managed to control his irritation at that restraint only after Hammond applied plenty of admonitory counsel. But, back in South Carolina, Rhett quickly threw off the shackles at a dinner of his friends and supporters to honor the fiery politician and hear his thoughts on the Nashville event.

"I see but one course left," he declared, "for the peace and salvation of the South—a dissolution of the Union." He described a strong and prosperous southern nation, free of onerous tariffs, free of insult and pressure from Pecksniffian northerners, free of the threat of devastation through forced emancipation. "By our physical power we can protect ourselves against foreign nations," he said, "whilst by our productions we can command their peace or support." He hailed industrial Europe and its markets for the South's staple crops in a free-trade environment. "Wealth, honor, and power, and one of the most glorious destinies which ever crowned a great and happy people await the South," he declared.

As for the treason charge, he scoffed at it. "[L]et it be that I am a Traitor," he proclaimed. "The word has no terrors for me." He extolled famous ancestors who had opposed tyranny in the long Anglo-Saxon struggle against arbitrary government. "I have been born of Traitors, but thank God, they have ever been Traitors in the great cause of liberty."

Rhett's brazen words swept across the country and stamped their author as a leading figure among southern fire-eaters. Seizing the leadership mantle, he crisscrossed the state, stirring disunionist passions, then traveled to Alabama to join that state's firebrand secessionist, William Lowndes Yancey, to incite fervor there. In the process he outraged establishment politicians everywhere. Washington's Democratic *Daily Union*, generally sympathetic to southern sensibilities, declared the speech to be "so full of the demagogue, and indicates so little of the statesman . . . that we are induced to pity rather than condemn its author." Henry Clay, on the Senate floor, proclaimed that, if Rhett actually had raised the flag of disunion and if he were to take action in furtherance of those words, "he will be a traitor, and I hope he will meet the fate of the traitor."

Hammond, who shared much of Rhett's ardent fealty to states' rights and considered secession inevitable, labeled the speech not just "injudicious" but "criminal." He suspected Rhett's motivation was a hope that the South Carolina legislature would "send him to the Senate."

It was true that Rhett's passion for disunion was shared by many members of the South Carolina legislature, scheduled to elect a senator to succeed Calhoun in December (following two placeholder senators in the meantime). Thus Rhett certainly had boosted his prospects. But, even if the state were ready for secession, as Rhett calculated and hoped, could it proceed without courting disaster? Would a go-it-alone approach leave it isolated and vulnerable? Would other southern states join the adventure?

Such questions preoccupied South Carolina governor Whitemarsh Seabrook, who busied himself in communications with other southern governors who might be receptive to secession. A lot of bluster emerged in these exchanges but also words of caution. It wasn't clear that any other state would take the lead or even follow if South Carolina declared itself the vanguard state. The result was a new political fault line between those who wanted immediate and bold action, called "disunionists," and those who urged caution, labeled "cooperationists."

Disunionists were ready to follow Rhett into the roiling cauldron of secession even if no other state would join the cause. These men calculated that other states, most likely Georgia, Alabama, and Mississippi, would take courage in South Carolina's boldness and follow suit. Then, if the North responded with coercive aggression, additional southern states would react by joining up as well. But, even if that never happened and South Carolina became a nation unto itself, it would get along just fine, in this view, with its agricultural prowess, efficient harbor, and vibrant culture.

The cooperationists, by contrast, embraced the ultimate likelihood of South Carolina secession but opposed any go-it-alone action as foolhardy and probably disastrous. They included Senator Butler and former U.S. representative and Rhett cousin Robert Barnwell.

With these lines drawn and the momentous year of 1850 nearing its close, South Carolina moved rapidly through four major developments.

First came the follow-up session of the Nashville convention in November. It fizzled after most moderates stayed away and only seven states sent delegations. The session did, however, declare a general right of secession and proposed a southern congress to ponder the matter further.

Hammond boycotted the session as unworthy of his time and because he didn't want to align himself with Rhett and other immediate secessionists. "The fruit is not ripe," he wrote to his diary—acknowledging, though, that he had been a secessionist for nearly twenty years and avoided issuing overt calls for disunion only in anticipation of "a more propitious season."

Next came an intense legislative battle between disunionists, who demanded a state convention to declare immediate South Carolina independence and force the issue with both Washington and other slave states; and cooperationists, who favored a southern congress called to forge a coalition of slave states into a new southern nation. Unionist sentiment was almost nonexistent in the legislature as it convened in December 1851. "I am here in the very focus of sedition," wrote James Petigru, a brilliant South Carolina lawyer and leading nationalist of the day, in a letter to Daniel Webster. "Disunion is the prevailing idea."

After days of legislative wrangling, a compromise was struck to set in motion actions for both a state convention (for the disunionists) and delegation selection for a proposed southern congress to be held in Montgomery, Alabama, in early 1852 (for the cooperationists).

The third development was the gubernatorial selection. The legislature chose John Means, not particularly prominent in the state, but a longtime Fairfield District agitator for resistance to troublesome federal actions and advocate of a new southern nation. He was a disunionist of the first order.

Finally, there was the legislative selection of a senator to fill the Calhoun slot. The two leading candidates, it quickly became clear, were Rhett and Hammond, with Barnwell and James Chesnut, a young comer, well behind. On the first ballot, Rhett led with fifty-six votes to Hammond's fifty, and the gap only widened from there—to a final majority vote of ninety-seven for Rhett on the fourth ballot. Advocates for immediate disunion had captured both statewide positions on the ballot, and it appeared that South Carolina had chosen its fate—and Hammond's.

"My career as a public man is over, I am crushed—*annihilated forever*," wrote Hammond to his journal, adding he long had "entertained the hope that the State would some day raise me from the dust and cleanse me from every stain." But, no, he conceded, it probably wasn't likely that, with "a heart so proud and sinful," he would ever be saved "from the ruin I have brought upon myself."

Not surprisingly, he didn't expect much leadership from Means or Rhett beyond "*abortive violence*. For they are both of the violent bugle blast section" and lacked "all the requisites of Leaders and Statesmen." The dual selection, he speculated, likely would create a wave of sentiment for immediate secession, with devastating consequences.

Indeed, as 1850 ended, South Carolina stood at the threshold of a portentous rush into the unknown. "What Does South Carolina Intend to Do?" asked the *Daily Union* on December 17. The mechanisms of official power now resided primarily in the hands of men who despised the constitutional system, the Constitution itself, the Union, even the mystique of the American story. The state's ancestors had entered into a deal with the fates when they embraced, at the dawn of that fledgling society, the Barbadian slave culture. Now the descendants of those people were trapped in that culture, facing a quandary that posed only ominous choices.

6

RHETT IN WASHINGTON

|||||||||||||||||||||||||||||||||||||||||||||||||||||||||||||||||||||||||||||||||||||||||

"I AM A SECESSIONIST; I AM A DISUNIONIST"

R. Barnwell Rhett walked onto the Senate floor on the morning of January 6, 1851, to have his credentials presented to the legislative body by Pickens Butler and to take the senatorial oath of office. Then, having sworn allegiance to a constitutional system that he truly despised, he took his seat at the desk previously assigned to John C. Calhoun. Barnwell Rhett finally reached the political station that had been his life's ambition.

He had turned fifty a few weeks before. Taking stock of his circumstances, he worried about his health, which had never been robust and now seemed brittle; he sometimes experienced a sensation of being persistently cold no matter how much he bundled up. He harbored greater concerns, though, about his wife, Elizabeth, who had given birth to eleven children in twenty-two years and who now, at forty-one, seemed to be withering under the strain of persistent child-rearing and manor-house duties. Rhett didn't know what to suggest, except that she should eat more to gain weight and spend more time outside in fresh air.

In the Senate he resolved himself to rise above the rancor that had characterized his twelve-year tenure as a congressman. He told Elizabeth that he would maintain "a holy state of mind" toward his colleagues, and to his son Alfred he wrote, "I intend to assail no one." Elizabeth endorsed the idea and particularly warned him about avoiding frictions with two troublesome unionists, the stiletto-tongued Henry Clay and Mississippi's irascible Henry S. Foote. As Elizabeth wrote to her husband, "I fear they will annoy you excessively this winter."

True to his intent, Rhett maintained a low Senate profile during the second session of the 31st Congress, which was set to adjourn in March. He engaged with Clay amiably on minor matters and stayed clear of Foote. He also developed a cordial association with Mississippi's Jefferson Davis, who was emerging as the South's key spokesman. Rhett appeared to accept Davis's regional stature despite viewing him as too accommodative toward the North.

His first opportunity for an extended address emerged on February 24, during a Senate debate on whether northerners would honor the Fugitive Slave Act by assisting in the apprehension and return of runaway slaves. This provision of the Clay/Douglas Compromise, particularly offensive to many northerners, had been inserted into the Compromise package to mollify the South.

But Rhett wasn't mollified. Seeing the issue as one of states' rights vs. "consolidation" of federal power, he believed that consolidation lay at the root of the sectional frictions—and at the root of the spreading abolitionist movement. Like Calhoun, he viewed the country as a compact of largely independent states, and therefore he considered the constitutional language requiring the return of runaway slaves to be a matter for state adjudication, without federal involvement. Citing the Tenth Amendment, which held that powers not delegated to the federal government were reserved to the states and the people, he argued that the Fugitive Slave Act represented unconstitutional federal usurpation.

"[T]his government has it not in its power to enforce this law," proclaimed Rhett, adding, "I believe that by the action of the States, and the States alone, the rights of the South can be maintained and enforced."

This confused many southerners, who had welcomed the Fugitive Slave Act as favoring their region. Generally it had been antislavery northerners, such as Sumner and Ohio's Salmon Chase, who had questioned the constitutionality of the runaway slave measure they despised. But for Rhett a paramount concern always was consistency of principle, and the principle of state sovereignty superseded all others.

"Sir, I protest against this doctrine," he declared. "I protest against this usurpation. . . . It is fatal to the rights of the South." Then Rhett unfurled his usual apocalyptic warnings. "I fear . . . that this Union will soon come to an end under the mighty sweep of the free States," he declared. "The wheel is destined to roll on, crushing . . . all faith, brotherhood, and peace until the whole fabric falls a vast pile of ruin and desolation."

Sitting at his Senate desk was Henry Clay, who rose calmly to apply a dose of his famous ridicule. Like a schoolmarm patiently instructing a slow-witted student, he chided Rhett for going on at length about the Constitution's delegated powers as if his colleagues didn't already understand this fundamental element of the American system. It reminded him, said Clay, of the Supreme Court justice who complained when a petitioner seemed incapable of making his argument without beginning at the flood of Noah's time. "Why, Mr. Counsel," admonished the justice (as recounted by Clay), "I really think there are some things which this court may be presumed to understand."

Clay identified the "difficulty with the Senator and his school" as their tendency toward preachy discourse on delegated powers. "And if all others do not concur with them they are consolidationists, Federalists, Whigs, precipitating the country into ruin." Clay playfully lumped Rhett with politically pious Salmon Chase, saying that perhaps they held opposite opinions on nearly everything, but joined together "in expressing the opinion that there is no power in the Congress of the United States to pass the fugitive slave law, and that Washington, and that all of us, from the Commencement of the government down to this time, have been wrong."

It was a devastating put-down, and Rhett felt stung. Down in South Carolina, an amused James Hammond noted that southern politicians were threatening secession if the fugitive slave measure were repealed, and now here was Rhett implicitly urging its repeal. "It would be a bright idea," mused Hammond to his diary, "to separate from the Union for the repeal of an Unconstitutional Law."

But in this instance Rhett didn't seek consistency. Determined to reply to Clay's rebuke, he waited in his seat every morning for five days, positioned to speak when the resolution at issue came up again for floor debate. But the crunch of late-session legislation precluded any reply before adjournment, and on March 12 a disappointed Rhett left Washington for his home state.

It was widely understood in South Carolina that the state rested upon a knife's edge as disunionists and cooperationists struggled over the question of immediate secession even without other state allies. But not even the Deep South cotton states seemed prepared to take the fateful plunge. The Clay/Douglas Compromise had had its effect.

The Alabama legislature actually endorsed the Compromise as a fixed settlement to be protected. Georgia soon followed with a state convention vote, while signaling that it didn't appreciate other states trying to pull Georgia into the secessionist maelstrom. Representative Howell Cobb, his House speakership behind him now as he prepared for a Georgia gubernatorial run, warned in a Macon speech against outside intrusions. The *Macon Telegraph and Messenger* quoted Cobb indirectly as declaring that Georgia could "never consent to be dragged into a conflict by any State"—meaning, of course, South Carolina.

That left Mississippi, where Governor John Quitman was known as an ardent secessionist. But, responding to a South Carolina query regarding his intentions, Quitman said he wouldn't lead his state out of the Union unless joined by neighboring states, and no neighboring states seemed ready to act unless prodded by the bold action of a vanguard state—again, meaning South Carolina. "So long as the several states wait for one another," suggested Quitman, "their action will be overcautious and timid." But, if South Carolina seceded alone, it would "startle the whole South, and force the other states to meet the issue plainly." In that event, he predicted, "all the states south of you would unite their destiny to yours." And, should the federal government respond with force, it would usher in "a complete Southern Confederacy."

The Quitman formula quickly became the rallying cry of South Carolina secessionists, embraced fervently by Rhett as he set about to establish himself as the state's premier secessionist leader. In that endeavor he had two institutional allies of considerable influence.

One was the South Carolina legislature, controlled by the state's low-country planter class through long-standing institutional power arrangements. Plantation regions were divided into many small legislative districts that were given greater representation than the larger—and fewer—nonslaveholding yeoman districts. Property ownership and net worth requirements for legislators further ensured the low country's legislative hold. The planter-controlled legislature in turn dominated state politics, selecting not just senators (as required by the Constitution) but also governors, state and local officials, and presidential electors. South Carolina, said an itinerant writer after traveling through the state, is "the most aristocratic state in the Union."

Barnwell Rhett was the darling of these low-country aristocrats and their handmaiden legislators. They had given him his senatorial seat the year before, and now they hailed his vehement desire for disunion and willingness to hazard a go-it-alone strategy. Rhett, noting their longtime dominance over state decision-making, felt certain that they would prevail also on the disunion question.

His other institutional ally was the widely read and influential *Charleston Mercury*, founded in 1822 and for decades the paper of South Carolina's tidewater aristocracy and also the leading proponent of John Calhoun's career. One of the paper's early editors and financial backers had been Rhett's devoted brother-in-law, John Stuart. Now, with Calhoun's death and the paper firmly in the hands of veteran newspapermen and proslavery advocates John Carew and John Heart, Rhett's connection was as firmly fixed as ever. The novelist William Simms complained to his friend Hammond that Rhett enjoyed "too prevailing an influence" on the paper's editorial positions.

The struggle between secessionists and cooperationists gained intensity during Rhett's time in Washington following a February 10 to 11 election for delegates to the state convention called by the legislature the previous December and scheduled for winter or spring of 1852 (eventually scheduled for April 26–30). Secessionists fully intended to push through that convention a disunion resolution, with cooperation if possible but separately if necessary. They took heart in the delegate-selection outcome, which indicated that some 127 of the 167 elected delegates would favor independent secession.

"Secession, and the withdrawal of the State of South Carolina alone from the Union," lamented the ardently unionist *National Intelligencer*, "seems now to be the settled purpose of those who are able to command a majority of votes in the Convention." The *Charleston Mercury* agreed. "South Carolina," declared the paper, "is the only State where this bold and decisive step can be taken with the general approval of the people."

But a new interpretation soon gained currency. Some noted that few citizens had turned out for the scattered preelection promotional events designed to gin up political excitement. Further, remarkably few citizens had actually voted in the elections. That suggested a level of apathy that didn't square with such a potentially hazardous decision. In Charleston, only 873 votes were cast, compared to 2,743 in the state's most recent legislative elections. Hammond calculated that voter turnout hadn't reached half of eligible voters in any of the voting districts. "This manifested so great an apathy," he wrote, "that in Charleston it is regarded as settled, that the Convention will not carry Secession."

Whatever the eventual outcome, it seemed that the Palmetto State now held the nation's fate in its hands. "South Carolina . . . has claimed the leadership of the South," declared the *Mercury*. But for now it lacked followers among its sister southern states, and within its own borders it wasn't clear what kind of mandate could be legitimately claimed by the forces of separate secession. Cooperationists argued that, yes, the delegates to the state convention would favor lone secession overwhelmingly, but they questioned whether this actually represented the will of the people. Voter apathy and the low turnout had left the question unanswered.

So state leaders turned to another special election called by the legislature and scheduled for October 13–14, 1851. This was for selection of South Carolina's delegates to the southern congress that had been advocated by the initial regional convention at Nashville back in June of 1850. In light of the recent actions by Georgia, Alabama, and Mississippi, few expected this southern congress to actually convene. But the South Carolina delegate-selection balloting had been scheduled, and it offered a neat opportunity to acquire a considered assessment of voter sentiment for or against independent secession. Rhett and other secessionist leaders, confident that they would prevail handily in the election, accepted cooperationist pleas that the outcome be considered definitive.

That unleashed furious efforts on the part of the factions to sway the state electorate. A key strategy of the secessionist faction was to leverage a looming informal convention of the state's thirty-six local Southern Rights Associations, with some 450 delegates, scheduled to convene in Charleston on May 5 to 8. Radical disunionists held sway over most of those associations, and they sent to Charleston large numbers of like-minded delegates. The aim was to demonstrate that the state had been captured thoroughly by the radicals.

In fact, however, Rhett and other firebrands harbored deep concerns about the voter-apathy problem and Charleston's growing fear that secession would disrupt harbor commerce and unleash a federal armed response. Thus the radicals viewed the Southern Rights convention also as an opportunity to educate voters not just on the necessity of disunion but also on prospects for a smooth and peaceful separation.

The convention overwhelmingly embraced an "Address" calling for immediate secession. But opposition arguments came from prominent cooperationists, including Pickens Butler, who contended that secession wouldn't likely unleash a federal military response of the kind that would bring other states to join the action. Rather, he argued, the federal government probably would strangle South Carolina economically, which would be less incendiary than military action, but just as effective.

"It will be a war of dollars and cents," said Butler, "a war of . . . embargoes, or of blockade," with federal officials taking "such measures as to divert and drive the commerce from Charleston, either by blockade, or by its influence exerted on foreign nations." Would such an economic assault, without bloodshed or martial fervor, stir other southern states to follow a beleaguered South Carolina out of the Union? Butler doubted it. "This is an age more of utilitarian sagacity than romantic honor," he said.

Romantic honor stirred the South Carolinian imagination, though, and it appeared to many that separate secession was now inevitable. As the *Richmond Examiner* put it, "If ever men had reason to expect with certainty an event which depends on moral causes, we have cause to believe that South Carolina will leave the Union." Governor Means agreed.

But opposition was growing. On July 29, some 1,200 citizens gathered for a public meeting in Charleston to support southern cohesion and the cooperative spirit. Butler and Robert Barnwell addressed the gathering, which approved four resolutions. They justified dissolution in light of northern hostility to southern customs and institutions; committed the state to unite with other southern states "in council and action to obtain redress for our common wrongs"; but characterized separate action as arrogant, premature, and an assault on the state's cooperative spirit.

The meeting kicked off a civic contention more intense and acrimonious than anything seen since the nullification debates of the 1830s. The two sides organized rallies, speeches, dinners, and parades, and one historian later suggested it wasn't easy to tell whether the combatants reserved their most hostile language for the North or their in-state rivals.

At the center of it was Barnwell Rhett, who crisscrossed the state delivering speeches in his blunt-spoken manner, issuing dire warnings about South Carolina's calamitous fate at the hands of northern abolitionists if it didn't soon extricate itself from the infernal Union. "My friends," he intoned, "time, resistless time—the great discloser of our destinies—the iron instrument of Providence in working his decrees—has settled at least one branch of this policy. Southern co-operation is at an end."

Responding to the fears of Senator Butler and others about a federal blockade shutting off trade, Rhett dismissed it as a "humbug" threat. "Blockade is war," he said, adding, "If war is made upon us, we will fight." Even if vanquished, the South would still win because the North couldn't force South Carolina to be a state or to send senators and representatives to Congress. "By our secession," he declared, "the Union is dissolved, and will stand dissolved by our mere non-action."

Much of this was delusional, but it quickened the hearts of many Carolinians and created a tight knot of fiery civic sentiment. Bent on capturing every available vote, Rhett expanded his travel schedule and placed himself before every Carolinian he could find. At one point he traveled a hundred miles to address one sparsely attended rally. Through his frenzied travels he enervated himself so completely that he developed various ailments attributed to exhaustion, and by September 25 he had to cancel his remaining engagements and sit out the last two weeks of the campaign.

When the votes were counted, Rhett and the secessionists took a fearsome blow. Cooperationist candidates captured 25,045 votes throughout the state to just 17,710 for secessionist candidates. The cooperationists elected their men in six of the state's seven congressional districts and in twenty-five of the forty-four assembly districts. In Charleston, cooperationists collected 2,454 votes to 1,018 for Rhett's movement. In the low country, bastion of the slaveholding aristocracy, disunionists carried all but three parishes, but they lost all but three parishes in the up-country. Essentially, the up-country carried the day in league with Charleston's merchant class.

The results destroyed, at least temporarily, the lone-secessionist movement. Not even the most ardent secessionists could argue now that South Carolina was a vanguard state, poised to lead the South out of the Union. Horace Greeley's abolitionist *New York Tribune* crowed, "South Carolina will not secede, nor even make a feint of so doing." The paper added that the South Carolina vote was a "substantial counterpart of the 'Union' victories in Georgia, Alabama and Mississippi."

Not quite. Those cotton states had embraced, however tenuously, the Compromise of 1850. Not so with South Carolina, where unionist sentiment was hardly discernible in the state's discourse. The cooperationists were themselves secessionists who merely wanted disunion accomplished through a pan-southern movement. As the *Mercury* put it, the cooperationists' "burning words" had stirred the people to resistance. "They will not, they cannot, take back their words," said the paper. "They will not be allowed to forget them."

The outcome stunned Rhett, who now became an easy mark for

critics and foes. Returning to Washington on December 8 for the opening of the 32nd Congress, he quickly came under fire from the man his
wife had warned about, Mississippi's combative Henry Foote.

Foote, once a southern firebrand but now an ardent defender of
the 1850 Compromise, introduced a resolution declaring that the Clay/
Douglas measures "should be acquiesced in and respected by all good
citizens." In supporting his resolution on the Senate floor, Foote suddenly launched into a bitter denunciation of Rhett as a hater of the
hallowed Union and a possible traitor.

When Pickens Butler, in an effort to defend Rhett, interpreted
Foote's words as an attack on the people and legislature of South Carolina, the Mississippian corrected him. He expressed his "high gratification" toward South Carolinians, including Butler, who successfully
opposed Rhett and his secessionist allies in the recent delegate elections.
He elaborated, "I felt that the real people of South Carolina had come
nobly to the rescue of the honor of the State in the contest lately in
progress there between them and certain demagogues."

Rhett sought to defend himself in the Senate by scoffing at Foote's
"epithets," while also embracing them. "I am a secessionist—I am a
disunionist," he declared, adding that so long as his sovereign, South
Carolina, should remain in the Union, "I am bound, as I am sworn, to
support the Constitution . . . ; but, in my opinion, the compact of the
Constitution is violated—the Union of the Constitution is dissolved."

By the time Rhett concluded his remarks, it was clear that Foote
had smoked him out to reveal just how far he had ventured beyond
conventional discourse and into his own political zone. Since Polk's war
and the emergence of Wilmot's proviso, outraged southern politicians
had been warning incessantly of secession if the North's threatening behavior continued. But now Rhett was declaring that the point of secession's justification had already arrived. And his behavior during the
delegate-election campaign in the fall had demonstrated further that
secession was his overarching aim.

The Foote-Rhett exchange, extending over three legislative days,
gained more and more attention as it became increasingly contentious
and nasty. The *Mercury* reported that Rhett's declaration as a secessionist

was received by the northern press "with something like holy horror." The *Baltimore Republican* suggested that, if the entire South should embrace Rhett's view, "there will be an end of the present Union." James Gordon Bennett's influential *New York Herald* said Foote deserved credit for guiding Mississippi toward accepting the Compromise, but "in doing a good thing, he overdoes it," in part by directing his ostentatious bluster toward Rhett after he had already been humiliated by his own constituency in the recent October elections.

During the Christmas holidays in South Carolina, Rhett pondered his situation with hopes that he could return to a higher plane of Senate discourse upon his Washington return. But he was a marked man now, and in his absence he came under a fearsome Senate-floor attack from Alabama's blustery Jeremiah Clemens, described by the *Mercury*'s Washington correspondent as "an eloquent man, and at times a strong reasoner, but swayed by impulses, and therefore unreliable." A weakness for alcohol contributed to his erratic nature.

Like Foote, Clemens had been until recently a strong Compromise opponent, almost a fire-eater, but now he hurled his newfound unionist convictions around with abandon. In a bizarre flight of rhetoric, he accused Rhett of aligning with abolitionists Sumner, Seward, and Chase in seeking a dissolution of the Union and reported falsely that the three northerners had responded to Rhett's "I am a secessionist" speech with "applause, cheers, and encouragement." Declared Clemens: "There is a sympathy in treason as well as in knavery."

Upon his Washington return, Rhett was urged by many friends to ignore the attack; instead he ignored the advice, attacking Clemens with such venom that the Alabamian suggested obliquely that perhaps a duel would be the best way to settle things. Rhett demurred on the basis, he said, of his religious convictions. It was in many ways a sordid exchange.

But Rhett had become a lightning rod for controversy and demonstrated that human contention brought to the surface of his persona an instinct for invective and pugilism that could be unbecoming. He paid a high price for his stark altercations with Foote and Clemens.

That became clear when the four-day South Carolina state convention, called by the legislature back in December 1850 to determine the state's response to perceived northern abuse, convened in Columbia on April 26. The question hovering over the proceeding from day one was what the convention could do in light of the cooperationists' electoral victory in October. "It cannot dissolve the bonds which bind the State to the Union," said the *Cheraw Gazette*. "This the people have instructed it not to do."

One possible approach, devised by James Hammond and called his "Plan of State Action," was a kind of middle way in which South Carolina would remain in the Union but refrain from any participation in it— no senators or representatives sent to Washington, no presidential electors named, no appropriations from the federal government accepted, etc. Following the October balloting, some secessionists embraced the Hammond plan, but the concept of being partly in and partly out of the Union never took hold. The convention ignored it amid much dissension, confusion, and frustration on the part of delegates.

When a group of strong secessionists met in caucus at Hunt's Hotel on the convention's first night to devise a strong approach embracing eventual dissolution under a cooperationist spirit, there didn't seem to be any prospect for consensus, much less enthusiasm. Rhett, though not a delegate, seemed pleased when his friend Maxcy Gregg suggested that he be invited to address the caucus. But a delegate named James Drayton Nance rejected the notion outright. "I hope not," he interjected, "we are twenty-one years old and capable of making up our own minds." Amid a murmur of assent, Gregg promptly withdrew the suggestion. "Thus the party refused to hear my views or to be counseled by me," complained a humiliated Rhett.

In the end, the convention produced merely a mild report, adopted 136 to 19, saying the state had good cause to secede but didn't do so merely out of expediency; and declaring that the state had a right to secede at any time and in doing so would be judged only by God and the world. The language didn't amount to much, despite the *Mercury*'s effort to put a stern face on it by saying the convention had "engrafted, as it were, the right of secession, by an almost unanimous vote, upon our body politic."

But Barnwell Rhett had had enough. On April 30, the convention's final day, he resigned his Senate seat in a letter to Governor Means. "In consequence of the proceedings of the Convention which has just adjourned," he wrote, "I deem myself no longer a proper representative of the position and policy of the people of South Carolina with respect to the aggressions of the General Government." He had not managed to bring his state to his way of thinking on the slavery crisis, even after a tireless and sometimes truculent drive that had left him diminished in the eyes of many. As a southern rights zealot, he had calculated that most of his fellow South Carolinians shared his zealotry. He wasn't far wrong, but that didn't mean they were prepared to follow him into the dark and dangerous unknown posed by immediate and independent secession. In venturing so far into that hazardous territory, he had lost his constituency and his political standing.

7

SUMNER IN THE SENATE

||||||||||||||||||||||||||||||||||||||||||||||||||||||||||||||||||||||||||||||||||||||||

"PROVIDENCE HAS MARKED OUT MY CAREER"

On December 2, 1851, the *Boston Evening Transcript* published an article about the opening day of the 32nd Congress and noted that Michigan's senator Lewis Cass had presented to the Senate the credentials of Charles Sumner, who was duly sworn in and took his seat in the body. What the paper didn't say was that Sumner's senatorial debut was marked by a certain awkwardness and embarrassment.

The credentials of new senators normally were presented by their senior state colleagues, as Pickens Butler had done for Barnwell Rhett. But Massachusetts senator John Davis apparently overslept and wasn't on hand to perform the traditional courtesy. Sumner hurriedly turned to Cass, whom he had known for years, but with whom he shared no particular mutual regard. Cass obliged but, eschewing the normal gracious language ("I beg leave to present . . ." or "I am pleased to present . . ."), said merely, "I have been requested to present the credentials of Charles Sumner. . . ."

The ill-disguised dig wasn't lost on Sumner's new colleagues. Given the raucous tenor of Massachusetts politics and Sumner's reputation for sometimes brutish rhetoric, some wondered if Davis had stayed away to avoid any cordial connection with his new colleague. Davis's leading political benefactor back home, after all, was the Cotton Whig Abbott Lawrence, a strong Sumner adversary. In any event, the senator's first-day embarrassment seemed to portend rough times ahead.

Looking at the new congressional term more broadly, the *Evening Transcript* also published a dispatch from Washington enumerating three national developments of note. First, it reported that Henry Clay, who had been in town for several days, had "evidently become much enfeebled in his physical powers," though the paper quickly assured readers that "the brightness of his mind remains undimmed." In fact, he was dying, apparently of tuberculosis, and would be gone within seven months. He wouldn't be back in the Senate again.

Second, the *Evening Transcript* noted a "prominent fact . . . apparent to every eye here"—namely, that despite the normal partisan conflicts, "everything seems to be merged in a determination to preserve the Constitution and Union inviolate." The paper acknowledged the ongoing agitations of "the Secessionists of the South and the Anti Slavery demagogues of the North." But it rejoiced that, notwithstanding those sectional rabble-rousers, the new "union spirit augurs well for the country."

Finally, the *Evening Transcript* reported that "many good judges" in Washington were suggesting that the Whig Party should forgo a presidential nominating convention in 1852 because potential candidates had been narrowed down to a single commanding figure. "The fact is," said the dispatch, "no one is talked of or thought of here for the Presidency, but Mr. Webster," who alone could draw to his unionist banner "the true patriotic men of all parties." Even Democrats, predicted the paper, "will flock to the Union standard regardless of the regular Democratic nomination."

This was fanciful in the extreme, a product of the *Evening Transcipt*'s staunch Whig allegiance and fawning Webster regard. The country's on-going frictions of ambition and ideology weren't about to be suspended in favor of a sixty-nine-year-old man whose political standing was severely reduced even in his own state. But the item captured a significant political reality. Daniel Webster intended to be a compelling factor in the 1852 presidential contest.

Back in the Senate, meanwhile, Sumner sized up his political circumstances. As one of only three Free Soilers in the chamber, unaffili-
ated with either of the nation's two major political parties, he anticipated
no prominent committee assignments that could enhance his political
standing in Congress or back home. Besides, he entered the country's
great deliberative body without any legislative background and hardly
any real political experience.

Further, he faced lingering outrage in Massachusetts over his election at the hands of the controversial Democratic–Free Soil coalition,
considered by many to be aberrant and underhanded. Added to all this
were persistent demands from antislavery constituents that he unfurl his
abolitionist sentiments in the Senate, when nearly the entire political
establishment, as the *Evening Transcript* had noted, strongly opposed
any such assault on the 1850 Compromise.

Typically, Sumner responded to such challenges with false modesty
mixed with hollow professions of having been plucked by the fates for
service beyond his desire or interest. As he wrote to a close acquain-
tance after his victory, "Most painfully do I feel my inability to meet the
importance which has been given to this election and the expectation
of enthusiastic friends." Just before leaving Boston for Washington, he
wrote to his sister, "For myself, I do not desire public life; I have neither
taste nor ambition for it; but Providence has marked out my career."

This was nonsense, of course, as reflected in his stealthy maneuvering for the job as the Democratic–Free Soil coalition was taking shape.
And he demonstrated his self-concept as a man of destiny by suggesting
to a friend that any failure due to a lack of commitment "should go far
to destroy all confidence in man."

Arriving in Washington in November, Sumner secured "well appointed" lodgings at a private home on New York Avenue, between Fourteenth and Fifteenth streets, for $35 a month. He quickly
settled into a routine that included a seven o'clock wake-up, a cold bath
followed by a cold-water shave, a robust breakfast of tea, eggs, toast,

pancakes, and fruit, and official work at his lodgings before a brisk mile-long walk to the Capitol. For evening meals he settled on a local French restaurant, where he dined with the Swedish minister to Washington and a former Connecticut congressman named John Rockwell. His dinners, often a porterhouse steak with oysters or corned beef and cabbage, generally included a glass or two of wine, but he almost never drank hard liquor. His tobacco use was confined to an occasional evening cigar. After-dinner activity most often centered on Senate work or social outings.

Arriving at the Capitol each morning, he conscientiously positioned himself at his desk when the Senate was called to order and for the chaplain's daily prayer, then remained there throughout most of the proceedings as a demonstration of his legislative seriousness. As a backbencher without time-consuming committee duties, he had time to apply his absorbent mind to mastering the intricacies of parliamentary procedure and assessing his colleagues. Thus did he quietly accumulate the tools to emerge eventually as a consequential senatorial voice (though he never developed much of a capacity for behind-the-scenes dealmaking).

Along the way he studiously sought to cut a distinctive figure, already evident in his tall, lean frame and smooth good looks. He effected just a touch of flamboyance by shunning the black frock coat worn by most senators in favor of less formal English tweeds, along with "light waistcoat, lavender-colored or checked trousers, and shoes with English gaiters." For a man who professed to having had little interest in becoming a senator, he devoted considerable time and thought to cultivating a particularly dignified congressional image.

His study of fellow senators began with his two Free Soil colleagues, John P. Hale of New Hampshire and Salmon P. Chase of Ohio. Hale, a former Democrat, had been a leading figure in founding the Free Soil Party and had vied for its presidential nomination in 1848, before the party's Buffalo convention turned to New York's Martin Van Buren. Despite his fiery opposition to James Polk's Mexican War, his Free Soil leadership, and his consistent antislavery passion, he never seemed entirely serious. He struck Sumner as an unlikely Senate ally.

Chase was something else entirely, a man of mark known for his stolid intellect, fearless purpose, and strong religious and moral sensibilities. He projected a natural forcefulness, enhanced by the rugged features of his oval face. But he was tormented by persistent feelings of inadequacy and fears that he wouldn't fulfill his potential or gain appropriate recognition for his attainments. As a young man, he lamented to a friend, "My life seems to me to have been wasted." Later, at age twenty-two, he wrote to his diary, "I almost despair of ever making any figure in the world."

Even as he matured and prospered as a lawyer and politician in the frontier Lake Erie city of Cleveland, this clash between boundless ambition and debilitating insecurity spawned a deep-seated feeling that internal serenity could be achieved only through fulfillment of his silent ambition to become president of the United States. In the meantime, he captured his Senate seat as a Free Soil candidate in 1849 and promptly emerged as one of the most forceful abolitionists in Congress. Sumner viewed him as "a tower of strength."

Sumner didn't immediately gravitate to many other northern colleagues. Cass's subtle put-down on Sumner's first day reflected a characteristic aloofness that precluded any warmth between the two men. And the Massachusetts newcomer considered Stephen Douglas to be a cold-blooded political manipulator lacking any moral sensibility. He did develop a fondness for the New Yorker William Seward, a master legislator and leading antislavery exponent.

Sumner discovered that he liked a number of southern colleagues, with their flowery discourse and friendly-faced demeanor. He felt a strong affinity for Louisiana's Pierre Soulé, who projected a vehement states' rights outlook. And he developed a particular appreciation for Pickens Butler, whose desk was next to Sumner's on the Senate floor and whose zesty bonhomie charmed the younger man. Somewhat patronizingly, Sumner felt that if Butler had been brought up in the culture of New England rather than in South Carolina, he "would have been a scholar, or, at least, a well educated man." For his part, Butler esteemed Sumner's erudition and enjoyed seeking his counsel on classical quotations for his floor speeches.

Always intent on promoting himself socially, Sumner cultivated cordial relations with Washington's prominent southern women, who dominated the city's social scene with lighthearted banter. This was sometimes a challenge, as the man once described as "impervious to a joke" couldn't always keep up with the witticisms of these social butterflies. But he developed a knack for crafting in advance little set speeches and digressions that could be pulled out at strategic moments to demonstrate his breadth of knowledge and intellectual verve. The wife of Mississippi's senator Jefferson Davis reported that Sumner could talk authoritatively about "the Indian mutiny, lace, Demosthenes, jewels, Seneca's morals, intaglios, the Platonian theory" and "the history of dancing."

Soon Sumner enjoyed a standing in Washington society that far outstripped his Boston stature, which had been crimped for years because of his intemperate and often insulting attitude toward those who disagreed with him. Biographer David Donald reports that in a single week during his first month in the Senate, Sumner dined with the French minister, President Fillmore, the influential Francis P. Blair, lawyer, diplomat, and literary figure Robert Walsh, and Virginia's prominent Henry A. Wise, soon to be governor. The man who always managed to supplant his alienated Boston friends with new friends found in Washington a vast supply of potential new friends.

Sumner wasted little time in delivering his maiden Senate speech. On December 10 he addressed the controversy that had emerged with the visit to America of Louis Kossuth, the exiled Hungarian revolutionary committed to democratic reforms in his country and its independence from Austria. Traveling through America at the invitation of President Fillmore, the dashing freedom fighter instantly stirred the imagination of many U.S. citizens with his eloquence and commitment to liberty. The *New York Herald* called his speeches "sublime in simplicity" and "dazzling to the brain."

But the Hungarian also generated discomfort by advocating U.S. military intervention in his faraway cause, while some southerners feared his liberal sensibilities might suggest latent antislavery views. Sumner staked out a middle ground by hailing the Hungarian as "the dread of Despots," a latter-day Lafayette who employed "words of matchless eloquence" to project himself as "the fiery sword of freedom." But Sumner added that America must not abandon the warnings of its revered first president against foreign wars and entanglements. Addressing his words to Kossuth, he proclaimed, "Leave us to tread where Washington points the way."

Though not particularly distinctive in thought, the speech impressed colleagues and editors with its essential soundness and fluency of language. The *Massachusetts Spy* praised the senator's "scholarship, good sense, and soul," while even Boston's *Daily Atlas*, which had opposed Sumner's Senate elevation, called the speech "highly polished and eloquent." Cass offered praise and allowed that he now felt pride in having presented the Massachusetts newcomer to the Senate.

With his Kossuth speech and a subsequent address on a proposed federal land grant for an Iowa railroad (which he supported), Sumner sought to demonstrate a capacity for expounding on matters beyond the expected slavery preoccupation. In the process, he also demonstrated his particular facility for rhetorical eloquence and piquancy. Over many years he had diligently developed his particular rhetorical style, which was formal and direct, with ample repetition of central points and a certain organizational rigidity. There were few flights of eloquence, no jokes or casual asides, limited metaphors, and absolutely no colloquialisms. There was usually at least one Latin quote or reference.

He also devoted immense time to memorizing large portions of his speeches and honing techniques of delivery for maximum impact. Such efforts breathed life into both the Kossuth and railroad addresses, and soon Sumner was viewed as a leading Senate orator among antislavery legislators.

But to fulfill that role Sumner needed to project his famous antislavery oratory from the Senate floor, and the chamber's leadership didn't want any such agitations disturbing the 1850 Compromise. Back home in Massachusetts, though, Sumner's core constituency was getting restless—and hostile—over his silence on the slavery issue. Now that he was nicely entrenched in the Senate, these people suggested, he seemed to be backsliding on the cause that had propelled him to his elevated status in the first place.

Then the clever and tireless Lloyd Garrison stepped in. He sent to Sumner a petition in behalf of two antislavery men, Daniel Drayton and Edward Sayres, languishing in a D.C. jail for violating the Fugitive Slave Act. The idea was that Sumner should present the petition to the Senate and thereby gain floor access for a forceful assault on slavery.

But Sumner didn't present the petition for reasons that were entirely defensible and necessarily secret. Knowing that Fillmore was considering a presidential pardon for the two men, Sumner supported the pardon quietly through high-level government channels. He knew that any public pressure would backfire, while any effort to explain his approach privately would be quickly exposed. But, while Fillmore ultimately granted the pardon, he was in no hurry to act, which left Sumner politically exposed.

His friend Wendell Phillips, a leading Boston abolitionist, warned that pressures were mounting. And, sure enough, Garrison's *Liberator* weighed in on March 19 with an editorial expressing "surprise and regret" at Sumner's inaction. Within a month Garrison had thoroughly lost his patience. At a meeting of the Norfolk County Antislavery Society, he helped secure a motion censuring Sumner for his "inexplicable" silence on the Drayton-Sayres matter.

Then, in an April 23 editorial titled "Inquiry after a 'Back-Bone,'" the editor turned pugilistic. He quoted from Sumner's famous speech of October 1850, when he had excoriated Fillmore in typically intemperate language, suggesting that by signing the Fugitive Slave Act the president had stained the good name of his own children. Now, according to reports, Sumner had actually met with Fillmore in Boston and had dined with him in Washington. In that same 1850 speech, noted the *Liberator*, Sumner had inveighed against the lack of backbone among northerners who remained aloof from the abolitionist cause. And yet now he was himself standing aloof from the cause even as a U.S. senator. "Is not this silence to be complained of?" asked Garrison. "Is this to have a 'back-bone'?"

As the congressional session stretched into summer, with an anticipated late-August adjournment, Sumner could see he was in a bind. Garrison was joined increasingly now by other Free Soil newspapers

and political leaders, already dismayed at what appeared to be diminishing party prospects both in Massachusetts and throughout the country.
Outside of New England, Wisconsin, and Ohio, in fact, the Free Soilers
seemed to be in total eclipse as the 1850 Compromise continued to
assuage tensions over slavery. "The moral tone of the Free States never
was more thoroughly broken," lamented Charles Francis Adams. "The
morale of our party is *chloroformed.*"

All this generated a sense of urgency among Free Soilers and intensified their demands on Sumner. But now his traditional adversaries
among Massachusetts Cotton Whigs and Democrats also joined the assault. Robert Winthrop, more contemptuous than ever, jabbed at the
senator's hypocrisy in demonstrating the kind of hesitancy on the slavery
issue that for years he had reviled in others. The prominent Boston cleric
and political activist Theodore Parker, who had defended Sumner in a
July 5 speech, nevertheless considered him to be in "imminent deadly
peril" if he didn't speak up soon. Meanwhile, the Democratic *Boston
Statesman* questioned Sumner's motive in allowing the matter to linger
into the crowded final weeks of the congressional session, when the crush
of legislative business would dim prospects for a lengthy and effective effort. The best possibility now, said the paper, was for a mere "whining
and feeble" address. "Is not the result exactly as Mr. Sumner might have
expected?" asked the *Statesman.* "Is it not exactly what he *wanted*?"

In late July Sumner sought to mollify his critics by presenting to
the Senate a resolution that stated: "*Resolved,* That the Committee on
the Judiciary be instructed to consider the expediency of reporting a
bill for the immediate repeal of . . . the Fugitive Slave Act." The next
day Sumner defended his resolve to press the issue at session's end and
pleaded with his colleagues to "yield to a brother Senator the opportunity which he craves . . . to express convictions dear to his heart and dear
to large numbers of his constituents."

Virginia's James Mason quickly objected on the ground that such
matters always arrived at the chamber "in the form of a fire-brand," and
firebrands were best left out of late-session deliberations. Pickens Butler,
whom Sumner considered a friend but whose proslavery commitment
always superseded his friendships on the Senate floor, elaborated on the

Mason view. "I believe the honorable Senator from Massachusetts is pledged to agitate," he said, adding that wouldn't necessarily preclude his assent to Sumner's request. "But," he continued, "if this subject is taken up, the fact cannot be disguised that the Senator himself will be found to make allusion to South Carolina and her laws—"

Sumner cut him off. "I shall not," he promised.

"Then I shall be clear, perhaps," said Butler, stirring laughter in the chamber. "I do not know how it can be discussed very well without some allusion of the kind."

Butler asked rhetorically whether Sumner's initiative wasn't designed primarily to "wash deeper and deeper the channel through which flow the angry waters of agitation already?" The Senate voted 10 to 32 against allowing consideration of Sumner's resolution.

After the defeat, Senator Mason assured his new colleague with a bit of a bite, "You may speak next term."

"I must speak this term," replied Sumner.

"By God, you shan't."

"I will, and you can't prevent me."

The defiance seemed ill-placed, given the nearly nonexistent chance of Sumner getting the floor for an extended antislavery speech. Garrison dismissed the failed effort as feckless and, referring again to the backbone question, declared, "Even gristle would be better than nothing." He decried particularly the senator's assurance to "overseer Butler" that, if allowed to speak, he wouldn't make reference to South Carolina or its laws. "What can be more humiliating?" he asked.

But Sumner's critics and detractors underestimated his resolve and wiles. Sitting on the Senate floor, closely taking in the proceedings, and waiting for his opportunity, he harbored within his desk drawer a nearly four-hour speech, all practiced and ready, on the evils of slavery and the imperative of repealing the Fugitive Slave Act. On August 26, just five days before the session's adjournment, his opportunity materialized when Senator Robert Hunter of Virginia offered an appropriations amendment to authorize payment for what the amendment cryptically called "extraordinary expenses"—actually for enforcement of the fugitive slave law. Sumner rose to amend the amendment by adding language prohibiting any such payment for executing the noxious law, "which said act is hereby repealed."

The amendment was germane to the discussion at hand, and no one could intercede now as Sumner remained standing to explain and defend his amendment. He absorbed three hours and forty-five minutes in doing so. Detractors later would disparage his arguments as unoriginal and derivative of previous discourses in the campaign literature of the antislavery 1840s Liberty Party and in the speeches of Salmon Chase, Joshua Giddings, and others. But Massachusetts congressman Horace Mann, a Sumner ally, argued that the senator's expansive antislavery crusade required "not originality . . . but skill in using, and this is his *forte*." Indeed, the speech's distinctive qualities were its comprehensiveness and logical compactness.

In crafting his dialectic, Sumner avoided any connection to Garrison or other abolitionists who assailed the Constitution as a covenant with death and an agreement with hell, as Garrison's newspaper expressed it repeatedly. While these men could never accept the Constitution's protections for slavery, crafted through compromises necessary to produce the document and get it ratified, Sumner set out instead to craft an antislavery polemic based on a strong constitutional reverence.

That meant also that he must avoid the pitfall that had tripped up the more moderate William Seward during the emotional 1850 debates over the Clay/Douglas Compromise. The New York senator famously had declared that there was "a higher law than the Constitution" and that compromise of the kind that Henry Clay wanted was "radically wrong and essentially vicious." Critics promptly attacked Seward as just another anti-constitutional provocateur. The Democratic *New York Herald* likened Seward's views to "those of the extreme fanatics of the North." Even Seward's valued friend and mentor, New York publisher and political boss Thurlow Weed, privately told Seward that the speech had "sent me to bed with a heavy heart" and a "restless night and an anxious day have not relieved my apprehensions." Seward himself recognized his mistake "with sorrow and shame."

Sumner had long perceived the political folly in "higher law" thinking. Beyond politics, though, he viewed the concept as philosophically repugnant. He embraced the sanctity of tradition and ancient protocols in guiding civic affairs and curbing governmental abuse. "Institutions are formed *from within, not from without*," he once wrote. "They spring from custom and popular faith, silently operating with internal power." Thus, he viewed the Constitution as a hallowed bulwark of tradition.

And so he fashioned an elaborate argument aimed at demonstrating that the early writings and actions of the Founders had been aimed at establishing liberty and justice as national principles, while slavery was confined to sectional or state jurisdictions. He began with the Constitution's preamble. "[A]ccording to undeniable words," he declared, "the Constitution was ordained, not to establish, secure, or sanction Slavery—not to promote the special interests of slaveholders—not to make Slavery national, in any way, form, or manner; but to 'establish justice,' 'promote the general welfare,' and 'secure the blessings of Liberty.' Here surely Liberty is national."

Next he explored "the explicit contemporaneous declarations" of the framers at the 1787 Constitutional Convention, where Elbridge Gerry of Massachusetts pronounced that, "though we had nothing to do with the conduct of the States as to Slavery, but we ought to be careful not to give any sanction to it." Sumner traced the discussions that led to avoidance of any reference to slaves as "property," but referred to them instead as "persons." He noted also the language of the Declaration of Independence that "all men are created equal" and a pronouncement of the Continental Congress that the rights bestowed by the people were "the rights of human nature."

Further, Sumner explored principles of liberty going back centuries in English common law and a U.S. Supreme Court ruling that supported the view of slaves as persons and not as property. He detailed the sentiments of the leading figures of the founding generation, including slaveholders Washington and Jefferson, who decried the institution and favored its eventual end. "Not encouragement but discouragement of slavery was their rule," said Sumner.

All this, he argued, proved that popular thinking had it precisely backward in perceiving slavery as a national institution that must be protected by the federal government based on a constitutional mandate, while freedom was an issue of state jurisdiction. No, said Sumner, history demonstrated "that Slavery is in no respect national—that it is not within the sphere of national activity—that it has no 'positive' support in the Constitution." Slavery rather should be seen as strictly "a local institution, peculiar to the States and under the guardianship of State Rights," including rights bestowed to the states by the Constitution's Tenth Amendment, which reserved to them all powers not specifically granted to the federal government.

The implications of this historical interpretation, as articulated by Sumner with literary eloquence and syllogistic rigor, were immense. Under the rubric of "Freedom National," as he called his speech, Sumner contended that the Constitution was, at its heart, a freedom document under which Congress had no power to legislate either for slavery's abolition in the states or to support it anywhere else. But it had a positive right and indeed an obligation to contend for freedom at the national level wherever it was threatened.

According to this interpretation, the Fugitive Slave Act was not only morally wrong but "doubly unconstitutional"—because Congress had no legitimate power to involve itself in matters regarding slavery in the states; and because it deprived fugitive slaves of due constitutional protections, such as trial by jury, before being returned to their presumed masters. Sumner devoted nearly half of his speech to dissecting and denouncing that despised law. "Repeal this enactment," he implored his colleagues. "Let its terrors no longer rage through the land."

The speech drew an immediate floor reaction. Alabama's Jeremiah Clemens assured his colleagues that "the ravings of a maniac may sometimes be dangerous, but the barking of a puppy never did any harm." More solemnly, Iowa's Augustus Dodge argued that the fugitive slave law clearly was consonant with the Constitution, since the document unambiguously demanded that runaways "shall be delivered up, on claim of the party to whom such service may be due."

Not surprisingly, New Hampshire's John Hale offered high praise, saying Sumner was "side by side with the first orators of antiquity" and had established "a new era in the history of politics." But Stephen Douglas refused to credit Sumner's insistence that his argument was grounded in the Constitution. "All that is said," he proclaimed, "about the crimes of slavery—about a higher law than the Constitution, which forbids obedience to human laws in conflict with the Divine law—the whole tenor of the objections that have been urged, are objections against the Constitution rather than the law."

Lloyd Garrison attacked from a different angle. He conceded that the speech would "enlarge and consolidate the already wide reputation of its author" and praised Sumner's analysis of the Fugitive Slave Act's unconstitutionality. But he rejected the senator's effort to draw a distinction between freedom as national and slavery as sectional. The distinction reflected no real difference, said Garrison, and it did "nothing to relieve the [central government] from the guilt of upholding the slave system." He concluded: "This is not statesmanship."

Sumner's disquisition didn't sway many colleagues. When the vote was taken on his amendment, he had the support of only three other senators—Hale, Chase, and Ben Wade of Ohio, a strongly antislavery Whig. The Senate moved on to its adjournment a few days later.

New Hampshire's Hale engaged in serious hyperbole in suggesting Sumner's speech had ushered in a new era in national politics. But a new era was dawning, and Sumner would be part of it. The mere four votes for his amendment demonstrated that the Compromise of 1850 continued to hold sway in the land and that the country, as the *Boston Evening Transcript* had reported on December 2, truly wished to preserve the Constitution and the republic. But it was a fragile consensus that kept the Union together, and it wouldn't take much to shake it. Massachusetts remained among the states least committed to the consensus, and now Sumner offered his state a dialectic more palatable and less assailable than the zealous anticonstitutional castigations of the radical abolitionists. Garrison's attack merely accentuated the point.

Stephen Douglas could ignore Sumner's distinction between higher law and national freedom in his effort to smother Sumner's essentially conservative political construction before it could gain a footing in the discourse of slavery. And other critics could dismiss his approach as not original to him, which was true. But the Sumner speech added force to the arguments already crafted by Chase, Ohio's Joshua Giddings, and others bent on attacking slavery without attacking the Constitution.

For Sumner himself, the speech presaged a possible new phase in his fledgling political career. Under immense pressure back home and surrounded in the Senate by rivals bent on marginalizing him, he had emerged, on the basis of a single speech, as an antislavery figure to be reckoned with. The question for many now was whether he would respond to the expanded attention and acclaim by getting "big, and pompous," as a friend had warned against when Sumner became a senator. The warning was apt. Even before the speech, some of Sumner's Boston friends found the freshman legislator to be "more egotistical than ever."

8

1852

||||||||||||||||||||||||||||||||||||||||||||||||||||||||||||||||||||||||||||||||||||||

"THE WHIG PARTY WILL
EXIST ONLY IN HISTORY"

D aniel Webster was in no fettle to run for president in 1852, much less to serve in that capacity. The secretary of state suffered from intermittent digestive problems, painful gout, and a persistent inflammation of his throat and nose. One insensitive contemporary described him as a "poor, decrepit old man, whose limbs could scarcely support him; whose sluggish legs were somewhat concealed by an overhanging abdomen." Too often did he indulge his fancy for alcohol and lavish meals. Indeed, when he addressed a large audience at a cornerstone-laying ceremony for a new Capitol Building wing, some spectators thought he was drunk. More likely his poor performance reflected his many nettlesome infirmities and perhaps the regressions of age. He would turn seventy in January and if elected would be the oldest president up to that time.

But he couldn't resist the lure of the political summit that had eluded him throughout two decades of presidential ambition. And so on November 25, 1851, his friends and supporters congregated at Boston's famous Faneuil Hall to inaugurate Webster's presidential quest. In earlier times, he began his campaigns with efforts to galvanize the support of Massachusetts Whigs, only too happy to swarm to his side and provide a powerful boost. But he commanded no such Whig fealty now, as party officials struggled against the powerful coalition of Democrats and Free Soilers that had upended the state's old Whig ascendancy. In recent local elections, the coalition took control of the state house of representatives, and it purged from the legislature all Democrats who had voted against sending Charles Sumner to the U.S. Senate.

Webster had created a campaign "Central Committee" of nineteen prominent Massachusetts figures, including Edward Everett, known for his soaring eloquence. He produced an "Address to the People of the Union," which was read at Faneuil Hall and embraced unanimously.

It emphasized that Webster intended to run as the country's leading champion of unionism. "Belonging to the party of the Union, by whatever other name we may be called," said the Address, "we believe that the preservation of the Union is the greatest political object to be pursued." By accepting "whatever other name we may be called," the statement signaled that Webster intended to solicit votes from across partisan lines and build a new coalition, perhaps a new party, based on the imperative of saving the constitutional system.

Despite Webster's unionist coalition strategy, he still needed to capture the nomination of the national Whig Party, his political home since 1832. That meant he faced two prominent party figures seeking the same prize—General Winfield Scott, widely heralded for his military exploits in the late war with Mexico; and President Fillmore, who opted for a presidential run only after months of characteristic indecision.

Scott became a national hero when he landed a large army at Vera Cruz, captured the city, then pushed into the country's interior, devastating enemy armies along the way and conquering the Mexican capital. In that final battle, with fewer than 11,000 troops and facing a well-dug-in force of 30,000, Scott killed or wounded 7,000 enemy troops, captured 3,730 prisoners, and seized 75 cannons. Britain's Duke of Wellington, probably the world's most renowned military man at the time, called Scott "the greatest living soldier."

A towering bulk of a man with an animated face, he displayed plenty of human magnetism. But he slipped into impetuous hostility whenever he felt insulted, which was easily triggered. And he was a man of extravagant vanity, reflected in the story of his action as a young man when he first obtained his cherished officer's uniform. He placed two large mirrors at diagonal corners of his largest room and strutted back and forth for two hours of self-indulgent preening. If anyone had seen him, he later quipped, the embarrassment would have forced him to kill the person.

Such vanity and related behavior traits—pomposity, peevishness, a tendency toward impulsive blunders—never remained in check for long. "The chief ruling passion of the general," wrote a junior officer who served under him, "was ambition and its uniform attendant, jealousy."

Now to fulfill his White House ambition, Scott turned to two of the nation's most cunning Whig operatives, New York senator William Seward and Albany newspaper publisher and political boss Thurlow Weed. These men knew what they wanted: to find a compelling Whig presidential candidate whom they could support; to gain influence by attaching themselves to that candidate (and, they hoped, to the later Whig presidency); to preserve the increasingly fractious Whig Party; and to position Seward eventually for his own presidential run in 1856 or beyond.

But as sworn enemies of the Fugitive Slave Act, Seward and Weed saddled Scott with a difficult dilemma. How could he unite the fractured Whig Party when he was aligned with men despised by the South? As Washington's *Daily Union* explained, if the Whig national convention embraced the fugitive slave legislation, the party would lose the North; without doing so it would lose the South. The solution for some northern Whigs, wrote the *Charleston Mercury*'s Washington correspondent, was to select a southern candidate who was also "uncommitted and unpledged on the Fugitive Slave law." They found their man, the reporter added, in General Scott.

But it wasn't clear Scott could finesse the issue. It was possible that the party was simply hopelessly split, and there wasn't much Scott or anyone else could do about it.

As for Fillmore, throughout much of 1851 he had assured Webster that he didn't intend to seek his own presidential term. But by the fall he seemed inclined to run. That posed a problem for both men. If Webster were to run against his own president—and the man who had salvaged his career by giving him the State Department portfolio when his home state political standing was collapsing—the secretary would look like an ingrate. And if Fillmore were to retain Webster as secretary even as the two men competed for the nomination, he would look like a weakling.

But Fillmore entered the race, and Webster stayed in. That created something of a spectacle as the two men sought to maintain a proper professional relationship in the heat of their rivalry. Like Webster, Fillmore sought to position himself as a unionist who could bridge the gap between the North and South, and he soon became a favorite of southern Whigs, who saw him as a northern man with southern sympathies.

Democratic prospects looked bright in 1852. The party had managed to avoid the intensity of North-South tensions that afflicted the Whigs. Its greater commitment to the 1850 Compromise allowed it to appeal to southerners intent on protecting the Fugitive Slave Act, while also placating northerners who embraced the popular sovereignty principle of letting territorial settlers decide their own slavery policies. Also, after three years of the Taylor-Fillmore presidency, the Whigs seemed like a spent force, as reflected in recent congressional elections. From the 30th Congress to the 32nd, the Whig Party lost twenty-nine House seats, while the Democrats picked up twenty-one. Democrats now enjoyed a forty-seat House advantage in Congress.

Further, the Democratic Party boasted numerous candidates of high stature, including Michigan's Lewis Cass, Pennsylvania's James Buchanan, and Stephen Douglas.

Cass, a rich and erudite frontier empire builder with a wide girth, weary eyes, and a demeanor that suggested he wasn't to be trifled with, had served his country as Ohio legislator, Indian fighter, army general against the British, governor of the Michigan Territory, secretary of war, minister to France, and now senator. By Inauguration Day, Cass would be seventy, and his 1848 capture of the Democratic presidential nomination had led to a disheartening general election defeat. Some party bigwigs felt he should step back from the fray, which he had no intention of doing.

Buchanan, son of an Irish immigrant storekeeper, became wealthy as a Pennsylvania lawyer and then pursued a civic career that included stints as legislator, diplomat, and cabinet secretary. With his six-foot frame, unruly white hair, and large jutting chin, the sixty-year-old Buchanan brought instant attention to himself when he entered a room. But he had demonstrated over the years a tendency to place his own political interests ahead of all other considerations, and his self-serving intrigues betrayed a lack of conviction and a willingness to dissemble when it served his purposes.

Stephen Douglas, now thirty-eight, was known affectionately by his followers as "the Little Giant," reflecting the outsize appetites and ambitions that emanated from his diminutive, blockish body. They loved him for his vast energies and populist passion in behalf of ordinary folk, whom he saw as building up the country from below by pushing west, subduing the wilderness, generating wealth, and building churches, schools, and towns. But his many detractors decried his self-assured strut, his often brutish rhetoric, his manipulative ways, and his indulgence with liquor and tobacco. Thomas Hart Benton, the colorful Missourian, considered him a maddeningly elusive target. "He will not do, sir," complained the longtime senator. "His legs are too short, sir. That part of the body, sir, which men wish to kick, is too near the ground."

Events leading up to the parties' national conventions in June brought about shifts in the political landscape. Henry Clay gave Fillmore a boost in March when he identified the president as his preference for the Whig nomination. The nation still listened to Clay, perhaps particularly now in the knowledge of his looming death. He would die on June 29, shortly after the party conventions.

Webster's campaign, by contrast, seemed stagnant. "All is apathy," lamented a friend. Webster himself wrote to his son that "things are not in a good way. Nobody does any thing on our side." Matters worsened in May when the secretary suffered a serious head injury and sprained his wrists severely in a carriage accident.

Meanwhile, Scott continued to struggle with the dilemma of what to say about the Compromise. Embracing Seward's advice, he decided to continue the finesse and say nothing of substance. The *New York Herald* decried the approach as cowardly and counterproductive. "Can General Scott, as the candidate of Seward," asked the paper, "receive the support of the Whigs of the South, and continue dumb as an oyster on the Fugitive Slave law?" The *Herald* thought not and added in another editorial that Scott "could not place himself in worse hands" than those of the Seward "clique."

On the Democratic side, Douglas suffered a blow when a fiery provocateur named George N. Sanders purchased the venerable *Democratic Review* magazine and used it to spray venom upon all the Democratic contenders save his own favorite, the Little Giant. It was time for the "Old Fogies" to get out of the way, wrote Sanders, and let "Young America" manage the national destiny. The party needed "young blood" and "young ideas," which weren't available from the likes of Cass and Buchanan.

The Fogies, blaming Douglas, unleashed a relentless counterattack, portraying the Little Giant as a self-absorbed upstart incapable of appreciating the talents and triumphs of his elders—hence not someone his elders should bother with. Turning away in large numbers, they significantly curtailed Douglas's prospects for fashioning a coalition of support. It was, wrote historian Allan Nevins, a "heavy calamity."

While politics preoccupied America in 1852, the nation also experienced a literary event of immense cultural impact. On March 20, 1852, the abolitionist publisher John P. Jewett brought out an antislavery novel called *Uncle Tom's Cabin; or, Life among the Lowly*, by Harriet Beecher Stowe. Within a year sales had topped 310,000 in America and a million in Britain. Multiple translations pushed worldwide sales to 2 million. The Boston minister Theodore Parker characterized Stowe's work as "more an event than a book."

The country had become familiar with Stowe's narrative through its serial publication in Gamaliel Bailey's abolitionist newspaper, the *National Era*, from June 1851 to March 1852. But publication in book form rocked the nation as no newspaper series could. It was estimated that each copy had an average readership of ten persons, and the book generated a torrent of related plays, essays, reviews, and even tie-in merchandise. "No book in American history," writes historian David S. Reynolds, "molded public opinion more powerfully than *Uncle Tom's Cabin.*"

On its literary merits, Stowe's book wasn't particularly great. Sentimental at times to the point of being sappy, it presented characters that often seemed one-dimensional. But she rendered a poignant and accurate portrayal of the plight of American blacks caught in the vise of bondage, with all the pain, anguish, and inhumanity of that experience. And she did so while avoiding the thundering anti-South invective often employed by many northern abolitionists.

In recounting the travails of Eliza, who is forced to flee bondage and seek freedom in order to keep her five-year-old son, Harry, from being sold away from her, Stowe excoriates the 1850 Fugitive Slave Act more forcefully than Charles Sumner could with his outraged polemics, as eloquent as he often was. And in capturing the vicissitudes of life experienced by the saintly Uncle Tom—benevolent ownership one moment, monumentally cruel ownership the next—Stowe personalizes her central point, which was that slavery was evil, and so were the institutional forces that sustained it.

Thus did Stowe's scenes and images arouse many northerners into rethinking their previous live-and-let-live neutrality on southern slavery; they also generated a reactive anger on the part of defensive southerners. Her morality narrative seeped into the nation's political consciousness, unsettling the efforts of unionists to ensure that the 1850 Compromise represented "finality" on the slavery issue. For Stowe and her growing numbers of assentors, there could be no finality so long as there was slavery.

The book's significance, however, went deeper than that. Stowe was born in 1811 into a family of famous clergymen, including her father, Lyman Beecher, and a brother, Henry Ward Beecher. She was herself imbued with a deep religious sensibility, and as a New Englander she identified with her region's Puritan tradition, the austere Calvinism brought to America by those Massachusetts Bay colonists beginning in 1630. But she was also a reformer, caught up in the progressive ethos that emanated from New England in the nineteenth century, fixed on human improvement in the realms of temperance, women's rights, education, public health and, of course, slavery.

Stowe's father and brother focused their own reformist zeal in part on church doctrine itself, on the Calvinist preoccupation with depravity, the austerity and inaccessibility of God, and the notion that even babies are destined for hell if born among the unelected. The Beechers viewed God as a loving presence, accessible to all, and a deity who issued his judgments on the basis of behavior, on good works, rather than random destiny. Harriet Stowe embraced this new and uplifting religious vision and meshed it with her zeal for humanitarian reform. She merged the early Puritans' concept of Providence with the later concept of human progress, as developed by contemporary New England thinkers such as Emerson and Thoreau.

This intertwined religious and secular sensibility inevitably led to another concept that was becoming more and more vexing for American thinkers as they perceived just how intractable the slavery issue was. This was the concept of a higher law that transcended the laws of humans, even the U.S. Constitution and certainly the 1850 Compromise. William Seward, of course, had stumbled into this doctrinal thicket to his regret back in 1850, but others were taking up the cudgel, none more emphatically than Stowe. She singled out Daniel Webster particularly for having "moved over to the side of evil" when he "scoffed at the idea that there was a law of God higher than any law or constitution of the United States."

However powerful those words were from the pen of the century's most successful novelist, their impact paled in contrast to the novel itself, whose message continued to reverberate through the country as Americans grappled with the relentless torment of slavery.

On June 1 some eight hundred to a thousand delegates and alternates assembled in Baltimore's Maryland Institute Hall for the Democratic National Convention. Every state was represented except South Carolina, which traditionally stood aloof from such gatherings to avoid any obligation to abide by convention decisions. "We see nothing to be gained," pronounced the *Mercury*, "in mingling in the struggle for Presidential nominations."

But those who did arrive filled Baltimore's hotels "to their fullest capacity," as one newspaper reporter wrote, and generated "a perfect whirl of excitement." One of the convention's first actions was to approve procedural rules, including the traditional requirement that the winning candidate collect at least two-thirds of the delegates. This posed difficulties in selecting a nominee, but the eventual winner was presumed to be a strong consensus candidate. It did mean, though, that while the South wouldn't have sufficient strength to select the winner, it could veto any candidate. An attempt to do away with the two-thirds rule was rejected overwhelmingly by the delegates.

It didn't take many ballots to reveal that getting to two-thirds wouldn't be easy. With 192 votes needed for nomination, Cass led in the first ballot with 116. He edged up slightly from there, then began a slow decline, dropping below 100 on the eleventh ballot and hitting just 60 on the twenty-first. Buchanan began the balloting at 93, then slipped slightly, but soon jumped up to above 100 for a number of ballots before slipping back again. That fluctuation suggested the delegates faced a possible convention deadlock.

That's when a group of Buchanan delegates concocted a scheme of spreading their votes among the lesser candidates as a way of blocking Cass and Douglas, while placing their man in a kind of reserve status. They hoped the Pennsylvanian might rise again with evidence that Cass and Douglas couldn't win. The plan backfired. One of those lesser candidates was former New Hampshire senator Franklin Pierce, who began a slight upward trajectory just as it became clear that none of the major candidates could get to two-thirds. On the forty-sixth ballot, Pierce received forty-one votes, up from twenty-nine on the previous ballot. In subsequent voting he rose to forty-nine, then to fifty-five.

That was all it took. Pierce, the fresh face, came into focus just as fatigue and frustration generated a widespread feeling that the party needed a fresh face. On the forty-ninth and final ballot, a stampede to Pierce gave him 283 votes, all but five of the sitting delegates. The party had its man. The delegates then nominated William R. King of Alabama for vice president, despite his declining health, and approved without debate the party's platform.

The platform offered no succor to northern abolitionists. It swore full fealty to the 1850 Compromise measures, including the Fugitive Slave Act, and denied that Congress had any authority to interfere in state matters beyond what was spelled out in the Constitution. It added the party "will resist all attempts at renewing in Congress or out of it, the agitation of the Slavery question, under whatever shape or color."

The nation's attention was now riveted on Franklin Pierce. Born in 1804, the son of a Revolutionary War hero who became New Hampshire governor, Pierce grew up in favored circumstances, attended private schools, and graduated from Bowdoin College in Maine. A winsome lad with a commanding voice, he displayed a wholesome exuberance and a knack for easygoing leadership among his peers. Adults responded avidly to his polite and somewhat formal bearing. Academically, he displayed a marked inconsistency, slacking at times but recovering with frenzied study when necessary. He liked sporting activity, hijinks with friends, and, in his college years, drinking in bars. As a young man, in fact, he developed what seemed to many like a drinking problem, which friends later insisted had been conquered.

Upon graduation he returned to his hometown of Hillsborough, New Hampshire, and entered the law. But politics beckoned, and he began an electoral career that proved meteoric—four years in the state legislature, including two years as Speaker of the lower house; four years in the U.S. House; and five years in the U.S. Senate—all before his thirty-eighth birthday. He resigned his Senate seat in February 1842 to return to his New Hampshire family life and legal career. But he remained head of the state Democratic Party, formally and informally, through the next decade, with time out for the war with Mexico, when he secured a command as colonel and then brigadier general of a New England regiment and saw considerable early combat. But serious military glory eluded him when a riding accident and an illness kept him from the center of action.

Politically, Pierce adhered to the fundamental tenets of Andrew

Jackson's Democratic Party—low tariffs, hard money, a limited federal government, territorial expansion. He sympathized with the South and harbored a severe dislike for northern abolitionists who put emancipation over societal stability and insisted that those who disagreed with them were morally unfit. He believed that if the abolitionists would back off, then southern rabble-rousers would settle down. Southerners generally applauded the selection. The *Charleston Mercury* said he belonged to that "respectable portion" of the Democratic Party that "never made terms with the Free Soilers" and was "in all respects as good a man for the South as any of those he has superseded." Lloyd Garrison's *Liberator* promptly reprinted those words as a warning of what to expect should Pierce become president.

The Whig National Convention convened on June 16 in the same Baltimore hall that had housed the Democratic gathering two weeks before. The delegates quickly approved a platform that echoed the Democratic document in stating that the 1850 Compromise measures, including the fugitive slave law, "are received and acquiesced in by the Whig party . . . as a settlement in principle and substance" and that Whigs "deprecate all further agitation of the slavery question as dangerous to our peace." This was a big victory for party moderates bent on avoiding a southern rebellion, and one disgruntled abolitionist delegate wondered aloud whether this wasn't the result of an intrigue to mollify the South in exchange for its acquiescence in Scott's nomination.

Unlike the Democrats, Whig delegates traditionally opted for a mere majority outcome. With 296 delegates, victory thus required 149 votes. In the first balloting, Fillmore received 133; Scott, 131; and Webster, 29. That general breakdown of convention sentiment held through three days and fifty-two ballots. Scott took much of the West and North, while Fillmore took the South (save for one vote). Webster received no southern support.

It was quickly perceived that if Fillmore and Webster could combine their support, or most of it, they could overwhelm Scott. Various efforts at negotiation failed. "My friends will stand firm," said Webster, who seemed humiliated and hurt to be reduced to such a lowly station after twenty years of party loyalty. When a Fillmore associate named John Barney, meeting with Webster in Washington, entreated him once again to release his delegates so they could vote for Fillmore, Webster again refused. "All I ask," he moaned, "is a decent vote that I may retire without disgrace."

It wasn't to be. As Webster finally relented and began preparing to release his delegates, a number of Pennsylvanians broke for the general on the fifty-third ballot, ending the logjam and giving the nomination to Scott. The convention then nominated William Graham of North Carolina for vice president and adjourned.

Northern Whigs generally applauded the Scott selection on the theory that he was a Free Soiler at heart, though in accepting the nomination he endorsed the party platform. "We accept the candidate, but we spit on the platform" became a popular phrase. Southerners, attacking the selection as a serious threat to their region, portrayed Scott as a phony "with a padlock on his lips, and his principles in Mr. Seward's breeches' pocket," as the *Savannah Republican* put it.

Massachusetts Free Soilers and Conscience Whigs took a morbid delight in Webster's humiliation. "We have dirked him!" exclaimed Henry Wilson, the Free Soil operative and former shoemaker who now served in the Massachusetts legislature. When a group of boisterous Whigs appeared at Webster's Washington home on the convention's final night to serenade him as a show of affection, he shrouded his true feelings in studied nonchalance: "The result has caused me no personal feeling whatever. . . . Gentlemen, there is not one among you, who will sleep better to-night than I shall." Garrison had fun with that. "Nothing could more plainly evince the utter disappointment he felt," said the *Liberator*, "than this attempt to seem indifferent to it. . . . 'Sour grapes,' said the fox." Webster's friends would put together an independent general election campaign in his behalf, but he was finished. The sad politician, once a giant but no longer, returned to Marshfield, where he died four months later.

Through all the political tumult of 1852, one thing was becoming clear: the Compromise of 1850 was taking hold in the country—under assault around the edges, yes, as northern abolitionists and southern secessionists continued to carp and seek avenues of weakness for exploitation. And the moral sensibilities driving antislavery forces were slowly gaining currency, posing a possible future challenge to Compromise adherents. But most Americans wanted calm and tranquility, which meant embracing the Compromise and subduing the slavery debate.

The major parties' campaign platforms, using nearly identical language in bolstering the Clay/Douglas accommodation, reflected this reality. Antislavery Whigs recoiled at their party document, but couldn't change it even with the wily William Seward pulling strings behind the scenes. And the recent actions of southern states, resisting the clarion call of fire-eaters and disavowing disunion in unmistakable terms, represented a serious desire to settle matters through constitutional means. Even South Carolina, for years under the sway of the ultra-secessionist Barnwell Rhett, had finally renounced the idea of precipitous action and repudiated Rhett's zealotry—along with the man himself.

Then there were the parties' presidential candidates. Franklin Pierce was nearly the archetype of the northern politician with southern sympathies. And, while Winfield Scott's coyness on the matter raised eyebrows on both sides before the convention, his ultimate endorsement of the 1850 Compromise reflected the party's majority sentiment.

One lingering question centered on whether the Free Soil Party, preparing for a national convention at Pittsburgh in August, would emerge as a significant political factor. The Pittsburgh gathering drew hundreds of avid antislavery men from every free state except California, and also from slave states Delaware, Maryland, Virginia, and Kentucky. Massachusetts sent the dedicated Free Soiler Charles Francis Adams and party leader Henry Wilson.

The Free Soil platform denied that the federal government had any constitutional right to involve itself with slavery in any way and denounced the 1850 Compromise as "inconsistent with all the principles and maxims of Democracy." In dismissing the idea that any law could have "finality," it called for repeal of the Fugitive Slave Act. In a passage that veered close to endorsing higher law, the platform stated that "slavery is a sin against God, and a crime against man, the enormity of which no law nor usage can sanction or mitigate, and that Christianity, humanity, and patriotism alike demand its abolition."

The convention then selected as its presidential candidate New Hampshire senator John Hale, that tower of conviction and bluster who had been fighting slavery for most of his career. It wasn't clear if Hale's vote total could hit or exceed the 291,501 popular votes garnered by Free Soil candidate Martin Van Buren in 1848. But it seemed clear to most observers that, whatever he collected, he would get it largely from Scott.

When the votes were counted in November, Pierce scored a blow-out Electoral College victory with 254 votes and twenty-seven states to Scott's 42 votes and just four states. The popular-vote distribution was 51 percent for Pierce, 44 percent for Scott, 5 percent for Hale. It was a monumental Whig debacle in every respect. The *Boston Daily Atlas*, a Whig paper, called it a "Waterloo defeat" and lamented that "the Whig banner trails in the dust." Indeed, it wasn't just the presidential outcome that slammed into the Whig Party. It won only three of twelve gubernatorial elections that year, giving it control of only five governorships in the country's thirty-one states. Further, back in 1848, Whigs had won 57 percent of contested House seats; in 1850, 42 percent; and now, in 1852, just 29 percent.

Democrats had no difficulty in assessing the election's meaning, with particular attention to William Seward. The *Daily Union* said the country had "repudiated and abjured forever, both that sectional policy, of which Mr. Seward is the special representative, and also that mere military *eclat* which was supposed to constitute the whole of Gen. Scott's personal availability." The *Boston Post* attributed the local results to the Whigs' misreading of voter sentiment in New England. "This is a Whig city," said the paper, "and it can, when it chooses, carry . . . a Whig majority. It is not, however, an abolition city." In this view, the party merely needed to return to the "high-toned patriotism of its mechanics and merchants" and abandon "such arch political intriguers as Seward and the men around him."

But others suggested it might not be that simple for a Whig Party that didn't seem in step with the prevailing political sentiment of the day. Reverberating in the minds of many were the words that Daniel Webster uttered on his deathbed shortly before his October 24 demise. After Election Day on November 2, predicted the great Whig statesman, "the Whig party, as a National party, will exist only in history."

9

PRESIDENT PIERCE

||||||||||||||||||||||||||||||||||||||||||||||||||||||||||||||||||||||||||||||||

"NO SECTIONAL OR FANATICAL EXCITEMENT"

Charles Sumner and Pickens Butler represented a study in contrasts in the U.S. Senate. Certainly their views on slavery couldn't have been more in conflict. But the contrasts extended also to matters of temperament, political style, social bearing, and their general views of the world and of themselves.

Sumner seldom could find the humor in a joke; Butler was a jokester who saw the humor in just about everything. Sumner spent weeks preparing for a major speech and sometimes flinched at the prospect of extemporaneous verbal combat; Butler thrived in off-the-cuff legislative exchanges. Sumner couldn't resist administering sharp thrusts at adversaries that often heightened political tensions; Butler enveloped friend and foe alike in rousing good cheer. Sumner's stock-in-trade was tightly reasoned and meticulously crafted oratory that captivated listeners; Butler's more varied specialties included backroom maneuvering, coalition building, and the well-timed quip.

But the two senators also enjoyed certain affinities, including a common interest in history, classical literature, foreign affairs, and the law. Thus, throughout the three-month congressional session that began in early December 1852, they maintained the cordiality that had developed between them following Sumner's Senate arrival. This was buoyed by the determination of congressional leaders, in the wake of the 1850 Compromise, to keep the emotion-laden slavery issue off the legislative agenda and to focus congressional attention on other matters. But the two men genuinely liked each other, and the friendship even inspired Sumner to develop a resolve, which he proved incapable of honoring for long, "to shun harsh and personal criticism of those from whom I differ."

Down in South Carolina, meanwhile, Butler's stature as his state's leading politician seemed secure now in the wake of Calhoun's death and Barnwell Rhett's Senate resignation, as well as Butler's own courage in pressing the cooperationist cause when most political observers believed disunionist sentiment represented the state's prevailing outlook. When the special delegate elections of October 1851 proved otherwise, Butler's political standing soared. The *Charleston Mercury*, no friend of the cooperationists, praised the judge's "skill and dignity of demeanor" and said that, "although addicted to humorous repartee, no man, when proper occasion presents itself, can rise to the full height of his subject better than he." Politically secure at home, Butler now was positioned to play an increasingly prominent role in Washington.

He magnified his senatorial clout through a lodging arrangement with three like-minded and highly influential senators: Virginians James M. Mason and Robert M. T. Hunter, and Missouri's David Rice Atchison. In 1853 the four senators jointly purchased a house at 361 F Street, between Ninth and Tenth streets, which would serve as their Washington living quarters, and foster a tight political and personal bond. The foursome's living arrangement became known as the F Street Mess.

These men embraced the political ethos of John C. Calhoun, particularly his view that slavery must be protected or the Union would dissolve. Mason, broad-faced, blunt-spoken, and highly educated, was a true Virginia aristocrat whose New World forebears stretched back to 1651 and included the U.S. Founding Father James Mason. Highly successful as a lawyer, he also distinguished himself in Congress as chairman of the prestigious Senate Foreign Relations Committee. During the political battles surrounding the 1850 Compromise, he wrote the fugitive slave legislation that generated so much northern dudgeon.

Hunter—imposing in physical appearance, reflective and courtly in demeanor—also enjoyed an aristocratic heritage. Educated in the law at the University of Virginia and under the tutelage of the celebrated legal scholar Henry St. George Tucker, he eschewed aggressive legal pursuits in favor of plantation management, politics, and financial speculations (many of which turned sour). Elected to the U.S. House at age twenty-eight, he became Speaker just two years later. In the Senate, he captured the chairmanship of the Finance Committee, with its jurisdiction over crucial and often incendiary tariff policies. The *Charleston Mercury* extolled "the great amiability of his character" and added, "Detraction has never dogged his footsteps."

Atchison's background and temperament differed markedly from those of his messmates. The product of three generations of Scotch-Irish Kentucky farmers, he grew up in middling economic circumstances within a rustic culture suffused by strict Presbyterian devotion. Seeking financial betterment, he gravitated to the western frontier of Missouri, took up the law and politics, and served as a Missouri militia general during the state's 1838 "Mormon War." After two terms in the U.S. House and a judicial stint, he entered the Senate in 1843 at age thirty-six. Quick of tongue and temper, rugged in appearance and temperament, he seemed to be something of a wilderness gamecock, not altogether tamed but adept at survival in any habitat. In the Senate he was elected repeatedly to the position of president pro tempore, in which he presided over the Senate in the absence of the vice president and also was second in line to presidential succession.

By the 33rd Congress, which convened in December 1853, the F Street messmates constituted an estimable senatorial force. With their command over three powerful committees and influence over senatorial procedure, they were well positioned to pool their power for increased leverage and apply that leverage to backroom dealmaking as well as emphatic Senate floor contention. They demonstrated little interest in addressing the galleries, much less the great mass of Americans beyond Washington, in the manner of Sumner or Rhett. Historian Alice

Elizabeth Malavasic even suggests that the Mess's "dexterous blend of fealty, institutional knowledge, and political acumen was the true source of the Slave Power." This may be a bit overstated. Slave power influence came from many sources. But the F Street Mess was one of them, and an important one.

While Butler was enhancing his political position at home and in Washington, Sumner faced political crosscurrents in Massachusetts that endangered the controversial coalition of antislavery Democrats and freewheeling Free Soilers that had ushered Sumner into the Senate. So long as the coalition held sway in the legislature, Sumner enjoyed a strong base of support. But it wasn't clear the coalition could last.

First, Massachusetts Whigs staged a comeback in the 1852 elections and got their man elected governor over the coalition candidate. This was a serious blow, all the more serious for Sumner because many Free Soilers and coalition members blamed him for the defeat. They had expected that, upon his return to Massachusetts following his triumphant Freedom National address, he would help rally the faithful through extensive speeches and public appearances. But he proved reluctant to interrupt his leisure and devote as much time and energy to the cause as many colleagues wanted. Sumner's close friend Samuel Gridley Howe warned that "many influential men are already disaffected toward you in consequence of your reluctance to come forward."

Sumner also had to contend with the hostility of more purist Free Soilers, including Charles Francis Adams and others, who were uncomfortable with alignments forged strictly for political power and viewed the coalition as unprincipled. Thus had Sumner placed himself in a precarious position—caught between, on one hand, traditional Free Soilers who disliked him for his alignment with Democrats and, on the other hand, coalition Free Soilers, under Henry Wilson's leadership, who disliked his sometimes indifferent party attitude. Adams expressed the view of many in suggesting the senator "was never formed to be a political leader." Meanwhile, the Garrison forces viewed him as an inadequate abolitionist because of his fealty to the Constitution, as expressed in his Freedom National speech. As Parker Pillsbury, a Garrison man, declared at an antislavery meeting, "Webster's fall was not so deplorable as that of Charles Sumner."

Another problem emerged when coalition Democrats pursued an agenda that further scrambled up the currents of Bay State politics. They wanted a new Massachusetts constitution designed to enhance the political clout of the state's rural western portions at the expense of the more densely populated east, bastion of the old Whig ascendancy. This power play unified defensive Whigs throughout the state, while splitting Democrats along geographic lines after they already had been fractured along political lines by the emergence of the coalition. It didn't help that Caleb Cushing—the state's fiercest anti-coalition Democrat, now about to become Franklin Pierce's attorney general—issued what became known as the "Cushing Ukase," which declared that the new administration would award no jobs to Massachusetts Democrats who continued to dally with the coalition.

Not surprisingly, the coalition's imperious ambitions generated a backlash. In the autumn elections of 1853, Whigs retained the governorship, recaptured the legislature, and defeated the proposed new constitution by some five thousand votes. Sumner called the defeat "a calamity to the Liberal cause." It was also a calamity to Sumner. The elections finished off the coalition and obliterated the senator's legislative base of support. That posed a political challenge: he must galvanize the state's antislavery voters into a new base of support before facing the legislature in a reelection bid four years hence.

The second session of the 32nd Congress began on December 7, 1852, and was set to adjourn on March 3, the day before Franklin Pierce's inauguration. Nobody expected the lame-duck session to tackle major issues or generate much political passion. And it didn't. A Senate debate emerged over whether the country should initiate efforts to purchase the island of Cuba from Spain. Congress also took up the visionary concept of fostering construction of a railroad to the Pacific coast, a civic ambition fraught with delicate questions involving which route to choose, how the rail line should be financed, and what role the federal government should play in the project. These questions had been percolating in Congress for a number of years, and many influential lawmakers felt the time was ripe now for aggressive action setting the project in motion.

Prominent among these railroad enthusiasts were Stephen Douglas, always at the center of any push for westward expansion; David Rice Atchison, focused on getting St. Louis designated as the eastern departure point so he could leverage the triumph in his next reelection campaign; Thomas Hart Benton, the great Missourian and Atchison antagonist, still smarting from the 1850 loss of his Senate seat; and Asa Whitney, a wealthy dry-goods merchant and inveterate promoter of the transcontinental dream.

Whitney became obsessed with the idea after a business initiative in the early 1840s, when he transported merchandise to China from the American East Coast via an ocean voyage that lasted more than three months. With railroad development gaining force and the United States positioned to acquire a large part of the Oregon Territory (and later California), he fixed on the idea of cutting weeks of travel time from his transport route by slicing through North America by rail. He studied various routes, produced pamphlets extolling the concept, and importuned politicians at every opportunity. His concept was that the federal government would sell him, at bargain prices, a strip of land sixty miles wide along the chosen route and then he would build the line using proceeds from the resale of much of the property. He favored a route from Milwaukee to the Columbia River.

His proposal never gained acceptance, but three elements of it congealed into settled concepts among many who later took up the cause: the Pacific railroad was a national necessity; the financing mechanism should be federal land grants along the route; and the builders should be private industrialists willing to leverage the land grants to construct and maintain the line. Aside from the civic benefit of a more closely knit nation, the concept posed rich opportunities for railroad builders to accumulate substantial wealth with little up-front investment. It also posed prospects for lesser but still substantial financial success for those who managed to acquire property and establish businesses along the chosen route. The entire concept, noted historian David M. Potter, "was like a giant lottery."

The lottery's big question, which preoccupied Congress and eastern industrialists, was which big city would become the eastern terminus, funneling massive numbers of people and large amounts of goods into the West. Cities vying for the bonanza included Minneapolis, Chicago, St. Louis, Memphis, and New Orleans. All took heart in the fact that U.S. railroad mileage was expanding at a feverish pace, from 8,600 to 21,300 in four years.

No one pursued the dream more persistently than Douglas, the great optimist and civic booster of Chicago and the West. As early as 1845, when he was a thirty-two-year-old freshman congressman, Douglas gained attention with an open letter heralding the project and pushing his hometown for the departure-point designation.

It wasn't just national greatness on his mind. In 1850 he had fostered legislation extending federal land grants to Illinois, Alabama, and Mississippi for construction of a rail line from Chicago to Mobile, Alabama. He made a financial killing by purchasing strategically located property in the Chicago area and selling it later for use on the rail route. Douglas was not unmindful of prospects for an even bigger score if he could get Chicago designated as the takeoff city of the Pacific railroad. In fact, he invited into his venture his Senate colleague Robert Hunter, Pickens Butler's messmate on F Street, who also had been Douglas's vice presidential designee during his aborted 1852 presidential run.

But Douglas and other railroad enthusiasts faced a serious impediment. A vast landmass at the center of the country had been designated by Congress in 1834 as "Indian Territory," reserved for tribes indigenous to the West as well as those that had been pushed there from the East. Whites were forbidden to settle or travel through those lands, which encompassed some 60 million acres and included nearly all U.S. territory between the Mississippi River and the Rocky Mountains, except for Missouri, Louisiana, Arkansas Territory, and small portions of four other states. President Andrew Jackson blessed the Indian-land designation in 1835 by embracing "the moral duty of the government of the United States to protect, and, if possible, to preserve and perpetuate the scattered remnants of this race, which are left within our borders."

Hardly anyone in 1835, however, conceived of the nation that would emerge within just a dozen years, stretching across the continent from ocean to ocean. New imperatives related to settlement, trade, national cohesion, and national security now argued for the federal takeover of the Indian lands and their incorporation into the rest of the country. Thus, any transcontinental railroad project that envisioned a central or northern route would require legislation authorizing negotiations with the Indian tribes for such a transfer. Several measures were introduced in the 1852–53 congressional session calling for the reorganization of the portion of the Indian lands called Platte Territory, sometimes referred to as the Territory of Nebraska. Douglas felt confident that this would be the session when Congress finally would initiate his cherished railroad project.

In February representative Willard Hall of Missouri introduced a bill to organize Nebraska Territory, and Chairman William Richardson of the House Committee on Territories promptly reported it to the floor. It passed 98 to 43. That generated plenty of jubilation among railroad advocates, but complications arose on the Senate floor after Douglas reported the bill out of his own committee on February 17. First, it was clear that the legislation couldn't pass if it denoted a preferred route, for advocates of the other routes would combine to defeat it. A plan to include numerous terminal points at both the East and West was rejected as being "entirely too magnificent," as Lewis Cass put it. Finally, Thomas Rusk of Texas offered an amendment leaving the choice of route and terminals to the president. It passed and seemed to solidify support for the measure.

But then Cass and others demanded new language stipulating that no portion of the $20 million provided for rail construction should be expended within any existing states, as opposed to territories. The argument, embraced traditionally by Democrats, was that the Constitution precluded intrastate internal improvements by the federal government, whereas improvements within territories could pass muster. The amendment passed, scotching any prospect for a southern route, as any such line would have to go through the state of Texas. Several southern senators promptly turned against the bill, and crucial votes needed to get floor approval evaporated. The congressional session ended without a Nebraska bill, and lawmakers had to content themselves with getting merely a $150,000 authorization for surveys on the various rail routes.

But the southern defections hinted at another problem that would face Pacific rail advocates in the next Congress, set to convene in December. The effort to organize Nebraska Territory appeared to be on a collision course with the persistent slavery issue. The reason was the Missouri Compromise of 1820.

That famous accommodation, part of Henry Clay's lasting legacy, was designed to quell tensions arising from the prospect of Missouri entering the Union as a slave state and thus upending the equilibrium that existed at the time between slave and free states. In addition to fostering the entry of free-state Maine to balance off Missouri, the compromise also established a demarcation line at latitude 36°30', with no new slave states allowed north of that line. But now, with Nebraska above the compromise line and hence barred from allowing slavery, some southerners hesitated to embrace the rail project and the related territorial initiative.

David Atchison reflected that sentiment even as he voted to take up the Douglas bill—as one of only two southern senators to do so. "Now, sir," said Atchison, "I am free to admit that at this moment, at this hour, and for all time to come I should oppose the organization or the settlement of the Territory, unless my constituents and the constituents of the whole South . . . could go into it upon the same footing, with equal rights and equal privileges, carrying that species of property [slaves] with them." But he added he saw no prospect for a Missouri Compromise repeal, and therefore he would opt for the territorial bill even with the 36°30' line intact. "So far as that question is concerned," he said, "we might as well agree to the admission of this Territory now as next year, or five or ten years hence."

Having accepted the Missouri Compromise restriction, Atchison almost immediately saw the political danger his action posed to his

senatorial career, particularly with Thomas Hart Benton positioned to
challenge him at his next election. On March 4, the day after the congressional session ended, Benton announced his candidacy for Atchison's Senate seat. Douglas, meanwhile, was left to ponder a reality of
his Nebraska defeat—namely, that northerners had killed the possible
southern routes by insisting on the proscription against intrastate federal assistance, while southerners had killed the Nebraska routes because
of the slavery proscription instituted by the Missouri Compromise. It
wasn't going to be easy getting the railroad project back on track at the
next Congress.

A light snow descended upon Washington on the day after the congressional adjournment, but it didn't diminish the celebratory
mood of Democrats, who were about to reclaim the White House with
Franklin Pierce. An estimated seventy-five thousand persons gathered
for the inaugural festivities, and the *Baltimore Sun* reported that people
thronged Pennsylvania Avenue with such density that "pedestrian progress in either direction was almost impossible." The paper added that
Chief Marshal J. D. Hoover led twelve special aides, four marshals, and
eighty-two assistants—"mounted and designated by rich regalia and appropriate implements of their respective offices."

Pierce's inaugural address combined appropriate expressions of humility with the requisite declarations of resolve—and added an assertion
that he stood there "in obedience to the unsolicited expression of your
will." Hinting at reports that he would pursue the U.S. annexation of
Cuba, he promised that his administration "will not be controlled by
any timid forebodings of evil from expansion."

On the slavery issue, he declared the 1850 Compromise to be
"strictly constitutional" and added that "involuntary servitude, as it
exists in different States of this Confederacy," was also "recognized by
the Constitution." In a nod to the Fugitive Slave Act, he averred that
the slave states "are entitled to efficient remedies to enforce the [act's]
constitutional provisions." And he expressed a hope that "no sectional,
or ambitious, or fanatical excitement may again threaten the durability

of our institutions." But he took care to avoid any mention of slavery expansion into the territories. On states' rights, he embraced standard Democratic language in declaring that the "dangers of a concentration of all powers in the general Government . . . are too obvious to be disregarded."

Washington's *Daily Union*, reflecting its Democratic fealty, said the speech demonstrated that "the art of the scholar is as conspicuous as the wisdom of the statesman and the devotion of the patriot." Charleston's *Mercury* bumptiously chided the *Union* for its extravagant prose, but characterized the address as "for the most part, neat, appropriate, and sufficiently explicit for the occasion." Of course, Garrison's *Liberator* disagreed, saying the speech demonstrated that Pierce "has never had a pulsation of his heart which did not beat in unison with the Slave Power." The paper said the new president's own "image and superscription" exposed him as "two-faced, brutal, and murderous."

Generally, though, the speech captured what many considered to be the prevailing post-Compromise sentiment of the nation, which favored acceptance of slavery where it existed, adherence to the Fugitive Slave Act, and popular sovereignty for territorial governments on the question of whether to opt for slave or free status. The Clay/Douglas handiwork seemed secure on that snow-swept Inauguration Day.

But the new president soon unleashed political resentments that threatened his ability to govern effectively. The issue was the age-old conundrum of patronage, the distribution of political spoils in the form of plum governmental jobs meant to reward and unify the party rank and file. Rather than giving his most ardent campaign supporters and Compromise adherents the greatest share of largesse, Pierce sought to pull the party together by distributing the jobs as equally as possible to all party factions. This resulted in what historian Michael F. Holt called "an unmitigated disaster."

Pro-Compromise southerners who had worked assiduously in behalf of southern moderation chafed at patronage jobs going to anti-Compromise dogmatists. Anti-Compromise southerners hated seeing largesse go to northern abolitionists. Midwestern Douglas supporters complained about distributions to Cass men, and a Democratic faction in Pennsylvania declared war on the administration based on patronage going to a rival faction. Pierce's allocation of federal jobs generated ire and belligerence in nearly every state, with New York being the most troublesome.

The New York imbroglio involved three power-hungry factions vying for party dominance. Though they despised each other they now directed much of their ire at the president, seen as having ducked his responsibility for party leadership. It was quickly perceived by many that the intraparty bickering in New York and elsewhere could sap Democratic strength leading up to the next election. A Missouri democrat warned Stephen Douglas that the national party faced being "shivered to atoms."

Sure enough, just two weeks later the New York elections dealt a heavy blow to Democrats. The Whigs' share of legislative house seats increased to 61 percent from just 33 percent in the previous session, while the party's senate share went to 72 percent from 50 percent. Seward's reelection in the coming legislative balloting now seemed guaranteed.

Many Democrats, fearing their fractured party would unravel further, wanted President Pierce to unleash a major initiative that would "raise invective from the other side and compel us to quit our domestic squabbles," as one Pennsylvania official put it. A Missourian warned party officials that, unless Pierce "promptly marks out a line of sound national and Democratic policy . . . , it will be impossible for him to save his Administration."

But Pierce, whose ambitions as president seemed focused primarily on foreign policy and the acquisition of Cuba, didn't show any interest in proposing bold domestic programs. His first Annual Message to Congress, in December 1853, presented just one such initiative: reductions in tariff rates. This had been a Democratic fixation since Andrew Jackson's day, but the nation's tariff rates already were quite low by historical standards (thanks to the leadership of Democratic president James K. Polk in the 1840s), and the Democratic Congress ignored the proposal.

Another possibility could have been the Pacific railroad. Just as James Polk had stirred the nation with his territorial expansion, some Democrats suggested, Pierce could pull America together with a cross-country

railway and help tame the wilds that now beckoned adventurers and settlers bent on pushing American civilization westward. Pierce described
himself in his Annual Message as "solicitous that the Atlantic and Pacific
shores of the Republic may be bound together by inseparable ties of
common interest." But he then tossed discouragement upon the idea by
suggesting the Constitution forbade any federal involvement in building
nonmilitary infrastructure in the states and it would be of "more than
doubtful propriety" to construct a railway even through territorial lands.
He didn't seem interested in finding a way to make it work within the
framework of his constitutional scruples. That meant leaving it to private
interests to pursue the project without any governmental involvement,
an approach that didn't seem likely to bear fruit.

Discerning political observers were beginning to perceive serious
limitations in Pierce's executive capacity. He lacked vision and imagination, brought to the office little policy coherence, and was easily swayed
by the last person he talked to. The patronage imbroglio particularly
had been a product of his own political naivete in not seeing that his
approach, while perhaps laudable for its "fairness," would bring down
upon him the wrath of all factions. Far better to reward those who had
rallied to his banner during the late campaign in order to firm up his
base of support as president.

But Pierce's discouraging words on the railroad initiative didn't
dampen the resolve of lawmakers determined to push the dream once
again in the next Congress. They would return to the issue with added
dedication in December and into 1854, with or without the president.

10

KANSAS AND NEBRASKA

||||||||||||||||||||||||||||||||||||||||||||||||||||||||||||||||||||||||||||||

FROM RAILROAD DREAMS
TO SLAVERY DISCORD

W hen the first session of the 33rd Congress convened on
December 5, 1853, everyone knew that organizing the
Nebraska Territory and building a Pacific railroad would dominate the
agenda. Few perceived that this dual vision would undermine the Clay/
Douglas Compromise in the name of sanctifying it. But powerful events
soon would reveal that the 1850 measures couldn't pacify the country's
sectional passions for long.

The continuing political drama surrounding Nebraska is best understood through the interests and aspirations of the prominent players
involved, including, of course, Douglas, Atchison, and Benton, from the
previous congressional session; but now also including new figures such
as Franklin Pierce, Salmon Chase, Charles Sumner, and the southern
members of the F Street Mess, Mason, Hunter, and Butler. All would
participate in a political saga that would reignite the slavery debate with
unexpected fury.

For nearly a year Douglas had suffered from depression brought on
by the January 1853 death of his twenty-eight-year-old wife, Martha,

from childbirth complications, and the subsequent death of his infant daughter. He managed to get through the congressional session and then set off on a six-month European journey in search of solace. He returned to Washington in November, energized and ready to shepherd through his committee and the Senate a comprehensive Nebraska bill. To that end he sought out his good friend, the blunt-spoken David Atchison. Douglas well understood that his Nebraska defeat in the last Congress stemmed from southern opposition, and Atchison, with tentacles of friendship and alliance throughout the Senate, was well positioned to advise Douglas on the state of southern sentiment, as well as his own thinking.

Douglas discovered that Atchison was a new man now. Never again would he vote for organizing Nebraska for eventual statehood with any slavery exclusion, explicit or implied. He wanted a definitive repeal of the Missouri Compromise as it applied to the entire Nebraska expanse. Further, he was well positioned, as the Senate's president pro tempore and a member of the influential F Street Mess, to press his case with his southern colleagues.

Though not a slaveholder, Atchison identified with the predicament of Missouri slave owners, clustered mostly in his home region of some seventeen western counties. The state's slave population represented only about 10 percent of Missouri inhabitants, and thus slaveholders there lacked serious political leverage in the state government. They felt besieged, a declining minority in their own state and nearly surrounded by free states—Iowa to the north and Illinois to the east. If Nebraska, to the west, were to become a free state (or states), the isolation would be nearly complete. The fugitive slave problem would worsen, slave prices would plummet, and the institution would wither away.

In their anxiety, Missouri slaveholders turned to Atchison. Already he had proved his political mettle by fashioning a statewide coalition that captured the Missouri legislature and passed resolutions instructing Missouri's U.S. senators to support the right of slavery in all territories. The resolutions promptly were denounced with outrage and contempt by Atchison's great rival, Thomas Hart Benton.

Though a slave owner, Benton never defended bondage and opposed all policies that would extend it beyond the states where it already
existed. He considered it "a temporary blight," as biographer Elbert
Smith put it, destined to succumb to economic realities and a spreading
moral revulsion. In the meantime, he urged northerners to ease up on
their attacks upon the South. The inexorable process of slavery decline,
he argued, couldn't be speeded up without tearing the country apart.
This measured approach angered Missouri slave owners and intensified
an already nasty competition between Benton and Atchison.

Now, as the 33rd Congress commenced, Benton was back—as a
House member. But he had fixed his sights on capturing the Atchison
Senate seat in 1855 and destroying his rival's career. The rival welcomed
the coming battle with reciprocal venom. As he wrote to a friend, referring to Benton's approach to the Nebraska controversy, "Of all the humbugs the old sinner has ever mounted, of all the lame blind windbroken
and spavined policies the old villain ever bestrode he has now mounted
the shabbiest." In public Atchison repeatedly denounced the Missouri
Compromise and vowed in one jarring speech that if the territory were
opened to settlement, "we pledge ourselves . . . to extend the institutions
of Missouri over the Territory at whatever sacrifice of blood or treasure."

Franklin Pierce, meanwhile, still showed little interest in the Nebraska situation. He didn't mention it in his Annual Message, and many
assumed his lukewarm regard for a Pacific railroad also suppressed his
interest in pulling Nebraska Territory into the Union.

As for Mason, Hunter, and Butler, they viewed the slave states as
Calhoun had: beleaguered and threatened by the North's growing power
in population, wealth, and industrial might. To them, the spread of
slavery into the territories, to whatever extent possible, represented a
necessity of survival. And standing in opposition to that sentiment,
bent on preventing any slavery expansion whatsoever, were the growing
numbers of antislavery politicians of the North—particularly Seward,
Chase, and Sumner.

The Nebraska drama in the 33rd Congress began on January 4, when Douglas brought to the Senate floor from his committee a new Nebraska bill he had fashioned himself. Employing the language of popular sovereignty previously used in the Utah and New Mexico measures of the 1850 Compromise, Douglas specified that "when admitted as a State or States, the said territory, or any portion of the same, shall be received into the Union, with or without slavery, as their constitution may prescribe at the time of their admission."

This vague language raised nettlesome questions: What about the Missouri Compromise line of 36°30', above which no slavery was to be permitted? Was Douglas trying to finesse that question by suggesting implicitly that the 1850 approach had superseded the Missouri Compromise? If so, would such a finesse mollify southerners, who wanted a clear avenue for slavery extension and who had killed Douglas's Nebraska effort the year before because it hadn't adequately addressed their Missouri Compromise concerns? And what kind of reaction would he get in the North if he permitted slavery where it had been prohibited for thirty-three years?

Whatever the answers, the Douglas legislation was silent on how the Missouri Compromise could be squared with the later 1850 measures. But on January 7, the *Washington Sentinel*, a Democratic newspaper with strong ties to the F Street messmates, published without comment the Douglas bill, S. 22. Then, on January 10, the paper published it again, this time with an added section of uncertain origin. Called Section 21, it stated that, "in order to avoid all misconstruction," the measure declared its "true intent and meaning" to be that "all questions pertaining to slavery in the Territories, and in the new States to be formed therefrom, are to be left to the decision of the people residing therein, through their appropriate representatives."

On the same day that Section 21 appeared in the *Sentinel*, a freshman congressman from Alabama named Philip Phillips, an accomplished lawyer, approached Robert Hunter with a legal analysis positing that Section 21 didn't accomplish what its adherents apparently intended. Unless repealed outright, he said, the Missouri Compromise would still effectively preclude bondage in a territory pending a decision by officials there regarding the status of slavery. In the meantime there would be no slavery, which meant there would be no slavery interests with sufficient political clout to enact a slave policy when it came time to settle the question. The antislavery people of the territory would always win by default. On the other hand, repeal of the Missouri Compromise would mean that slavery could be introduced into any territory at any time, thus putting slave interests on an equal footing with antislavery people at any point during the territorial phase.

Intrigued and disturbed, Hunter relayed the problem to Atchison, who called a meeting for January 12 of himself, Phillips, and Douglas in the vice president's chamber off the Senate floor. Atchison wanted the chairman to understand fully the dilemma, but Douglas didn't want to hear it. He maintained that his Section 21 language served his purposes quite well. Still, he prudently asked Phillips to draft language explicitly repealing the Missouri Compromise language so he could keep it handy as events unfolded.

On Saturday, January 14, the *Sentinel* weighed in again with an editorial that interpreted the Section 21 language as "intended to place the Territory of Nebraska under the shelter and protection of the compromise acts of 1850, as if the Missouri compromise had never been adopted." But, following the Philip Phillips logic, the paper added that some still feared misconstruction as to the legislative intent and that therefore the Missouri language "cannot be set aside or weakened in any manner except by a direct and specific repeal." The *Sentinel* urged Douglas to embrace such a repeal and added that "no room should be left for doubt, or cavil, or dispute."

Then Kentucky's Whig senator, Archibald Dixon, a close Atchison associate, inserted himself into the controversy by pressing for a definitive Missouri Compromise repeal. On Monday morning, January 16, Dixon introduced an explicit amendment to the Senate bill, thus forcing the question into the open. His new language surprised many senators, Dixon later noted, adding that "no one appeared more startled than Judge Douglas himself." The chairman walked across the Senate floor to engage the Whig senator on the issue and argue calmly that congressional action permitting slavery in the territories under his popular sovereignty doctrine amounted to an implicit Missouri Compromise repeal.

The next day Douglas announced to the Senate his plans to have his Nebraska legislation called up before the body on Monday, January 23. Charles Sumner promptly offered an amendment affirming the Missouri Compromise ban on slavery above 36°30'. Unlike Philip Phillips, Sumner believed Douglas's Section 21 language did in fact repeal the Missouri Compromise, and he wanted that language expunged from the bill. Sumner couldn't command anything approaching the necessary votes for legislative success on the matter, but he could generate plenty of agitation among antislavery northerners.

Now Douglas had a problem. After all his efforts to get the slavery issue out of congressional deliberations through the 1850 popular sovereignty doctrine and to finesse the delicate matter of the Missouri Compromise repeal, he faced an ominous choice: maintain the finesse and lose the South or bow to southern demands and reignite the slavery agitation.

The chairman made his choice on Wednesday, when he invited Dixon on a carriage ride to probe more fully his views on the necessary repeal language. After an extended display of reluctance on the issue, Douglas finally relented. "By God, sir," he exclaimed, "you are right! I will incorporate it in my bill, though I know it will raise a hell of a storm." The next day Douglas instructed Phillips to draft new language on repeal based on popular sovereignty. But he didn't want it to be incendiary to northern Democrats, hence no explicit use of the term "repeal." He also wanted Phillips to get approval from Atchison and the influential F Street Mess on anything he produced.

On Friday morning the messmates—Atchison, Butler, Mason, and Hunter—walked five blocks down F Street, from their home off Third Street, to Eighth Street, where they entered the huge new Patent Office building for a meeting with Phillips and representative John C. Breckinridge of Kentucky, a top Pierce ally in the House. Phillips presented for F Street review his proposed language, which stated that the people of the territories could legislate on slavery "in any manner they may think proper not inconsistent with the Constitution" and that "all laws or parts of laws inconsistent with this authority or right shall . . . become inoperative, void and of no force and effect." The F Street men unanimously embraced the language. Now Douglas needed just one more endorsement before he could present his revised bill to the Senate on Monday morning. He needed the president.

At the White House, Pierce was grappling with the same dilemma that had bedeviled Douglas: Should he resist southern pressure for an explicit repeal in the interest of national tranquility? But, since the president harbored no particular desire to organize Nebraska into states, through which to build a rail line, or rail lines, he seemed better positioned to opt for fealty to the Missouri Compromise line. Besides, Pierce had received strong warnings from Senator Cass and Secretary of State William Marcy, among others, that this issue could ensnare him in a treacherous political thicket. The president seemed to heed the warning, as reflected in a White House cabinet meeting on Saturday, January 21.

It lasted most of the day, and a strong consensus emerged that the president must reject the repeal. Among the seven cabinet members, only war secretary Jefferson Davis of Mississippi and navy secretary James Dobbin of North Carolina argued for revoking the Missouri Compromise. The rest strongly favored Douglas's initial Section 21 language as appropriately vague, hence not likely to stir up sectional passions. Pierce finally agreed that he shouldn't attack the Missouri Compromise, though he considered it unconstitutional. Instead, he collaborated with Caleb Cushing on alternative wording designed to kick the matter up to the Supreme Court as a means of avoiding a legislative repeal and a convulsive Democratic split. The president's language stated that "the rights of persons and property shall be subject only to the restrictions and limitations imposed by the Constitution of the United States and the acts giving governments, to be adjusted by a decision of the Supreme Court of the United States."

The president asked Breckinridge to deliver this language to Douglas and the F Street men for review. Douglas accepted it in deference to his party leader, but the messmates rejected it outright. They had set their sights on a full and clear Missouri Compromise repeal, and they had no intention of backing down. This placed Douglas in yet another decision vise, caught between the president, whom he considered largely ineffectual, and the F Street men, who could destroy his dream of a transcontinental railroad. He sought to avoid the vise with one final effort to change the president's mind.

But he had only one day in which to do it before the scheduled introduction of his bill on the Senate floor. And that day was a Sunday, posing the awkward requirement of asking Pierce to waive his usual refusal to conduct business on the Sabbath. Douglas sought to exploit Atchison's longtime friendship with Jefferson Davis, stretching back to their college days, and Davis's very cordial friendship with Pierce. He asked Atchison to ask Davis to intervene with the president in order to schedule a Sunday meeting. Davis did, and the president assented. But he wasn't happy about it. The subsequent exchange in the White House library unfolded in an atmosphere of what Philip Phillips called "cold formality."

Attending were Douglas, Davis, Breckinridge, and Phillips, as well as the F Street men (though it appears Butler was absent). Thus, without consulting his cabinet, Pierce had consented to face alone, except for his war secretary, a contingent of congressional lions who favored a policy he had rejected and who could make or break his top legislative goals. Only a political naïf would do such a thing. Without anyone present to counter the arguments of his visitors, the president reversed course and embraced the approach advocated by Phillips and Dixon. Knowing of Pierce's tendency to change his mind (and having just witnessed an astounding display of it), Douglas asked the president to write down his preferred language. Pierce wrote out a statement that the Missouri Compromise "was superseded by the principles of the legislation of 1850, commonly called the compromise measures, and is hereby declared inoperative and void."

The deed was done. Douglas now had a clear path for bringing to the Senate, on Monday the twenty-third, an entirely new Nebraska bill that would transform the terms of debate on slavery and alter the course of American history. Fixated on his vision of uniting the country

Kansas and Nebraska || 153

physically through ribbons of railroad track and unmindful as ever of the moral dimension of slavery, he rushed forward with his plan.

Douglas didn't know it, but already his rumored assault on the Missouri Compromise had stirred the ire of powerful northern figures, including Salmon Chase, Charles Sumner, and Joshua Giddings. They quietly joined with three other antislavery congressmen in drafting an impassioned attack on Douglas and his allies for their effrontery in seeking to allow slavery in territories that had been established as free for decades based on the Missouri Compromise. Chase produced the nearly 2,400-word document from a rough draft by Giddings, while Sumner and the others applied literary polish.

Entitled "Appeal of the Independent Democrats in Congress to the People of the United States. Shall Slavery Be Permitted in Nebraska?," the statement was written with stark polemical pungency. It condemned the emerging Nebraska measure as "a gross violation of a sacred pledge," a "criminal betrayal of precious rights," and an "atrocious plot." By discouraging the influx of free labor in the vast Nebraska expanse, predicted the statement, the slavery incursion would tilt the balance of power to the slave forces and thus eventually "subjugate the whole country to the yoke of slaveholding despotism." This was absurd on its face, as prospects for slavery taking hold in most of Nebraska were slim indeed based on climate, topography, and cultural sensibilities.

The statement was on firmer ground in tracing the history of the Missouri Compromise and the South's success in getting Missouri admitted into the Union as a slave state and also in getting slavery permitted in lands below 36°30'. But the North got the slavery exclusion above that line, and now the South wanted to retain its winnings from that distant negotiation, while depriving the North of what it had achieved during the Missouri controversy. "Not without the deepest dishonor and crime," stated the Appeal, "can the free States acquiesce in this demand." The Appeal's authors carefully calculated the most opportune time for its release.

On the morning of January 23, Douglas called a meeting of his committee and placed before its members an entirely new bill, hurriedly fashioned overnight by himself. It encompassed the new Pierce language (slightly revised by the chairman) declaring that the Missouri Compromise proscription of slavery north of 36°30' had been superseded by the 1850 Compromise and was therefore "declared inoperative." Another major new feature was the division of Nebraska into two territories— Kansas, west of Missouri, anchored by the Kansas River Valley; and Nebraska, west of Iowa and Minnesota, encompassing the Platte River Valley. Several committee members protested that they lacked sufficient time to study the bill's new provisions or even to read them. But Douglas, on a tight schedule, rebuffed those concerns and hurried to the Senate floor to present the new measure as a committee bill.

After presenting his revised bill to the Senate on January 23, Douglas returned to the floor the next day to initiate the Nebraska debate. That's when Salmon Chase slyly rose with a request. The initial bill had been quite simple, he said, while later versions added significant complexity requiring time for study and consideration. Chase asked for a delay of a week or so. Douglas acquiesced, and it was agreed that the Senate would take up the measure on the following Monday, January 30, and stay with it until the matter was settled.

Later that day, the *National Era*, Washington's abolitionist paper, published the Appeal produced by Chase, Sumner, and the others. Though widely viewed as what it was, a brilliant piece of propaganda, it crystallized the antislavery demonstrations and expressions already springing up in the North in reaction to the Douglas formulation. The *Baltimore Sun* speculated that, while the Douglas bill likely would clear the Senate, it was a different situation in the House, where "the agitation of the question at the north will not improve its prospects." The *Charleston Mercury* complained that renewed antislavery agitations at the North, whatever their origins, proved that the 1850 Compromise was merely "a hollow truce, by which the South was put to sleep for further robbery."

Douglas reacted to the Appeal with rage. He felt he had been played by Chase, and he particularly despised a "Note" attached to the Appeal

that characterized the language accepted by Pierce as "a manifest falsification" and suggested Douglas's presidential ambitions motivated his
Nebraska actions.

Everyone knew that when Douglas took the floor on January 30 to
initiate the Nebraska debate, he would not be gentle. The galleries over-
flowed with spectators anxious to witness the fireworks, and so many
representatives attended the session that the House couldn't do business
for lack of a quorum. As expected, Douglas's volcanic nature erupted
into a torrent of angry invective directed primarily at Chase and Sumner,
whom he referred to as the "Abolitionist confederates." One news reporter said he "lost his temper before he began," and another suggested
his "defiant tone and pugnacious attitudinizing" reflected "the terrific
tornado raging within him."

Douglas castigated Chase and Sumner for bad faith in snookering
him to get the debate delay so they could ambush him with their Appeal. After rejecting multiple efforts by Chase to speak, the Little Giant
summarized the reasoning behind the 1850 Compromise and its "leading feature"—congressional nonintervention in the territories and states
regarding slavery and the right of citizens to settle the issue locally for
themselves.

Indeed, argued Douglas, that 1850 legislation already had superseded the Missouri Compromise with language employed in organizing
Utah and New Mexico into territories and establishing the principle of
popular sovereignty as a basis for all future efforts to stitch new states
into the fabric of the nation. But it wasn't merely a matter of the 1850
Compromise or the Democrats' Baltimore platform, said Douglas; the
issue extended to "a higher and a more solemn obligation" related to
"that great, fundamental principle of Democracy and of free institutions
which lies at the basis of our creed."

The Senate debate began in earnest on February 3 and extended
through the month. Through it all, Douglas met with Democratic Party
leaders most mornings to plan debate strategy, and at times the leaders
invited into the discussions southern Whigs, in an effort to divide the
opposition and persuade the southerners to join the cause. The debate
itself was at various times raucous, emotional, enlightening, granular,

and repetitive. Not surprisingly, Chase, Sumner, and Seward emerged as
prominent opposition leaders, while the F Street men took a key role in
supporting the bill. Douglas and Atchison effected some further refine-
ments in wording to tighten up the repeal language and solidify southern support. Newspapers covered the proceedings in minute detail, and
the country soon became fixed on the Senate discourse as evidence of a
gathering political storm. Throughout the North, a wave of anger and
revulsion was building.

The stark nature of the renewed North-South conflict took form in
the floor speeches of those two cordial rivals, Charles Sumner and Pickens Butler, who personified the slavery chasm between their states and
within the nation. In a tightly crafted and smoothly delivered address
on February 21, Sumner combined flights of eloquence with polemical
precision. Slavery in America, he declared, was doomed:

> Art, literature, poetry, religion—everything which ele-
> vates man—all are on our side. The plow, the steam-
> engine, the railroad, the telegraph, the book, every
> human improvement, every generous word anywhere,
> every true pulsation of every heart which is not a mere
> muscle . . . gives new encouragement to the warfare with
> slavery.

Sumner dismissed Douglas's contention that popular sovereignty, as
applied to New Mexico and Utah in the 1850 legislation, had repealed
the Missouri Compromise. The two approaches, he contended, were
crafted at two different times for two different parcels of territory—the
Louisiana Purchase and the Mexican cession—and could coexist just
fine. And, anyway, he added, nobody had even whispered such an interpretation during the extensive 1850 debates. It was all coming up
now as a kind of afterthought, in legislation that seemed to be ever-
changing—"now, like a river, and then like a flame," but always "with
but one end and aim—. . . the overthrow of the prohibition of slavery."

Sumner rejected the Kansas-Nebraska project on the basis of two
distinct grounds: first, as "an infraction of solemn obligations assumed

beyond recall by the South" when Missouri became a state; and, second, "in the name of Freedom, as an unjustifiable departure from the original Anti-Slavery policy of our fathers." As he often did, Sumner rose to his highest fluency in denouncing the brutality of bondage: "For the husband and wife there is no marriage; for the mother there is no assurance that her infant child will not be ravished from her breast; for all who bear the name of Slave, there is nothing that they can call their own. Without a father, without a mother, almost without a God, the Slave has nothing but a master."

Butler, himself a master, harbored philosophical views far removed from Sumner's humanitarian embrace of equality. The South Carolinian denied any such thing existed. "Is the black man equal with the white man under human judgment?" he asked in his Senate speech, delivered on February 24 and 25. His answer: "All history refutes it." Indeed, if Sumner considered slavery unnatural, Butler considered the pursuit of equality among men (other than in a religious sense) to be unnatural. "The effort to confound castes between whom God has made an indelible distinction," he pronounced, "would result in but the destruction of one, or the base degradation of the higher caste."

Butler sought to vindicate the racial prejudice associated with such views with a story, designed to be humorous in his characteristic way, about a man unaware of the African race who is elated to learn he is to be awarded a princess—but then is repelled in beholding that she is black. Though ripples of laughter arose from some colleagues, reflecting the tenor of the times, it was the kind of whimsy that would become widely considered repugnant in U.S. polite society (and was demonstrably fallacious in any event given what was known at the time of the behavior of many slave masters toward their female slaves).

Butler denounced the Missouri Compromise as the primary cause of the sectional strife over slavery that had plagued the nation since 1820. Echoing his mentor, Calhoun, he lamented that "the Missouri controversy gave rise to a discussion which for the first time opened to the north the certainty that it had power to interfere with slavery." He waxed nostalgic for those northerners of old—Gouverneur Morris, John Hancock, Samuel Adams, Alexander Hamilton—who "were not agitators and intermeddlers" and who "never thought it necessary or proper to make any such allusions [to southern mores] as have been made by the honorable senator from Massachusetts [Mr. Sumner]."

On March 3, the Senate approved the Kansas-Nebraska measure, 37 to 14, and sent it to the House, where crafty opponents managed to bypass the friendly Committee on Territories and assign it to the Committee of the Whole. There it languished for weeks behind fifty other measures until administration officials and congressional supporters managed to amass enough votes to get it released. That required the tabling of the preceding bills, one after another, until Kansas-Nebraska emerged at the top. After fifteen days of raucous and sometimes slashing debate, floor manager Alexander H. Stephens of Georgia brought it to a vote. It passed 113 to 100. President Pierce signed it into law on May 30.

When proponents of that heady dream of a transcontinental railroad came together in the 33rd Congress to establish the Nebraska Territory as a crucial first step, slavery didn't loom large in their calculations. The 1850 Compromise seemed to be holding those old emotions in check in both the North and South, although the Fugitive Slave Act stirred ongoing political acrimony in the North and southern fire-eaters continued their fulminations about southern rights and southern pride. But through 1853 the Clay/Douglas Compromise seemed to be functioning nicely as a national adhesive.

All that was gone now. Throughout the North, outrage welled up within a citizenry that couldn't accept congressional action reversing thirty-three years of free status for a vast territory that now would be opened to the prospect of slavery. Northern rage descended upon Douglas with such force that he sought to make light of it by suggesting he could travel from Boston to Chicago by night with his own burning effigies lighting the way. Moreover, the northern inflammation wrought by the Nebraska legislation also intensified antislavery passions stirred by other issues related to slavery—most notably, of course, the fugitive slave controversy.

Many southerners took heart in their victory in getting rid of the despised Missouri Compromise, considered a blight on the Calhoun doctrines of states' rights and state equality. But the South for years had enjoyed the succor of the Democratic Party, guided by the likes of Andrew Jackson, James Polk, Lewis Cass, and Franklin Pierce—all men, whether of the South or North, with strong southern sympathies. Now the party faced the kind of regional split that for years had eroded Whig unity. As one southerner declared, "The Democratic Party has been literally slaughtered in the Northern, Middle and Western States, whilst the Whig party there is not left even a monumental remembrance." The old party system was breaking up, and the biggest threat facing the South was the prospect of a northern coalescence of antislavery forces injecting ever greater potency into the Free Soil movement.

Douglas had set out to repeal the Missouri Compromise as a way of maintaining domestic tranquility through the doctrines of popular sovereignty and congressional noninterference. But when he told Archibald Dixon back in January that he would embrace repeal even though it would generate "a hell of a storm," he didn't seem to have any notion of just what kind of storm he was about to unleash.

11

THE MASSACHUSETTS SHOEMAKER

||||||||||||||||||||||||||||||||||||||||||||||||||||||||||||||||||||||||||||||||

A POLITICAL TIDAL WAVE
FORESHADOWS REALIGNMENT

For the first twenty-one years of his life, Henry Wilson, the Massachusetts Free Soil operative, went by the name of Jeremiah Jones Colbath. He changed it legally at reaching adulthood because he didn't like it. Nobody seemed to know why. Some speculated that he wanted to distance himself from his father, a man of intemperate ways and lowly financial circumstances. Others suggested he held an aversion to his nicknames, "Jed" and "Jerry." Whatever the reason, the name change represented a life demarcation.

Born in February 1812 in Farmington, New Hampshire, young Jeremiah worked as an indentured laborer for ten years beginning at age ten. It was an austere existence, but he managed to borrow a few books from neighbors and enter the world of American and European history. Completing his indenture, he received six sheep and a yoke of oxen, the first and only recompense, beyond meals and lodging, for his decade of service. He sold the animals for $85 and set out to make his way in the world.

In search of opportunity, he walked a hundred miles to Natick, Massachusetts, where he met a shoemaker named William Legro, a gracious fellow willing to teach young Wilson the cobbler's trade. Wilson hired himself out to Legro for an apprenticeship, then set up his own shoemaking shop. Eventually he built a shoe-manufacturing business with a hundred employees and solid profits. Along the way he read widely and accumulated a smattering of formal learning at a number of New England academies.

Early in his business career Wilson suffered an illness that necessitated a retreat from his arduous work schedule. Traveling to Virginia for recuperation, he stopped off at Washington, D.C., where he witnessed the spectacle of a black family being separated at a slave auction. Shocked at the sight, he left Washington, as he later recalled, "with the unalterable determination to give all that I had, and all that I hoped to have, of power, to the cause of emancipation in America." Back at Natick, he joined a debate society, honed his public-speaking skills, and ventured into politics. Still in his twenties, he captured a seat in the Massachusetts house of representatives. That led to his Free Soil Party involvement and eventually to national political prominence.

They called him "the Natick Shoemaker," reflecting his humble origins. It also reflected, more subtly, his improbable rise in a political milieu dominated by pedigreed figures with Harvard diplomas and tentacles of connection throughout Boston's rarefied high society. The dichotomy became vivid when Wilson suffered a political defeat, whereupon his followers blamed Charles Francis Adams and his allies for harboring "aristocratic prejudices" against such men as Wilson, while favoring their own well-born friends. An offended Adams denounced the allegations as "tricks of demagogues to undermine better men!"—thus lending credence to the disparagement that Adams had wished to refute.

No doubt some class consciousness crept into the relationship of Wilson and Adams, but their frictions went beyond that, reflecting their civic temperaments and the increasingly unstable political dynamics of their state. Adams's politics of asceticism led him to strive always for purity of motive and avoidance of political crassness (as defined by Adams). As a Whig in a time of the Whigs' Massachusetts dominance, young Adams could afford his high-toned political sensibility and adherence to what he considered the spirit of his father and grandfather.

And when the issue of Texas annexation in the 1840s spurred the rise of the Young Whigs, motivated by opposition to slavery expansion, Wilson and Adams found themselves on the same side, along with other Young Whigs (nearly all Harvard graduates). Wilson's strong antislavery convictions gave him a standing with such men that superseded his background. They all stood together in opposing the more traditional politics of the Cotton Whigs, such as Webster, Winthrop, and Everett, whose slavery opposition was more a matter of academic attitude than a call for action.

But now the Massachusetts political scene was buffeted by new swirls of political passion in stark conflict with each other. Nobody knew just where these swirls would take the state, but it was clear that the old days of relative political gentility within the Whig ascendancy were gone. Indeed, the national Whig Party, split between its northern and southern wings, seemed threatened as well. The Democrats enjoyed greater success in straddling the sections, as evidenced by Franklin Pierce's presidency, but the Kansas-Nebraska legislation now was driving a wedge through that party also. The Free Soilers offered an alternative, but their party was new and frail, and it wasn't clear just how it should seek to gain leverage in a fluctuating political environment. And over on Cornhill Street, Lloyd Garrison's *Liberator* continued to gin up increasingly radical passions with its attacks on the Constitution and calls for breaking up the Union to extricate the North from the evil of slavery.

This was not a hospitable environment for the asceticism of Charles Francis Adams and some of his cohorts within the Harvard set, who often lacked the wiles and audacity to gain control over unpredictable events within an unruly political atmosphere. Adams himself often abandoned the cause in favor of his scholarly pursuits when he feared that the new Free Soil project wouldn't remain above the rough-and-tumble of politics.

But the rough-and-tumble posed no problem for Henry Wilson. He accepted the chaos and messiness of politics as inevitable elements of the game—and potential avenues of opportunity. Tireless, full of artifice, with uncommon organizational skills to go with his ardent antislavery conviction, he demonstrated a relentless purpose in building the Free Soil Party into a powerful institution to rival or perhaps even replace its competitors. His interest was not ascetics but power—how to get it; how to wield it; how to leverage it to the benefit of the Free Soilers. And he understood that power was derived from the votes of citizens (or of legislators), pooled from whatever source was at hand, and also from inside dealmaking, maneuvering, and compromising.

Hence it wasn't by coincidence that he embraced and helped foster the coalition between Free Soilers and antislavery Democrats. And it wasn't surprising that Charles Francis Adams would complain to friends about Wilson's characteristic "duplicity" or lecture the Natick Shoemaker about politics having a higher purpose "than the mere bargaining for Offices."

But Wilson, undeterred by Adams's protestations, responded to the coalition's demise by looking for new alliances for the Free Soilers, perhaps with antislavery Whigs or even with a new political movement that washed over Massachusetts and a number of other states unexpectedly in 1854. That was the so-called Know-Nothing movement, a nativist backlash against large numbers of immigrants, mostly Irish Catholics, flooding onto American shores in pursuit of financial betterment. Unlike most of the well-born Harvard grads who clustered around Charles Francis Adams, Wilson would have no scruples about aligning himself with that new and powerful political force. He was always looking for ways to enhance the political standing of his cherished Free Soil Party—and perhaps, in the process, of himself.

Down in South Carolina, politicians grappled with a different challenge. Their state wasn't in political chaos so much as in political drift. Having rebuffed Barnwell Rhett's call for immediate secession, particularly on a stand-alone basis, the state now defined itself politically not by what it stood for but by what it didn't. It wouldn't leave the Union in the foreseeable future and certainly wouldn't do it alone. But not even the standpat cooperationists would forswear disunion when the circumstances were more desperate and other states would join the action.

That left South Carolina in a state of suspension, exhausted from the intense political battles that had raged prior to the cooperationist victory of 1851. The state seemed to be waiting expectantly now for events to determine its fate, within or outside the Union. In the meantime, a certain political lassitude prevailed. James Henry Hammond wrote in his diary in August 1852 that a "dead apathy in regard to politics pervades the State. . . . The General Election now near at hand appears to excite no interest any where."

Thus the state legislature selected an up-country man of bland temperament to fill the Rhett Senate seat, which was more widely viewed as the Calhoun seat. The new senator was Josiah J. Evans, sixty-seven, a former state legislator and longtime judge on the South Carolina Supreme Court. He was an 1850 Compromise adherent who harbored strong unionist sentiments. Indeed, he had been the favored candidate of the state's two leading unionists, Benjamin Perry and James Orr, who wanted South Carolina not only to remain aligned with the North but to actually compete with it as a vibrant, modern region brimming with confidence and guided by a vision for the future.

Perry, born in 1805, was the elder of the two by seventeen years. Though trained as a lawyer, he gravitated to journalism, edited the *Greenville Mountaineer*, and later founded the *Southern Patriot*, South Carolina's only unionist newspaper at the time. He gained notice in the 1830s as a strong anti-nullification man and parlayed his speechmaking skills into a legislative career at Columbia, both in the state house and senate. Square-faced, bespectacled, with thin lips and a high forehead, he projected the countenance of a schoolmaster.

Orr, round-faced, bearded, and portly, entered the law and became a state legislator at a young age, then in 1849 captured a seat in the U.S. House. There he demonstrated political sagacity and legislative dexterity, as well as a jovial demeanor. He was the primary architect of the political vision promoted by himself and Perry as an antidote to the state's—and the South's—nagging predicament.

The predicament, argued Orr, was that the South couldn't compete with the North and hence was reduced to just two possible responses to the North's antislavery agitations—secession or submission. South Carolina's plantation owners, he continued, wanted it that way because they favored secession. And the planter class could enforce this persistent dilemma because it enjoyed outsize political power relative to its actual popular support. But the South wouldn't be locked in this subordinate position, said Orr, if it would expand and diversify its industrial base, build railroads and other industrial products, modernize its financial system and its outdated agricultural practices, create a more unified and open school operation, and bust up the planter oligarchy through electoral reforms.

Then, according to this view, the South could compete with the North on an equal footing and could protect its interests even within the Union. Orr wanted South Carolina to exploit the current political pause by transforming its civic discourse, away from fiery talk of secession and toward more lofty goals of modernism, nationalism, and regional leadership of a more constructive and less combative kind. And a good beginning, he believed, would be for South Carolina to abandon its traditional political aloofness on the national scene and become tightly aligned with the national Democratic Party, sending delegates to party conventions and vying for leadership positions.

In other words, just as Wilson of Massachusetts was a new-breed politician for a new and more complex era of politics in his state and region, Perry and Orr offered a new concept of southern politics and southern life designed to keep the idea of secession out of consideration, while directing the way toward southern prosperity and security.

Just about every element of the Orr vision repelled Barnwell Rhett. Orr wanted to save the Union while Rhett sought to destroy it. Orr favored Democratic Party loyalty while Rhett viewed partisan politics as a threat to southern unity. Orr wanted to upend the rotten boroughs of the state's parish system of political representation while Rhett embraced that system as a guarantor of political supremacy for the state's plantation oligarchy. Orr was a nationalist in a nation despised by Rhett.

But Rhett didn't have much political leverage now as the state grappled with its political identity. That was reflected in the vote totals when the legislature selected Josiah Evans for senator. Though Rhett's name had been placed into nomination by friends hoping for a return to stature for their man, he received only seven votes on the first ballot and none thereafter. It was a tough blow and gave rise to feelings of inadequacy. "My who[le] life," lamented Rhett, "seems to me to have been a failure and to have ended in vanity." But the political disappointment was overwhelmed on December 14 by a shattering personal blow, the death of Elizabeth from childbirth complications, followed by the death of their infant son. "His admiration and love for [Elizabeth]," wrote biographer Laura A. White, "had been unbounded and their life together had been one of singular beauty and happiness."

Rhett turned his attention increasingly to private pursuits: his Charleston law practice (which didn't stir much enthusiasm), his Ashepoo River plantation, a rice plantation he acquired in Georgia (along with 190 slaves), and his personal finances, which always seemed on the verge of unraveling under the weight of persistent debt. His 1850 rice-crop profit of more than $47,000 all went to canceling burdensome financial liabilities, and still plenty of debt remained. Eventually he found a measure of serenity in his second wife, Katherine Dent, from a prominent Maryland family.

As for politics, he would bide his time in the expectation that his dream of an independent southern empire would reemerge at some point as a slave state imperative in the face of the North's accelerating pressures. He took heart in the conviction that "the Southern people have but one alternative—Independence or ruin." He couldn't conceive that they would ever choose ruin. And, in choosing independence, he calculated, they likely would turn to him once again for leadership.

No such expectation animated the fevered mind of James Henry Hammond, who viewed himself as having been cast down among the lowly, consigned to a life of regret, humiliation, and anguish. "Every hope of life has now utterly failed," he wrote in his diary in early 1853. "Every ideal crushed and forever destroyed, I have no inspiration." The diary reveals Hammond's occasional flirtations with suicide as he contemplated his torturous flaws and the consequent wrath of God. "The result of my experience of Life and Him is that I pant for *Annihilation*," he wrote. "Would it might come and *easily this night*."

The focus of Hammond's torment was, once again, whiffs of scandal emanating from his own "animal propensities" and, this time, widespread whisperings throughout plantation society about Catherine's decision to flee the Hammond household with two young daughters and live with relatives in Charleston and later in Augusta, Georgia. The curiosity among friends and acquaintances became unbearable, he explained to the diary in describing the syndrome in hypothetical terms. A person in such a vise is persistently goaded for an explanation, he explained, but he cannot respond because "matters of too much delicacy" are not fit for discussion by "any but a brute." But the mystery couldn't be ignored because "the vulgar appetites of scandal" are universal among humans. Meanwhile, his best friends flee his presence. The embarrassment becomes torture. "He falls and is crushed forever. It is a horrible fate. *Yet it is mine*."

The answer to the mystery was that Hammond for years had been having sexual relations with two slave women—first with Sally Johnson, a seamstress purchased along with her one-year-old daughter, Louisa, in 1839 for $900; and then with Louisa, after she had reached age twelve. It is likely, based on documents, that he fathered children with both of them.

Catherine, who had responded with a certain forbearance when she eventually learned of her husband's dalliances with their nieces, took an entirely different attitude toward his behavior with female slaves, which she learned about through what Hammond called his "want of caution." Surviving documents indicate she demanded that Sally and Louisa be sold. He refused because, as he said with a lofty self-regard, he wouldn't accept "injustice and cruelty to others." And so he languished in self-pity and loneliness, contemplating the meaning of his having three hundred human beings dependent upon him and yet being "more solitary than any hermit." He feared he would be "plunged hereafter into a 'still lower depth'" if he could not atone through good works, and yet he felt incapable of any good works. "I am now too old, too infirm, too heart broken to do any thing with spirit or look forward to any earthly enjoyments."

In Massachusetts, meanwhile, Henry Wilson attacked the challenge of leading his Free Soilers to some kind of new alliance that could enhance their political leverage, as the old coalition had done in 1851 and 1852. But the Democrats didn't figure in his calculations in the wake of the Whigs' statewide triumph of 1853. More recently the national Democrats' controversial Kansas-Nebraska Act had tainted the party in the eyes of most antislavery men throughout the land. And so Wilson and his allies proposed a "fusion" with the Whigs.

Conservative Whigs, uncomfortable with antislavery agitations, were aghast at the prospect. They wanted their party to retain its independence and build on its 1853 victories, using the despised Kansas-Nebraska Act as a political cudgel against Democrats. Ultimately the Whig leadership officially rejected the fusionist idea in mid-1854 and girded for the political battles ahead. In doing so, though, it embraced a decidedly antislavery outlook. The state convention called for repealing the Kansas-Nebraska Act, watering down or rescinding the Fugitive Slave Act, and nominating committed party figures up and down the ballot, without any political coalitions.

The anti-southern provisions disturbed many of the old-guard Whigs of the Daniel Webster stripe who wanted their party to maintain the effort to bridge the North-South gap as a strategy against opposition Democrats. A good example was Edward Everett, now sixty, probably the state's greatest living embodiment of statesmanship—an ordained Unitarian pastor, former professor of Greek literature at Harvard, former Harvard president, and former U.S. House member, Massachusetts governor, U.S. secretary of state, and minister to Great Britain. Now he represented his state in the U.S. Senate as a Whig, having been sworn in the previous March.

He was heartened when his party rejected the fusion idea with Wilson's Free Soilers, but now felt downcast that the party was adopting a generally anti-southern Free Soil attitude. "The Whig party is . . . completely demoralized," Everett complained, "and will have little else to do for some time to come but to follow a 'freesoil' lead." He sadly accepted the reality that the northern Whig Party was "used up."

For Wilson, the Whigs' internal tensions spelled political opportunity. He and a small group of Free Soil officials called a party convention for July in Worcester, Massachusetts. One aim was to lure antislavery Whigs and disaffected Democrats away from their traditional political moorings and into the Free Soil camp. That didn't happen to any significant extent, as Democrats remained loyal to President Pierce and Whigs anticipated a resurgence by hammering away on Kansas-Nebraska. But two developments of interest occurred at the convention: it adopted the name "Republican" to replace the Free Soil appellation, thus aligning with a zesty group of antislavery fusionists that had met recently in Wisconsin to foster a new national party; and it nominated for governor the party's indefatigable leader, Henry Wilson.

Since ending his eleven-year tenure as a state legislator a couple years before, Wilson had sought to mesh his party responsibilities with his own political ambitions. He ran unsuccessfully for a U.S. House seat in 1852, then captured his party's gubernatorial nomination the following year. Not surprisingly, that nomination didn't please Charles Francis Adams. "If we are to have Mr. Wilson for governor," wrote the haughty critic to his diary, "I will make no lamentation at the desecration of an office which has seldom had very distinguished incumbents." But he told his friend Richard Dana that he wouldn't vote for Wilson and seethed at the Free Soilers becoming what he considered a party of "dirty, negotiating, trading politics."

Wilson lost the gubernatorial election that year to Whig Emory Washburn. The question now was whether, in his second try, his Free Soil Party could muster enough political strength as a stand-alone entity to thrust him into the governorship. The answer was probably not. But the Shoemaker of Natick was nothing if not resourceful, and for months he had been positioning himself and his party to exploit the powerful new wave of Know-Nothing sentiment welling up from the American heartland.

When the Know-Nothings began as a secret society of nativist sentiment, society leaders instructed members to respond to queries about the stealthy organization by saying simply, "I know nothing"—hence the name. But everyone knew what it was about. In Massachusetts during the decade following 1846, some hundred thousand Irish migrants entered the state, and Irish residents now constituted 25 percent of Worcester's population and more than half of Boston's. Seeking financial betterment, they clustered in urban ghettos and served as the backbone of the state's emerging industrial development. They became what historian David Donald called "a visible symbol of the forces that were transforming an unwilling New England." Know-Nothing adherents harbored stark elements of xenophobia that resonated in states with large numbers of immigrants.

But the political party that emerged from the movement, sometimes called the Native American Party and later simply the American Party, represented sentiments that extended beyond ethnic and religious bigotry. Populist in outlook, the party projected hostility to exploitative titans of industry and entrenched elites, favored government intervention to ensure worker rights, and embraced such causes as alcohol temperance and women's suffrage. And it took a strong stand against slavery, which particularly impressed Henry Wilson.

Throughout 1854 the Know-Nothings gained political strength in Massachusetts as more and more citizens gravitated to the party banner, including large numbers of Free Soilers chagrined at the Whigs' rebuff of the fusion concept. Wilson himself joined a Know-Nothing lodge in the spring as a means of educating himself on the movement and gaining access to its leaders, particularly Henry Gardner, a Boston dry-goods merchant and former Websterite state legislator of no particular prominence until he switched positions on numerous issues and embraced Know-Nothingism.

All this created a new political fault line in Massachusetts between those willing to deal with the rising Know-Nothings and those who abhorred the movement. The old aristocracy abhorred it. Robert Winthrop considered the movement's leaders to be "of a very repulsive character." Everett dismissed the Know-Nothings as "small traders, mechanics, &

artisans, wholly unknown to the public," and characterized Gardner as "a man of some cleverness, but no solidity of character." An antislavery Whig named Ezra Lincoln warned that the movement had "spawned upon us the veriest race of spaniel ministers, lying toothpullers & bargaining priests that were ever showered upon an unoffending people."

But Ezra Lincoln could see reality when it loomed before him. In late summer he predicted that "the result of our state election will depend upon the Know Nothings." And Wilson saw no point in resisting such a political storm. He entered into discussions with Gardner about combining Free Soil and Know-Nothing forces for the coming fall elections.

At this point Wilson's fate became entwined with that of Senator Everett, whose health was waning and whose congressional responsibilities were becoming less and less satisfying. Elected by the Massachusetts legislature in part to serve as a counterweight to the often out-of-control Sumner, he discovered that this was an impossible task. Relations between the two men soured quickly when Everett worked behind the scenes to thwart Sumner's quest for a meaningful committee assignment. "Ehew! Ehew!," Sumner sighed. "For a while we must eat our political bread in great humility."

But humility was not a natural attitude for Sumner, and soon he managed to nudge Everett aside as he emerged as a leading voice against Stephen Douglas's Kansas-Nebraska bill. Everett, uncomfortable with noisy polemical fireworks, expressed his opposition with a certain caution, careful not to agitate the bill's forceful floor manager, Douglas. That didn't impress Massachusetts's increasingly antislavery citizens, who responded far more enthusiastically to Sumner's combative rhetoric. Even Everett's brother-in-law pronounced him "stuff not good enough to wear in rainy weather, though bright enough in sunshine."

The gulf separating the two senators became even wider after Harriet Beecher Stowe financed an effort to collect clerical signatures on an anti-Nebraska petition that vilified the Douglas measure as "a great moral wrong, . . . a breach of faith, . . . a measure full of danger to the Union." When Everett was asked to present the petition, presumably to give the initiative an air of statesmanlike evenhandedness, he did so without any fire or manifest conviction.

Increasingly distressed with his senatorial duties, Everett returned to Massachusetts and a few weeks later resigned his Senate seat. A disgusted Sumner got a few more signatures attached to the petition so he could introduce it once again and heap praise upon the ministers, while suggesting that such senators as Pickens Butler, James Mason, and Stephen Douglas might learn from the clerics something about wisdom, grace, and "the privileges of an American citizen."

In the meantime, Wilson had been negotiating with Gardner about how the Know-Nothings and his Republicans might combine their interests for maximum mutual benefit in the coming elections. The talks went well despite Gardner's refusal to give the Know-Nothing endorsement to Wilson's gubernatorial candidacy; the Know-Nothing leader planned to run for the office himself under the American Party banner. But Wilson could still run as a Republican, and Gardner granted Know-Nothing endorsements to seven of eleven Republican congressional candidates. Also, the two wily pols entered into a private pact of vast significance to both men.

In early November the *Boston Traveller* reported that Wilson had announced to the Republican State Committee that he was bowing out of the gubernatorial contest. The *Boston Courier*, in explaining the action, said Wilson "declines in favor of Mr. Gardner, and surrenders all his chances for the office . . . to his brother of the 'Know Nothing' order." The paper added, "What consideration he is to receive for this surrender is not yet stated." It never was stated publicly, but the secret agreement stipulated that if Gardner won the governorship and his party captured the legislature, Henry Wilson would emerge in the new year as the occupant of Everett's old Senate chair (following the interim appointment of former congressman Julius Rockwell).

The balloting of autumn 1854 turned out to be a spreading electoral wildfire. The Know-Nothing Party captured all the seats in the state senate and nearly all in the house. Gardner glided into the governor's chair with 63 percent of the vote, while Emory Washburn, the Whig incumbent, garnered only 21 percent. In addition, the Know-Nothings swept out every Whig candidate for the U.S. House and expelled the delegation's only Democratic member. In the new 34th Congress, set to convene in early December 1855, the state's entire delegation would be members endorsed by the Know-Nothings, including seven Republicans who had been put forward by Wilson. Even Whig incumbents who had voted against the Kansas-Nebraska Act went down.

The big new reality was that the Whig Party was crippled in the Bay State. "Poor old Massachusetts!" moaned Robert Winthrop, who hadn't seen much to smile about in his state's politics over the past few years. "Who could have believed the old Whig party would have been so thoroughly demoralized in so short a space of time?" No doubt his spirits declined further in January when the Massachusetts legislature, now the domain of the Know-Nothing Party and its opportunistic allies, sent the former cobbler Henry Wilson to the United States Senate to fill out nearly four years of a six-year term.

The events of 1854 jolted Massachusetts. The Know-Nothing phenomenon turned out to be remarkably brief, a tidal wave that crashed upon the scene with awesome force, but within just a couple years receded back into the sea. The landscape it left behind, however, was utterly changed. For years there had been calls for combining various strains of antislavery sentiment into a single tightly defined party that could move state and national politics in the favored direction. But partisan loyalties always seemed to militate against such a movement. And lingering unionist sentiment generated hesitancy toward hard-line abolitionism, still considered by many to be incendiary to the South and hence counterproductive to the aim of calming the troubled waters of sectionalism.

But now the electorate had stripped away any remaining hopes that Massachusetts Whigs could parlay the Democrats' Kansas-Nebraska fiasco into a return to statewide political dominance and governmental sway. And the Know-Nothing onslaught had battered Massachusetts Democrats with equal force. All this suggested political realignment. A vacuum had been created. Voters would have to find new homes, develop new loyalties, navigate a new landscape. And hanging over the entire puzzle was that incessant slavery tension, once thought subdued by the 1850 Compromise, but now newly inflamed by Kansas-Nebraska.

Thus it seemed impossible to overstate the significance of Massachusetts having in the U.S. Senate two of the country's leading antislavery figures, both provocateurs but of different stripes—one, an earnest rhetorician with a flair for eloquence mixed with a tendency toward ice pick–sharp rhetoric; the other, a cunning political tactician whose strong convictions meshed with an instinct for the inside political game. Together they represented a dawning new era for their state, a shift in the balance of power toward a new level of antislavery vigor and aggressive agitations against the slave power. The *Charleston Mercury* greeted Wilson's Senate election by labeling him "the very embodiment of the fierce spirit of war upon the South."

That view was widely shared in South Carolina. But throughout the state, in the wake of the secessionist sputter there, the political scene remained in a kind of civic inertia lacking passion or boldness. Passion and boldness represented powerful elements of the state's heritage, however, and events in Massachusetts and other northern locations weren't likely to leave that situation untouched for long.

12

BOSTON BLOOD

||||||||||||||||||||||||||||||||||||||||||||||||||||||||||||||||||||||||||||||||

STRIFE OVER THE FUGITIVE SLAVE ACT

In late October 1854, residents of Worcester, Massachusetts, noticed in their midst a Boston man whose face and reputation were familiar to many. He was Asa O. Butman, a "notorious kidnapper" who hunted down fugitive slaves and returned them to southern bondage. Butman had gained infamy for his actions in three sensational Boston cases involving desperate runaways, including one just a few months before. To many he personified the evil at the heart of the 1850 Fugitive Slave Act.

A buzz of excitement spread through Worcester as Butman, now under close watch from members of the antislavery Vigilance Committee, registered at the American House hotel and then visited the armory of the City Guards, "evidently in search of information . . . connected to his line of work," reported the *Worcester Spy*. The paper added that Butman also visited a police officer and a number of lawyers and sent out various telegraph dispatches. Clearly, townsfolk concluded, he was on the trail of another fugitive from bondage, and they weren't about to let any such capture ensue if they could thwart it.

They distributed handbills in black communities, warning of the danger. They suggested to a proprietor of the American House that perhaps he should inform Mr. Butman that he was not welcome there (the proprietor declined the suggestion). They surrounded the hotel so Butman's every move could be watched, and some Vigilance Committee members, who had never seen the man, entered the hotel "for the purpose of familiarizing themselves with the features of the noted bloodhound" so that they could monitor his movements.

The hotel stakeout continued from dusk to dawn, and toward morning Butman, anxious for his safety and having hardly slept through the night, drew a pistol as a sign of his resolve to defend himself. That was a mistake. Soon a warrant was issued for his arrest on a charge of carrying a concealed weapon. The next morning he was taken before a magistrate and, at his lawyer's request, was granted a two-week continuance, secured by a hundred-dollar bail. By this time vast crowds had gathered in the courtroom and outside streets, where cries of "Bring out the Kidnapper" and "Kill the scoundrel" rang out.

Concerned about Butman's safety, the city marshal, a man named Baker, placed him in the marshal's own office. But a group of angry young blacks charged into the Butman hideaway, and one of them decked the slave catcher with a potent blow to the head. Baker promptly arrested the assailant and placed him under guard along with Butman. The assailant escaped through a window, while Butman remained trapped in the courthouse as the growing mob outside called for his head.

Then out stepped young George Hoar from inside the courthouse, where he had been talking with the slave catcher. Everyone knew who Hoar was, in part because everyone knew about his famous father, Samuel, a former congressman, longtime state legislator, and fervent antislavery advocate. Everyone also knew about the incident that occurred a decade earlier when the elder Hoar was commissioned by the Massachusetts governor to travel to Charleston and pursue a court challenge against a South Carolina law that was roiling relations between the two states.

It was an unconscionable law, prohibiting state entry of free blacks and allowing state officials to arrest free black seamen entering Charleston Harbor on merchant ships and to confine them while their ships remained in harbor. If the seamen or their captains didn't pay assessed fines for the illegal entry, the seamen could be sold into slavery to cover the monetary assessments.

This was during the days of James Henry Hammond's governorship, and he promptly sent word of Hoar's imminent arrival to the state legislature, which declared that the state enjoyed the right to exclude persons who might disrupt civic tranquility, that free blacks were not in fact U.S. citizens, and that Hammond must "expel from our territory the said agent, after due notice to depart."

Hammond sent a young planter and politician named Preston Brooks to escort Hoar and his daughter, Elizabeth, out of town as undesirable visitors. But a number of sympathetic citizens, fearing mob violence against the Hoars, rushed to their hotel and spirited them to a departing ship. The sting of the episode still rankled the people of Massachusetts ten years later.

And now here was the son of Samuel Hoar appearing before an angry Massachusetts mob with an entreaty to be heard. Given his family history, the throng settled down to listen. Reporters for the *Worcester Spy* later wrote down his words "as near as we can recollect." He said:

> Fellow-Citizens,—It is some ten years ago, that my father and sister were driven out of Charleston, South Carolina, . . . because, in obedience to a commission issued by the authority of the State of Massachusetts, he had gone thither to test, in the courts of the United States, the validity of those laws under which they imprison our citizens, for no crime but the color of their skins; and none of you, I think, will accuse me of having any great sympathy for slaveholders. It is gratifying to see such a feeling of indignation manifested against an individual whose acts have rendered him so odious in your eyes; but yet, I trust none of you have come here to do him any personal injury. Even in Charleston . . . some persons were found to sustain the majesty of the law, and to their interference, my father and sister owed

the preservation of their lives. . . . Let us remember that
the cause we all have so much at heart cannot but suffer,
if we engage in acts of violence against this obnoxious
and odious individual, who, whatever may have been
his past course, assures me that he came here with no
intention of molesting a slave. Believing that your sentiments upon this subject are in unison with mine, I have
ventured to assure Mr. Butman, in your behalf, that he
may depart from the city unmolested and in peace; and
I have offered to accompany him to the depot, so that
he may leave by the earliest train.

Hoar's remarks generated applause from some, while others shook
their heads in displeasure and wondered if tar and feathers wouldn't
make for a more gratifying send-off. Meanwhile, some blacks in the
crowd, according to the *Spy*, "growled their dissatisfaction, in smothered
words of indignation and hate."

Hoar reentered the courthouse and shortly returned with Butman.
Some in the crowd parted to make way for the small entourage, but
others pressed forward in efforts to get their hands on the slave catcher.
Some noted abolitionists joined Hoar in fashioning a human cordon
of protection as Butman struggled his way through the crowd. When
one furious colored man managed to land "a tremendous blow" behind
Butman's left ear, he staggered forward "like a drunken man." Others
merely threw eggs at the slave catcher's head.

At the depot it was discovered that all the trains had left for the day,
which necessitated that Butman be tucked away in the depot privy, with
protective guards positioned at the door. But Marshal Baker, fearing the
crowd's rising rancor, obtained a horse and wagon to whisk away the beleaguered man, described by the *Spy* now as "the poor, abject, debased,
degraded and trembling white fugitive." Before departing he promised
Hoar that he would never again set foot in Worcester. His words seemed
entirely sincere.

The Butman episode reflected an emerging new reality in the Massachusetts slave controversy. Violence in behalf of the cause was becoming more and more acceptable in the minds of many antislavery activists, incensed at such southern triumphs as the Fugitive Slave Act and the Missouri Compromise repeal.

Of course, the state for years had been at the vanguard of the northern antislavery movement, and many Massachusetts agitators had pushed the abolitionist argument well beyond what most northerners considered judicious. Lloyd Garrison continued to emblazon upon his newspaper's front page every week the defiant words "No Union with Slaveholders"—meaning America should get rid of slavery by getting rid of the South. A *Liberator* headline soon declared, "The Dissolution of the Union Essential to the Abolition of Slavery."

And many prominent Massachusetts figures had grappled for years with that nettlesome concept of higher law—whether citizens were justified in shunning governmental laws that violated their own consciences or their perception of God's will. Many recoiled at the concept on the ground that, if individual consciences prevailed in such matters, the principle of majority rule would lose its meaning, and the nation's social compact would break down. Violence and chaos would ensue. And yet with a moral issue as profound and overladen as slavery, many considered the question of higher law to be unavoidable.

Particularly sophisticated in his exploration of the concept, not surprisingly, was Charles Sumner, whose increasingly recognized capacity for elegant reasoning on highly charged topics verged on the acrobatic. In a letter to the editors of the *National Intelligencer*, he sought to wend his way through the intellectual thicket posed by the issue, beginning with the observation that laws and even court decisions are never final because new rulings and subsequent legislation can supersede old precedents. He added: "Of course, the judgment in the 'case' actually pending is final, as the settlement of a controversy, for weal or woe to the litigating parties; but as a precedent, it is not final even in the Supreme Court itself"—or in any legislative setting. Hence a bad court ruling or legislative law need not be considered sacrosanct. "In both instances, the power to interpret the Constitution is incident to other principal duties, as the trial of cases or the making of laws."

Thus did Sumner reject the notion of "passive obedience" to tyrannical power, "whatever guise it may assume and under whatever *alias* it may skulk." He asserted instead "for every citizen, whether in public or private station, the supremacy of conscience, as the final arbiter of all duty." But here Sumner inserted a caveat with the words "to the extent of braving the penalties of an unjust law rather than obeying it." He quoted Judge E. Rockwood Hoar (brother of George Hoar of the Asa Butman incident) in an instruction to grand jurors: "A man whose private conscience leads him to disobey a law recognized by the community must take the consequences . . . although it may be to his grievous harm." In other words, those who disobey laws they disdain on moral grounds can't escape—and shouldn't escape—the sanctions imposed by law for such defiance.

Beyond that, proclaimed Sumner, each citizen, "after anxious examination, without haste, without passion, solemnly for himself, must decide this great controversy. Any other rule attributes infallibility to human laws; places them beyond question, and degrades all men to an unthinking passive obedience." Then, as he always did, Sumner brought the question down to the current moment and to what he considered the greatest outrage of the slave controversy, the Fugitive Slave Act:

> The good citizen, as he thinks of the shivering fugitive, guilty of no crime, pursued, hunted down like a beast, while praying for Christian help and deliverance, and as [this good citizen] reads the requirements of this act, is filled with horror. Here is a despotic mandate. . . . Not rashly would I set myself against any provision of law. This grave responsibility I would not lightly assume. But here the path of duty is clear. By the supreme law, which commands me to do no injustice; by the comprehensive Christian law of brotherhood; by the Constitution which I have sworn to support, I AM BOUND TO DISOBEY THIS ACT. Never, in any capacity, can

I render voluntary aid in its execution. Pains and penalties I will endure; but this great wrong I will not do.

It was vintage Sumner—meticulously crafted, studiously disclaim-
ing any disrespect for the Constitution or the American system. As he
had in his famous Freedom National speech, he expressed faith that
moral authority eventually would overwhelm bad precedents, either judicial or legislative. Invoking implicitly the higher law concept by refusing to accept the Fugitive Slave Act, he circumscribed his defiance
by applying it narrowly to "tyrannical" laws and by accepting the legitimacy of resulting penalties.

But Sumner's nuanced approach to the higher law concept didn't assuage southerners outraged by the assault on the one element of the 1850
Compromise that they considered marginally beneficial to their region.
Their anger flared when movements emerged in several northern states,
including Massachusetts, for enactment of "personal liberty laws" designed to thwart local officials seeking to comply with the Fugitive Slave
Act. Inevitably, these were denounced as "nullification" laws of the kind
that had brought the wrath of Andrew Jackson down upon John C. Calhoun and the people of South Carolina in the 1830s. The Massachusetts
proposal sought to disbar lawyers who represented slaveholders in fugitive cases and prohibit persons from holding state office if they sought to
assist in the rendition of slaves. The *Charleston Mercury* said these efforts
exposed the Fugitive Slave Act as "a worthless cheat, over which Southern
submissionsists made a great hurrah, and persuaded the South to believe
that she had gained much, when she had gained nothing."

Further, it was becoming increasingly clear to *Mercury* editors and
other impetuous southerners that some fiery Massachusetts citizens
were willing to threaten or employ force in their efforts to negate the
country's fugitive slave policy. They pointed particularly to three fugitive slave episodes that rocked Boston between 1851 and 1854.

The first involved Shadrach Minkins, a thirty-three-year-old Nor-
folk slave who escaped from his master in 1850 and made his way to
Boston, where he worked as a waiter at Taft's Cornhill Coffee House.
On February 15, 1851, some four months after passage of the fugitive

slave legislation, U.S. marshals tracked him down and arrested him at the coffeehouse. While his case was pending before a U.S. commissioner, a mixed-race group of armed protesters burst through the doors of the U.S. courthouse and rescued Minkins from custody. They hid him in a Beacon Hill attic, then spirited him away to Montreal, Canada, where he became a restaurateur and barber. Northern agitators subsequently pulled off similar rescues in New York, Pennsylvania, and Wisconsin.

The Minkins case prompted President Fillmore to issue a statement on February 19 condemning "these unexpected and deplorable occurrences in Boston." The president vowed it wouldn't happen again: "I use this occasion to repeat the assurance that so far as depends on me the laws shall be faithfully executed and all forcible opposition to them suppressed."

Six weeks later, Fillmore's assurance would be tested with the Boston arrest of Thomas Sims, a Georgia slave who had worked as a bricklayer on a rice plantation owned by one James Potter. After fleeing to Boston, Sims was apprehended on April 3 by a trio of slave hunters, including Asa Butman, who was stabbed in the thigh by Sims as he resisted capture. This time federal and local officials embraced the Fillmore admonition to thwart mob action. During the Sims legal proceeding, up to two hundred police officers surrounded the courthouse, which was secured further by extensive lengths of chain.

Enraged Bostonians quickly noted the jarring symbolism of the chains. That heightened angers already stirred by Fugitive Slave Act provisions designed to streamline procedures for adjudicating cases, but viewed by many as depriving alleged runaways of full justice. There was no guarantee of a jury trial; cases could be tried before court-appointed commissioners rather than judges; there were no explicit habeas corpus provisions; and commissioners earned $10 when an alleged runaway was returned to his master, but only $5 when a ruling went against the slave owner. These procedures were challenged by Sims's lawyers, to no avail. Sims was marched to a Boston Harbor ship, past throngs of angry protesters decrying his plight.

But down in Charleston, the *Mercury* pointed out that the cost of recovery for Sims exceeded $5,000, most of which fell to the slaveholder, Potter, and which far exceeded Sims's value as a slave. The paper added that the Sims rendition, "at such a price, encourages the Abolitionists, while it discourages the owners of fugitive slaves from repeating so costly an experiment." It wondered: "[O]f what use is such a law?"

No fugitive slave case generated more civic acrimony than the Anthony Burns case in the spring of 1854. Lloyd Garrison set the tone of northern outrage with a provocative headline, all in capital letters, over his coverage: "Another Sims Case in Boston—Slave Hunting Depended on the Point of the Bayonet—Civil Liberty Prostrate before Military Despotism—Massachusetts in Chains, and Her Subjugation Absolute—the Days of 1776 Returned."

The episode reflected the pitch of emotion welling up in New England and other regions of the North over the fugitive slave issue generally and now the Burns case in particular. The alleged fugitive, reportedly the slave of an Alexandria, Virginia, merchant named Charles Suttle, was apprehended in Boston on Wednesday, May 24, and assigned to the jurisdiction of Edward Loring, a probate judge who also served as a commissioner in fugitive slave cases. Two nights later Boston's venerable Faneuil Hall was filled to overflowing for a rally to "consider what steps should be taken to save Massachusetts from the disgrace of having a man . . . taken by violence from her metropolis," as the *Liberator* put it.

Among the speakers were two of the state's most vehement and renowned antislavery partisans, Wendell Phillips and Theodore Parker, whose fiery words frequently graced the pages of Garrison's *Liberator*. Phillips, lawyer and peripatetic lecturer, agitated the crowd by recounting that, once Burns had been confined "between four walls, with a dozen special officers . . . about him," and with his proceedings before Loring pending, "his master appeared. Mark me! his master appeared. [Cries of 'No!,' 'No!,' 'He has no master.']" Phillips raised his voice to a high timbre and shouted, "'See to it, fellow-citizens, that in the streets of Boston, you ratify the verdict of Faneuil Hall tonight, that Anthony Burns has no master but God!' [Sensation, followed by enthusiastic cheers]." Then Phillips issued what could only be considered a call to action:

Now, fellow citizens, in the celebrated case of Boston
and the slave Shadrach, . . . Mr. Shadrach took up his
residence in Canada on that occasion—in that celebrated case, we settled the slave law one way—that
slaves were not to go back. Well, [later] they settled the
slave law the other way, and sent Thomas Sims back
to bondage. Tomorrow the question is which way will
you stick? Will you adhere to the precedent of Thomas
Sims? ["No! No!"] Carried down State Street betwixt
two or three hundred men . . . ? Or will you adhere to
some other precedent of the year before . . . ? [Cries of
"that's it," and cheers.]

Parker, a Unitarian minister and leading New England transcen-
dentalist, went further in calling for action to save Burns from a return
to bondage. "Gentlemen," he intoned, "I am a clergyman and a man of
peace. . . . But there is a means, and there is an end; liberty is the end,
and sometimes peace is not the means toward it [Applause]. Now I want
to ask you what you are going to do [A voice—'shoot, shoot']." Parker
quickly discouraged any gunplay, but added that government officials
enforcing the fugitive slave policy were essentially cowards and would
buckle under any resolute stand from Boston's antislavery citizens. He
added: "Now, I am going to propose that when you adjourn, it be to
meet at Court Square, to-morrow morning at nine o'clock. As many are
in favor of that motion raise their hands."

A large number of hands went up, but many shouted their preference
for immediate action. In fact, immediate action already had begun when
a crowd of several hundred persons arrived at the courthouse with an apparent intent of breaking into the building to free Burns. Officers locked
the building doors as two gunshots rang out from the third floor. That
provoked a rush to the building's western entrance, and soon the door
was battered down. As antislavery men rushed to subdue the marshal's
deputies and extract the fugitive, several pistol shots were heard. One
killed Deputy James Batchelder, a twenty-four-year-old Irish immigrant

who apparently had been impressed into temporary guard service by local officials.

A dozen policemen promptly rushed to the scene, along with a military company. Arrests were made and order restored, although hundreds of protesters remained on the scene, and the arriving soldiers were greeted with "hisses, groans, and other marks of derision." The Shadrach approach had failed; Sims's fate would be Burns's fate.

At nine o'clock on June 2, Commissioner Loring began the reading of his ruling. He rejected arguments that the Fugitive Slave Act's administrative procedures violated the Constitution. There was no doubt, he added, that the respondent was in fact the Anthony Burns named in record. Thus the commissioner concluded, "On the law and facts of the case, I consider the claimant entitled to the certificate from me which he claims." Burns would be returned to Virginia.

"Great sensation was manifest in the Court Room," reported the *Boston Evening Transcript*, adding that many of those present evinced "much disappointment" and abundant "sympathy for the unfortunate man."

An immense outpouring of Burns support quickly welled up, with downtown residents and business owners hanging black streamers from their buildings. "[A]ltogether," reported the *Evening Transcript*, "the vicinity around the Court House wore the appearance of a day of public mourning." Shops and other businesses closed at ten o'clock as some fifty thousand Bostonians began lining the streets in anticipation of the procession later in the day to escort Anthony Burns to his waiting ship. It took an hour for local officials to clear the procession route, and still spectators could be seen everywhere.

The procession began at two o'clock, and local officials took no chances that the escort could be overwhelmed by the crowd. Surrounding Burns on the route was a detachment of Boston Lancers, an army infantry company, two U.S. Marine companies ordered to the scene by President Pierce, and some sixty local volunteers armed with pistols and cutlasses. Rolling along at the rear was a six-pound cannon manned by a contingent of marines. Boos, hisses, and groans rose up from the crowd intermittently, but the operation came off without incident.

Passions unleashed by the Burns case reverberated throughout Boston and beyond. In the North, antislavery people decried the outcome, while others condemned the violence. "A grave crisis has arrived, which ought to be firmly met," declared the *Worcester Transcript*, "but not by lawless multitudes." The *Springfield Post* accused antislavery protesters of advocating "the open rebellion of this Commonwealth against a law of the United States." But the harshest attack came at a meeting of the Common Council of Boston from a man named Pat Kelley, described by the *Liberator* simply as "an Irishman and an unmitigated blockhead." Kelley accused Phillips and Parker of "treason against the laws and the government" and demanded that Faneuil Hall be proclaimed off-limits to such figures operating under "the so-called 'higher law'!"

The higher law question posed a particular challenge to antislavery politicians. It was one thing for journalists or activists such as Garrison, Phillips, or Parker to embrace the concept to the point of attacking the Constitution or even dismissing it as morally flawed. But, for a U.S. senator who had sworn allegiance to the country and its founding document, that constituted dangerous territory. Any politician who stumbled into it would be greeted with a quick and severe attack from proslavery forces hurling weapon-words such as "treason" and "sedition," never mind that the opposition's secession threats could be construed in much the same way. Even many antislavery moderates had trouble with higher law when adherence to the Constitution was at issue.

This fraught political reality was on full display in Congress in late June, with passions over the Anthony Burns episode still simmering throughout society. It began when Massachusetts senator Julius Rockwell, Edward Everett's interim successor, introduced a petition from his constituents urging repeal of the fugitive slave law. He asked that the matter be assigned to Pickens Butler's Judiciary Committee, and soon the Senate floor rumbled with denunciations and counter-denunciations centered on whether senators could seek to undermine the Fugitive Slave Act while maintaining fealty to the Constitution.

Sumner rose in the Senate to blast the fugitive slave legislation as unconstitutional on several grounds, and likened its opponents to the heroes of the American Revolution. Yes, he said, Boston may be a hotbed of "fanaticism," as Tennessee's senator James Jones had proclaimed, but "[i]t is the fanaticism that finally triumphed on Bunker Hill." Responding to a Jones query of whether the country could exist without the fugitive slave law, Sumner declared that if America needed a law as "revolting in every regard" as that one, perhaps the country "ought not to exist."

Then Pickens Butler entered the chamber. By now the passions of the slavery debate had cooled the Sumner-Butler friendship to a point of mutual wariness. Butler reflected the change when he accused Sumner of displaying "a species of rhetoric" intended to "feed the fires of fanaticism which he has helped to kindle in his own state—a species of rhetoric which is not becoming the gravity of this body." Butler posed a sly question to Sumner: If the despised law were repealed and states could institute whatever legal protections they deemed appropriate for runaways—jury trials, habeas corpus, no more commissioners—would Massachusetts honor the constitutional requirement that fugitive slaves be returned to their masters? And would the senator seek to ensure adherence to that constitutional provision?

Then Butler summed up his query with the words "Will the honorable Senator [Mr. Sumner] tell me that he will do it?"

Sumner replied: "Does the honorable Senator ask me if I would personally join in sending a fellow man into bondage? 'Is thy servant a dog, that he should do this thing'?"

The quote was from the Bible's second book of Kings, reflecting Hazael's expressed shock at his own temerity in deciding to kill his monarch in order to usurp the Syrian throne. The allusion reflected Sumner's delight in parading his expansive erudition. But he selected the wrong senator for such ostentation, given Butler's facility in the arts of ridicule.

> **Mr. BUTLER:** These are the prettiest speeches that I ever heard. [Laughter.] He has them turned down in a book by him, I believe, and he has them so elegantly fixed that I cannot reply to them. [Laughter.] They are too delicate for my use. [Renewed laughter.] They are beautiful things; made in a factory of rhetoric somewhat of a peculiar image. . . . Well, sir, it was a beautiful sentiment, no doubt, as he thought, and perhaps

he imagined he expressed it with Demosthenian abruptness and eloquence. [Laughter.] I asked him whether he would execute the Constitution . . . without any fugitive slave law, and he answered me, is he a dog—

Mr. SUMNER: The Senator asked me if I would help to reduce a fellow-man to bondage? I answered him.

Mr. BUTLER: Then you would not obey the Constitution. Sir, [turning to Mr. SUMNER], standing here before this tribunal, where you swore to support it, you rise and tell me that . . . it is a dog's office to execute the Constitution of the United States.

Mr. [THOMAS] PRATT [OF MARYLAND]: Which he has sworn to support.

Mr. SUMNER: I recognize no such obligation.

Mr. BUTLER: I know you do not.

By getting Sumner to spurn a law that most people believed had been enacted to fulfill a constitutional mandate, Butler opened up a torrent of abuse upon the Massachusetts senator from agitated colleagues, as he no doubt intended. Senator James Mason denounced Sumner as a "fanatic . . . whose reason is dethroned!" John Pettit of Indiana added that anyone who would take a solemn oath to support the Constitution "and then boldly proclaim that he will not do it, has sunk . . . to a depth of humiliation and degradation which it would not be enviable for the veriest serf or the lowest of God's creatures to occupy." Alabama's Clement Clay, not to be outdone, suggested Sumner should be "shunned like a leper and loathed like a filthy snake."

Sumner did not retreat mildly from the fray. In an extensive rebuttal on June 28, he presented an elaborate justification for his insistence that he had not violated his loyalty oath to the Constitution. "I swore to support it *as I understand it*; nor more, nor less," he declared, citing Andrew Jackson's famous dictum that the document is subject to various interpretations, and officials are free—indeed bound—to support it as they perceive its meaning. Harking back to his Freedom National thesis, he argued that the framers carefully had consigned slavery to state jurisdiction while keeping it away from the general government. It was under that doctrine, he insisted, that he viewed the slave rendition law as unconstitutional.

And in attacking his tormentors, he displayed his characteristic scorn, vengeance, severity, and swagger. He excoriated the "plantation manners" of Butler and Mason, speculating that they fancied themselves not in the Senate but on "a plantation well stocked with slaves, over which the lash of the overseer had full sway." He directed particular invective to Mason, saying he conducted himself "with imperious look, and in the style of Sir Forcible Feeble." He compared Mason unfavorably to himself, based on the fact that he knew "something of his conversation, something of his manners, something of his attainments, something of his abilities, something of his character."

Though many southerners predictably recoiled in horror at Sumner's performance, his stature soared throughout much of the North and particularly in his home state. Henry Wilson, soon to join Sumner in the Senate, wrote to him, "You have given the heaviest blow you ever struck to the slave-holding oligarchy. Dont I feel proud to think that I had a humble part in placing you in the Senate?" The *New York Times* praised Sumner's "matchless eloquence and power," while the senator's Boston friend Richard Dana, a prominent lawyer and author, exclaimed, "You have done gallantly."

Sumner himself took delight in his enhanced prominence. "I find myself 'a popular man,'" he wrote to a friend, adding that, if his reelection bid were taking place that year, "I should be returned without any opposition." He also enjoyed knowing that the Washington political establishment now viewed him as not just a learned and eloquent orator but also as a fighter who could dish it out in heated political battles. This carried a corollary reality, however: like his many friends in Boston who had abandoned him over the years, some Senate colleagues now treated him warily. As biographer David Donald put it, "Henceforth Southern senators tended to leave him alone in respectful silence, while cutting him socially."

13

PRAIRIE TENSIONS

||||||||||||||||||||||||||||||||||||||||||||||||||||||||||||||||||||||||||||||||||||||

A NEW PHASE AND A NEW FOCUS

On May 25, 1854, in the wake of the emotion-suffused congressional debate over the Kansas-Nebraska bill, New York's William Seward rose in the Senate to taunt his southern colleagues with an observation about American demographics. Slavery, he said, was destined to be overwhelmed by masses of immigrants pouring into the country—hundreds of thousands per year—bent on making their way as freemen in a land of free labor. Rich western territory beckoned, declared Seward, and news of the Kansas-Nebraska opening would draw these people thither in ever greater numbers. Thus would the fate of the Kansas Territory be determined by this inexorable inflow. Slavery couldn't compete with it.

"Come on, then, gentlemen of the slave States," exhorted Seward. "Since there is no escaping your challenge, I accept it on behalf of the cause of freedom. We will engage in competition for the virgin soil of Kansas, and God give the victory to the side which is stronger in numbers as it is in right."

That was a bit much for the Little Giant, operating now on a hair trigger of outrage at northern rancor toward the South and consumed with anxiety about the possible emergence of a powerful northern party of antislavery resolve. To Stephen Douglas, such words from Seward and his allies represented an assault on the status quo that could only lead to violence and disunion. "I accept your challenge," declared the feisty combatant. "[R]aise your black flag; call up your forces; preach your war on the Constitution. . . . We will be ready to meet all your allied forces."

Such words of mutual belligerence reflected a fresh reality in the politics of slavery: the debate had entered a new phase and had taken on a new focus. Of course, the Kansas-Nebraska Act and its Missouri Compromise repeal were generating geysers of animus throughout the North, adding to angers already wrought by the Fugitive Slave Act and subsequent anguishing episodes involving captured slaves. But now the fate of slavery seemed to be intertwined with the fate of the Kansas Territory. Many southerners reckoned that, if Kansas became a slave state, slavery might expand farther west and perhaps survive—so long as southern slaveholders could take their slaves into the new territories, as they were demanding with increasing intensity. If Kansas were to become free, on the other hand, slavery in neighboring Missouri, already on a precarious footing, likely would wither away, setting in motion a slow inexorable slavery decline in other border states and an eventual collapse of the institution throughout America in the face of overwhelming northern power.

Washington's *Weekly Union* perceived the same phenomenon as Seward, although the paper pointed out that much of the looming Kansas influx would comprise native-born Americans as well as foreigners. It reported that "the tide of population has already begun to set in for the regions of Nebraska and Kansas." In fact, there weren't enough boats in St. Louis to convey the crowds waiting for passage to the new territories, said the *Union*, while immigrant-assistance companies were springing up at Wheeling, Louisville, Chicago, and various Iowa towns.

Would these new arrivals embrace slavery or prohibit it? That was the choice handed to them by the popular sovereignty thrust of the Kansas-Nebraska Act. But most of those who would decide hadn't arrived yet, and so the high-stakes outcome would be determined by such questions as who would be arriving, who could be barred from arriving, who could be intimidated into leaving or not voting, who would manage the process of land claims, how would residence be defined, and how would the sanctity of elections be protected.

It was a situation fraught with possibilities for civic mischief, tension, and violence. A smooth transition to statehood would require firm, adroit, and judicious leadership—from newly installed local officials, from the presidentially appointed territorial governor soon to arrive, and from the president himself. Unfortunately, that kind of leadership proved elusive.

The *Weekly Union*'s prediction of coming multitudes soon became reality. In May 1854, Kansas territory contained about eight hundred whites; over the next nine months the number shot up to more than eight thousand. Almost immediately frictions emerged among the various groups of settlers, particularly Missourians, New Englanders, and midwesterners. Many of these frictions centered on competing land claims that arose because of slipshod procedures hurriedly crafted by local officials to manage the influx of settlers. But percolating just below the surface was the ever-present slavery issue.

The Missourians, given their state's proximity to Kansas, quickly gained a numerical advantage, causing some to mock Seward's earlier bravado. Of the initial eight thousand settlers, about half were Missourians, with another 7 percent from other southern states. While these were mostly proslavery folks and slave owners, they also included significant numbers of nonslaveholding southerners. Few slaveholders brought their slaves into the new territory, however, given the uncertainty surrounding the bondage question; thus, when the population reached 8,000, fewer than 250 were slaves. But southerners felt confident that slavery eventually would thrive in Kansas. "This is [as] fine a country as any on the face of the earth," wrote territorial judge Sterling G. Cato to his brother in Alabama, "and the profits of its productions would far exceed those of the cotton fields of the South." He cited specifically hemp, corn, and grain.

The unchallenged leader of the Missouri forces was Senator Atchison, who absented himself from his Senate duties in December to devote his energies to a struggle that he believed would determine "the prosperity or the ruin of the whole South." He helped establish the Platte County Self-Defensive Association, designed to recruit Missourians as volunteers to enter Kansas and ensure a slave state outcome. Indeed, some Atchison friends felt that his devotion to the Kansas contention exceeded his own reelection hopes in the forthcoming legislative balloting in January 1855. Even with Thomas Benton nipping at his heels, Atchison made plans to expand his recruitment and fundraising efforts to the broader South if he should lose his reelection bid.

He did lose. The legislature struggled through forty-one ballots in an effort to resolve a three-way deadlock that also involved a Whig candidate named Alexander Doniphan. The stalemate couldn't be broken, so lawmakers finally decided to postpone the election indefinitely and leave the seat open until at least the fall. Atchison and Benton, the great antagonists of Missouri politics, went down together in an embrace of mutual enmity.

That left Atchison free to pursue his Kansas obsession. "If we cannot get Kansas by peaceful means," he declared, "we must take it at the point of the bayonet." What riled Atchison particularly was a report in the *New York Tribune* in early June about efforts in Boston to establish an organization called the Massachusetts Emigrant Aid Company (later the New England Emigrant Aid Company). Its leader, a Massachusetts teacher and state legislator named Eli Thayer, envisioned a private joint-stock company drawing investors with the promise of solid financial returns and satisfaction at helping establish Kansas as a free state.

It soon became clear that Thayer's enterprise was less an investment opportunity than a charity case. Under persistent financial pressure, he kept his company alive through the support of wealthy benefactors, most notably Amos A. Lawrence, son of the rich textile kingpin and Cotton Whig, Amos Lawrence, who died in 1852. The father, in the spirit of Daniel Webster or Robert Winthrop, had decried northern agitations against southern bondage, while the son had embraced the more aggressive Conscience Whig sensibility. Now he was extending financial benefactions to Thayer of up to $6,000 at a time.

Atchison became consumed with ill-founded rumors that Thayer's operation would funnel up to twenty thousand New England abolitionists into Kansas and thus overwhelm the proslavery forces. He needn't have worried, as it turned out that New Englanders weren't traveling to Kansas in significant numbers. "We are too far off," Lawrence told his friends in Kansas. "[W]e can pay some money, and we can hurrah; but we cannot send you men—men of the right stamp." Indeed, Thayer's enterprise sent only some 750 people to Kansas in 1854, with another 900 or so the next year. An 1855 census pegged New Englanders at just 4.3 percent of the territorial population, a percentage that would hold firm even as the influx of settlers expanded year by year.

A greater threat to Atchison was the influx of midwesterners from free states such as Indiana, Iowa, Ohio, and Illinois. These were people close enough to brave the hardships of the westward migration without much hesitancy, and they soon constituted some 30 percent of the Kansas population, with prospects of becoming a territorial majority in the near future. They were industrious folk, rugged in appearance and deportment, considerate of others but quick to call out encroachments. Kansas offered them prospects for precisely the life they sought as small-farm operators exploiting the rich soil and favorable climate for the production of cattle, wheat, corn, beans, potatoes, and pumpkins.

Slavery didn't figure in this kind of farming or this kind of life, and these arrivals opposed it implacably, but not because of any concern about the plight of black Americans. They didn't want slavery because they didn't want blacks and they didn't want to compete with slave labor. Some even favored a proposed "black law" prohibiting free African Americans from entering the territory.

These free-state midwestern settlers soon perceived their main problem to be proslavery western Missourians bent on ensuring, by whatever means necessary, that Kansas would never become a free state. Most of these Missourians didn't plan to settle in the new territory, but rather to organize cross-border forays and raids, under the guise of actual settlers. With an aim to intimidate and neutralize free-staters in the crucial early months of territorial governance, they quickly became known as "Border Ruffians," a characterization they readily embraced.

In Missouri they established secret organizations called "Blue Lodges" or "Self-Defensives," dedicated to sending Missourians across the border to vote in forthcoming Kansas elections and otherwise disrupt efforts of free-state men. For those willing to participate they offered "free ferry, a dollar a day, & liquor." The greatest of the Blue Lodges was the Platte County Self-Defensive Association, led by Atchison.

The looming turmoil in Kansas could be seen in the language used by proslavery and antislavery men in describing the Ruffians. The Kansas correspondent for a southern newspaper waxed rapturous in describing them. "Imagine a fine looking man with a heavy beard and moustache, felt hat, red shirt (no coat) . . . immense Spanish spurs . . . a Sharp's rifle slung over one shoulder . . . charging down upon you across the prairie on a fine bay." The writer added that they always managed "to win the hearts of their fellows." But an eastern journalist pegged them with disdain as typically having tobacco juice trickling from their mouths, with bowie knives in their boots and six-shooters on their belts. Antislavery Kansans took to calling them "pukes."

Such was the situation in Kansas and neighboring Missouri when President Pierce's handpicked territorial governor arrived on October 7. He was Andrew Horatio Reeder, a forty-seven-year-old Pennsylvania lawyer and Democratic loyalist with no experience as a public officeholder. Though he had supported the Kansas-Nebraska Act and was viewed as a southern sympathizer, he gave every indication upon arrival that he intended to govern without favor. He ordered a census and scheduled elections for the territory's nonvoting delegate to Congress (on November 29) and for territorial legislators (the following March 30).

The census revealed 8,601 Kansas residents, of whom 2,905 were eligible voters. But the official language purporting to define voter eligibility suggested merely that any "resident" could vote, without a clear definition of residence. That invited both sides to take frenzied actions designed to plump up their voting rolls. The Missourians exploited the opportunity most aggressively. In the November 29 election for a congressional delegate, some 1,729 Border Ruffians crossed over to vote illegally, according to a later congressional investigation. Of 2,871 votes cast, only 1,114 were legal. One polling place recorded 604 voters, only twenty of them legal.

The electoral victory, such as it was, went to J. W. Whitfield, an Atchison associate, Mexican War veteran, and former Tennessee state legislator. The proslavery *Washington Sentinel* described him approvingly as "thoroughly identified with the interests of the South." But the *Hartford Republican*, in a piece reprinted in the *Liberator*, declared that Kansas "is lost to freedom" because of the "shamefully atrocious" incursions of the Ruffians.

Land-claim tensions also roiled the fledgling territory. "There is a good deal of trouble everywhere among the squatters," reported the *Missouri Democrat*. "They are jumping each other's claims every day." An antislavery settler, writing from Lawrence, Kansas, told the *Milwaukee Sentinel* of an incident "which occasions great commotion in our camp." After a member of his company staked a claim and put up a cabin, eight Missourians showed up complaining that "the d—d Yankees were taking everything they could get." Two of them tore down the cabin and set it ablaze, while their companions, "armed and mounted on horseback, lay back as a corps of reserve if needed."

The next day another group of Missourians removed a land-claim tent, placed it in a wagon, and drove off. When a squatter party confronted the miscreants, guns were drawn and a standoff ensued. The Missourians finally backed down, but the settlers retained a lawyer to draw up papers for the formation of a military company. "Everything betokens war," reported the letter writer. "God grant that it may not come! but the passions of desperate men are the most unreasonable things in the world."

With attention turning now to the March 30 balloting for legislative representatives, the squatter frictions merged with slavery emotions to produce a bitter brew of civic anxiety. The Ruffians came back in force and tilted the outcome through illegal voting and massive intimidation. Atchison himself led into Kansas a force of some eighty men, "armed to the teeth," who "demolished considerable whiskey" along the way. A census earlier in March had identified 2,905 eligible voters, but more than 6,307 actually cast ballots, and 5,427 of them were proslavery votes. Douglas's principle of popular sovereignty looked like a farce.

On April 6, Reeder set aside the results in only six disputed districts despite substantial evidence that the abuse had been much more widespread. When the governor ordered special elections for May 22 to fill the six disputed seats, the voting unfolded without serious disruption, in part because it wouldn't materially affect the legislative balance of power.

Increasingly distressed by the turn of events, Reeder left Kansas for the East, where he intended to place the debacle before the president and the American people. Back in his hometown of Easton, he castigated the Missouri intruders and declared in a speech: "Kansas has been invaded, conquered, subjugated by an armed force from beyond her borders."

Visiting with Pierce numerous times during a two-week Washington visit, Reeder described the magnitude of the Missouri insurgency and called for federal action to undo the fiasco and redeem the idea of popular sovereignty. Typically, the president offered words of encouragement but took no action on the matter beyond chiding Reeder for the pointedness of his Easton speech.

Back in Kansas, the governor encountered a legislature bent on neutralizing his executive authority and taking full control over the territorial government. Spurning Reeder's decision to place the territorial capital at Pawnee City, well into the interior of the state, lawmakers promptly relocated the seat of government to Shawnee Mission, just a few miles from the Missouri border. Then they enacted a string of laws, over the governor's veto, demonstrating just how determined they were to suppress any activity or open expression reflecting antislavery sentiment.

The measures included the imposition of the death penalty for anyone who helped a slave escape bondage or who distributed printed materials that incited slaves to conspiracy or rebellion. Ten-year sentences would be meted out to those who harbored or concealed a fugitive slave. And simply to argue that slavery wasn't legal in Kansas carried a two-year sentence of hard labor.

Kansas events now riveted the nation as people discerned the emergence of an almost hopeless struggle. The *Charleston Mercury* crystallized the southern attitude in celebrating the outcome of the March 30 balloting and arguing that the Ruffian incursions were justified by the North's resolve, "as a master stroke of policy, to force the colonization [of Kansas] by a hired inundation of Abolition adventurers." Missourians and southern settlers, in this view, had been "challenged to a trial of strength," and they had met the challenge. "[T]he free-soilers are *nowhere*," crowed the *Mercury*.

One Atchison associate argued that slavery had been established in Kansas by the simple fact of slaves having been taken there. Only a specific prohibition by the legislature could reverse it, and that wasn't possible now with the proslavery legislature firmly established and Missouri's Border Ruffians on the scene. "Such laws will never be enacted!" he pronounced.

Up in Boston, Lloyd Garrison expressed his usual moral dudgeon at such temerity. "Violence, outrage, force and fraud are the open, unhesitating instruments of these border forays," declared the *Liberator*, predicting "a severe and desperate struggle" in Kansas. Garrison demanded action from President Pierce: "He must undo this great wrong, or share in its guilt."

But the president demonstrated little inclination to do anything that would rile the South. In June he succumbed to pressure from prominent southerners and proslavery partisans by firing Reeder. Pierce learned that the governor had engaged in unsavory Kansas land speculations, including the purchase of property at Pawnee City that likely would have increased in value substantially had his plans for placing the territorial capital there not been rejected by the legislature. Such land speculations were not uncommon among politicians of the time and probably weren't illegal. But it exposed Reeder to intensified attacks from his enemies and rendered him an easy target for Pierce's disfavor.

Reeder promptly joined up with the territory's frustrated antislavery men, who were coalescing into a resistance force bent on amassing political power by leveraging their growing settler numbers. One leader of this new movement was Dr. Charles Robinson of Massachusetts, who joined the earliest Kansas settlers to arrive under the auspices of Eli Thayer's New England Emigrant Aid Company. Earlier he had gone west in search of California gold and led squatter protests in Sacramento. Bearded, lucent-eyed, and austere looking, Robinson displayed a dexterous and clearheaded intellect. When he talked, men listened.

It soon became clear that Robinson, Reeder, and the free-state movement faced a dilemma. Should they defy what they considered an illegitimate government and set up a rival civic entity of their own? Or should they avoid any appearance or intent of subverting the authority of an officially recognized territorial government, however questionable that recognition was or however abhorrent the government's actions? The dilemma spawned disagreement, and the disagreement gained intensity throughout 1855 as the free-staters prepared for a convention at Topeka charged with drafting a state constitution, with a ratification vote envisioned for December.

From Boston, Amos Lawrence warned that the free-staters couldn't create a civic authority to rival the Shawnee Mission government "without coming in collision directly with the United States." Thus did free-state organizers initially take pains to emphasize that any laws they might devise would be considered unofficial until the point of statehood. At a free-state convention at Big Springs on September 5, a moderate faction put forth a resolution disavowing as "untimely and inexpedient" any intent to establish a free-state government in competition with Shawnee Mission.

But that kind of forbearance didn't satisfy the more militant free-staters, including the increasingly combative Reeder and a free-state firebrand named James Lane. Declared Reeder, "We owe no obedience to the tyrannical enactments of this spurious legislature." Soon the free-staters found themselves moving toward the creation of a rival government. A September 5 convention at Big Springs embraced a number of Reeder resolutions calling for the Free-State Party to spurn what members considered the bogus territorial legislature and to establish their own assembly. To that end delegates endorsed a follow-up convention at Topeka later in the fall.

The Topeka gathering, with Lane as president, convened in late

October and extended to mid-November. Delegates, through arduous drafting sessions, fashioned a constitution for the new state that would outlaw slavery after July 4, 1857, locate a temporary capital at Topeka, and establish official positions of government. A ratification vote on the document was set for December 15, with balloting for state offices scheduled for January 15, 1856. The ratification election, airily ignored by proslavery men, yielded 1,731 votes for the Topeka constitution to just 46 against. The free-state men promptly sent the document to Washington, where it was expected to receive approval from the House but stern opposition from Pierce and the Senate.

But this coalescence of the antislavery forces unnerved the pro-slavery men and their Missouri allies, who had become accustomed to dominating events but who now saw an effective opposition bolstered by the kinds of demographic trends that Senator Seward had heralded. Perceiving the need for a greater political presence to counteract the appearance of their ruffian ways, they met at Leavenworth on November 14 to establish their own organization, which they called the Law and Order Party. Present at this conference was President Pierce's new Kansas governor, Wilson Shannon of Ohio.

The fifty-three-year-old Shannon was a stocky, blunt-spoken Cincinnati lawyer with a political pedigree as Ohio governor and congressman as well as U.S. minister to Mexico. Even before arriving, he displayed his political sentiments by suggesting that Missouri and Kansas institutions should "harmonize," which was widely interpreted as a call for slavery in Kansas. After arriving, he confirmed the interpretation by aligning closely with the Shawnee Mission government and pronouncing its laws to be entirely legal, while showing open disdain for the Topeka constitution.

Now it could be seen that Douglas's vaunted popular sovereignty had spawned in Kansas two rival governments, each viewing the other as illegitimate and offensive to the fundamental tenets of representative democracy. It was a confrontation almost guaranteed to generate civic tension. And it quickly burst into what became known as the Wakarusa War—better labeled, in the view of noted historian Allan Nevins, as "the Wakarusa Demonstration" because actual violence was averted.

It began with the widespread feeling among southern settlers, vented at the November 14 Leavenworth meeting, that the "unprincipled Abolitionists" were forming into well-armed paramilitary groups bent on thwarting Shawnee Mission governance and assaulting southern settlers. The cry went up for a stern demonstration of force that would discourage these provocateurs from carrying out their dastardly intentions. It was thought that the militia force being formed by Shannon could administer the show of resolve.

Then came a precipitating event that, while unrelated to the slavery issue initially, ignited sectional passions and shattered much of the remaining goodwill in the territory. On November 21, a southern settler named Franklin Coleman, enraged over a claim dispute, killed a free-state man named Charles Dow. Coleman, claiming self-defense, fled to safety in Missouri. As men from both sides gathered menacingly, a free-state figure named Jacob Branson, a party in the claim dispute and leader of a free-state military group, organized a "vigilance committee" to exact justice. His men ignited the dwellings of two proslavery men and destroyed Coleman's empty house.

Some two hours later the Douglas County sheriff arrived. He was Samuel J. Jones, a bumptious Ruffian sympathizer, and he came with a posse and arrest warrants for Branson and others involved in the destruction. He arrested Branson on a charge of disturbing the peace and proceeded to escort him to Lecompton for legal proceedings. But Branson's outraged friends, led by a lawyer and free-state provocateur named Samuel N. Wood, rescued him from custody in a tense roadside standoff. That prompted the sheriff to call on Governor Shannon to raise a citizen army and deliver a lesson to the free-state folks gathering at the fledgling town of Lawrence (named after the Boston benefactor).

Shannon wasn't able to raise much of a militia force, but Missouri's Border Ruffians rushed to the center of action in large numbers, perhaps twelve hundred or more. They swarmed along the Wakarusa River, south of Lawrence, dispersing livestock, torching haystacks, harassing travelers, and threatening to raze the town entirely. "My deliberate opinion," wrote one Missourian leader, "is Lawrence will soon cease to be a habitable place."

But free-state men weren't about to be cowed by the Missourians. They rushed to Lawrence in large numbers; one participant, in a letter to his wife, estimated that the defending volunteer force eventually approached two thousand men, all heavily armed. "Our fighting spirit is fully up," reported another free-stater in a letter to the *New York Evening Post*. "The great difficulty is to restrain our men from making a sally upon the camp on Wakarusa."

But the spectacle set off a powerful alarm siren in the mind of Governor Shannon, whose view of the free-state men had softened as he got to know them. Atchison, for his part, worried about the likely negative impact that a violent clash would have on his broader proslavery program. The two men rushed to Lawrence on December 7 to forestall, if possible, a bloody battle. Their presence eased tensions on both sides, and they managed to deflate the situation further through a negotiated settlement between the governor and free-state leaders Robinson and Lane. The free-state men accepted Shannon's disavowal of any participation in events leading to the Missourian incursion, while the free-state leaders vowed obedience to laws enacted by the recognized territorial government, though they declined to acknowledge the government's legitimacy. Soon the belligerents of both sides began a slow decampment.

The negotiations had averted bloody violence, but it had been a near thing. And the Kansas controversy wasn't going away. Just eight days after Atchison's participation in the December 7 negotiations, the former senator penned a letter to the *Atlanta Examiner* in which he distanced himself from his own actions during that delicate bargaining. "I was a peace-maker in the difficulty lately settled by Gov. Shannon," he wrote. "I councilled the 'Ruffians' to forbearance, but I will never again council peace." Looking to the future, he declared, "I do not see how we are to avoid civil war." He called for money, men, and moral succor from southerners to support the southern cause in Kansas.

Meanwhile, free-state leaders Robinson and Lane faced their own difficulties in controlling their men, many of whom wanted to attack Border Ruffian camps. Shannon could see that he couldn't count on either side in the Kansas contention to maintain peace; only federal troops could do that. But Pierce remained inert, even after Shannon revealed his "forebodings as to the future."

The gathering Kansas disruption was becoming a touchstone issue for more and more Americans. The political passions unleashed in the territory were seeping increasingly into the American consciousness, and it was becoming clearer by the day that the issue could not be avoided. Everyone eventually would have to choose sides—and, having chosen, would have to muster a rationale of justification. Thus was Kansas pushing increasing numbers of Americans to one side or the other of a widening national divide.

14

SECTIONALISM RISING

||||||||||||||||||||||||||||||||||||||||||||||||||||||||||||||||||||||||||||||||||||

FROM KANSAS TO BOSTON TO WASHINGTON

Sadness mixed with adulation flowed in Boston and throughout Massachusetts following the August 1855 death of Abbott Lawrence at age sixty-two. A large crowd gathered at Faneuil Hall to hear the heavyhearted eloquence of such figures as Robert Winthrop and Edward Everett in praising the generous spirit and extensive good works of the great textile industrialist, civic leader, congressman, and U.S. minister to London. Even Garrison's *Liberator* joined in the praise—up to a point. "All that is claimed for Mr. Lawrence," said the paper, "on the score of urbanity, a genial temperament, a kind disposition, a generous distribution of his means, enterprise in business, and fidelity in all his official trusts, may be readily conceded."

But Lawrence had been a Cotton Whig whose antislavery pronouncements never meshed with antislavery action and who had accumulated much of his wealth by making textile products from cotton secured through slave labor. Thus, declared Garrison's newspaper, Lawrence's many achievements and fine qualities "cannot atone for profound insensibility to national criminality, for moral cowardice in the midst of popular wickedness, for connivance at oppression on a gigantic scale, for hostility to the cause of freedom, borne down to the earth by all the powers of darkness."

William Lloyd Garrison hadn't changed a jot since he founded his newspaper in 1831. He was still the moral absolutist, still rejecting conventional politics as a squalid search for the possible, as opposed to his untainted pursuit of what most Americans considered the impossible. And yet his many followers had reason to lionize the man as one of the country's most effective abolitionists. As the *Weekly Transcript* of Providence put it in a piece reprinted in the *Liberator*, "everyone considered him a fanatic" during his famous Baltimore imprisonment in 1828. "But what a change has come over the nation."

Similar sentiments, though drenched in venom, emanated from southern newspapers, irate over the election or reelection of senators such as Henry Wilson and William Seward. The *Mobile News* of Alabama declared (in a piece also reprinted in the *Liberator*): "Abolitionism, the offspring of crazy preachers and foolish women, the bantling of dirtiest demagogues, now takes a seat in the Senate Chamber" and "controls the political destiny of . . . States like New York." The paper called these developments "ominous."

As the antislavery movement gained prominence and force, so did the reputation of Lloyd Garrison. He was known throughout the nation as a major figure of his time, and biographer Henry Mayer notes that near the end of the decade he received more space in a comprehensive encyclopedia of political and cultural life than the combined space given to Emerson, Thoreau, Stowe, Phillips, and the famous free black activist, Frederick Douglass.

Garrison settled into middle age with his unconventional career intertwined with an entirely conventional personal life of simplicity and stability, though always on the cusp of financial difficulty. In 1834 he married Helen Benson, a merchant's daughter six years his junior, who shared his antislavery passion. The couple produced five sons and two daughters, though the childhood deaths of a son and daughter caused immense anguish for the couple. But Garrison never lost the sunny disposition that had sustained him through the travails of childhood and early adulthood. During household chores, which he avidly embraced, he could be heard belting out his favorite songs, and he interacted with his children in a loving spirit devoid of paternal austerity.

Now, as he entered his fifties, the marks of age could be seen in his baldness and deep facial lines. A New York newspaper, in covering a Garrison speech, estimated his age at about sixty, when in fact he was fifty-one. Helen worried about the effects of his frenzied work pace and long hours at the newspaper and in public discourse. Financial concerns naturally took a toll, with his income stuck for nearly two decades at just $1,200 a year. But a fund for the family established in 1847 by a group of supportive patrons built up enough capital by 1855 to put the Garrisons into a relatively commodious house on Boston's Dix Place. It also greatly reduced his living expenses, and the improved financial situation, though still modest, left Garrison "feeling both prosperous and grateful," wrote Mayer.

Around this time Garrison confronted a new philosophical challenge. He recoiled at the rhetoric of violence and martial spirit increasingly evident in the antislavery movement, particularly during fugitive slave episodes such as the Anthony Burns case and in the gathering Kansas tensions. The abolitionist editor embraced a philosophy of "nonresistance," meaning he opposed violence as a tool of civic contention. Though he despised organized religion and church hierarchy, he revered the teachings of the Bible, including the admonition to turn the other cheek, and sought to conduct himself according to such strictures. He brought to that principle the same uncompromising spirit that guided his antislavery crusade.

But it seemed to be a losing proposition. Even Amos A. Lawrence, Abbott's nephew and the noted antislavery patron, pronounced his acceptance of violence in the cause when he shipped a hundred Sharps rifles to free-state Kansans, then followed up with another 225. The minister Henry Ward Beecher caused a stir when he raised money for Kansas weaponry that he suggested would have greater "moral agency" than Bibles. He added that "you might just as well read the Bible to buffaloes" as to Kansas Border Ruffians. Sharps rifles soon became known as "Beecher's Bibles."

Alarmed by such actions and pronouncements, Garrison joined

others in reviving a dormant organization called the New England Non-Resistance Society, which convened a symposium on the topic at Worcester. Garrison denied that any losses arising from fidelity to nonresistance would disprove the nonresistance principle. "As a general rule," he said with considerable naivete, "obedience to God, on the part of an individual or a nation, will be attended with safety and prosperity."

He recoiled when an abolitionist organizer named Stephen Foster generated applause at the symposium by arguing that, when the right to life and liberty is threatened, the aggressor "ought to be put out of the way, by the least amount of suffering possible; but out, at the sacrifice of his life, if necessary." Garrison suggested that attendees didn't appreciate what they were saying when applauding such pronouncements. Since slavery negates liberty, he declared, "[y]ou say by this act that all slaveholders ought to be shot down." Indeed, he added, since all citizens are complicit in slavery, "you are saying that you yourselves ought to be put into your graves." Violence begets violence in an endless cycle, Garrison argued, unless interrupted by nonresistance.

But the Worcester discussion was an academic one, as opposed to the Kansas situation, where those Beecher's Bibles were being distributed to angry men vowing more and more fervently to use them to protect themselves and their rights as settlers. The distinction hit home with a stark change of attitude expressed by a Garrison friend named Charles Stearns, who had gone to Kansas to survey the situation and report back to Boston through news-packed letters to the *Liberator*. Writing as the Wakarusa standoff commenced, Stearns reported that he was joining the free-state militants to help fortify the town of Lawrence against any proslavery attack. But he was still a nonresistance man, he averred, even if he had to shoot a Ruffian.

"God never made these fiends—they are the devil's spawn," he wrote, adding, "I have always said I would shoot a wild beast. If I shoot these infernal Missourians, it will be on the same principle." In publishing the letter, Garrison affixed a note saying it seemed that "our impulsive friend Stearns has got thoroughly frightened out of his peace principles." He added he felt "no disposition to utter a reproachful word," but hoped his friend would recapture his conviction, as did the apostle Peter after he "denied his Lord to save himself from impending danger," but later "lamented his apostasy."

It was a rejoinder of sorrow more than anger. But it reflected a fundamental inconsistency in Garrison's political framework. He was the master of fiery, mesmeric rhetoric designed to rouse emotion on the most inflammatory issue of the day, and yet his call to action ultimately boiled down to just words and a turning of the cheek. He ridiculed those who believed that precluding slavery expansion in the territories would cause the evil institution eventually to wither and die. Too timid and too slow, declared the impatient editor. But nonresistance certainly couldn't work any faster, if at all. This dichotomy posed what biographer Mayer called "a terrible paradox: the more successful he became at persuading the society to take decisive action, the more it turned to modes that he rejected."

On December 3, lawmakers descended upon Washington for the start of the 34th Congress, and almost immediately the House found itself once again unable to elect a Speaker, much like the fiasco of December 1849. While the previous episode had shocked unsuspecting legislators, this one seemed almost inevitable; and, whereas the 1849 standoff had lasted just three weeks, this one would extend beyond two months.

It reflected the undulating politics of the day as parties old and new grappled with fast-moving political developments. Following the congressional elections of 1854–55 and the Know-Nothing wave of those years, Democrats controlled barely a third of House seats in the 234-member chamber. They faced what historian Michael F. Holt called a "polyglot opposition" consisting nominally of 108 Republicans and 43 Know-Nothings. But within those broad categories resided many subcategories, including "straight Whigs, Know Nothing/Whigs, Know Nothing/Democrats, Know Nothings of Free Soil or nonpartisan background, and anti-Nebraska fusionists, many of whom . . . sought an exclusively northern and overtly anti-southern Republican party." In such a welter of political alignments, getting to a majority vote of 118 wouldn't be easy.

It proved to be impossible. As in 1849, members ultimately voted to accept a plurality outcome, and on February 2, 1856, Massachusetts Free Soiler (and soon to be Republican) Nathaniel P. Banks captured the speakership on the 133rd ballot with 103 votes to 100 for the fifty-year-old Democrat William Aiken of South Carolina. Banks, a tall, mustachioed figure with deep-set eyes and wavy gray hair, prevailed in the contest without getting a single southern vote.

The election capped nine weeks of indignity, frustration, and anger, though members did manage to avoid violence on the House floor. Outside in the street, though, Arkansas's representative Albert Rust, a hulking six-footer, attacked New York's representative Horace Greeley, the newspaperman, with fists and a cane when he responded to a Rust argument in a dismissive tone. Other members interceded quickly enough to spare Greeley serious injury.

After the vote, Aiken, a National Democrat in the mold of his anti-secessionist South Carolina colleague James Orr, demonstrated his amiability by escorting Banks arm in arm to the Speaker's chair, an above-the-fray courtesy duly appreciated in the chamber. But the outcome carried powerful implications that quickly superseded Aiken's gesture. It was widely seen by both jubilant and disappointed Americans as a strong signal of Republican ascent. Ohio's Giddings, the fierce abolitionist, murmured after the vote, "I have attained the highest point of my ambition. *I am satisfied.*"

Southerners predictably decried the result. The *Charleston Mercury* attacked Banks as "unscrupulous, selfish, and unprincipled; true to none, false to all; a politician by trade, and a fanatic by calculation." Even some Banks allies noted the political inconstancy of the man, who, as the *Boston Courier* put it, "changes his politics with as little remorse as he would change his flannels." Within three years, the paper noted, he had been "a Democrat, a Know Nothing and a Free Soiler, and has betrayed each."

More troublesome for southerners was a trend noted by the *Mercury*, which pointed out "that Abolition, which has been constantly growing, only needs a little more growth to be dominant and irresistible in the House." Virginia's Know-Nothing congressman John Carlile declared on the House floor that the Banks vote represented an unprecedented development—the emergence of a purely northern party in the House, "willing to elect a Speaker . . . by sectional votes alone." No such party could claim to be national, he added, "and its success would produce a state of feeling that would shake this glorious Union to its very foundation."

Indeed, the Speaker race crystallized a seminal development in American politics—the emergence of a new political force, the fusionist Republicans, without need of a national identity or any intent to forge one. And yet even as a regional party it aimed to supplant the fading Whigs as the country's premier opposition to the Democrats, who were struggling to maintain their own national identity. These Republicans clearly had become a party of serious contention. As Maine's representative Israel Washburn said of the Banks triumph, "The importance of this victory cannot well be overestimated."

From Washington, Franklin Pierce watched developments in Kansas with a certain detachment even as the Wakarusa standoff nearly erupted into a bloody battle on the Great Plains. He faced the predicament of two governments claiming legitimacy, with each denouncing the other as a phony product of villainous interlopers. Widely viewed as a northern "doughface" with southern sympathies, Pierce seemed likely to favor the Atchison program over that of Robinson. But he also had embraced popular sovereignty as a hallowed principle for settlers seeking to transform territories into states. Could he reconcile those two attitudes, considering that true popular sovereignty had been trampled in Kansas?

It was clear that the two sides in Kansas were heading to war unless the situation could be brought under control. That suggested a few imperatives of presidential leadership: avoid taking sides absent a clear understanding of events; send in troops from Fort Leavenworth to maintain order; create a presidential commission to investigate the recent chaos and assess responsibility; and foster a new election, fair and untrammeled, to be overseen by federal troops. The president did none of those things.

Pierce's doughface sensibility was reflected in his Third Annual Message to Congress in late December, which heralded the good times prevailing under his leadership. "It is a matter of congratulation," said the president, congratulating himself, "that the Republic is tranquilly advancing in a career of prosperity and peace." And, while the peace of Kansas may have been threatened by what Pierce called "acts prejudicial to good order," he didn't see any need for federal intervention, as these acts were merely "exaggeration of inevitable evil, or over zeal in social improvement, or mere imagination of grievance." He would intervene, the president emphasized, only if such acts veered into "obstruction of Federal law or of organized resistance to Territorial law, assuming the character of insurrection."

Thus did the president signal his tilt toward the southern cause in Kansas by vowing to protect territorial law, meaning Atchison's law. Further, he railed against northerners who "engage in the offensive and hopeless undertaking of reforming the domestic institutions of other States, wholly beyond their control and authority." Such people, he declared, "peril the very existence of the Constitution."

The Message thrilled southerners and enraged northerners. The *Charleston Mercury* predictably hailed "its force, its originality and its suitableness." But the *Dedham Gazette* of Massachusetts said the document's slavery portions read like they had been written by a "South Carolinian fire-eater to whom the crack of the whip and the clank of chains are the sweetest music."

The *Boston Journal*, in excoriating Pierce, said he "merited the title of *the first sectional President*"—a particularly provocative observation and probably true. But, of course, Republicans and prospective Republicans also were seeking to fuse themselves into the country's first purely sectional party. From both sides American politics was becoming increasingly sectionalized.

Meanwhile, new violence erupted with the approach of the January 15 elections for state officials under the antislavery Topeka constitution. In the Leavenworth area, a two-day confrontation led to a ten-minute exchange of gunfire in which two men were wounded and prisoners were taken. Subsequent hatchet attacks resulted in numerous injuries and the death of a free-state settler. The victim, bleeding profusely, was taken home and deposited at his doorstep, where his wife found him. His last words were "They murdered me like cowards."

Despite that skirmish and the civic passions it generated, the balloting for state officials unfolded without further incident (though proslavery men declined to participate), and voters chose Charles Robinson as leader of the embryo government. He proved an able administrator—measured in rhetoric and cautious in action but steadfast in his defense of the Topeka constitution. Nevertheless, that election and the violence that attended it stirred President Pierce to issue a special Message on Kansas, this time leaving no doubt that he considered the proslavery government "duly constituted" and the Topeka entity illegitimate. While saying he didn't impugn the patriotism of antislavery settlers, he condemned their "misdirected zeal in the attempt to propagate their social theories by the perversion and abuse of the powers of Congress." And he suggested their effort to establish a shadow government was "of revolutionary character" and would become "treasonable insurrection" if it reached the point of organized resistance.

Two weeks later he announced that he had put federal troops at Governor Shannon's disposal and warned that resistance to the original territorial government would be "firmly withstood." He also called on Congress to enact legislation empowering the people of Kansas, under the proslavery government, to craft a state constitution and apply for statehood.

By taking sides in the ambiguous and highly charged situation, Pierce emboldened proslavery forces to defend their governmental institutions against the upstart Topeka men, who now faced mounting pressure from heavily armed law enforcement officials and militia groups bent on suppressing what the proslavery forces considered treasonous action. But the Topeka men weren't about to back down. As an antislavery settler named E. P. Fitch wrote to his parents in the East, "Pierce says we are traitors so of course the Missourians are to put us down but if they try it we shall have a bloody time out here."

The free-state men who emerged as leaders in the antislavery government now fully expected to be arrested as traitors. When they gathered to inaugurate their dominion at Topeka, Sheriff Jones, the ardent proslavery lawman, was there to take down names for possible future action. Topeka officials, under Robinson's leadership, proceeded cautiously with an approach they hoped would spare them the charge of insurrection and get the territory to statehood without slavery or violence. Rather than creating a fully functioning territorial government in competition with the proslavery one, they would send their proposed constitution to Congress in hopes lawmakers would accept the document and, on that basis, welcome Kansas into the Union. Further, the Topeka legislature enacted resolutions deferring the effective date of any legislation it passed until after Congress granted statehood.

But the free-staters didn't shrink from defiance, as reflected in Robinson's inaugural address. He declared that antislavery Kansans, and not the president, were the true defenders of popular sovereignty and were justified in enforcing the doctrine even to the point of revolution. But revolution wouldn't be necessary, he added, as Congress would see the virtue of their cause and respond accordingly. Thus they would not embrace violence in resisting territorial authority but wouldn't shrink from it, either. "Let what will come," proclaimed Robinson. "[N]ot a finger should be raised against the Federal authority until there shall be no hope of relief but in revolution."

Still, Robinson and his followers refused to accept the initial territorial government, and that in itself, as many proslavery men viewed it, constituted treason. David Atchison distilled this attitude in a letter to Amos Lawrence. "[Y]ou and your people are the aggressors upon our rights," he declared. "You come to drive us and our 'peculiar' institution from Kansas. We do not intend, cost what it may, to be driven or deprived of any of our rights." Atchison's words were backed up by ongoing Missourian harassment of antislavery Kansas settlers.

The nation's attention now turned to Congress and particularly the Senate, where Stephen Douglas took charge of efforts to heed Pierce's call for legislation to effect Kansas statehood. He crafted a report on the Kansas situation along with a statehood bill, got them approved by his Committee on Territories, and reported them to the Senate on March 17. Debate commenced three days later with a two-and-a-half-hour speech by the chairman in which he endorsed Pierce's argument that primary responsibility for the Kansas mess resided with northern immigrants and their antislavery maneuverings. The claim of widespread voter fraud by Missouri Ruffians, he insisted, was vastly overblown.

In opposition to Douglas, Vermont's freshman senator Jacob Collamer, a Whig-turned-Republican, crafted a minority report defending the free-state movement and advocating Kansas statehood under the Topeka constitution. As the Senate debate unfolded off and on over several weeks, William Seward announced that he intended to introduce legislation along the lines of Collamer's recommendation. Meanwhile, over in the House, Speaker Banks took action to get clarification on the entire Kansas story and its implications. He commissioned a three-member House investigative committee and dispatched it to Kansas to conduct an extensive series of interviews. The chairman was William Howard of Michigan, with Mordecai Oliver of Missouri and John Sherman of Ohio also serving.

As the Senate debate unfolded, Pickens Butler emerged as a prominent southern voice agitated by the storm of criticism leveled at his good friend David Atchison and at President Pierce for their actions regarding Kansas. The South Carolinian was approaching sixty now and enjoying the stature he had attained back home and in Washington. In South Carolina, he seemed secure in his Senate seat for as long as he wanted it, and his manor house in Edgefield, presided over by his mother since the death of his second wife so many years before, served as an upland center of convivial hospitality and spirited conversation. It was a good life. "My Dear General," he wrote Atchison in the spring of 1856, "I have just returned from my plantation where I have been spending some time talking to practical men on practical affairs—eating well baked cornbread and well cured bacon, and . . . delicious fishing . . . finally shooting ducks."

In Washington his popularity remained undimmed. A contemporary journalist who had followed his Senate career hailed his "dignity of mind" and his "abilities which give him a towering eminence among his brother Senators."

On March 5, he rose on the Senate floor to deliver his version of Kansas events, his defense of Atchison and Pierce, and his general support for the southern cause. It was a typical Butler speech—well argued, blunt spoken, and devoid of personal animus. "I do not intend to use the language of asperity in this debate," he began, and he largely adhered to that stricture. But he did allow his political prejudices and personal feelings to undermine at times his accuracy in recounting events.

"I have known General Atchison long and well," he said, adding that his knowledge of the man didn't align with the portrayal of him by such senators as Hale of New Hampshire, who had "attributed to him a ferocity and vulgar indifference and recklessness in relation to the affairs in Kansas, which is refuted by every confidential letter which he has written to me." Butler hailed his friend's actions at Lawrence the previous December in helping defuse the Wakarusa confrontation. Without his involvement, said the senator, "the houses of the settlement would have been burnt and its highways drenched with blood." He didn't mention that Atchison later vowed publicly that he would never again seek peace in Kansas in such a manner.

Butler lamented the Kansas turmoil particularly because it was destroying prospects for the territory to evolve naturally based on climate and geography, "with many white men and few negroes—with labor capable of being usefully and profitably employed—a community of farmers, using labor as they thought proper. In this way, by accretion, Kansas might have become a State." Again, such a bucolic vision didn't comport with the actions and aims of Border Ruffians over the previous two years.

Butler's speech wasn't particularly fiery, nor did it seem calculated to give serious offense to colleagues. The senator, true to his stated aim of avoiding asperity, presented his generally conventional arguments in conventional terms. But sitting on the Senate floor that day was a man who did take offense. For Charles Sumner, events in Kansas had ignited a simmering anger that flared up periodically into bursts of rage. And he seemed to be directing his rage more and more these days toward Butler, once his unlikely friend, then his friendly adversary, then his nettlesome foe, and now his political enemy.

DECADE OF DISUNION

The tensions roiling the two senators' relationship went deeper than the slavery issue, as fundamental and emotional as it was. They stretched back into the divergent cultural attitudes, mores, and folkways of the two states they represented—the austere Calvinism of the old Massachusetts Puritans vs. the Cavalier sensibilities of the early Carolina swashbucklers. A key point of disparity could be seen in the two men's view of the American Revolution and the founding of the American system. For Butler, those hallowed events epitomized a valorous struggle against governmental tyranny; for Sumner, an ongoing fight for freedom and equality.

Sumner now turned his attention to the writing of his own "elaborate speech" on Kansas and the broader slavery issue. And he saw Butler, among others, as a convenient foil for his address, an embodiment of the despised slave power from the state most vehemently committed to the odious institution. "I shall pronounce," he informed Theodore Parker, "the most thorough philippic ever uttered in a legislative body."

15

SIX DAYS IN MAY

||||||||||||||||||||||||||||||||||||||||||||||||||||||||||||||||||||||||||||||||||||||

BLOODY TIMES EAST AND WEST

May 1856 was a pivotal month for America. Within just six days, May 19 through May 24, a cluster of events in Kansas and Washington shook the nation and raised questions about its stability. Blood flowed at both locations, political passions intensified, and fiery new figures emerged. One new figure was South Carolina congressman Preston Brooks, thirty-six, an Edgefield planter and lawyer. Dark-haired and square-faced, with a pleasing countenance until it clashed with his hot-blooded temperament, Brooks was related to Pickens Butler, who was a first cousin of Brooks's father. Preston Brooks considered his kinsman Butler to be a statesman of the highest order.

As a young man, Brooks enjoyed his well-born status but sometimes pushed against the confines of respectability. South Carolina College expelled him twice for skipping class and frequenting local taverns. Near the end of his final term, he got into a fistfight with a fellow student that led to a final expulsion and debarment from graduation. Barely into his twenties, he fought a duel with former classmate Louis Wigfall, later a U.S. senator from Texas, in which both men sustained gunshot wounds.

These multiple altercations reflected Brooks's strong sense of Cavalier honor—the imperative of redressing even minor affronts directed at him, his family, or his state. But he also projected in normal times a compelling good humor, rather like his cousin Pickens Butler, though without Butler's rousing comedic touch. A *New York Times* editor described him as "a man of generous nature, of kindly feelings and of manly impulses, warmly attached to his friends."

Upon entering Congress in March 1853 at age thirty-three, Brooks identified with the moderate National Democratic faction led in South Carolina by his House colleague James Orr. But he believed that southern bondage benefited both whites and blacks and certainly was superior to what he considered the grinding worker exploitation of the North. "Let Free-Soilers come to the South, sir," he said in his first House address, "and we will show them the white and black man in a relation of friendship never dreamed of in their philosophy." But, of course, that relation of friendship rested firmly, in his view, on the intrinsic superiority and necessary dominance of the Caucasian race.

Another figure of growing prominence was Samuel Jones, the proslavery sheriff in Douglas County, Kansas Territory, who embraced the role of anti-Lawrence enforcer for the territorial government. Tall, slim, and beady-eyed, the sheriff fancied himself a man of boldness, but when confronted with threatening adversaries he often lost his swagger. A contemporary in the Kansas controversies said of him, "He seldom looks those with whom he is conversing full in the face, [and] his eye constantly wanders about as if he were apprehensive of some unknown danger."

A Virginia native, he moved with his family to Westport, Missouri, in 1854 and became postmaster there. He joined forces with the Border Ruffians and entered Kansas in March 1855 to disrupt free-state voting in the territorial elections. He helped steal the ballot box at one polling station and, according to later congressional testimony, gave election judges five minutes to resign or be killed.

He subsequently moved to Kansas and helped establish the town of Lecompton, designated in August 1855 as the new territorial capital. There Jones engaged in land speculations, timber harvesting, and lumber sales.

He became sheriff in late 1855 and promptly projected a strong enmity toward free-state forces. The enmity intensified in the new year when the sheriff entered Lawrence on April 19 with arrest warrants for several free-state men charged with various offenses against the proslavery Lecompton government. Jones and a deputy became enraged when a hurriedly formed mob disarmed them and sent them on their way. The next day the sheriff returned with a small posse, but menacing townsfolk again prevented him from fulfilling his mission.

Lawrence residents backed away three days later, when Jones reappeared with a party of army troops. Under military protection, the sheriff made six arrests, but still failed to capture a particularly elusive fugitive. Later, camped outside the town for the night, Jones was shot in the back by an unknown assailant. Though he wasn't seriously wounded, early reports that he had been murdered inflamed proslavery men throughout the territory. Even after the true outcome became known, a Lecompton newspaper declared, "Continued Resistance to Our Laws!!" and denounced "this clan of assassins—this sworn, secret organization, against law, against order, against the true pillar of our government."

Hailed by Lecompton and reviled by Lawrence, Jones now became the man in Kansas whose name called forth the most vehement passions, pro and con. He harbored a seething hostility toward his adversaries, born of his embarrassments at the hands of those he considered treacherous governmental usurpers.

Finally there was John Brown, desperate to prove to the world, at age fifty-six, that he wasn't to be defined by his multiple business failures, his embarrassing personal bankruptcies, his history of embezzlement, his inability to provide adequately for his family, or his congenital deviousness. He wished instead to be viewed as he viewed himself—as a man of destiny, aligned with the Almighty in purposes soaring far above the tribulations of ordinary life and the constrictions of man-made laws and customs. His brother-in-law, the Reverend Samuel Adair, noted his preoccupation with "the idea that God had raised him up on purpose to break the jaws of the wicked."

And nothing was more wicked than slavery, as Brown's deeply

religious father had taught him and as he himself felt to the depths of his consciousness. According to family lore, in 1837 he had stood up in church following a sermon on human bondage and declared his resolve to "consecrate my life to the destruction of slavery!" He also embraced violent action in the cause. Lloyd Garrison's nonresistance notions didn't resonate with Brown.

He was in fact a throwback to the austere Puritanism that dominated the sensibilities of early Massachusetts. As the Bay State abolitionist and writer Franklin Sanborn put it, "He was, in truth, a calvinistic Puritan . . . as ready as those of Bradford's or Cromwell's time . . . to engage in any work of the Lord to which he felt himself called." Brown biographer David S. Reynolds writes that the man embraced his Calvinist doctrines whole and pure, as preached by the famous Massachusetts cleric Jonathan Edwards, who viewed God as absolutely sovereign and man as absolutely helpless before God's power. For Edwards, writes Reynolds, "[t]here was no middle ground. Nor would there be for John Brown, who believed that God determines everything."

But New England's old Puritan preoccupation with providence had given way now to the reform spirit of the transcendentalists and their embrace of the "antinomian" view that Christians are released by grace from observing conventional civic laws. Here we encounter once again the higher law concept and particularly New England's embrace of a kind of "individual sovereignty" superseding societal norms. Brown, it could be argued, represented the furthest extension of these doctrines, where even proscriptions against wanton violence or murder could be flouted in deference to a greater morality defined by the individual conscience and by any man's perception of God's will.

John Brown was born in 1800 in Connecticut and moved with his family at age five to Ohio, where his father's often imprudent land speculations left the family struggling financially. At age twenty, the younger Brown began a series of vocations that included tanning, surveying, farming, sheepherding, land speculation, and wool brokerage. He succeeded at none of it, yet always came up with new schemes designed to wipe away past disappointments and place him finally in the lap of position and wealth. Unfortunately he lacked a capacity for the kind of steady toil necessary for frontier success. But he succeeded in producing a large family: twenty children in two marriages, though only eight survived him.

In 1848 he entered into a transaction with a wealthy New York abolitionist named Gerrit Smith, who had set aside lands at North Elba for a community of free blacks. Brown offered to clear and develop the lands, using black labor, in exchange for an opportunity to purchase his own land at favorable terms. But the harsh New York winter and the project's magnitude soon sapped his enthusiasm, and he returned with his family to Ohio, whence five of his sons, with their families, had set out for Kansas in 1855 in search of opportunity and a chance to demonstrate their antislavery passion. The father soon followed.

He took with him, in addition to a wagon full of supplies and weapons, a bundle of traits and attributes that would set him apart in the territory. Despite his many failures, he projected himself as a man of mark, with a purposeful gait, often with his hands clasped behind his back, and an air of resolve and tenacity that captured the attention of those he met. Egotistical, hardheaded, impatient, he tossed his opinions about like spears and showed little interest in social banter. He fancied himself a leader of men and carried himself like one, employing his considerable gift of vivid expression fortified by deep conviction.

The momentous Six Days in May began on the nineteenth of the month when Charles Sumner rose in the Senate to deliver the first installment of his two-day "philippic." Entitled "The Crime against Kansas," it consumed fully three and a half hours of eloquence, erudition, and vituperation. In print form it ran to 112 pages, and he memorized its entirety in order to ensure a commanding delivery. He quoted giants of Western thought such as Cicero, Livy, Dante, and Milton, and closed by invoking passages from the famous judicial oration "On the Crown," by the Athenian statesman Demosthenes. Spectators filled the galleries and jammed doorways in their desire to hear what everyone knew would be a rhetorical tour de force. "No such scene has been witnessed in that body since the days of Webster," reported the *New York Evening Post*.

True to his reputation, the senator quickly set a battering-ram tone by proclaiming the crime against Kansas to be "the rape of a virgin Territory, compelling it to the hateful embrace of Slavery; and it may be clearly traced to a depraved longing for a new slave State, the hideous offspring of such a crime, in the hope of adding to the power of slavery in the National Government."

Tracing Washington and Kansas events leading to the crisis, he declared that there was only one way to avert a horrible war—"fratricidal, parricidal war—with an accumulated wickedness beyond the wickedness of any war in human annals; justly provoking the avenging judgment of Providence and the avenging pen of history." The only tenable solution, said Sumner, was "the remedy of Justice and Peace"—namely, the immediate admission of Kansas as a free state under the Topeka constitution and as prescribed in the pending legislation of New York's senator Seward.

Sumner directed his ire particularly at three opposing figures—Butler, Douglas, and Virginia's James Mason. Though Butler was absent from the Senate and couldn't defend himself, he took the brunt of Sumner's malice in ridicule and bludgeon words:

> The senator from South Carolina . . . believes himself a
> chivalrous knight with sentiments of honor and cour-
> age. Of course he has chosen a mistress to whom he
> has made his vows, and who, though ugly to others, is
> always lovely to him; though polluted in the sight of the
> world, is chaste in his sight—I mean the harlot, slavery.
> For her his tongue is always profuse in words. Let her
> be impeached in character, or any proposition made to
> shut her out from the extension of her wantonness, and
> no extravagance of manner or hardihood of assertion
> is then too great for this senator. . . . He is the uncom-
> promising, unblushing representative on this floor of a

flagrant sectionalism, . . . and yet with a ludicrous ignorance of his own position—unable to see himself as
others see him—or with an effrontery which even his
white head ought not protect from rebuke.

The rebuke continued the next day, May 20, when Sumner, al-
luding to the slight paralysis in Butler's lower lip that caused him to
spit somewhat when talking, ridiculed the "incoherent phrases" and
"loose expectoration" of his oratory. Sumner added that Butler "touches
nothing which he does not disfigure with error" and that he could not
"open his mouth, but out there flies a blunder." Sumner also maligned
South Carolina, saying that if its whole history were blotted out, civilization would lose less than it had gained through the two-year effort of
right-thinking Kansans to create a state without slavery.

It was a remarkable bit of oratory, far outside Senate rules of decorum, and it was doubly remarkable that no colleagues called him down
for being out of order. As Sumner spoke, Stephen Douglas, pacing at the
back of the chamber, muttered, "That damn fool is going to get himself killed by some other damn fool." When the senator finished, Lewis
Cass, the gray eminence from Michigan, denounced the speech as "the
most un-American and unpatriotic that ever grated on the ears of the
members of this high body." Douglas decried "the depth of malignity
that issued from every sentence" and the "lasciviousness and obscenity"
of Sumner's sexual allusions.

He particularly condemned Sumner's attack on Butler as "an outrage." He added, "Every Senator who knows him loves him."

Defending himself, Sumner turned even more bellicose. Attacking
Douglas, he declared, "I say, also, to that Senator, and I wish him to
bear it in mind, that no person with the upright form of man can be
allowed . . . [Hesitation.]"

Mr. DOUGLAS: Say it.
Mr. SUMNER: I will say it—no person with the upright form
  of man can be allowed, without violation of all decency, to

switch out from his tongue the perpetual stench of offensive personality. . . . The noisome, squat, and nameless animal, to which I now refer, is not a proper model for an American Senator.

Sumner's speech and subsequent exchanges generated in Washington a buzz of disbelief mixed with foreboding. The senator's defiant and venomous abandonment of decorum struck many as yet another manifestation of the rending of America's civic fabric. Sumner appeared to delight now in clothing his arguments in the garb of fighting words, while seeming oblivious to the implications of such brutal discourse.

Over in the House, Preston Brooks reacted with the simmering rage of a Cavalier gentleman who feels himself publicly wronged. He was doubly incensed—at Sumner's attack on his beloved home state and at his insulting assault on the revered Butler. He worked through his anger by working through the precepts of the Cavalier honor code: first, that a duel challenge would be inappropriate because duels were for gentlemen and Sumner didn't qualify as one; second, that Sumner therefore would have to be horsewhipped or beaten with a cane for redress, according to the code; third, Pickens Butler wasn't in Washington to administer the punishment and, besides, lacked the youth and strength for such an encounter; fourth, Brooks therefore would undertake the attack in behalf of his cousin.

On Wednesday, May 21, the day after Sumner's final remarks, Brooks waited an hour and a half on the Capitol grounds in hopes of intercepting Sumner on his way toward the building, but no opportunity to accost the senator presented itself. He would have to wait for another opportunity.

On that same day, more than a thousand miles to the west, Lawrence, Kansas, became the scene of big events, set in motion by earlier developments beginning on May 5. That's when the territory's chief judge, Samuel Lecompte, decided to squeeze the Topeka free-state government by getting a grand jury in Lecompton to issue indictments for all free-state officials who had committed "constructive treason" by resisting territorial laws. The grand jury also returned indictments against two free-state newspapers in Lawrence for journalistic sedition and against the new Free State Hotel, viewed by Lecompton officials as suspiciously fortresslike and thus a possible instrument of rebellion.

Six days later federal marshal Israel Donaldson issued a call for volunteers to join a posse charged with serving the indictments and taking down the newspapers and hotel. Soon the grounds surrounding Lecompton were filled with paramilitary forces imbued with a proslavery martial spirit. After days of organizational planning and military drills, Donaldson moved his force of some five hundred to eight hundred men, including many Missourians, to Lawrence, surrounded the town, and planted big guns on nearby highlands. Accompanying him was the now-recovered Sheriff Jones, along with Atchison, leading their personal militia groups.

The situation appeared ominous. A southerner living near Lawrence wrote to his relatives, "I expect before you get this Lawrence will be burnt to the ground." And settler Edward Fitch reported, "We never have been quite so near a war as we now are."

But with the town surrounded, free-state officials informed Donaldson on May 21 that the locals would not buck federal authority. Donaldson assured him that, absent resistance, no attack would ensue. Free State Hotel owner Shalor Eldridge even prepared a lavish meal for Donaldson and his top leaders as a way of easing tensions. The marshal responded by arresting a few free-staters and then dismissing his men.

Jones's thirst for vengeance had not been slaked, however, and he promptly deputized the Donaldson posse under his own command. He ordered the town to relinquish its weapons, placed his artillery in position to destroy the hotel, tore apart the newspaper offices, and generally unleashed a torrent of plunder. Local folks didn't resist, as they had promised not to do, but they cheered when the cannonballs from Jones's field guns failed to bring down the hotel and when efforts to blow up the building also failed. Finally a frustrated Jones set the building ablaze and burned it to the ground. "This is the happiest moment of my life," he shouted.

The Sacking of Lawrence, as the episode became known, didn't generate bloodshed on the Kansas plain. Only one man died, and he was the accidental victim of falling debris from the battered hotel. But town damage was extensive. In addition to the hotel and the newspaper offices, the home of Charles Robinson was destroyed, and extensive looting left the town in shambles. Robinson was arrested, along with twenty or so other free-state officials.

Predictably, southerners and southern sympathizers applauded the onslaught. "The Law and Order party in Kansas Territory have at length succeeded in queling insubordination at Lawrence," crowed Missouri's *Independence Messenger*. The *Doniphan Constitutionalist* celebrated the victory over "that notorious abolition hole, Lawrence."

But the degradation of the little town actually represented a moral victory for free-state families, seen more widely now as peaceful but beleaguered settlers in the tradition of America's time-honored westward push. Proslavery leaders emerged with tarnished reputations, as perpetrators of what many considered a grave injustice committed under the auspices of a phony democracy.

Back in Washington on May 22, Preston Brooks once again positioned himself outside the Capitol in hopes of encountering Charles Sumner. Once again he missed his quarry. So Brooks made his way to the Senate floor, where, sure enough, there was Sumner at his desk. The congressman waited until adjournment and then lingered another hour as Sumner busied himself with paperwork and a number of women conversed with friends in or near the chamber. He had with him a "gutta percha" cane, made from a hard Asian-tree substance, well suited for violence.

With the ladies gone, Brooks approached Sumner's desk and stood over him. "Mr. Sumner," he said, "I have read your speech with care and as much impartiality as was possible and I feel it my duty to tell you that you have libeled my State and slandered a relative who is aged and absent and I am come to punish you for it." Even as he spoke, Brooks delivered his first blow, then landed several more in rapid succession upon the victim's bare head. "Every lick went where I intended," recalled the congressman. "For about the first five or six licks he offered to make fight but I plied him so rapidly that he did not touch me."

Stunned into temporary blindness, with blood flowing from head wounds, Sumner sought to rise from his desk. But it was bolted to the floor, and the assailant's blows blocked his only escape route. Acting now "almost unconsciously . . . under the instinct of self-defense," as Sumner later recalled, he wrenched the desk from the floor with the leverage of his knees and thighs, then spun around and staggered backward and sideways, seemingly about to fall to the floor. But Brooks held him up by the lapel of his coat with one hand as he continued the beating with the other. The congressman ultimately delivered some thirty blows, by his own estimate, splintering the cane into three pieces. The assault continued until Sumner collapsed, "bleeding and powerless," as a later congressional report described him. The report concluded that Sumner's wounds were "severe and calculated to endanger the life of the Senator." Blood was everywhere, his clothes soaked and the floor slippery.

New York congressmen Ambrose Murray and Edwin Morgan, in conversation on the floor when the assault began, rushed over to stop the violence. But South Carolina representative Lawrence Keitt, circling Sumner and Brooks as the assault continued, deterred the congressmen by brandishing his own cane menacingly and yelling, "Let them alone, God damn you." Finally Murray managed to pull Brooks away from his victim as Kentucky senator John Crittenden admonished the congressman, "Don't kill him." Replied Brooks, "I did not intend to kill him, but I did intend to whip him."

Sumner, barely conscious and still bleeding profusely, was taken to an adjoining anteroom and placed on a sofa, where a local doctor tended his wounds, stitching up two gashes. Henry Wilson, hearing of the episode, rushed to the Senate to get his colleague into a carriage and back to his lodgings for quiet and rest. "I could not believe that a thing like this was possible," Sumner mused as he dropped off to sleep.

Embedded in the aftermath of this sensational development was a recognition that it reflected an ominous reality of American politics: the country was so divided over slavery now that it couldn't agree even on the proper attitude toward such a heinous crime in the Senate chamber. The episode thrilled many throughout the South, while most northerners were aghast. A case in point involved two public meetings on the matter, one in Massachusetts and the other in South Carolina.

At Boston's Faneuil Hall, a "Sumner Indignation Meeting" drew an overflow crowd to what the *Liberator* called "one of the most enthusiastic and marked gatherings ever held within its famous . . . walls." The throng cheered enthusiastically when Governor Gardner declared that the participants had come together not just as supporters of Sumner or as defenders of the rights of Massachusetts or as members of any party or faction, but "as citizens of this broad land, all of us, I trust and believe, determined and prepared to defend the constitutional right of every section and every quarter, be they menaced where they may or by whom they may."

No such sentiment of national unity, nor any sympathy for the afflicted senator, animated the citizens of Bishopville, South Carolina, when they gathered to celebrate Brooks's "prompt and chivalrous" response to the "fanatical tirade of the notorious . . . Sumner." The Edgefield congressman, they added in a resolution, acted "as becomes a high-toned gentleman toward an arrant poltroon." Southern newspapers, avoiding the words "attack" or "assault" to describe Brooks's action, employed instead such euphemisms as "chastisement," "castigation," "salutary discipline," and even "transaction."

Even before news of Brooks's attack on Sumner reached Kansas, John Brown seethed with anger over the Sacking of Lawrence. While despising proslavery aggressors, he also felt contempt for free-state leaders who lacked the fighting spirit to protect the little town. He viewed Charles Robinson as a "perfect old woman" and dismissed Topeka leaders as "broken-down politicians" who displayed "more talk than cider."

If they wouldn't take action in righteous retribution, then he would. He became, said a friend, "wild and frenzied."

What came next is best understood in the context of the Brown family's Kansas experience. After Brown had entered the territory to join family members who had come some months before, the clan spent the brutal winter of 1855–56 in a three-sided lean-to in southeastern Kansas, near Osawatomie, which also happened to be proslavery territory. Brown's son John Jr., an energetic and amiable young man, captured a seat in the Topeka legislature and formed a military company of some thirty-four men, called the Pottawatomie Rifles. Though the elder Brown didn't seek a leadership role in the free-state movement, he helped fortify Lawrence against attack during the Wakarusa War and participated in activities of the Pottawatomie Rifles. He also attended free-state gatherings, such as the convention that nominated John Jr. for legislative office.

The Browns quickly established themselves as vocal antislavery warriors, eager to force the issue of human bondage into open belligerency. John Sr.'s spirited calls for action during the Wakarusa War, before that December standoff was settled through negotiation, got him marked as a "gun-happy nonconformist."

In late April the proslavery judge, Sterling Cato, issued warrants for the arrest of John Brown and his sons, apparently for violating provisions of the draconian territorial slavery code. During a subsequent court session near Osawatomie, several Brown sons disrupted the proceedings in hopes of getting themselves arrested. John Brown's aim apparently was to then bust them out of jail and "*hurry up the fight*," as one of the brothers put it. When John Jr. summoned his rifle company just outside the court proceeding as a show of force, Cato promptly closed down the session and returned to Lecompton.

Brown took note of those assisting Cato on that day, including William Sherman, the brother of the man whose tavern served as the site for the court session; James Doyle, a member of the grand jury that handed down the indictments; a Doyle son named William, a court bailiff; William's brother Drury; and Allen Wilkinson, a district attorney at Cato's court. For John Brown these were now marked men.

When the Browns heard of the looming Sack of Lawrence on May 21, they mustered the Pottawatomie Rifles and headed for the scene, only to learn the next day, as they continued their ride, that they were too late. That night, at his camp near Lawrence, Brown crafted a plan of retribution. The next morning, on May 23, he assembled his men and called for volunteers. With his welkin eyes flashing, he declared, "Something is going to be done now."

Then a messenger entered the camp with news of the Sumner atrocity, and the men "went crazy–*crazy!*" as Jason Brown later recalled. "It seemed to be the finishing, decisive touch." When one of the men, noting the burst of rage in the camp, urged caution, John Brown declared, "I am eternally tired of hearing that word caution. It is . . . the word of cowardice." He assembled a party that included four of his sons (John Jr. stayed back), his son-in-law Henry Thompson, and rifleman James Townsley.

That night, around eleven o'clock, Brown and his band arrived at James Doyle's cabin near Pottawatomie Creek and yelled through the door that they needed directions to their destination. When Doyle opened the door, he was seized along with his two sons by the Brown party, heavily armed with rifles and broadswords sharpened to a razor's edge. Doyle's younger son, just sixteen, was spared only through the tearful pleas of his mother. But the other three were taken outside, hacked up, and shot, their mutilated bodies left in the dirt as a savage sight for their loved ones in the morning.

Similar scenes unfolded at the cabins of Wilkinson, whose throat was slashed and whose body was so hideously disfigured that friends wouldn't allow his wife to see the corpse, and of the Shermans, where Henry Sherman wasn't to be found, so the Brown party contented itself with destroying his brother William, splitting his skull open and nearly severing his hand from his arm. Then members of the Brown party, having completed their work before daybreak and taken horses and other possessions of the victims, washed their hands and sabers in the creek and returned to their daily routines.

News of the massacre soon seeped into the public consciousness, with the names of Brown and his men often linked to the terrible deeds.

A Lecompton court issued a murder indictment against Brown, but the slow pace of territorial justice amid the Kansas chaos allowed him to avoid the law for four months before leaving the territory to pursue other avenues of antislavery activity. Eventually the indictment was amended to name just Townsley, who was arrested. The charges against him were later dropped for lack of evidence.

Reflection brought remorse to most of the participants. Owen Brown wept inconsolably for an extended period, while son Jason labeled the massacre "an uncalled for, wicked act." John Jr. suffered what seemed like a mental breakdown. But John Sr., not one to suffer remorse when in service to the Almighty, responded to Jason's characterization by declaring, "God is my judge. It was absolutely necessary as a measure of self-defense, and for the defense of others."

The Six Days in May transformed the tenor of American politics. Sumner's crude discourse and the corollary acts of destruction and violence inflamed the nation, dividing its citizens as never before and raising questions about whether civic passions over slavery could be quelled peacefully through the constitutional system. Northerners became even more agitated now over the South's recent institutional victories such as the Fugitive Slave Act, the Missouri Compromise repeal, and the apparent Ruffian triumph in Kansas. And southerners became increasingly indignant over the North's intensifying resolve to curb the spread of human bondage—reflected, as they saw it, in the kind of carnage unleashed at Pottawatomie.

In terms of political influence, the proslavery forces had on their side the institutional power of the U.S. presidency, the Senate, and the southern-dominated judiciary, while antislavery northerners enjoyed a growing sectional coalescence of public opinion reflected in Republican dominance of the U.S. House and the rise of antislavery stalwarts such as Seward, Sumner, Wilson, Hale, and Chase.

Kansas served as a kind of microcosm example. The proslavery forces enjoyed President Pierce's support and the cover of the popular sovereignty doctrine (though it had been in reality eviscerated by the

DECADE OF DISUNION

Ruffians). But popular opinion within the territory had been trending inexorably toward the antislavery cause with the arrival of new immigrants. That had guided Charles Robinson's delicate policy of peaceful acquiescence to Lecompton, while refusing to accept its underlying legitimacy. "Nothing remained," he later explained, "but to fill up the Territory with *bona fide* settlers, and to take possession of the government at the election of the legislature, when the day should arrive."

The Sacking of Lawrence and the caning of Sumner fortified that strategy by pushing public opinion in the desired direction, in Kansas as in the northern states. And the Brooks attack fortified it further. Northern outage increased when the congressman was arrested on a mere assault charge and fined just $300. A Senate committee condemned his behavior but said any disciplinary action must come from the House. That chamber took up a censure motion but lacked the two-thirds vote necessary to pass it, whereupon Brooks defiantly resigned his seat to give his constituents an opportunity to judge his behavior. They did so a month later by overwhelmingly returning him to the House.

All this bolstered the antislavery cause in the North. But then John Brown upended the situation with his butchery. His actions inflamed and emboldened the proslavery forces in Kansas and Missouri while forcing the antislavery men on the defensive. Robinson's strategy of patience now lay in shambles while he languished in jail and the Lecompton government escalated its offensive against Topeka.

Thus peace in Kansas appeared more remote than ever. "The war seems to have commenced in real earnest," wrote a Kansas settler. A Missouri newspaper emblazoned across its front page, "WAR! WAR!" Kansas was entering yet another new phase, as was the nation.

16

CAMPAIGN OF '56

||||||||||||||||||||||||||||||||||||||||||||||||||||||||||||||||||||||||||||||||||||

THE PARADOX OF A "VICTORIOUS DEFEAT"

James Buchanan had plenty of time to contemplate his political future during a two-week steamship voyage from England to America in April 1856. The Pennsylvanian had just completed a three-year stint as U.S. minister to Great Britain, and his return coincided nicely with the start of the presidential canvass. Should he enter the fray and seek the Democratic nomination? That was the question he pondered as he retreated frequently to the solitude of his stateroom and pulled from his travel trunk the Madeira wine and robust cigars he always kept readily available for moments of leisure and contemplation.

Few acquaintances harbored any doubt about the final decision. Buchanan had never shrouded his presidential ambition, though he once told President Polk that he would rather be a Supreme Court justice than U.S. president. He certainly had the background for either, with ten years as a U.S. congressman; minister to Russia, in which role he successfully negotiated a commercial treaty with St. Petersburg; a decade as U.S. senator; secretary of state under Polk; and the just-completed London mission. One New York newspaper extolled his "powerful intellect" and added that he "acquired knowledge for use, not for display." But many of his friends and supporters didn't fully realize the mixed nature of his traits and attributes.

Born in 1791 near Mercersburg, Pennsylvania, he attended Dickinson College, became a lawyer at age twenty-one, participated in the defense of Baltimore during the War of 1812, and eventually settled in Lancaster, Pennsylvania. Bright, hardworking, and gregarious, he never faltered in his rise to the pinnacle of Pennsylvania politics and national stature. Though devoid of wit or imagination, he projected himself as a man of consequence with his physical size, wavy blond locks, resonant voice, and political wiles. Because of a slight vision defect, sometimes called wandering eye, he tended to compensate in conversation by leaning his head forward and to the side—a mannerism that gave him an attractive appearance of uncommon social attentiveness.

He also displayed a certain effeminacy, accentuated by soft features and a beardless face. Andrew Jackson dismissed him as "an inept busybody" and referred to the lifelong bachelor as an "Aunt Nancy," hinting at possible homosexuality. Buchanan's close friendship over many years with the handsome and foppish Senator William King of Alabama stirred whispers in some social quarters, but historians who later sought evidence of a sexual relationship never could answer the question definitively.

More significantly, Buchanan often indulged in outlandish whims and puzzling inconsistencies. He manifested these tendencies most starkly during his years as Polk's chief diplomat, stirring in the president both puzzlement and irritation at his persistent wavering on important policy matters. Over time, Polk concluded that Buchanan's troubling behavior reflected his desire to position himself for his own presidential run. "He has been selfish," Polk wrote to his diary, "& all his acts and opinions seem to have been controlled with a view to his own advancement, so much so that I can have no confidence or reliance in any advice he may give."

Contemplating his political situation during his oceanic voyage, Buchanan inevitably focused on two key elements: his competition for the Democratic nomination, to be awarded at the party's national convention in Cincinnati in June, and the dynamics of the nation's party system, which had been in a state of flux for years.

Buchanan's analysis of his Democratic opposition began with Frank-lin Pierce, who wanted another White House term and enjoyed wide-spread southern support. But his general ineptitude and divisive Kansas interventions had shredded his political standing throughout the North. The *Charleston Mercury*'s political coverage reflected the slow realiza-tion among southerners that Pierce couldn't be reelected. In January the paper called the president "the natural and almost necessary candidate of the South." But by April it was a different story. "Every day, and each new development," said the *Mercury*, "confirms the hopelessness of president Pierce's re-nomination." The South, the paper added, "is divided against him, while the entire North demands his sacrifice."

But if he couldn't get renominated under the Democrats' two-thirds requirement, he still might garner enough convention support to deny an early victory to anyone else, most notably Buchanan. That could create a deadlock and open the way for a dark horse. This was a partic-ularly feasible scenario given the similar circumstances surrounding the irrepressible Little Giant.

The fires of presidential ambition burned within Stephen Douglas as furiously as ever. But he would avoid his mistake of 1852, when he had established an early high profile and drawn the fire of "old fogy" Democrats angry over his upstart airs and those of his "Young America" supporters. This time he would operate quietly and unobtrusively. That might also help him bridge the gap between those who had favored the Kansas-Nebraska legislation and those who had opposed it—a difficult task for someone as closely identified with the pro-Nebraska faction as Douglas.

Thus did the political passions swirling around the Illinois senator suggest that he also, like Pierce, probably couldn't muster the two-thirds vote necessary for an early nomination in Cincinnati. But if Pierce and Douglas together could garner enough support to thwart Buchanan in the early balloting, they might manage to generate an unforeseen out-come, perhaps even with one of them emerging as a late-ballot victor.

As Buchanan contemplated the American party system, he perceived a number of realities. First, the Whigs were practically dead, reduced to a scattered and ill-defined collection of die-hard loyalists described by

New York congressman Solomon Haven as the "fossil remains of too low and ancient a strata to stir up the surface in the least." But some dogged Whigs still wanted to organize a party convention in the fall, nominate a candidate, produce a platform, and honor the party heritage. Perhaps, it was thought, they could keep the flame alive for a postelection Whig revival.

In the meantime, a big question facing the country was where old-line Whig voters would go now. Some certainly would end up with the new Republican Party, which had coalesced around a provocative principle: that Congress had every right to outlaw slavery in the territories and should do so, while leaving the institution untouched where it already existed. It was the old Wilmot Proviso concept, dusted off and thrust into the debate as a cudgel against Douglas's cherished popular sovereignty.

Some Republican leaders argued that slavery couldn't survive for long if confined to its southern base, outnumbered and outflanked by more and more free states (a view shared by plenty of apprehensive southerners). Many former antislavery Whigs found the concept enticing. One was Charles Francis Adams, the oft-frustrated but still-ambitious Massachusetts Conscience Whig. He had spent the previous three years largely away from politics, pursuing private endeavors such as a biography of his grandfather. But now, agitated by events in Kansas and the Sumner caning, he got himself selected as a delegate to the forthcoming Republican convention in Philadelphia in mid-June. He was back in the game and fully committed to Henry Wilson's Republicans. Many other former Whigs joined his political migration.

The Republican Party wasn't the only destination for wayward Whigs. Most southern and some conservative northern Whigs had gravitated to the Know-Nothing (or American) Party over the previous year or more, and now they hoped to position that nativist institution as a new unionist party bridging the North-South divide with a program that included a clampdown on Catholic immigration and opposition to abolitionist agitations. Back in February, even before Buchanan's departure from England, the party had met in convention in Philadelphia and selected as its standard-bearer former president Millard Fillmore, who was out of the country at the time and had never even flirted with Know-Nothingism. But upon his return he seized the opportunity and embraced the party's nativist and anti-abolitionist sentiments.

Finally, there was the Democratic Party, the nation's dominant political force for nearly three decades. Starting with Andrew Jackson's 1828 presidential run, the party had won five of seven presidential elections and appeared well positioned to win again in 1856. Its general governmental philosophy—curtailment of federal authority, strict interpretation of the Constitution, low tariffs, fiscal austerity, continental expansionism—had resonated with voters and given the party a national identity. But just as sectional strife had destroyed the Whigs as a bisectional political entity, that festering conflict now threatened to upend also the Democrats' ability to straddle the North-South divide.

The Democratic strategy had been to adjudicate the slavery issue through compromise, which inevitably entailed a certain solicitude toward the South and acceptance of bondage as an ongoing American institution. That had yielded the Fugitive Slave Act, the Missouri Compromise repeal, Pierce's proslavery tilt on Kansas, and the ongoing effort to curtail the slavery debate altogether. Such policies were becoming more and more unacceptable to more and more northerners, however, and already the Republican Party was drawing significant numbers of antislavery Democrats into its fold. That posed a question: Could the Republicans gain enough electoral strength as a strictly northern party to actually win presidential elections? If so, the Democrats were in serious trouble.

On April 24, Buchanan's steamship, the *Arago*, reached New York, where the celebrated passenger avoided all fanfare as he made his way to Philadelphia. But there he received a rousing welcome, with cannon blasts, fireworks, and bands playing sprightly marches. The politician delivered a three-minute speech before an outdoor crowd of three thousand. Then it was on to Lancaster, where a similar celebratory welcome extended over two days and where Buchanan's operatives, led by

Louisiana senator John Slidell, busied themselves in strategy sessions and political maneuvering. Soon it was apparent to all that the Pennsylvanian wanted the job.

The Democrats' looming Cincinnati convention, meanwhile, set off a firestorm of political controversy in South Carolina, where congressman James Orr's effort to forge a coalition of National Democrats seemed to be gaining favor, much to the chagrin of old-line disunionists such as Barnwell Rhett and his followers. Orr's concept—that the South could protect its interests and thrive within the Union if it would fortify itself through economic and political reforms—rested upon the proposition that a unified South must bolster the Democratic Party as a bulwark against northern antislavery aggression. That meant South Carolina must strive always for southern unity and Democratic Party strength. A corollary was that the state's Democrats must participate in national Democratic nominating conventions, beginning with the Cincinnati gathering in June.

That assaulted the traditional notion, going back to Calhoun, that South Carolina's participation in those conventions inevitably undermined the state's political independence. In this view, convention attendance implied a commitment to support the eventual party candidate even if he turned out to be hostile to South Carolina interests. "There is no reason why we should sacrifice the independent consideration of our position to the blind passions of Presidential partisanship," declared the *Mercury*, emerging as the state's most ardent opponent of convention participation. "There are fools enough engaged in this chase."

The controversy unfolded against the backdrop of the state's ongoing struggle to define itself politically in the wake of the 1851 cooperationist triumph and the humiliation of the state's secessionists. Those events still exercised a strong psychological tug on the public consciousness, dispelling serious interest in secessionist turbulence and generating cautious favor toward Orr's hopeful formula.

But some men still harbored nostalgia for the days when secessionist fervor seemed to dominate the state. Barnwell Rhett, though a voice in the wilderness now, certainly represented that lingering sentiment. So did the *Charleston Mercury*. The two converged in the spring of 1856 when Rhett's fourth son, Edmund, took a job as a *Mercury* editor, working under his cousin, William Taber (son of Barnwell Rhett's sister Emma), who had bought an ownership position in the paper four years earlier. Now Rhett's son and nephew both held prominent positions at the paper, and Edmund was known as a loyal adherent of his father's outlook and interests.

Barnwell Rhett disliked Taber, however, and considered him "a low-reckless debaucher," a heavy drinker with a reputation for pursuing sexual interactions with slave women. "I have no faith in his morals and pride of character," Rhett confided to his oldest son, Barnwell Jr. But Taber and Edmund steered the *Mercury* in the direction of Barnwell Rhett's fiery outlook, hammering away on the anti-convention theme and attacking those who supported the Orr view or even displayed a lack of firmness on the issue. Their vehemence increased when South Carolina Democrats met in convention and named delegates to the Cincinnati gathering.

The *Mercury* directed much of its ire toward Pickens Butler after the senator revealed that, while in principle, he remained opposed to convention participation, he also recognized that public opinion in the state had swung against that view. Therefore, he added, South Carolina "should send a full, able and responsible delegation to insist on a man of principles, &c." That spurred Taber and young Rhett to intensify their attacks on Butler.

The senator was not having a good year. The crosscurrents of political emotion that swirled around the state as it sought to establish its identity on the issues of slavery and secession inevitably generated criticism of sitting politicians, including Butler. "These strictures are hard to bear," he told a friend, pointing to critical notices in a South Carolina newspaper, "yet, I suppose, a public man must submit to the fate of his position." And, while the recent Sumner-Brooks travesty hadn't undermined his political standing in South Carolina or elsewhere in the South, it remained a divisive blot on the nation, not something that anyone would want to be associated with.

In discussing the matter on the Senate floor on June 12, Butler refused to concede even a small portion of the moral high ground. Sumner, he said, "should be held exclusively responsible to his country and his God" for the episode. Had he been present during Sumner's speech, added the senator, he would have interrupted to ask Sumner to cease such an attack. If the Massachusetts senator had refused, Butler said further, he would have later demanded retractions to bring Sumner's speech "within the sphere of parliamentary propriety." Butler conceded that he couldn't know in hindsight what he would have done in response to a further Sumner rebuff, "yet I can say that I would not have submitted to it."

Butler argued that nothing he had said or done "could have called for, much less justified, the gross personal abuse, traduction, and calumny" of Sumner's "compound poison of malignity and injustice." Hence he felt that Brooks acted appropriately in delivering a "castigation . . . according to the old-fashioned notion, by caning him." Butler also disparaged the seriousness of the assault, saying Sumner received merely "two flesh wounds" not sufficiently serious to keep him out of combat, for example, had he suffered such blows while in the military. Butler conceded that Brooks deserved to be punished for his action, but only lightly. He embraced the southern view: Sumner got what he deserved.

Butler's underlying anger surfaced starkly when he embarrassed himself on the Senate floor in the immediate aftermath of the caning episode, after he had rushed back to Washington from Edgefield to deal with the controversy. The South Carolinian lost his composure when Henry Wilson castigated Brooks's action as "brutal, murderous, and cowardly."

"You're a liar!" shouted Butler in an uncharacteristic violation of Senate decorum. When colleagues urged him to withdraw the remark, a chastened Butler expressed hopes that it would not be put down into the record. "I have never used an epithet on this floor," he said, "and therefore ask that I may be excused."

But Brooks was not so willing to accept Wilson's characterization of cowardice. True to form, he challenged the Massachusetts senator to a duel. The Shoemaker of Natick refused to back down and dismissed the challenge as not just illegal but silly. In a note to Brooks he repeated the offending language and added: "I have no qualification whatever to make in regard to those words." He emphasized that he had "always regarded dueling as the lingering relic of a barbarous civilization, which the law of the country has branded a crime." Therefore, while he believed strongly in the right of self-defense, he would not meet Brooks anywhere "for the purpose indicated in your letter."

As a precaution, Wilson had the letter delivered by a congressional colleague and took to arming himself in the course of fulfilling his senatorial duties. To his wife he wrote that he would "defend my life, if possible, at any cost." Wilson reported years later that a group of southern politicians had met at Washington's National Hotel to discuss the idea of attacking him, but they were dissuaded from carrying out the plan by earnest entreaties from James Orr.

But the old-fashioned notion referenced in Butler's Senate speech, of southern honor and pride, generated subsequent violence involving the *Mercury* and its editor, Taber, as well as a longtime Rhett adversary named Andrew G. Magrath, selected as the Democratic candidate for an open U.S. House seat. Magrath, a federal district judge, was a longtime cooperationist and National Democrat, just the kind of moderate despised by the Rhetts. Edmund Rhett unleashed a torrent of *Mercury* invective on the man—"scathing even by the paper's own incendiary standards," according to a later historian. Though Edmund Rhett expected a duel challenge from Magrath, the challenge came instead from the judge's brother Edward and was directed not to young Rhett but to Taber as the paper's co-owner. In the gunshot exchange that followed, Edward Magrath killed Taber. The episode shocked Charleston society, and Andrew Magrath promptly abandoned his House campaign, while the Rhetts and the *Mercury* stepped up their contentious ways.

In late May large numbers of boats from Kentucky and Ohio towns began arriving in Cincinnati via the Ohio River for the June 2 start of the Democratic convention. The boats and other conveyances brought to the city some twenty thousand delegates and other participants, and all hotels were thoroughly booked. The tony Burnet House spread three thousand cots across the floor of an adjoining warehouse for the overflow as representatives arrived from all thirty-one states, including South Carolina.

Various rumors quickly filtered through the convention floor—that the Buchanan men were "very confident"; that Douglas operatives were discussing their candidate's possible withdrawal; that Pennsylvania, Virginia, and Ohio were solidly in the Buchanan camp, while Pierce stood tall in Mississippi and Massachusetts.

Turning to the party platform, the Democrats declared that the Kansas-Nebraska Act embodied "the only sound and safe solution of the 'slavery question.'" Preservation of the union, it said, was the nation's "paramount issue," and popular sovereignty represented the best means of achieving that goal. The document subtly favored the Lecompton government in Kansas over the antislavery Lawrence entity by repudiating "all sectional parties and platforms concerning domestic slavery" that seek to incite settlers "to treason and armed resistance to law in the Territories." Employing capital letters for emphasis, the platform endorsed: "NON-INTERFERENCE BY CONGRESS WITH SLAVERY IN STATE AND TERRITORY, OR IN THE DISTRICT OF COLUMBIA."

When the nomination voting commenced, Buchanan led on the initial ballot with 135½ votes to 122½ for Pierce and 33 for Douglas. (Cass received 5 and was quickly eliminated.) That left Buchanan 65 votes shy of the two-thirds threshold. In subsequent ballots that day— fourteen in all—Pierce lost ground, while Douglas drifted upward, with the result that Buchanan ended the day with 152½ votes, Pierce with 75, and Douglas with 63. Overnight, the Buchanan men successfully lured many Pierce supporters to their banner, and the next morning Pierce collected only 3 votes, while Buchanan rose to 168½ and Douglas garnered 118.

It now seemed clear that the convention was deadlocked, with two candidates who couldn't be knocked out but who also couldn't reach the required two-thirds. Then Douglas's floor manager, William A. Richardson of Illinois, gained floor recognition so he could read a letter from his candidate. The Douglas letter informed the delegates that to avoid "an embittered state of feeling" and to foster "harmony of our party," he wished to withdraw his candidacy. The convention exploded in enthusiasm for the outcome and appreciation for Douglas's magnanimity. On the seventeenth and final ballot, Buchanan received the convention's unanimous support. Then delegates selected Kentucky's representative John C. Breckinridge as its vice presidential candidate and adjourned.

That night Cincinnati erupted into "a constant state of excitement" as various clubs from Pennsylvania and elsewhere paraded the streets with huge banners, fireworks, and occasional cannon blasts.

The Buchanan selection reflected the Democrats' view of themselves as the country's only truly national party, positioned to foster intersectional harmony with what they considered sound policies of moderation for both the North and South. In that regard, Buchanan wasn't much different from Pierce in terms of outlook or policies. Both projected themselves as northern men with southern sympathies.

The *Charleston Mercury* captured this neatly in producing three separate articles assuring readers of the Pennsylvanian's soundness on the slavery question. The paper called Buchanan "as acceptable a man as could be presented to support the Southern people" and added it could endorse his nomination "without grimace." Clearly, Buchanan would get most of his electoral votes from the South.

The first national convention of the fledgling Republican Party convened in the Music Fund Hall of Philadelphia on June 17. Waves of exuberance washed over the proceedings as participants contemplated the significance of antislavery sentiment coalescing now under a single party banner. Some two thousand delegates and spectators descended on the city from throughout much of the country, including four border slave states—Delaware, Maryland, Virginia, and Kentucky. None of the eleven states farther south sent delegations, however, because the party had no significant presence there and no prospect of ever having any. But the convention not only invited delegations from the territories of Kansas, Nebraska, and Minnesota, but welcomed them with thunderous cheers.

The hall reverberated with further applause when the names of prominent Republicans of various political backgrounds were called out, reflecting the stature and clear antislavery sentiment of the new party's leadership: Henry Wilson, David Wilmot, Joshua Giddings, Salmon Chase, and William Seward.

So strong was the coalescence that the party platform, just nine resolutions that could be read in less than ten minutes, was approved in a voice vote. It declared the party to be "opposed to the repeal of the Missouri Compromise, to the policy of the present administration, to the extension of slavery into free territory, [and] in favor of the admission of Kansas as a free State." The document further declared that the "dearest constitutional rights of the people of Kansas have been fraudulently and violently taken from them" and that the Constitution gave Congress "sovereign power over the Territories" and thus it had "both the right and the duty . . . to prohibit in the Territories those twin relics of barbarism—polygamy and slavery" (the former a reference to the marital practices of Utah Territory Mormons).

With Seward out of the nomination rivalry and with a similar demurral from Salmon Chase, the nominee candidates narrowed down to just two. One was Supreme Court associate justice John McLean of Ohio, known as a man always looking for the next opportunity. When working in the John Quincy Adams administration years before, he had carried on a political flirtation with Adams's great rival Andrew Jackson, who later gave the wayward functionary the court seat he coveted. He was seventy-one now and drab of temperament—ill-suited, in the view of many, to the zesty ebullience of the rising new party.

McLean's rival was the famous "pathfinder" of the American West, John C. Frémont, just forty-three and a man of impetuous boldness and unquestioned courage. He was an imposing figure, with a full black beard, fiery eyes, and a messianic mode of expression. And his unceasing vibrancy seemed much in keeping with the Republicans' yeasty optimism. The bastard son of a penniless French vagabond and a fallen woman of Virginia society, he set his sights early in life on the attainment of fame and glory. He got both as a U.S. army officer assigned to the Army Corps of Topographical Engineers, under whose auspices he led three remarkable expeditions of western exploration and mapping. (A fourth came later, after his departure from the army.)

It didn't hurt that he had married Jessie Benton, daughter of senator Thomas Hart Benton and a brilliant writer and promoter in her own right. She extracted his stories of adventure and derring-do in the western wilds, sprinkled in elements of human drama, and packaged them into magazine articles and pamphlets that reached wide audiences of avid easterners hungry for knowledge of the country's westward expansion. Soon his story was known throughout the land, generating inspiration for many.

But Frémont didn't always keep his impetuous nature in check. During his third western exploration, he ventured into California, then part of Mexico's sovereign domain, and treated the local military official there with such contempt that he placed his men in serious danger from a far superior Mexican force. Only a plea from the U.S. consul in the area and the specter of a Mexican military buildup persuaded him to slink away.

Later, after news of war with Mexico had arrived and U.S. general Stephen Kearny appeared with a contingent of overland troops, Frémont refused to accept Kearny's superior military status. Eventually he was court-martialed and convicted of three counts of misconduct, including "mutiny" and "conduct to the prejudice of good order and military discipline." His punishment was dismissal from the army. Though President Polk offered to commute the sentence, Frémont opted to end his military career and relocate to California, a state he represented for a time as U.S. senator. In that role he burnished his identity as a staunch slavery opponent by voting for the abolition of Washington, D.C., slave auctions and against legislation providing for stiff prison sentences for those convicted of encouraging or aiding slave escapes.

At the Philadelphia convention, the flamboyant pathfinder, his reputation rehabilitated, cruised to a first-ballot victory with 530 votes out of 567 cast. The party gave the vice presidential nomination to former New Jersey senator William Dayton.

Shortly thereafter, the so-called North American Party (northern Know-Nothings) endorsed the Frémont ticket and essentially merged with the Republicans. And in September the vestigial Whigs gathered in Baltimore with delegates from just twenty-one states and endorsed Fillmore's Know-Nothing candidacy, with Tennessee's Andrew J. Donelson on the ticket for vice president. The Whig platform focused exclusively on the imperative of fighting disunion from the North or South. Thus did the 1856 electoral contest come down to three candidates under five party labels.

Southerners everywhere and many northern Democrats decried the emergence of this new fusion Republican Party and took to calling its members "black Republicans" as a kind of political slur. James Gordon Bennett's *New York Herald* published a piece headlined "Black Republican Balderdash," accusing the new party of fomenting anti-southern hostility as a means of generating Republican votes in the fall election. "An abolitionist cannot lose his baggage without a groan from the same quarter to the effect that the entire North is being despoiled," said the paper.

The *Charleston Mercury* portrayed the political situation more starkly when it warned of the new power center represented by the fusionist Republicans and added that "their intensity has been increased by the war in Kansas, and the 'shrieks for freedom' over Sumner's bloody head." The result was that "the Democratic party will need all its strength in the South to save it from defeat. The contest will be deeply sectional."

The Electoral College calculus facing the candidates demonstrated the truth of that warning. The nation's free states, with 176 electoral votes, outnumbered the slave states in electoral strength by 56 votes. Theoretically, Frémont could win the presidency without any slave states, which he would have to do anyway, as he had no prospect of getting any. But with 149 electoral votes needed for victory, a loss of just 28 electoral votes in the North would spell defeat for the Pathfinder.

For Buchanan, the calculus meant he would have to sweep the South, or nearly so, and also pick up a number of free states—say New York (not likely), or Pennsylvania and Indiana (certainly possible), or some combination of Illinois, Indiana, New Jersey, Michigan, and

California. And even if he pulled that off, any Fillmore success in cutting into Buchanan's southern total could ensure his defeat or possibly throw the election into the House of Representatives. This was new Electoral College math. Since 1828, no presidential candidate had been elected without a bisectional coalition, meaning a majority of votes in both the North and South. Now the candidates were squaring off in what seemed to be largely a sectional contest with virtually no prospect that any of the three candidates could get a majority in both sections.

Attention turned now to Pennsylvania as probably the election's pivotal state, and both campaigns mounted all-out efforts to capture its twenty-seven electoral votes. Democrats spent a reported $500,000 in the state, and the South weighed in heavily, with former House Speaker and Georgia governor Howell Cobb delivering ten Keystone State speeches in ten days, including one in a driving snowstorm. Lancaster staged a rally that drew some fifty thousand persons, including nearly all nationally prominent Democrats and the sons of Henry Clay and Daniel Webster, both traditional Whigs.

Though Buchanan didn't communicate his views or plans to voters during the campaign, he privately expressed fears about the fate of the nation. All other issues became trifling, he wrote a friend, "when compared with the grand and appalling issue of union or disunion." If Frémont won, he added, disunion "will be immediate and inevitable."

He wasn't alone in thinking so. Southern secessionist warnings were rampant now, and many northerners echoed the sentiment, some with almost gleeful satisfaction at the prospect. House Speaker Banks said he was "willing . . . to let the Union slide." Horace Greeley of the *New York Tribune* wrote that the Union "is not worth supporting in connexion with the South." New York's Seward even expressed hopes that events would soon "bring the parties of the country into an aggressive war upon slavery." Joshua Giddings went further, calling for a "servile insurrection," with the black man waging "a war of extermination against his master."

It wasn't clear if such talk, so incendiary and even frightening to many southerners, would drive northern voters to Buchanan as a hedge against southern secession; or if the Democrats' abysmal performance in

Kansas under Franklin Pierce would drive more alienated party members to the new Republican Party.

When the votes were counted, Buchanan emerged the winner, with 174 electoral votes to 114 for Frémont and 8 for Fillmore. The Pennsylvanian secured his victory by capturing all slave states except Maryland (which went to Fillmore) and adding 62 electoral votes from five nonslave states, including the pivot of Pennsylvania as well as California, Illinois, Indiana, and New Jersey. Frémont captured a solid bloc of eleven northern states, but he needed to peel away from Buchanan at least 35 of his 62 nonslave electoral votes. He couldn't do it. In the popular vote, Buchanan garnered 45 percent, to Frémont's 33 percent, and Fillmore's 22 percent.

Buchanan, reflecting the Democratic smugness that emerged after the triumph, told friends that his central presidential aim was to "arrest . . . the agitation of the slavery question at the north, and to destroy sectional parties." This was a remarkable statement given the Republicans' success in getting their party deeply rooted in America's political soil, with 1.3 million votes cast for their candidate in a single region of the country and with a Republican House member sitting in the Speaker's chair.

But Republicans derived a different lesson: that their sectional power, well established now and growing, might actually be sufficient soon to win presidential elections without a single southern state. That was a heady concept. A Pennsylvanian named W. H. Furness wrote to Seward that the party may have lost an election but had gained an entire section of the nation. This represented, he said, the intriguing paradox of a "victorious defeat."

17

BUCHANAN AT THE HELM

|||||||||||||||||||||||||||||||||||||||||||||||||||||||||||||||||||||||||||||||||||

SUPREME COURT DEFIANCE
AND A NEW KANSAS PLAN

I n mid-June 1856, about a month after Preston Brooks's attack on Charles Sumner, Washington's *Weekly Union* published an article debunking reports that the assault had left the senator in a precarious state of health. The reports had been "systematically manufactured," declared the paper, adding, "At no time has Mr. Sumner's condition bordered on the serious."

This was false. Though Sumner appeared initially to be recovering nicely, serious complications quickly set in. He had suffered two deep head gashes reaching to his skull, and one didn't heal properly. A persistent fever and pus discharges suggested a dangerous "septicemia." Then came a new neuralgic pain at the back of the skull, brain sluggishness, difficulty in walking, and long bouts of debilitating fatigue. He went to Francis Blair's country mansion at Silver Spring, Maryland, for recuperation and found himself confined to bed for nearly twenty-two hours a day. William Seward, visiting on July 4, discovered that Sumner's normal "elasticity and vigor" were gone, along with his "vivacity of spirit."

At the end of September his doctor, Marshall Perry, concluded, "From the time of the assault to the present, Mr. Sumner has not been in a situation to expose himself to mental or bodily excitement without the risk of losing his life."

And yet Sumner detractors continued to accuse him of "shamming" his injuries to galvanize a Republican sympathy vote in the fall elections. The *Boston Courier* suggested he was "playing the political possum," while the *Boston Post* accused the senator's doctors of participating in a conspiracy of distortion regarding his health. Sumner complained that if anything could add to his misery "it is this supplementary assault on my character."

The ramifications of his ordeal went beyond his own medical condition or the partisan crosscurrents that had buffeted him throughout his Senate tenure. As a victim of villainy, he gained sympathy and hence influence. Before the attack, Governor Gardner had planned to challenge the senator when his reelection came up before the legislature early in the new year. That wasn't feasible now, so Gardner instead got himself elected to a third gubernatorial term. As George Hillard, Sumner's old law partner, mused, Providence favored Republicans, and "Sumner is not merely their champion but their martyr, and his election for the next six years is now certain."

That was accentuated on November 3, the day before the national elections, when Sumner's Boston backers staged a celebratory procession through the city to honor the fallen statesman. The parade stretched over a mile and a half and featured some eight hundred horsemen and untold numbers of festooned carriages. It began in Brookline at the home of Amos Lawrence, who suppressed for the day his longtime dislike of the senator, and snaked its way through the city to Beacon Hill and the statehouse. A Newton Street banner proclaimed: "Massachusetts loves and honors and will sustain and defend her noble Senator."

Along the way Sumner met with the venerable Josiah Quincy, a former state legislator, congressman, and Harvard president, who expressed satisfaction that "now, at last, the free States are beginning to awaken to a sense of their dangers and their duties" regarding slavery. In brief remarks, Sumner noted Quincy's kind reference to "the suffering which I have undergone" and labeled it a small matter "compared with that tale of woe which is perpetually coming to us from the house of bondage!"

At the statehouse, Gardner himself welcomed Sumner "from your field of intellectual victory—and . . . your bed of pain and suffering." Sumner replied that he felt "constrained to confess that I am still an invalid—cheered, however, by the assurance that I shall soon, with un-impaired vigor be permitted to assume all the responsibilities of my position." With characteristic felicity of phrase, he promised to "perse-vere, against all temptation, against all odds, against all perils, against all threats—knowing well that, whatever may be my fate, the right will surely prevail."

In reporting the day's festivities, the *Boston Evening Transcript* con-firmed that Sumner did indeed appear "like an invalid—pale, and suf-fering from weakness." At the State House he spoke only a few sentences before giving his notes to reporters for publication. But he ended the day with added stature, and the *Evening Transcript* even suggested the celebration represented "a popular demonstration equalling the ova-tions of civic triumphs in Rome during the palmy days of the republic."

When the Massachusetts legislature began its new session a couple months later, it promptly awarded Sumner a second term—with a vote of 333 to 12 in the House, unanimously in the Senate. Still suffering from intermittent pain and fatigue, Sumner delayed his Washington return until February, when an important tariff bill beckoned. He lin-gered in Washington long enough to be sworn in and then sailed for Europe on March 7, three days after the Buchanan inauguration, to begin what he hoped would be a convalescent sojourn.

Sumner's reelection revealed a powerful new reality of Massachu-setts politics: a decade of civic turmoil over slavery was ending. It had begun with the widening split between the Cotton Whigs and the Conscience Whigs, reflected in the controversies surrounding Daniel Webster's Senate speech of March 7, 1850, and in Robert Winthrop's subsequent career implosion. It continued with the emergence of the disruptive Free Soil movement under the state leadership of Henry Wilson; then with the Democratic–Free Soil coalition that had given Democrats a brief moment of ascendancy while ushering Charles Sumner into the Senate; then with the unexpected Know-Nothing tidal wave and Wilson's brief flirtation with Henry Gardner, making Gardner governor and Wilson a senator; then with the remarkable Whig decline and the Know-Nothing deflation; and finally with the Republican rise.

Now the state was moving into a new era of one-party dominance that would be both pronounced and long. In the 1856 presidential contest, Frémont collected nearly 60 percent of the Massachusetts vote with his resolve to quash any further extension of slavery, while accepting it in states where it already existed. Of course, fervent antislavery warriors such as Garrison, Phillips, and Parker dismissed the new party as feckless, but they didn't gain much favor against the Republicans' more moderate formula. The state's Democrats, meanwhile, couldn't get a foothold, and Fillmore's northern American Party fizzled as slavery expansion superseded the Catholic influx as the preeminent concern of the day.

All this placed Republicans in command of the state. Of the next seventeen Massachusetts governors after Gardner, fourteen would be Republicans. The Senate seat held by Sumner would remain in Republican hands for the next sixty-nine years; Wilson's seat, for the next sixty-two years. Of course, disagreements would emerge within the new party over the best approach of ending slavery, the acceptable pace of change, and the most effective means of building and maintaining a strong political base. And disunion abolitionists would continue to carp. But there was plenty of common ground now on the fundamentals: opposition to the Fugitive Slave Act; opposition to the Missouri Compromise repeal; and Congress's right to preclude slavery in the territories and the District of Columbia and the imperative of doing so. Republicans now enjoyed a sway in the state that for decades had been held by the powerful Whig Party of Daniel Webster.

James Buchanan's inauguration unfolded in typical fashion as a celebration of a democratic tradition that was "unequaled by that conferred by any imperial or royal crown," as the *Daily Union* expressed it. The paper added that the civic ritual drew to Washington "an immense concourse of citizens," including "gallant cavaliers of the Old Dominion . . . descendants of the austere Puritans of the Bay State . . . merchants of crowded Atlantic cities . . . [and] adventurous pioneers from the Pacific." Washington's *Evening Star* even noted the presence of two young Pennyslvanians who had walked sixty miles just to witness the spectacle.

It began "most auspiciously," added the *Star*, "with bright skies and a deliciously bland atmosphere." The day featured cannon salutes, martial music, prancing steeds, military units in formation, and a "mosaic of humanity" crowded upon Pennsylvania Avenue sidewalks as the inaugural procession made its way from the White House to the Capitol. The presidential carriage, carrying outgoing president Pierce, picked up Buchanan at Willard's Hotel, at Fourteenth Street, and the two Democratic heavyweights rode together to the Capitol, where thousands had gathered in front of the building's east portico to hear the new president's inaugural address and to witness his promise to "preserve, protect and defend the Constitution of the United States."

Buchanan's inaugural speech hailed the November electoral outcome as a harbinger of civic serenity. When the vote was rendered, he proclaimed, "the tempest at once subsided and all was calm." This was a tribute, he said, to the power of the democratic ideal, based upon fealty to majority rule and the Constitution.

"What a happy conception, then," continued Buchanan, "was it for Congress to apply this simple rule, that the will of the majority shall govern, to the settlement of the question of domestic slavery in the Territories," including Kansas. The doctrine of popular sovereignty, so fervently embraced by Democrats, would guide the nation through the crisis and into an era of civic harmony, so long as the government guaranteed to every resident citizen of the territories an opportunity to vote on the slavery question. "This sacred right of each individual must be preserved," said Buchanan, suggesting that mere legislative action or a vote of convention delegates wouldn't suffice to settle such weighty territorial questions.

Of course, he acknowledged, disagreements persisted as to the point within the territorial status when the people should decide, or be allowed to decide, whether the embryo state would accept or reject slavery. But this was a trifling matter, he averred, best left to the Supreme Court—which, as it happened, was about to issue a seminal decision regarding the status of slavery in America. "To their decision," declared Buchanan, "in common with all good citizens, I shall cheerfully submit, whatever this may be." And thus, concluded Buchanan, with popular sovereignty in place and timing details left to the court, "everything of a practical nature has been decided" and "[n]o other question remains for adjustment."

This passage betrayed two attributes of the incoming president destined to tangle up his leadership. One was an intellectual rigidity that clouded his perception of political reality, accentuated by a tendency to surround himself with like-minded figures disinclined to question his views. The other was a willingness to dissemble, even to the American people, when it served his purposes. Certainly his rigidity of thought contributed to his inability to perceive the significance of the rising Republican Party and the political threat it posed to Democrats and their cherished concept of popular sovereignty. He had dedicated himself to the political destruction of sectional parties at a time when the opposition was gaining enough strength in just one region to vie seriously for the White House and when his own party's status as a national institution was challenged by the election returns of the previous November.

And, in assuring the American people that he would "cheerfully submit" to the looming court decision, "whatever this may be," he neglected to mention that he already knew the gist of the decision because of inappropriate communications with two justices. He had in fact urged one of them to vote on the matter as he desired. Hence his promise to abide by the ultimate decision was an empty one resting upon a foundation of dishonesty.

The court case at issue, *Dred Scott v. Sandford*, was the culmination of a judicial drama that had rumbled through the legal system for eleven years without much notice until recently. It concerned the fate of the slave Dred Scott, who in 1830, at around age thirty-one, became the property of an army surgeon named John Emerson, who lived at the time near St. Louis, Missouri. In 1836 Emerson was assigned to a military installation in Illinois, rendered a free state by the 1787 Northwest Ordinance and also by the state constitution. A year later Emerson moved to Fort Snelling, in a portion of the Wisconsin Territory that later became the state of Minnesota. This also was a non-slave region, based on the Missouri Compromise prohibition of slavery above the latitude of 36°30'. Emerson took Dred Scott with him to both locations.

In 1838 the doctor returned to St. Louis along with Scott, who had married a slave woman in the interim. Five years later Emerson died, leaving Scott, his wife, and two daughters in the possession of his widow, Irene. Scott sought to buy his family's freedom from Mrs. Emerson, but she refused. So he sued her based on the legal thesis that his freedom had been conferred by virtue of his having been taken onto free soil for extended periods.

There was plenty of precedence for this. The Missouri Supreme Court had ruled numerous times that slaves taken from that state into areas of freedom would become free, and Scott won a favorable ruling from a Missouri court based on that principle. Mrs. Emerson promptly appealed, and the case reached the Missouri Supreme Court in 1852.

By that time slavery had taken on a far more emotional aspect, in Missouri as elsewhere, and the state's high court wasn't about to issue what amounted to an antislavery opinion. It ruled for Mrs. Emerson. The opinion, written by Judge William Scott, repulsed the idea that Missouri must accept the laws of free states or territories on matters related to slavery in Missouri. Judge Scott justified the court's turnaround by arguing that "a dark and fell spirit in relation to slavery" had descended upon America and threatened "the overthrow and destruction of our government."

Dred Scott's lawyer, Roswell Field, wouldn't give up, though. The antislavery advocate filed a new lawsuit in the U.S. Circuit Court in

St. Louis. Cleverly based on a constitutional provision that gave federal courts jurisdiction over controversies between persons from different states, the suit argued that Dred Scott was a free citizen of Missouri based on his previous residence in Illinois and the Wisconsin Territory. As such, he had standing to file a federal lawsuit challenging the contention that he remained a slave. The lawsuit identified a new defendant, New York resident John Sanford, Mrs. Emerson's brother and the executor of John Emerson's estate. Field's federal lawsuit accused Sanford of trespass in that he had held the former slave against his will. (A court reporter, in recounting the proceedings, misspelled Sanford's name—hence the discrepancy.)

Sanford's lawyer, Hugh Garland, argued that Scott wasn't a citizen of Missouri, and hence couldn't sue anyone in federal court, for the simple reason that he was black—or, as a Garland motion put it, "because he is a negro of African descent; his ancestors were of pure African blood and were brought into this country and sold as negro slaves."

When the case reached U.S. Circuit Court judge Robert Wells in 1854, the judge ruled that Scott's race didn't preclude citizenship and therefore didn't constitute a barrier to his right to file a federal lawsuit. But his jury instruction suggested that Scott had relinquished his status as a freeman when he voluntarily returned to Missouri and put himself under the jurisdiction of Missouri law. The jury embraced that reasoning in ruling for the defendant. Dred Scott could not sue because he was still a slave.

Field promptly filed an appeal to the U.S. Supreme Court and recruited Montgomery Blair, of the prominent Maryland family, to assist in the appeal. It was widely perceived by this time that the case now encompassed potentially far-reaching constitutional issues: whether a black freedman could be a citizen with a right to file a federal lawsuit; whether a slave's residence in a free state or territory conferred freedom; and even—if the Court chose to take up the question—whether the Missouri Compromise of 1820 was in fact unconstitutional, as argued by Sanford's lawyers, Reverdy Johnson and Henry Geyer.

Here's where the story of the illiterate but implacable freedom seeker Dred Scott intersected with the twilight career of Roger B. Taney, nearly eighty, a powerful presence on the political scene for the past three decades as Maryland attorney general, prominent cabinet official under Andrew Jackson, and chief justice of the U.S. Supreme Court for more than twenty years. He was a bookish, purposeful figure whose views and attitudes sometimes seemed subject to fluctuation and internal contradiction.

As a young man, for example, he embraced the Federalist faith in governmental power at the national level in the spirit of Alexander Hamilton and Henry Clay. Later he converted, with equal zeal, to the ethos of Jacksonian democracy with its call for limited government, low tariffs, and strict constitutional adherence. Also, although the scion of Maryland's old tobacco aristocracy, he nevertheless publicly abhorred the "galling chain of slavery" and the "wretched condition of the slave." Over time, and with no fanfare, he freed his own slaves. And yet he recoiled at the idea of social or political equality for blacks, whom he seemed to regard as appropriately consigned to a permanent underclass status.

When he became chief justice, anxious Whigs and former Federalists issued dire predictions that he would interject his Jacksonian zeal into court proceedings with such force as to shred the fabric of society. And yet, while he did in fact nudge the court away from the nationalist and pro-government sentiments of his predecessor, John Marshall, he did so with a light touch and respect for civic continuity and calm. So highly did members of Congress come to regard Taney's court leadership that William Seward at one point sought to get congressional authorization for the commission of a bust of the chief justice to be produced even as he sat on the bench, though such honors had never been awarded before death. Taney, said Seward, "has already earned the sculptor's reward. Let it be awarded by his contemporaries."

Now the chief justice, physically infirm but retaining his "alacrity and force of mind," faced momentous judicial decisions over how bold or how circumspect the court should be in adjudicating the fraught Dred Scott case. With five southern justices on the court and four northerners, Taney initially sought to avoid a far-reaching ruling that would unleash sectional passions and roil the nation. That meant a narrow opinion that would defer to Missouri's contention that Scott remained a slave despite his residence in free-state Illinois and free-territory Wisconsin. That in turn meant Scott, as a slave, was not a citizen and could not initiate a lawsuit. This approach would allow the court to sidestep more emotion-packed constitutional questions such as the constitutionality of the Missouri Compromise and the essence of black citizenship.

Taney's plan dissolved, however, when two northern justices, John McLean and Benjamin Curtis, signaled that they would write extensive dissents protesting the lack of full justice for Dred Scott. That prompted the five-man southern majority to insist on a broad opinion addressing the incendiary issues of black citizenship and Congress's constitutional prerogative to establish or prohibit slavery in territories.

At that point Taney assigned the writing of the opinion to himself with a firm intention of issuing a bold and broad ruling and with a clear anticipation that his four southern colleagues would go along. But a narrow 5–4 decision on such a weighty matter wouldn't likely command the desired public support, particularly if the aye votes were all from southerners. As the process unfolded at the court, Justice John Catron of Tennessee asked president-elect Buchanan to write to Justice Robert Grier of Pennsylvania, urging him to join in the Taney ruling. Buchanan did so and received a reply from Grier saying he had shared the Buchanan letter with Taney and another southern justice, James Wayne, and had made his decision. "On conversation with the chief justice," he wrote, "I have *agreed to concur with him.*" In recounting this inappropriate back-channel intrigue, historian Kenneth M. Stampp writes, "Thus, three southern justices, one compliant northern justice, and the President-elect made a pawn of Dred Scott in a game of judicial politics."

On the morning of March 6, 1857, just two days after the Buchanan inauguration, Chief Justice Taney entered the Supreme Court chamber on the Capitol's ground floor and commenced to read his fifty-five-page ruling in the case of *Dred Scott v. John F. A. Sandford*, an argument embraced by six of the nine Supreme Court justices. Feeble of body and weak of voice, he nevertheless held forth for two hours, issuing bludgeon words that were breathtaking in their sweep, dogmatism, defiance, and, for many, perversity. He sought to cut through the intensifying slavery contention of the past eight years by simply declaring one side of the debate to be largely outside the bounds of the Constitution. In the process he delivered a powerful blow to the Republican Party's fundamental rationale for existence and reduced all American blacks to a permanent state of subordination.

The ruling declared that Dred Scott could not file a lawsuit in a U.S. court because blacks in America, whether enslaved or free, "were not included, and not intended to be included, under the word 'citizen' in the Constitution." The ruling accepted the right of states to grant Americans of African descent privileges of citizenship equal to those of whites, but that would not confer any such status within the framework of the federal government or within any other state. The ruling acknowledged that public opinion regarding slavery and people of African descent had changed since the early years of the republic, with more sympathy and regard for them throughout much of the country. But the thoughts and feelings prevalent at the time of the founding must prevail, insisted Taney.

Purporting to review European thought upon the North American continent for at least a century before the Declaration of Independence and the U.S. Constitution were produced, Taney wrote that blacks had "been regarded as being of an inferior order, and altogether unfit to associate with the white race, either in social or political relations, and so far inferior, that they had no rights which the white man was bound to respect." This broad and stark statement was contradicted, of course, by vast amounts of history that Taney chose to ignore.

His reasoning was equally contorted and slipshod in his declaration that the Missouri Compromise was unconstitutional and that Congress lacked any legitimate power to prohibit slavery in the territories. Fully embracing the southern point of view, Taney stated that only the voters of each territory could make such decisions and only when they applied for statehood. Thus did he confer on southern slaveholders a constitutional right, superior to congressional prerogative or voter sentiment, to carry slaves into territorial lands prior to any statehood application. This meant, in practical terms, as Buchanan quickly declared, that all territories were essentially slave territories prior to statehood.

In rendering such sweeping judgments, Taney faced a nettlesome precedent: a statute enacted by the 1st Congress embracing the 1787 Northwest Ordinance, including its prohibition of slavery throughout those vast tracts of unorganized western lands known as the Northwest Territory. Taney simply brushed aside the precedent by declaring that no future Congress could do what the 1st Congress had done because the framers hadn't authorized it. Thus did he strike down the Missouri Compromise prohibition of slavery above latitude 36°30', already repealed by Congress, but now also placed beyond any congressional reach.

As for Dred Scott, Taney stated that he remained a slave because, as a Missouri resident, he was subject to Missouri law. This had been the judgment of the Missouri Supreme Court in 1852 and the U.S. Circuit Court in 1854. It also was consistent with an earlier Supreme Court decision, written by Taney, establishing that state law controlled the status of slaves within state boundaries. Many legal scholars at the time believed that this simple determination could be defended as a legal precept. But by grafting onto it his vast and sweeping legal and social pronouncements, with "strained reasoning and meager documentation," as historian James F. Simon has written, Taney shocked vast numbers of Americans, further inflamed intersectional tensions, and wiped away his own reputation for fairness and sound judgment, forged over two decades of jurisprudence.

The impact of the decision was immediate and immense. It devastated the philosophical underpinning of the North's antislavery argument, as expressed perhaps most eloquently by Charles Sumner in his famous Freedom National speech of 1852. This was the idea that freedom was national while slavery was local. As Sumner had argued, freedom was enshrined in the Declaration of Independence with its emphasis on equality, in the framers' avoidance of the word "slave" in the Constitution, and in the widespread view that slavery would wither away naturally, and certainly wouldn't expand, so long as the federal government remained aloof from what was essentially a state institution.

But now the court was inserting the national government directly into the slavery controversy in ways that designated the institution of bondage as distinctly national, to be protected by the federal government, while freedom was merely a state matter. The ruling, wrote the *New York Evening Post* in a piece reprinted in Garrison's *Liberator*, "has stripped Congress of a power to exclude slavery from the territories, which has been exercised by every President . . . from Washington." This, added the paper, meant that political control of the government had been transferred "to the hands of the slave oligarchy, beyond the possibility of a recovery by the free States for their fair share of influence." The *Milwaukee Sentinel* said the U.S. flag now "carries slavery wherever it waves!"

How to explain such a judicial ruling from a man who had expressed his abhorrence of bondage in unmistakable terms, had set free his own slaves, and had meticulously crafted an image as a particularly measured jurist? It seems that by 1857 he had developed nagging concerns about northern encroachments upon southern independence and the southern way of life, intensified by a growing hatred of fiery northern abolitionists bent on destroying slavery even if it meant destroying the South in the process and perhaps even the Union. As historian Simon has written, Taney thought he could help protect the Union from further destabilizing contention if he could expunge from the national debate the flammable issues of black citizenship, the Missouri Compromise, and territorial procedures for settling the slavery question. In the process he just might also checkmate the rising and threatening Republican Party.

This thinking meshed with President Buchanan's resolve to subdue the vexing slavery issue once and for all, while thwarting the Republican rise. The key, as the new president well knew, was Kansas, that suppurating canker of a territory that had infected the nation for nearly three years. Recognizing that the recent influx of northern settlers now rendered untenable the southern vision of a Kansas slave state, Buchanan calculated that, if he could get the South to accept that reality, he could lead the nation to a new post-Kansas equilibrium. Republican anxieties about the spread of slavery could be assuaged, while the South would be reassured that the institution would be protected where it existed. After all, slavery didn't seem to be economically feasible in the other western territories, so future Kansas-like embroilments appeared unlikely. And Taney's Dred Scott ruling, as Buchanan saw it, should reassure southerners that their cherished bondage system was protected.

Buchanan's first act regarding Kansas was to fire Pierce's third territorial governor there. He was John Geary of Pennsylvania, a Mexican War veteran and former California official who had managed to establish a tenuous peace in Kansas after arriving on September 9, 1856. But the president wanted a man of greater consequence and reputation.

He turned to Mississippian Robert J. Walker, a wisp of a man weighing barely a hundred pounds, with a "wheezy voice" and beset by chronic ill health. But he was one of his generation's most cunning political operatives, often at the center of intrigues of civic significance and, sometimes, personal financial gain. Born to wealth and prominence in Pennsylvania, he fled his state's sluggish elite to embrace the more open and raucous society of Mississippi, where he emerged as a successful lawyer, planter, and land speculator. He served in the U.S. Senate and in James Polk's cabinet, then pursued numerous high-stakes speculations in the areas of railroad development, mining ventures, and the construction of a canal through Central America. At age fifty-five, the bold visionary couldn't quite resist vague thoughts of someday winning the presidency.

The idea of going to Kansas sharpened those vague thoughts. Though initially reluctant to enter such a political snake pit, he soon began to envision the rewards of success in terms of added political stature. But, knowing of Buchanan's reputation for southern sympathies and bent on cutting through the welter of conflicting passions surrounding the fate of Kansas, Walker first wanted assurances that he would be allowed to foster a new election, entirely fair and unassailable, as the means of pacifying the territory.

He wrote a letter to Buchanan outlining his understanding that the president and his cabinet "cordially concurred in the opinion expressed by me, that the actual bona fide residents of the territory of Kansas, by a fair and regular vote, unaffected by fraud or violence, must be permitted, in adopting their State Constitution, to decide for themselves what shall be their social institutions." Buchanan replied that the question of slavery in Kansas would be "submitted to the people of the territory."

But Walker didn't leave it there. In a visit with Buchanan before his departure, he reviewed with the president the language of his proposed inaugural address. It contained a passage that read, "In no contingency will Congress admit Kansas as a slave state or free state, unless a majority of the people of Kansas shall first have fairly and freely decided this question for themselves by a direct vote on the adoption of the Constitution, excluding all fraud or violence." Again, Buchanan promptly concurred in the language without reservation.

Fortified by these assurances that his plan coincided with Buchanan's intentions, Walker set out to subdue the territorial turbulence of Kansas and give the president a signal political victory, while fashioning for the nation a new dawn of civic affinity—and enhancing his own national standing in the bargain.

BUTLER DEPARTS

|||||||||||||||||||||||||||||||||||||||||||||||||||||||||||||||||||||||||||||||||||||||

DEATH, AMBITION,
AND KANSAS MANEUVERING

When the final session of the 34th Congress adjourned on March 3, 1857, Pickens Butler returned to Edgefield, South Carolina, feeling ill. Doctors diagnosed his ailment as dropsy, an abnormal accumulation of bodily fluid. It can be serious, reflecting failure of the heart, liver, or kidneys. But the senator's doctors didn't perceive any such immediate threat, reported Butler's friend William Boyce, a South Carolina congressman, "so that the rapid and fatal termination of his disease was in a great degree unexpected." He died less than three months after his return home.

South Carolina courts adjourned all sessions for twenty-four hours, and the Charleston Bar convened a gathering for eulogies. An oft-repeated theme was that the senator's departure would leave a large gap in South Carolina politics and throughout official Washington. "It may be truly said," pronounced the prominent lawyer James Petigru, "that there is no man left in South Carolina whose death would create so great a sensation." Virginia's James Mason, from the old F Street Mess, added a recognition of his personal rectitude. "Distrust and suspicion were at once disarmed at his presence," said the senator.

Prospects for Butler's Senate seat soon narrowed down to three: Francis Pickens, former state legislator and nine-year congressman; the winsome young state legislator James Chesnut; and the old standby, James Henry Hammond, who greeted with deep ambivalence the prospect of returning to public life after thirteen years as a private citizen. Just three months earlier, Hammond had rejected entreaties that he seek the U.S. House seat vacated when Preston Brooks, still draped in controversy, died unexpectedly at Brown's Hotel in Washington, D.C.

It was a horrible death, brought on by what seemed initially to be merely an inflamed throat. But then a sudden attack of croup besieged his lungs and suppressed his breathing. According to reports, he suffered intensely and even sought to tear open his throat to get air. Highly polarizing in life, so also in death did Brooks divide the nation into those who lamented his passing and those who welcomed it.

Washington's *Evening Star*, a Democratic paper, called Brooks a "sincerely beloved hero" and framed its obituary in a mournful black border. The paper hailed the "sorrow-stricken citizens" who crowded into the lobby at Brown's to honor the deceased. But Garrison's *Liberator*, while conceding Brooks's following of "personal friends," suggested that most others felt that "the wrath of man was avenged in the justice of God." Garrison published a poem for the occasion that read in part:

Who, like a caitiff base and low
Came treacherously upon his foe,
And stunned him with a murderous blow?
Preston Brooks!

Who, sent, his country's laws to make,
And, bound to obey them for her sake,
Dared hers and Honor's laws to break?
Preston Brooks!

Who, when his victim senseless lay,
Cold and inanimate as clay,
His brutal hand refused to stay?
Preston Brooks!

Down in South Carolina the nearly universal acclaim accorded
Brooks didn't delay the selection of a successor. When other major candidates offered to withdraw in favor of James Hammond, he declined
"explicitly and decidedly," even getting Edgefield's leading newspaper to
publish a strong defense of his resolve to stay out of the fray. It wasn't
that Hammond's long consignment to private life had slaked his thirst
for fame and glory through civic achievement. He continued to brood
over his fate as a thwarted would-be statesman and to shift back and
forth between accepting responsibility for his circumstances and seeking
to avoid it at all costs.

Hammond attributed his decision to ill health, but that posed a persistent question: What exactly was this malady that he so often blamed
for his misfortunes and for his own wickedness? Certainly he suffered
from some sort of anxiety disorder, accompanied by an often debilitating
chronic fatigue. It is impossible to discern the origin of these problems
or any connection to the psychological despondency inherent in his
craving for a level of distinction that seemed increasingly unattainable.

So he wandered through the slough of despond with as much grit as
he could muster, while struggling to buck up his self-esteem in the face
of life's disappointments and what numerous diary entries suggested
was a powerful strain of subliminal guilt. In 1855, he bought a four-
hundred-acre estate at the little town of Beech Island, about six miles
north of the old family seat at Silver Bluff, and commenced to build a
mansion on the property, which he christened "Redcliffe." The project,
wrote Hammond biographer Drew Gilpin Faust, was a "diversion for
himself and . . . a gesture of reconciliation to his wife," who that same
year resumed living with her husband in what was an uneasy marriage.

To Hammond the property was a "beautiful situation, susceptible
of magnificent improvements and has the finest view in the middle
country." But he couldn't help wishing he had purchased it years before

instead of establishing his retreat at Columbia and entering into the fateful lechery with the Hampton girls. He speculated with a hint of self-reproach: "How would my career differed from what it has been!!" Though certain that he possessed talents "equal to, if not superior to, any public man in this country," he opted for a simpler life. "I want repose," he wrote to his diary.

R obert Walker arrived at Leavenworth, Kansas Territory, in late May and delivered his inaugural address at Lecompton on May 27. He sought conciliation within the context of the political and demographic realities of the territory, reflected in a series of numbers that Walker quickly pulled together into a report for Buchanan. According to Walker's analysis, Kansas settlers numbered around 24,000, with a breakdown as follows: free-state Democrats, 9,000; Republicans, 8,000; proslavery Democrats, 6,500; proslavery Know-Nothings, 500. Thus, the antislavery men outnumbered proslavery settlers 17,000 to 7,000, while Democrats outnumbered those from other parties by 15,500 to 8,500.

Those numbers cheered Buchanan, who wanted not only to stanch the bleeding of Kansas but also to forge it into a Democratic state. For Walker the numbers gave hope that he might be able to cajole the antislavery elements, under the leadership of Charles Robinson, to abandon their upstart Topeka government and ply their political talents within the Washington-recognized Lecompton structure. After all, the antislavery forces now commanded a strong territorial majority and therefore would ultimately prevail in territorial politics. Specifically, Walker wanted the antislavery forces to abandon their longtime boycott of Lecompton elections and to participate in the scheduled June balloting for delegates to a constitutional convention slated for September at Lecompton. Walker addressed this and other challenges in his inaugural speech with a number of sharply delineated points.

First, he sought to disabuse free-state settlers of any thought that their Topeka governing structure could ever supplant the Lecompton government, which was recognized by Congress as legitimate. Whatever abuses it may have committed in the past, it now must serve as the territory's government, with whatever reforms that might be necessary to prevent future abuses. By opposing the Lecompton government, Walker warned the Robinson forces, "you resist the authority of the Federal Government," a dangerous approach.

Second, if free-state men boycotted the convention-delegate elections, they must nonetheless accept the electoral outcome as legitimate. "[T]hose who abstain from the exercise of the right of suffrage," declared the governor, "authorize those who do vote to act for them in that contingency."

Third, the ultimate remedy for any abuse of process involving the convention-delegate voting or the actions of the convention lay in Walker's commitment, embraced by President Buchanan, to ensure that the constitutional document created by the Lecompton convention would be submitted to Kansas voters for ratification or rejection. "I repeat then, as my clear conviction," stated Walker, "that unless the Convention submit the Constitution to the vote of all the actual resident settlers of Kansas, and the election be fairly and justly conducted, the Constitution will be, and ought to be, rejected by Congress."

Fourth, Kansas wasn't likely ever to become a slave state because of what Walker called "the law of the thermometer, of latitude or altitude, regulating climate, labor and productions, and as a consequence, profit and loss." Kansas couldn't produce the kinds of staple crops that rendered slave labor economically feasible, and that reality needed to be understood and accepted by the proslavery men of Kansas as well as those of Missouri and, indeed, the entire South.

Finally, Walker hinted that southerners might pin their hopes for another slave state on the remaining Indian lands sandwiched between Kansas and Texas, which likely would be open to white settlement at some point in the future. That could greatly expand U.S. production of the slave crop of cotton.

Walker's five central points constituted the pillars of his plan to end the war in Kansas. It didn't take long for all five to crumble.

In June the free-staters adamantly refused to participate in the balloting for convention delegates because they didn't trust Lecompton officials. Thus, with many proslavery candidates running unopposed, voters sent to the September convention a large majority of avid proslavery men. This posed a big problem for Walker, as the convention now seemed certain to send to Washington a governing document establishing bondage in the new state, when in fact the prevailing sentiment in the territory was against slavery. But at least the governor had the backup assurance of "submission"—that the eventual constitution would be submitted to the people for ratification or rejection, thus protecting popular sovereignty and Walker's hope that the eventual outcome would reflect the majority feeling of Kansans.

But southern partisans, refusing to accept an antislavery outcome, quickly set out to kill the submission idea. Eliminate submission, they figured, and the constitutional convention could produce a proslavery document, get it approved by the Democratic-controlled Congress in Washington, and win the state for the South. It was transparently cynical and essentially undemocratic, but it reflected a new sense of urgency emerging throughout the slave domain.

Indeed, southern leaders were feeling both beleaguered and emboldened—beleaguered by the rise of the Republican Party as a northern juggernaut of antislavery zeal, and emboldened by a decade of institutional victories, including the fugitive slave law, the Missouri Compromise repeal, the bold Kansas initiatives, and the Supreme Court's Dred Scott decision. To survive, they calculated, they must leverage these victories into an expansion of the country's slave territory to counter the increasingly powerful Republican North. That meant Kansas must become a slave state, along with the remaining Indian lands south of Kansas and also nearby Cuba, which many southerners wanted America to acquire through purchase or war. A sentiment was building throughout the South that the region must pursue aggressive expansionism.

Thus did Robert Walker become the new southern villain, denounced and censured by Democratic state conventions in Georgia and Mississippi and by the Alabama senate. Newspapers throughout the region attacked him bitterly. "Governor Walker," declared the *Charleston*

Mercury, "can deceive no one by his bullying policy." The paper dismissed as "baseless vaporing" Walker's threat that Congress would reject a constitution that hadn't been submitted for approval by Kansas voters.

In fact it wasn't clear what Buchanan would do now with the South in revolt over the submission question. The president wasn't particularly known for steadfastness in the face of adversity, and the southern attack represented a serious thrust of adversity. As Georgia senator Robert Toombs wrote to a Baltimore friend, "Was there ever such folly as this Walker has been playing in Kansas? Buchanan intends to sustain him, and thereby ruin himself and his administration." The implication was clear: if Buchanan supported Walker's call for submission, the South would abandon him, upend his administration, and probably destroy Democratic prospects in the next presidential election.

But Buchanan displayed no sign of wavering. On July 12 he wrote to Walker, "On the question of submitting the constitution to the bona fide resident settlers of Kansas, I am willing to stand or fall." At stake, he said, was popular sovereignty, which he called "the foundation of all popular government."

It turned out that Walker's most menacing enemies were the president's closest advisers. In late July and early August, while Buchanan was away at Bedford Springs, Pennsylvania, recuperating from an infirmity, some cabinet members sought to traduce the Kansas governor with confidential communications to the president. The ostensible issue was a Walker request to the cabinet (in Buchanan's absence) for two thousand federal troops to confront what Walker considered a dangerous act of defiance by free-state Kansans at Lawrence.

Cass and war secretary John Floyd of Virginia considered the request excessive, reflecting poor judgment and perhaps revealing a self-serving desire by Walker to deflect criticism that he had become too cozy with free-state Kansans. Cass wrote the president, "We all fear that Governor Walker is endeavoring to make a record for the future." For good measure he forwarded to Buchanan a letter to him from Toombs saying that, if the president continued to support Walker, Toombs would abandon the party.

Floyd separately suggested that Walker, stung by the southern onslaught and fearful it would upend his efforts, was looking for someone
to blame, perhaps even Buchanan. "I doubt, now," wrote the war secretary to the president, "whether the investment in Governor Walker is
going to turn out very profitable."

B uchanan now faced a quandary: either respond to cabinet sentiment and fire Walker, with all the political chaos that likely would
ensue, or keep the Walker program in place with his closest advisers in
opposition. With the president in the grip of that dilemma, events unfolded in rapid succession through the remainder of the year.

On September 7, delegates to the much-anticipated constitutional
convention assembled at Lecompton, but promptly suspended deliberations until October 19, after legislative elections scheduled for October
1, so convention delegates could consider those ballot results in their
deliberations. Notably, antislavery settlers decided to participate, and
the result was that proslavery forces seemed headed to a narrow margin. But then evidence of massive fraud emerged in two counties: some
1,200 proslavery votes tallied in a location where no balloting had taken
place, and more than 1,600 votes counted where only thirty persons
had actually voted.

Kansas law had designated the territorial courts as arbiter in cases
involving alleged electoral fraud. But Walker, fearing chicanery by proslavery territorial judges, threw out the fraudulent ballots on his own
authority. The resulting recount ensured free-state dominance of the
territorial legislature at its next session. This constituted a pivot point
for Kansas—the first time the free-state majority prevailed in the councils of the territorial government.

But the action set off waves of indignation among proslavery men in
Kansas and elsewhere. They insisted that Walker had broken the law with
a willful intent to pollute the electoral outcome and hand the territory
over to abolitionists. The *Mercury* assailed his "usurpation and outrage,"
by which the Kansas legislature "was converted from a Democratic to a

Black Republican majority." The paper condemned even Buchanan for cowardice in countenancing Walker's actions.

On October 19 the constitutional convention reconvened at Lecompton to begin deliberations on a proposed state constitution. So outraged were proslavery delegates at Walker's election interventions that they nearly voted to send their proslavery draft document directly to Congress, bypassing any validation vote of Kansas citizens. There was little doubt that such an action would have precipitated a new Kansas crisis of fearsome intensity, while squeezing President Buchanan between his submission commitment and his crucial southern constituency.

In the end the Lecompton convention crafted what it considered a compromise approach, labeled "partial submission." It called for a vote of the people on the question of whether Kansas would be free or slave, but disallowed a vote of acceptance or rejection of the full constitution. In other words, the referendum proposed by the convention would be a vote strictly for the "constitution with slavery" or the "constitution without slavery." All other constitutional elements, including the constitution itself, would be sent to Washington without settlers having a chance to vote on them.

Those elements included a twenty-year residency requirement for Kansas governors, a seven-year prohibition on any constitutional amendments, and an exclusion of free blacks from state residence (similar to what the Topeka forces had drafted in their own proposed constitution). Most troublesome for antislavery people was an allowance for current slaveholders in Kansas to remain there with their two hundred or so slaves even if Kansas voters opted for free-state status. Thus the referendum on Kansas as a free or slave state would actually be an election on whether slavery in Kansas would be unlimited or limited. For those who considered the issue to be one of moral principle, this was abhorrent. But the Lecompton convention had framed the issue anew, and proslavery forces now fervently embraced partial submission, while many free-state settlers protested what they considered a repugnant and artfully crafted choice that wasn't really a choice at all.

As these developments unfolded, Robert Walker could see that events had flipped out of his control and that the hostile proslavery forces would never allow his Kansas-pacification program to succeed. Disillusioned, feeling the onset of ill health, and anxious about his investments with a financial panic converging on the nation, the governor retreated to the Leavenworth home of a friend, waited for the convention to adjourn, and then fled the territory for good. There wouldn't be any Walker legacy in Kansas.

But there would be a Frederick Stanton legacy of sorts. Stanton, Kansas territorial secretary under Walker, now was acting governor, and he perceived a desperate need for action designed to align events in the territory with the prevailing antislavery views of its citizens. Though a proslavery Tennessean, he had become disgusted with the bad-faith maneuvers of proslavery Kansans and particularly the action of the con- stitutional convention in crafting the partial-submission referendum. So he called into session the territorial legislature, which now was dom- inated by antislavery men, and recommended that the governing body schedule a separate referendum on the full constitution as crafted by the constitutional convention.

With the partial-submission referendum scheduled for December 21, Stanton argued, a subsequent legislature-sponsored balloting could serve as a kind of second channel of information on Kansas politics for Con- gress to consider in assessing the worthiness of the proposed Lecompton constitution. Both elections would be legal, he said, and neither would be binding on Congress. The legislature complied, and Stanton signed the measure on December 17. The referendum was scheduled for January 4.

Attention now turned to Buchanan. When the president heard of Stanton's action (from the newspapers), he promptly fired the man. The last thing he wanted was the complication of another election and increased prospects for an agitated South. What he needed now was to make partial submission work in order to mollify the slave states and protect his party's prospects in coming national elections. That meant extricating himself from his previous pronouncements implying a com- mitment to ensuring a vote on the full constitution. He would have to finesse the issue through artful argument, though he knew his earlier words would be thrown back at him with considerable vehemence. He set out to craft the finesse in his Annual Message, to be delivered to the new 35th Congress in early December. Soon he learned he was on a collision course with the one man possessing the influence and force to upend his plans. That was Stephen Douglas.

When the Little Giant learned of Buchanan's intention, he rushed to the White House to dissuade the president from what he considered a dangerous course that would undermine his cherished doctrine of true popular sovereignty. But Buchanan would hear none of it. He cautioned that he planned to designate the Lecompton constitution an administration measure when it came before Congress and enforce party loyalty through tough political sanctions. Invoking the names of two Democratic politicians from many years before who famously had run afoul of President Jackson to their detriment, the president warned, "Mr. Douglas, I desire you to remember that no Democrat ever yet differed from the Administration of his own choice without being crushed. Beware the fate of Tallmadge and Rives."

"Mr. President," retorted the feisty Illinoisan, "I wish you to remember that General Jackson is dead, sir."

That set the tone for a classic political struggle between the two most influential and powerful Democratic figures of the day, both accustomed to getting their way through famous attributes of magnetism, determination, wiles, and grit. The clash between the two men would dominate the first session of the 35th Congress from December through the following April.

In the meantime, many in South Carolina turned their attention to the forthcoming legislative balloting for Pickens Butler's old Senate seat. A groundswell seemed to be emerging for Hammond, notwithstanding his disavowal of any interest in the job. A letter writer to the *Mercury*, who signed his name simply THE UPPER COUNTRY, captured the sentiment when he urged state legislators to "go back to the good old days of the republic, when office sought men, and not men office." He added, "Who, of all the living statesmen of South Carolina, has made the mark which [Hammond] has?"

Not only had Hammond's long separation from public life left him free from the weight of recent controversies, but he was known for a political pedigree that went back decades and still resonated with many South Carolinians. It included his service as governor, his effective stint in behalf of John C. Calhoun's ill-fated nullification campaign, his defense of the gag rule against antislavery agitation in the U.S. House of Representatives, and numerous brilliant essays and public letters extolling the virtues of the southern culture and of slavery. Two famous letters to the British abolitionist Thomas Clarkson, writes South Carolina historian and Calhoun scholar Clyde N. Wilson, "constitute possibly the ultimate apologia for the slave system of the Old South." Hammond extolled southern society as a hierarchical order whose distribution of rights and duties, while certainly unequal, was designed "for the welfare of the whole," as Wilson explains it. However abhorrent and evil that concept was, and came to be viewed throughout America, Wilson writes, it "was seldom drawn with more artistry and conviction than by Hammond."

All that contributed to the attention accorded the man in South Carolina as the senatorial election approached in late 1857. When the legislative balloting began on November 27, Hammond led the field with sixty-seven votes, to thirty-nine for Pickens and twenty-four for Chesnut. (Barnwell Rhett, now clearly an also-ran, received just six votes on the first ballot and slipped from the field thereafter.) The following day Hammond captured seventy-one votes, just two short of victory, and the next tally gave him eighty-five votes and the Senate seat he had coveted in his fretful way for most of his adult life.

The Rhett-dominated *Mercury* hailed the victor as "one of the most refined scholars in the country—one of the most learned in its political history." Hammond himself called the development "the strangest and most unexpected chapter of my history, or of almost any history." In pouring his thoughts into his diary, he seemed to say that the victory absolved him of all previous transgressions and nullified every criticism ever leveled against him. "This is a signal triumph over all my enemies," he wrote, "and, speaking as a mere mortal, a full compensation and more for all I have endured. It wipes off every calumny and puts my name among the foremost of SoCa without a stain."

As happened following Hammond's gubernatorial triumph some fifteen years before, he ceased writing in his diary in the afterglow of success. But, in what turned out to be his last entry for two years, he presented himself in all of his self-absorption, self-deception, and bathos: "Oh Lord," he wrote, "I have struggled earnestly and honestly amid all my trials and temptations, my suffering and agony to do right and not to do wrong. Thou has fully repaid me already according to my estimate of deserts and overpaid me. Oh that having confidence in me Thou mayest see fit to enable me, with Thy support, to do *all* that one, placed as I am, might do, if in addition to my willingness, he had the required health, strength and inspiration."

In his gush of excitement at his unexpected good fortune, Hammond expressed his confidence that he could "regulate the affairs of this Country and thereby of the World better than any man living." The question he faced now, as he took his seat in the U.S. Senate, was whether he could help manage the affairs of South Carolina, leaving aside the country and the world, in a time of mounting turmoil and crisis.

1

JOHN C. CALHOUN

2

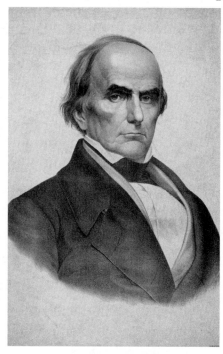

DANIEL WEBSTER

3

HENRY CLAY

As the 1850s dawned and America entered the fearsome slavery crisis, the greatest political figures of their generation—John C. Calhoun, Daniel Webster, and Henry Clay—neared the end of their careers and their lives. By October 1852 all three were gone, and the country grappled with the enveloping crisis without them.

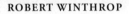

ROBERT WINTHROP

EDWARD EVERETT

6

CHARLES FRANCIS ADAMS

The decade began with Massachusetts dominated by "Cotton Whigs," who opposed slavery but didn't agitate against it. They included Senator Robert Winthrop and the eloquent statesman Edward Everett. But the more ardently antislavery "Conscience Whigs" soon upended their political careers. Charles Francis Adams switched sides and became a leading antislavery spokesman, congressman, and minister to Great Britain.

CHARLES SUMNER

HENRY WILSON

Massachusetts sent to the Senate
two of the nation's leading antislavery combatants: the slashing
rhetorician Charles Sumner and
the backroom deal-maker Henry
Wilson. Both revered the Constitution despite its acceptance
of slavery. The fiery and brilliant
polemicist William Lloyd Garrison, on the other hand, labeled
the Constitution "a covenant
with death and an agreement
with hell."

WILLIAM LLOYD GARRISON

ANDREW PICKENS BUTLER

JAMES HENRY HAMMOND

12

ROBERT BARNWELL RHETT

With Calhoun's death, South
Carolina split into factions personified by three major figures: Senator
Andrew Pickens Butler, a leader of
the "cooperationists" who accepted
secession only in conjunction with
other states; James Henry Hammond,
brilliant but psychologically broken
and prone to scandalous behavior;
and Robert Barnwell Rhett, who
longed for secession even on a
stand-alone basis, with himself at
the helm of a new southern nation.

FRANKLIN PIERCE

JAMES BUCHANAN

With Whigs in eclipse, Democrats sought to dominate politics as a truly national party. Presidents Franklin Pierce and James Buchanan pursued policies that many northerners considered distasteful southern favoritism. Then Chief Justice Roger Taney stunned the nation with his Dred Scott decision, which enraged northerners.

ROGER TANEY

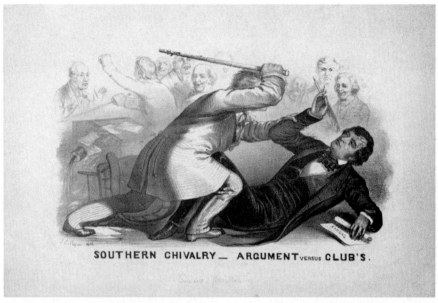

SOUTHERN CHIVALRY — ARGUMENT versus CLUB'S.

DRAWING OF BROOKS BEATING SUMNER

JOHN BROWN

In May 1856 came bloody episodes in Kansas, site of a bitter struggle over whether the territory would enter the Union as free or slave. The free-Kansas town of Lawrence was "sacked" by proslavery ruffians, and a party of cutthroats led by the messianic antislavery rustic John Brown slaughtered five proslavery settlers in cold blood. South Carolina congressman Preston Brooks brutally bludgeoned Senator Sumner with a cane on the Senate floor.

18

Stephen Douglas and
Abraham Lincoln sparred
often as young adversaries
in the Illinois legislature.
Douglas quickly became
a powerful senator while
Lincoln lamented that
"I . . . can hardly be
considered worthy of his
notice." But Lincoln went
after Douglas's Senate
seat in 1858. He lost but
gained national acclaim
for his measured and
eloquent performances
in their debates.

19

ABRAHAM LINCOLN

20

STEPHEN A. DOUGLAS

CHARLESTON

MERCURY

EXTRA:

Passed unanimously at 1.15 o'clock, P. M., December 20th, 1860.

AN ORDINANCE

To dissolve the Union between the State of South Carolina and other States united with her under the compact entitled "The Constitution of the United States of America."

We, the People of the State of South Carolina, in Convention assembled, do declare and ordain, and it is hereby declared and ordained,

That the Ordinance adopted by us in Convention, on the twenty-third day of May, in the year of our Lord one thousand seven hundred and eighty-eight, whereby the Constitution of the United States of America was ratified, and also, all Acts and parts of Acts of the General Assembly of this State, ratifying amendments of the said Constitution, are hereby repealed; and that the union now subsisting between South Carolina and other States, under the name of "The United States of America," is hereby dissolved.

THE

UNION

IS

DISSOLVED!

CHARLESTON MERCURY "EXTRA":
THE UNION IS DISSOLVED

In seeking the presidency in 1860, Lincoln vowed to protect slavery where it existed but also prevent its expansion. That wasn't enough for die-hard southerners bent on ensuring slavery's spread into U.S. territories. On December 20, 1860, South Carolina became the first state to secede. The *Charleston Mercury*, owned by Barnwell Rhett, hailed the action.

RISE OF THE RADICALS

||||||||||||||||||||||||||||||||||||||||||||||||||||||||||||||||||||||||||||||||||

INSURRECTION PLANS AND
A SLAVE-TRADE MOVEMENT

T he editors at South Carolina's *Edgefield Advertiser* became unsettled in late 1857 when it appeared that the forthcoming legislative election for Pickens Butler's old Senate seat wasn't generating the excitement that seemed warranted by the stakes involved. After all, said the paper, the state had always assumed a big civic role as a counterweight to the political philosophy of its great northern rival, Massachusetts. And that required solid representation at the highest governmental levels.

"From the foundation of our Republic there have existed two contending parties in the country, the one leaning to an absolute central government, the other to a simple confederacy of independent States," said the paper, adding that "Massachusetts has always led upon one side, and South Carolina upon the other." This sectional contention emerged in the first years of the republic and reverberated through all the subsequent great debates, including those involving the War of 1812, nullification, the federal bank controversy, and now the intensifying slavery issue.

But the sectional antagonism had spawned a new development affecting both states: the rise of radical thought and even radical action on the part of small but intense interests. In South Carolina a movement emerged to expand slavery throughout the country wherever possible under the imprimatur of the Supreme Court's *Dred Scott* decision—in Kansas, Nebraska, Oregon, the remaining Indian Territory, and also by adding new offshore lands, by conquest if necessary, in places such as the Caribbean and Central America. And, with more slave territory, there must be more slaves, and thus many South Carolinians now argued for resuming the importation of African slaves.

The indecency of this idea was reflected in a jarring, untitled item in the *Charleston Mercury* in January 1855. It noted that the African slave trade was flourishing in Cuba, where three or four slave ships had recently landed. "The last cargo heard of," said the paper matter-of-factly, "was landed near Santa Cruz, and consisted of 317 Africans, some two or three hundred having, it is understood, died on the passage from Africa."

For America, Congress had outlawed this brutal human commerce as of January 1, 1808, based on a provision in the U.S. Constitution barring federal interference in the trade prior to that date but allowing for restrictions afterward. By that time, a widespread opposition to the further importation of African captives had developed, and all states, including all southern states, had enacted prohibitions. In 1820 the U.S. government also declared the prohibited trade to be piracy, which carried the death penalty. But now, nearly forty years later, southern fire-eaters wanted to upend this old consensus in the interest of expanding southern power vis-à-vis the North.

This was a political pipe dream, highly incendiary and thus more likely to intensify the northern attack on slavery than to perpetuate bondage or foster its expansion. But it gained momentum through much of the South, with South Carolina as usual leading the way. And the argument often was accompanied by a threat that, if the plan didn't work, the inevitable next step would be the equally radical option of secession.

A similar embrace of national disunion gained momentum in Massachusetts as many abolitionists rejected the Republican contention that the Constitution protected slavery in the southern states. If that were true, more and more people now argued, then the Union wasn't worth saving. At a Worcester gathering to explore dissolution, Lloyd Garrison called the Union "an insane experiment to reconcile those elements which are eternally hostile." The quickest way to abolish slavery, he argued, was to break up the nation, remove that constitutional protection, and "paralyze the power of the master."

At the same gathering Wendell Phillips attacked Henry Wilson for his embrace of the Republican position. "[I]n no possible contingency, for no possible purpose, will he allow the Union to be touched," complained Phillips. "He is not a fit leader in the Anti-Slavery enterprise, if he lays down any such principle."

Advocating a breakup of the nation was one thing; helping to organize a violent insurrection against the government was quite another. Yet a number of prominent Massachusetts citizens gravitated to a man bent on leading such a revolt. He was the blood-soaked, messianic warrior of the Kansas tumult, John Brown.

F ollowing his murderous night of May 23–24 along Pottawatomie Creek, Brown lingered in Kansas for four months despite the arrest warrant that had been issued for him. This was the time, following the momentous Six Days in May, when Bleeding Kansas truly earned its nickname, and Brown plunged into battle determined to prove his military mettle and gain fame in the process. His anti-Ruffian passion soared when two sons, John Jr. and Jason, were captured by a militia captain and turned over to a federal cavalry officer named Captain Wood. Wood took them in chains to Lecompton in a brutal seventy-five-mile trek. Officials there released Jason, who hadn't participated in the Pottawatomie murders, but John Jr., still suffering from a mental breakdown, was held on charges stemming from his earlier free-state activities.

Brown himself returned to the family camp with eight other men, including four sons and a son-in-law, only to discover the camp had been plundered. A reporter for a free-Kansas paper who encountered the party in a subsequent camp described the scene in a *New York Tribune* piece, with weapons leaning against trees, saddled horses lingering near a creek, and the leader, with rolled-up sleeves, tending to a roasting pig. Displaying a week-old white beard, stained garments, and toes protruding from worn-out boots, Brown regaled the reporter with earnest expressions of defiance and purpose.

"Give me men of good principles; God-fearing men . . . ," he told the reporter, "—and with a dozen of them, I will oppose any hundred such men as these [southern] ruffians." His followers, God-fearing or not, weren't allowed to drink alcohol or swear in camp.

Connecting with various free-state militias, Brown participated in two pitched battles, one at a place called Black Jack, the other near the town of Osawatomie. At Black Jack, he employed effective guerrilla tactics and managed to trick a proslavery militia leader into thinking he was surrounded. The leader surrendered and turned over to Brown twenty-three prisoners. Four militia men were killed in the battle, while eight free-state combatants were wounded, two seriously.

The outcome at Osawatomie proved less impressive, and Brown paid a heavy price with the death of his son Frederick. He positioned his thirty-eight or so followers in an ambush thicket from which they rained devastating fire upon a large mounted proslavery column. But when the proslavery men dismounted and initiated a broad counterattack, the outnumbered Brown men turned tail, scrambled down a riverbank, and escaped. Brown, wrote biographer Reynolds, "hardly looked heroic in flight." But the irrepressible warrior's small force had taken on some 260 Missourians, killing twenty to thirty and wounding at least forty.

What's more, he now had a record of combat and a budding reputation as a figure of courage to accompany his antislavery zeal, although those rumors of his involvement in the Pottawatomie Massacre continued to dog him. He figured he could leverage his new persona and his showmanship talents to raise money in the East for further antislavery exploits. His area of greatest opportunity, he concluded, was Massachusetts.

As it turned out, many of Boston's ardent abolitionists were particularly receptive to John Brown's rustic appearance and blunt-spoken ways. Many were friends of the rich antislavery activist Gerrit Smith, from Peterboro, New York, who had befriended Brown in the 1840s and joined the entrepreneurial charlatan in that failed North Elba land transaction. But Smith didn't seem to hold that failure against Brown.

Smith lived in a mansion overlooking extensive lawns and gardens, with a book-lined study featuring a mahogany desk once owned by Napoleon Bonaparte. As a philanthropist he doled out untold thousands of dollars to cherished causes, including antislavery causes. He also was a hypochondriac who shuddered with apprehension at every sneeze. And he struggled with wildly fluctuating moods, from ebullient optimism to deep melancholia and even thoughts of suicide. He once attempted to kill himself.

Smith never managed to reach a conclusion on whether violence was justified in the antislavery cause. As a young man he embraced the idea of repatriating freed blacks to Africa; then as a founder of the old Liberty Party he advocated a gradual and peaceful process of emancipation; later he issued fiery calls for violent insurrection; eventually he reverted back to nonviolence. At present he was in his insurrection phase but sometimes got nervous about it. "He loved the idea of armed revolt," said a friend, "until armed revolt drew near."

It wasn't surprising that John Brown would approach Gerrit Smith in his search for money. But at a meeting with Smith in late January 1857, Brown found the philanthropist in one of his sour moods, feeling tapped out from past Kansas contributions and ongoing commitments to the cause. It didn't help that Smith was suffering from an anxiety-inducing winter cold.

Brown encountered better prospects in Boston, where he met a romantic young schoolmaster named Franklin Sanborn, serving at the time as secretary of the Massachusetts State Kansas Committee. The two men discovered an instant mutual affinity based largely on their shared passion for the antislavery cause, but also on Brown's glowing portrait of himself as a man of military brilliance destined to play a heroic role in the eradication of slavery. Brown cut a thrilling figure with his ramrod military bearing, tattered garb, religious intensity, and conversational brusqueness. Here was a man of action with little patience for the idle attitudinizing of Harvard intellectuals, a pose that many Harvard intellectuals found compelling.

Sanborn quickly perceived Brown as "a fighter and a purifier such as was long overdue." Referring to his circle of friends, he added, "We had felt in our heart to expect one such as he."

Sanborn asked Brown about rumors of a Kansas killing spree along the Pottawatomie Creek. The warrior denied any involvement, and the beguiled Bostonian promptly accepted the answer. Almost immediately he offered to help Brown get the money and weapons needed for his plans, described by the Calvinist fighter as the creation of a military company of a hundred men with enough firepower to subdue the Missouri Ruffians and help build a free-state Kansas.

Sanborn introduced Brown to some of his friends, including clergyman Theodore Parker. Instantly smitten by this compelling figure, Parker organized a Sunday reception at his Boston home to introduce Brown to important citizens of the city. Lloyd Garrison was there, along with Amos Lawrence, Wendell Phillips, a rich industrialist named George Luther Stearns, the famous physician and adventurer Samuel Gridley Howe, and Howe's wife, a well-known poet, Julia Ward Howe.

The occasion was a bit of a spectacle, with the Boston Brahmans, in all their upper-class finery and surrounded by Parker's lavish decor, displaying their studied graciousness toward this feisty gamecock of the West with the threadbare corduroy suit, scarred hands, and dirty fingernails. To many, Brown appeared ill at ease as he darted glances from one guest to another. But when the gamecock spoke, his eyes lit up and the words lacerated the room with sharpness and force. Many of the guests nearly swooned at the experience.

But not everyone. Garrison, upon meeting Brown, entered into a conversation in which each man warily probed the other in an effort to find common ground. They discovered that they viewed the slavery challenge through different lenses. It was Brown the rousing man of violence vs. Garrison the nonresistance advocate; Brown's wrathful God vs. Garrison's merciful one; Brown's Old Testament admonition of an eye for an eye vs. Garrison's New Testament precept of turning the other cheek. The two men never gravitated to each other.

Wendell Phillips developed a similar skepticism, nurtured by those persistent reports of Brown's participation in the Pottawatomie murders. In a letter to Garrison, Phillips said that such villainy "cannot be successfully palliated or excused." Both men feared that Brown likely would become a blot on the cause.

Brown pulled to his side plenty of ardent followers, though, and soon was making fundraising rounds throughout Massachusetts and nearby states and connecting with some of New England's most prominent figures, including Emerson, Thoreau, Sumner, and Henry James Sr. The Massachusetts State Kansas Committee appointed him as its agent and offered him two thousand rifles stored in Tabor, Iowa. The transfer needed consent from the Chicago-based National Kansas Committee, which convened a meeting in New York to discuss the matter. A delegate named Harvey Hurd objected, based on what Franklin Sanborn later called "some inkling that Brown would not confine his warfare to Kansas."

When Hurd asked Brown if he intended to attack Missouri or any other slave state, the Kansas warrior became defiantly vague. "I am no adventurer," he said. "You all know me. . . . I do not expose my plans. . . . I will not be interrogated; if you wish to give me anything, give it freely." He got the rifles, along with a promise of $5,000, only $150 of which he ever collected.

The episode reflected a pattern in Brown's efforts—plenty of encouragement, even adulation, but not much cash. But Brown became particularly close to six abolitionist figures who revered him as a man of greatness destined to become one of the most consequential figures of his age. They would come to call themselves the Secret Six, and they shrouded the fullness of their Brown connection because they suspected he intended to initiate a southern slave revolt.

Gerrit Smith became one of the Secret Six after reversing his sour attitude of early 1857 and giving Brown $350 for his Kansas mission and another $110 to settle a debt. It wasn't much, but it signified that he was fully in the insurrection camp now.

Franklin Sanborn was the youngest of the Six. Born in 1831, he studied at Phillips Exeter Academy and Harvard, then founded a prep school in Concord, Massachusetts, where the sons of Emerson, Nathaniel Hawthorne, and Horace Mann studied. His romantic spirit became widely recognized and extolled after his fiancée contracted a debilitating neurological illness and he married her anyway just days before her death. With his smooth good looks and calm demeanor, he seemed to be a picture of moderation—until aroused by the world's injustices. Thoreau said his "quiet, steadfast earnestness and ethical fortitude are of the type that calmly, so calmly, ignites and then throws bomb after bomb."

There was no moderation in the life of Dr. Samuel Gridley Howe, tall and wiry in appearance; brash, iron-willed, and vengeful in temperament. He was a polymath whose professional exploits included a stint as a military doctor in the Greek revolution against the Turks, during which he was noted for tending to wounded soldiers only after the battles had ended because he was too busy fighting during them. He also was a brilliant medical pioneer in helping blind and deaf persons overcome their handicaps, publisher of a feisty abolitionist newspaper, and tireless antislavery activist. "I do not like caution," he said. "It betokens little faith in God's arrangements." Julia Ward Howe privately decried her husband's "terrible faults of character . . . often unjust in his likes and dislikes, arbitrary, cruel, with little mastery over his passions." The couple had a tempestuous marriage, largely due to Howe's character flaws and indiscretions.

There was never any doubt that the clergyman Theodore Parker would embrace the Brown mystique. Tireless and driven, he had, in one recent five-month period, delivered eighty-four lectures, preached sermons every Sunday but two (when he was out of town), conducted six meetings a month at his home, and written a thousand letters—all in addition to his routine ministerial and scholarly work. As a theologian he brilliantly incorporated some of Emerson's transcendental views into his vision of Christ, an interpretation so radical for the day that he was barred from church pulpits. So he delivered his sermons instead at the Boston Music Hall.

The 1850 Fugitive Slave Act transformed Parker into a vehement adherent of higher law and of violent action when necessary in the cause of liberty. Thomas Wentworth Higginson, another Secret Six member, called Parker "God's fanatic" and labeled him "the greatest, most eloquent defender of the ideal of individual liberty in the modern era."

Higginson, born in 1823 into a prosperous Cambridge merchant family, was a product of the Harvard Divinity School and served much of his early life as a Unitarian minister—first at Newburyport, where he was forced to resign in 1848 because of his unorthodox views, and later at Worcester. Like Parker, Higginson participated regularly in public demonstrations against slavery and in behalf of runaway slaves. During the 1854 protests against the capture of the fugitive Anthony Burns, he received a saber gash on the chin that left a lifelong scar and a source of considerable pride.

Higginson despised the Constitution, even refusing to vote in elections for politicians required to take a loyalty oath upon victory. He called himself a "Disunion Abolitionist," and thrilled at the prospect of "the life of a Reformer . . . 'battling for the right'—glorious, but Oh how hard!" He declared in his journal, "To Disunion I now subscribe," even to the point of "obloquy and danger."

Finally, there was George Luther Stearns, born in 1809, a self-made industrialist who had generated a fortune in linseed oil production, then another in the manufacture of lead pipes. Now he lived in luxury, summoning his carriage for distances that most people would traverse on foot and hosting lavish dinners at his Medford, Massachusetts, mansion for luminaries of the antislavery movement, including Charles Sumner, Wendell Phillips, and Frederick Douglass. Sober-minded and methodical, he impressed people by speaking sparingly but with conviction and good sense. Stearns believed that bondage could never be abolished through constitutional means. "I would mortgage all I own," he told Samuel Howe, "to see the end of slavery."

B y late spring, as Brown made plans to return to Kansas via Iowa
(and take possession of those rifles from the National Kansas Committee), the association between the Kansas warrior and the Secret Six
had become inextricable, though not always amicable. Brown often
seethed at his patrons' inability to raise significant funds, while the Six
wondered why Brown was taking so long in getting back to the Kansas battlefront. But by this time Kansas governors Geary and Walker
had managed to subdue the fighting with their strong and largely evenhanded policies, and the free-state victory in the fall legislative elections
further persuaded antislavery men, including the Secret Six, that Kansas
could become a free state without further bloodshed. Stearns wrote to
Brown that the "true course now is to meet the enemy in the ballot-box."

Thus did Brown quickly turn to a more brash and far-reaching idea
that had animated his fevered brain for years: an insurrection against the
southern oligarchy designed to unleash a massive slave revolt, kill the
masters and their families, and destroy the South's hold over its 4 million slaves. Many would flee to the North or to Canada, he figured, but
some of the more adventurous blacks would join the guerrilla army he
planned to establish in the Allegheny Mountains of Virginia, a redoubt
of rugged terrain in which, he believed, government forces would have
difficulty in finding and quashing him.

The operation would begin at Harpers Ferry, Virginia (later West
Virginia), where Brown planned to seize the federal arsenal, which produced much of the government's military weaponry. Throughout the
fall he pulled together a small group of some twelve to twenty "misfits,
idealists, and charlatans," as historian Edward Renehan described them,
to effectuate the armory attack and begin the process of freeing slaves
and building the insurgent army. He secured winter lodging for his men
and headed east to drum up support and cash. Inevitably, he traveled
back to Peterboro and Boston, where in early March he discussed with
the Secret Six his insurrection plans. To a man, they embraced it enthusiastically.

By the time Brown left Boston on March 8, the loosely organized
Secret Six had become a formal committee, with a treasurer (Stearns),
financial commitments (amounting to several hundreds of dollars), and

a resolve to provide counsel and guidance as the plan unfolded. Smith, reflecting the general sentiment of the Six, told Sanborn that Brown— "our dear friend"—was determined to proceed with or without the Six, and thus they had a moral obligation to support him. "We cannot give him up to die alone," he said. Higginson declared to his friends, "I am always ready to invest in treason," though he conceded he didn't have much to invest.

Then a complication arose. The previous summer Brown had lured to Tabor, Iowa, a New York down-and-outer named Hugh Forbes, an alcoholic Scotsman with a checkered background as a European silk merchant, fighter for the Italian revolution of 1848, and New York newspaper editor. He fancied himself an expert on military tactics and had written a two-volume treatise on the subject. Brown hired Forbes as a military adviser for $100 a month, with a $600 advance.

But the two men couldn't get along. Brown wanted merely a drill instructor, whereas Forbes fancied himself a commanding officer. Further, Brown fell behind in the promised payments. The Scotsman left Iowa in a huff and soon began writing letters to the Secret Six attacking Brown as an unreliable phony and threatening to expose the Harpers Ferry campaign if he didn't get his back pay. More ominously, he traveled to Washington to air his complaints with senators William Seward (through a letter) and Henry Wilson (in a personal interview). Seward dismissed the excitable Forbes as an incoherent crank, but the Shoemaker of Natick understood enough of what he heard to develop concerns about what his friend Samuel Gridley Howe may be up to. He wrote to Howe warning that any weapons contributed to Brown for Kansas activity must not be used for other provocative purposes.

There followed a flurry of letter-writing, consultations, arguments, and hand-wringing among Secret Six members over what they now faced and how they should deal with it. The chance of exposure prior to Brown's action seemed perilously high, and a consensus emerged that they should pull back from the brink. Eventually it was agreed—and reluctantly accepted by Brown—that he should postpone his insurrection until the following winter or spring, giving time for the Forbes rumors and any suspicions emanating from them to die down and for the Six to raise some $2,000 to $3,000 for the venture. It was also agreed that the Six would not be informed of details of the plan as it developed, thus giving them sufficient deniability should they be charged with crimes related to Brown's revolt.

Brown, muttering about his collaborators' lack of courage, headed off to Kansas to establish his presence there as a kind of feint to draw attention away from Harpers Ferry and the targeted plantations of Virginia. He had a consolation, though: $500 from the Massachusetts State Kansas Committee for his antislavery campaign, the true nature of which was unknown to all committee members save the Secret Six.

I n South Carolina, Barnwell Rhett struggled with the meaning of his latest humiliation at the hands of his old rival James Hammond and the appearance that he was politically washed-up. "I seldom leave the house," he told a friend in early 1857, "and feel as if I have already passed out of the world."

Without any prospect of accumulating political power, he hit upon the idea of wielding journalistic power. Even in his beleaguered financial state, he raised enough money by mortgaging slaves to purchase the *Charleston Mercury* ownership share that had been held by the deceased William Taber, victim of that duel of the year before. That put Rhett in partnership with longtime *Mercury* principal John Heart in an arrangement whereby Heart ran the paper's business side, while Rhett's loyal and like-minded son Robert Barnwell Rhett Jr. served as editor. Some eighteen months later, Rhett Sr. bought out Heart and became the paper's sole owner. It was a rickety enterprise, struggling to stay afloat while paying off substantial debts, but the Rhetts, father and son, embraced the challenge of fashioning the *Mercury* into an uncompromising organ of southern nationalism.

Their first challenge, during the months of the Rhetts' partial ownership, was to determine their positions on the radical notions increasingly agitating the state's body politic: the slave trade, the acquisition of Cuba, and the idea of a Central American slave empire. The slave trade agitation was the product largely of two South Carolinians, Leonidas W.

Spratt, editor of the *Charleston Southern Standard*, and James H. Adams, the state's governor from December 1854 to December 1856.

Spratt purchased the floundering *Standard* in 1853 and turned it into a successful megaphone for his conviction that South Carolina's cherished "democratic aristocracy" and the southern way of life generally were doomed without a major influx of slave labor. He was not wrong. Indeed, he had developed a discerning perception of the social and economic forces pressing down upon the South and particularly on South Carolina.

The state had been losing slaves steadily throughout the 1850s as more and more planters, fleeing the weakened soil of the upper South, moved to more fertile lands in Mississippi and Alabama. Accompanying that trend was an influx of poor white immigrants, many of them artisans, who gravitated to the cities and didn't like competing with slave labor for their livelihoods. Charleston's slave workingmen had declined in number by 46 percent through the 1850s, while foreign-born white workers increased by 25 percent. Soon the whites were agitating for legislation barring slaves from menial work in the cities, and demographic trends indicated that their demands soon would be difficult to ignore.

Spratt could see that these trends represented an internal threat to slavery quite apart from any northern agitation. His answer was to import some ten thousand Africans designated for urban menial labor and thus to push out the whites before they could coalesce into a serious political challenge to the state's autocratic system. Further, with demand for southern labor growing and the supply suppressed, the price of slaves was rising to the point where fewer and fewer southerners could afford to be slaveholders. Spratt wanted to see more southern slaveholders, not fewer, so that a larger portion of the population would be invested in the system.

Massachusetts, noted Spratt, could tap into an endless supply of cheap labor through European immigration, while the South was stymied by the slave-trade prohibition. Just the South Carolina low country alone, he argued, needed tens of thousands of slave laborers to raze forests, construct and maintain roads and bridges, build urban structures, and rehabilitate declining plantations. Bring in those slaves, demanded

Spratt, and soon the South could compete with the North in enterprise, efficiency, and wealth creation.

A leading supporter of the Spratt cause was Governor Adams, owner of some two hundred slaves and a fire-eater of the first order. In November 1856 he called on the legislature to endorse the slave-trade revival. Both houses responded by creating special committees to probe the issue, and each produced a report favoring reinstatement. The reports were tabled, reflecting fears that opposition would bring allegations of abolitionism.

But Benjamin Perry didn't worry about that. The unionist editor of the *Southern Patriot* and leader of the National Democratic movement denounced the idea implacably. "If we have to turn pirates and kidnappers," declared Perry, "and fight the whole civilized world under a red and black flag, in order to defend slavery in the southern states, we are, indeed, in a most deplorable state of degradation as a people."

As for Rhett, though he had endorsed Adams for governor, he ultimately dismissed the slave-trade movement as a distraction. In a June 1857 editorial, the *Mercury*, under Rhett Jr.'s editorship, predicted that an inflamed North would crush any serious effort to enact slave-trade legislation. Besides, added Rhett's *Mercury*, the issue would divide southerners at a time when "[u]nity of purpose throughout the South should be the great object of all who look for redress, and security in the future, in or out of the Union."

The words "in or out of the Union" reflected the senior Rhett's lingering desire: southern secession and the creation of a new slave nation. Everything else was secondary. As the *Mercury* editorial concluded, "When the re-opening of the African Slave Trade is a practicable measure, by a dissolution of the present Union and the independence of the South, it will be time enough to consider the policy of renewing it."

For Rhett the secession imperative also superseded any interest in Cuban annexation or the vague notion of an American slave empire in Central America. Leonidas Spratt, too, considered those ideas to be impractical as well as irrelevant to the true needs of the South. Such grandiose visions, he argued, would not supply the slaves needed in the already established South for economic development and progress. He felt the same about Kansas, where the influx of white settlers—rabble, in Spratt's estimation—was sure to wrest the territory away from the southern ethos. Slavery could thrive, he argued, only in areas where the southern ethos prevailed.

And yet the idea of expanding slave territory as a means of perpetuating the domestic institution continued to animate the minds of southern partisans and some prominent northern Democrats. During Franklin Pierce's presidency, Secretary of State William Marcy urged three prominent U.S. ambassadors—Pierre Soulé in Madrid, James Buchanan in London, and John Y. Mason in Paris—to meet at Ostend, Belgium, to determine how America might acquire Cuba. The resulting Ostend Dispatch (later dubbed the Ostend Manifesto for its aggressive language) suggested that the United States should seek to purchase the island, but would be "justified in wresting it from Spain" should the Iberian nation refuse to sell and if Spanish rule over the island should constitute a threat to the United States.

When the highly confidential dispatch became publicly known, it kicked up a stir in the country and in foreign capitals. The controversy seriously undermined Pierce's political standing, as antislavery northerners quickly perceived the underlying interest in expanding slavery in order to perpetuate it. And yet Buchanan, as president, revealed his interest in the U.S. acquisition of Cuba on numerous occasions.

Southern firebrands and their northern allies weren't alone in their fevered pursuit of an ultimate strategic victory on the slavery issue. Up in Massachusetts, the Secret Six were flirting with a slavery-eradication plan that any ordinary intellect, unencumbered by such moral and political fervor, would see as entirely fanciful. Like frantic southerners searching for a way out of their predicament, these northern men, all highly intelligent and accomplished, had lost their ability to place their passions into a context of realism and moderation. For many, realism and moderation seemed inadequate to the intractable crisis gaining force within the nation.

20

35TH CONGRESS

||||||||||||||||||||||||||||||||||||||||||||||||||||||||||||||||||||||||||||||||

A KANSAS PAUSE AND A NEW HAMMOND

The epic struggle between President Buchanan and Senator Douglas began in earnest on December 8, 1857, the day after the opening session of the 35th Congress. That's when the president sent to lawmakers his First Annual Message. It contained not a hint of the old Robert Walker strategy of wooing antislavery leaders of the Topeka movement into participation in the officially recognized Lecompton government. Gone also was Walker's effort to get proslavery forces in Kansas and elsewhere to accept the reality that territorial demographics now presaged a free-state outcome for Kansas.

The four Kansas governors up to that time—Reeder, Shannon, Geary, and Walker—had all developed a sympathy for the antislavery men based on the abuses they had endured from Missouri's Border Ruffians and other proslavery forces. Those governors also, however, had issued stern warnings to free-state leaders that they risked getting caught in a treason trap if they undermined by force the recognized Lecompton government. And, although Robinson and others had been arrested for their free-state activity in defiance of the congressionally recognized

Lecompton government, President Pierce eventually ordered the case dropped on the ground that the treason allegation was tenuous. Under Robinson's leadership, the free-state people managed to avoid legal sanction while making their case that the established government had been formed through illegitimate means.

Buchanan now brushed aside any sympathy for the antislavery forces and any suggestion that Topeka leaders deserved to be part of the Kansas solution. Instead he castigated the free-state elements as a "revolutionary organization" itching to "put down the lawful government by force and to establish a government of their own." And the president now publicly endorsed the incendiary concept of partial submission—a vote of Kansas residents on the slavery question only. This required some artful rhetorical contortions.

Buchanan cited the Kansas-Nebraska Act's language specifying that territorial residents must be "perfectly free to form and regulate their domestic institutions in their own way." The term "domestic institutions," he argued with a stretch of the imagination, was "limited to the family. The relation between master and slave and a few others are 'domestic institutions,' and are entirely distinct from institutions of a political character." Thus, he continued, the constitutional convention was not required to call an election on any other provisions of its governing document besides the slavery issue.

He suggested further that his instructions to Walker just before the governor's departure for Kansas had reflected this distinction, though neither the instructions nor various other communications between the two men bolstered any such interpretation. Now, though, he faced the political imperative of finessing that inconvenient exchange, and he did so in typical fashion—without much concern about the appearance of it. More important was maintaining good relations with the South so his Democratic Party could continue its image as a national institution.

It worked. The *Charleston Mercury* said of the president that "we heartily support his policy" and expressed pleasure "that he has not soiled his fame by identifying it with Walker." The paper did carp a bit in wondering why the president felt any need to push for even a partial submission, as opposed to letting the proslavery convention speak for the people. Generally, though, the *Mercury* saw "so much to approve, and so little to condemn."

The next day Stephen Douglas rose on the Senate floor to rebut the president in a speech that many historians later regarded as one of his finest. In a tone of measured explication, curbing his famous instinct for rhetorical pugilism, the Little Giant picked apart the opposition arguments with precision and thoroughness. "I propose to examine this question calmly and fairly," he told his colleagues, "to see whether or not we can properly receive Kansas into the Union with the constitution formed at Lecompton."

He began by stating—"with profound respect to the President of the United States"—that Buchanan had "committed a fundamental error . . . which lies at the foundation of his whole argument." It was his conclusion that the Kansas-Nebraska Act had formulated a distinction between the proper disposition of the slavery issue and the disposition of all other issues, such as banking and tax policies, the judicial system, public education, the elective franchise, and more. "We repealed the Missouri restriction because that was confined to slavery," said Douglas. "That exception was taken away for the avowed and express purpose of making the rule of self-government general and universal."

In an elaborate review of precedence and law related to the government's acceptance of territories into statehood, Douglas argued that no territorial assembly or convention could establish a state; only Congress could do that. And Congress couldn't do it until it knew that the people of the territory had embraced its terms. Partial submission couldn't serve that purpose, stated Douglas, because under that approach "men must vote for the constitution, whether they like it or not, in order to be permitted to vote for or against slavery." Besides, continued the senator, any reasonable review of political sentiment in Kansas would reveal that the vast majority of settlers favored a free-state outcome.

Responding to the president's insistence that all Democrats must embrace his approach as a matter of party loyalty, Douglas turned defiant. "I have as much heart in the great cause that binds us together as a party as any man living," he said, adding he would sacrifice anything for party unity except "principle and honor."

T hus were the lines of contention drawn for a renewed struggle over slavery in Kansas, with Congress this time as the field of battle. It would consume legislators for nearly five months, with hardly any other congressional business taken up and with emotions at a fevered pitch. Most fevered of all was the southern reaction to the Douglas speech. It was, declared the Rhetts' *Mercury*, "the clap-trap of a demagogue, looking to his position with an anti-slavery constituency in Illinois, of whom he is afraid."

The congressional battle unfolded against the backdrop of two electoral events in Kansas that were seized upon by partisans of both sides as indices of territorial sentiment, but served mostly to heighten tensions. The first, on December 21, was the controversial partial referendum established by the Lecompton constitutional convention to determine whether Kansas would become a state with or without slavery. The second, on January 4, was the referendum put into place by acting governor Frederick Stanton and the new antislavery legislature on whether Kansans would accept or reject the constitution in its entirety.

On December 21, with free-state Kansans refusing to participate, the balloting came down to 6,226 votes favoring the constitution with slavery and 569 for it without slavery. Southerners quickly hailed the result as a signal victory. "We have made Kansas this day a Slave State," proclaimed the *Mercury*'s Kansas correspondent.

But the January 4 balloting presented a different picture. With proslavery men this time abstaining, the vote to reject Lecompton totaled 10,226, with another 138 votes for the proposed government with slavery, and 24 in favor of it without slavery. The two referendums together clearly demonstrated that antislavery sentiment in Kansas was the prevailing territorial attitude.

James Gordon Bennett's *New York Herald*, a paper highly attuned to southern interests, quickly perceived the broad significance of the two

votes. The South, said the *Herald*, held the tactical high ground, positioned to send to Washington a proslavery constitution for Kansas and
with prospects of getting it through the Democratic Congress under
the resolved leadership of a crafty Democratic president. But even in
victory, said the *Herald*, the South would be fighting a rearguard battle,
with little prospect that it could maintain Kansas as a slave state for
long with a large majority of its citizens favoring free-state status. Even
worse for the South, said the paper, would be a congressional repudiation of the Lecompton formula. That would be "tantamount to a decree
from the North that "there shall be no more slave States; but that the
South, henceforth, must depend entirely upon the protecting power
and abounding grace of her Northern masters."

In other words, according to the *Herald*, the South must contend
with its declining power vis-à-vis the North and with prospects that the
forces of northern ascendancy and southern subservience were becoming inexorable. If so, a short-term southern victory in Kansas wouldn't
amount to much.

But that didn't diminish the intensity of interest in the short-term
question of what Congress would do with the proslavery Lecompton
constitution once it made its way to the legislative body. In the Senate,
Democrats held thirty-nine seats to just twenty for Republicans and five
for the fading American (Know-Nothing) Party. Thus Buchanan and
the Democratic establishment appeared certain to win that battle.

The House posed a greater challenge. With 118 votes needed for
victory, the Democrats held 131 seats to 92 for Republicans and 14
for the Americans. But with many northern Democrats recoiling at
the thought of Kansas as a slave state and feeling pressure from equally
uncomfortable constituents, Buchanan could count on only about a
hundred committed members. That meant he would have to get the
remaining eighteen through cajolery, threats of retaliation, or backroom
deals in the currency of politics, including patronage jobs, government
contracts, social invitations, and campaign cash. That was a brand of
politics that Buchanan knew well and thrived in.

But he also utilized his White House megaphone in presenting an
entirely one-sided description of the recent Kansas wars. In transmitting

the proposed Lecompton constitution to Congress on February 2, he sought to puncture the "great delusion" of two parties in the territory, both "acknowledging the lawful existence of the government." No, said the president, the conflict was between "those who are loyal to this government and those who have endeavored to destroy its existence by force and usurpation." No mention of Ruffian violence or the Sack of Lawrence or the brazen efforts to establish Kansas as a slave state by poisoning the democratic process.

Douglas took command of the anti-Lecompton campaigns in both the Senate and House, much to the satisfaction of previous adversaries such as William Seward, Salmon Chase, and Nathaniel Banks. Henry Wilson said Douglas would give "more weight to our cause than any other ten men in the country."

The Illinoisan carefully crafted a tone of magnanimity in rebutting even his most effective adversaries. When James S. Green, Missouri's freshman senator, delivered a particularly well-reasoned floor address defending the Buchanan position, Douglas refrained from any harsh response. "I but do the senator justice," he began, "when I say that he has presented the question with marked ability and clearness; and I am inclined to think that the best view of the subject has been presented to-day."

When the Senate vote was taken on March 23, Buchanan sealed the anticipated victory, thirty-three yeas to twenty-five nays. The measure now went to the House, where early procedural votes indicated an extremely close outcome. Fearing defeat, anti-Lecompton Democrats—some nineteen to twenty-four in number—offered to support the measure, including the slave clause, if Buchanan would accept deletion of the language foreclosing any constitutional amendments for seven years. It was a signal opportunity for the president to settle the Kansas matter finally and decisively on largely his own terms. But he rejected the offer.

Then Representative William Montgomery of Pennsylvania dusted off a proposal that had been rejected earlier by the Senate when put forth by Kentucky's John J. Crittenden. It called for the resubmission of the Lecompton document to Kansas residents in yet another referendum—but this time, it was assumed, a carefully managed one. In a surprise vote on April 1, the House substituted the Crittenden-Montgomery proposal, as it was now called, for the old Lecompton constitution. The vote was 120 to 112. Then by the same vote margin the chamber embraced the substitute.

The result was a congressional deadlock between a Senate that vehemently opposed any resubmission and a House that wouldn't accept the Lecompton program without one. The only hope now was for some kind of face-saving compromise to be worked out by a House-Senate conference committee, but the House nearly nixed the conference idea. It required a tiebreaking vote by the chamber's new Speaker, South Carolina's James Orr, to open the way for House participation.

During conference deliberations, Indiana's Democratic representative William English hit upon the idea of a kind of backdoor resubmission, without tying it directly to the emotion-laden slavery issue. The Lecompton proposal had included an outlandish request for the transfer to Kansas of some 23 million acres of federal land, about six times the normal land grant for previous states entering the Union. English suggested that lawmakers should attach to the Lecompton proposal a related measure that would reduce the land transfer to a more appropriate level. Then the two intertwined measures would be submitted to Kansas voters so they could accept or reject the land-grant change in keeping with the doctrine of popular sovereignty. In the process they also would be accepting or rejecting the full constitutional language, including the slave clause.

Thus if Kansans accepted the change, the territory would become a state—without all the inappropriate acreage but as a slave state. If they rejected the change, according to the English formula, Kansas statehood would be placed on hold until the territory had reached a population equal to the population of congressional districts at the time, roughly ninety-three thousand. That would mean no Kansas statehood for at least two years and perhaps longer.

What followed was a political spectacle as members scrambled to put the best face possible on an ambiguous situation. Buchanan, seeing salvation from what appeared to be a looming defeat, quickly endorsed the English formula. Many Republicans initially rejected it as a sub-terfuge measure but later relented based on predictions of a favorable referendum vote. Anti-Lecompton Democrats slowly came around to the concept. Southerners were split but eventually tilted toward the Bu-chanan position, in part, it was surmised, because Douglas, considered a villain throughout the South, refused to endorse the backdoor ap-proach. In the end, on April 30, Congress embraced the concept, 31 to 22 in the Senate and 112 to 103 in the House. The president promptly signed the measure.

Three months later, when Kansans went to the polls once again to express their sentiments on the Lecompton constitution, they delivered a fatal blow, rejecting the land-grant change and hence the constitution itself by a vote of 11,300 to 1,788. The English proviso that a rejection would delay any prospect of Kansas statehood until at least 1861 now took hold. "Most of the people of Kansas," wrote historian Allan Nev-ins, "were willing enough to continue in territorial status if only they could have peace, security and fair elections."

Back on February 4, as Congress struggled with the Kansas contro-versy, James Henry Hammond delivered his maiden address to the U.S. Senate on the topic. The hour-long speech reflected a demarca-tion between Hammond and his predecessor, Pickens Butler, in tone, temperament, and turn of mind. In contrast to Butler's straightforward bluster and studied jocularity, always rushing to the heart of any issue, Hammond presented a more cerebral approach, intent on seeking the underlying meaning of issues through distinctive interpretations. As an intellectual, he found comfort in the world of abstraction.

Thus did Hammond present in his speech an elaborate rebuttal to Stephen Douglas's insistence that the popular sovereignty doctrine placed a vote of the people above the actions of a mere constitutional convention in establishing governmental legitimacy. No, said Ham-mond, referring to the Lecompton convention, that gathering was "an assembly of the people in their highest sovereign capacity, about to perform their highest possible act of sovereignty." This reflected

Hammond's devotion—and South Carolina's—to the ideal of an "aristocratic republic."

Hammond also quoted William Seward's provocative statement of some days before that "the battle has been fought and won," meaning that the South and its institution of slavery soon would be overwhelmed by greater northern power in population, wealth, and votes. Hammond agreed with Seward's statement and took it to mean that the North would be coming after southerners with crippling tariffs and export bounties, expensive public works, a meddlesome national bank, and eventually with a resolve to eradicate slavery everywhere in America. In other words, the powerful North would thrust the South into abject subservience. "We cannot rely on your faith when you have the power," Hammond told his northern colleagues. "It has always been broken whenever pledged."

But Hammond also enumerated what he considered the South's many assets, providing the region with the ability to protect itself—for example, its advantageous location, with many bustling harbors and the mighty Mississippi River cutting through it; its staple crops generating abundant wealth; its ability to man and equip an army as large and threatening as any in the world; and, not least in his view, the South's efficient and profitable system of slave labor, far superior to the North's brutal wage system. "Why," he said, "you meet more beggars in one day, in any single street of the city of New York, than you would meet in a lifetime in the whole South."

The speech elicited a favorable response from southern politicians and newspapers as a blast of defiance at northern aggression. "He leaps into the arena with an air of conscious supremacy," declared the *South*, a Richmond newspaper. "There is nothing timid in his tread."

Despite the favorable reaction to his speech and his vote for the Lecompton constitution, Hammond returned to South Carolina in June without any particular feeling of triumph. "I don't feel at home here yet," he wrote to his close friend William Gilmore Simms. He added that he hadn't exactly taken Washington by storm. "I have not put myself forward to lead," he wrote. "If I come back I *must* do it." Simms helped by organizing a "welcome home" barbecue for the senator on

July 22 at Beech Island, with fifteen hundred guests and Hammond as featured speaker.

No draft of the speech survived, but press accounts suggested a radical departure from much of the Senate speech. Both addresses hailed the inherent strengths of the South as a vibrant and wealth-generating region blessed with abundant natural and human resources. But at Beech Island the words dripped with a sentiment that most southerners equated to submission, and Hammond seemed to embrace unionism over southern security.

It would take many years, said Hammond, for the South, on its own, to build a country as strong and rich as the combined Union, now at the front rank of nations. Better, therefore, to remain within that powerful entity and seek southern protection and glory within the current federal framework. Even if an abolitionist were to become president, he didn't think the South would secede or should. That's because he didn't fear the North's abolitionist crusade, which he thought was deteriorating. Soon, he predicted, it would be merely "a corporal's guard of a few old maids and fanatics."

Hammond didn't see much significance in the ongoing southern conflict between National Democrats such as Benjamin Perry or House Speaker James Orr, on the one hand, and the states' rights men such as Barnwell Rhett or Maxcy Gregg, on the other. He declared, "We should address ourselves to the development of our own internal resources and the achievement of Southern harmony and power in the Union."

The speech jolted South Carolina and much of the South. "A dark and portentous cloud has certainly suddenly blown up upon our political horizon," said the *Mercury*, adding that "the announcement that Senator Hammond is for the Union, is a thunderbolt that burns up the very blood in our veins." Barnwell Rhett Jr. said Hammond had given "aid and strength to unmitigated unionists and submissionists."

Simms chided his friend for not foreseeing the coming firestorm and suggested that Hammond deliver a clarifying speech, to be distributed also to the press to avoid confusion about his views. Thus on October 29 at Barnwell, South Carolina, Hammond delivered a follow-up discourse on the nation's slavery crisis. Far from retreating from his Beech

302 || DECADE OF DISUNION

Island pronouncements, he sought simply to clarify and defend them by injecting some realism into the state's political consciousness.

Yes, said Hammond, the South had lost its political parity with the North in the U.S. Senate, and the disparity would only grow as more non-slave states entered the Union. Not even the acquisition of Cuba, which was highly unlikely in any event, could reverse the North's growing electoral strength. Further, the idea of resuming the U.S. slave trade was ridiculously unrealistic because it was opposed even by many southerners, while "the North is unanimously against it." He also debunked the idea of colonizing Mexico or Central America for slavery expansion, since the populations there lacked the qualities for success as either slaves or free men. "What . . . could we do with these people or these countries to add to Southern strength? Nothing."

Hammond reiterated his catalog of southern assets and his bold confidence that the region could more than hold its own within the Union. The South, he said, "has been lamenting her weakness, and croaking about the dangers that beset her, when she might glory in her strength and hurl defiance to her enemies."

But, he concluded, should the region fail in its resolve to fend off northern encroachment, then it could always turn to the ultimate solution of secession. And then, he promised, "I shall, without hesitation, go with her fully and faithfully."

It was a remarkable speech, a strange mixture of realism and naivete and seemingly designed to carve out for the senator a distinctive and intellectually seamless political perspective, uncontaminated by the views and perceptions of people he considered of lesser intellectual capacity. Like James Orr, Hammond advocated bolstering the South so it could fend off the North within the Union, but he separated himself from Orr by rejecting the Speaker's strategy of working within the Democratic Party, or any other party. And to the South's states' rights adherents he offered hardly a nod of approval.

Not surprisingly, many in the North perked up at the emergence of this singular southern figure who might emerge, it was thought, as a force for conciliation between the sections. The *New York Times* praised his attack on "the whole body of extreme Southern men and measures," while Bennett's *Herald* saw in Hammond a possible 1860 presidential contender. Hammond himself told Simms that "thinking & patriotic men" of the North seemed to be looking for just such a man as himself for higher office.

In the South, however, he came under a ferocious assault. One letter writer to the *Mercury* declared, "I am sorry to say that this speech is one of the most dangerous moves that has been made in our State for many years." Even before the attacks, the tensions of his new Senate life had regenerated hints of "those nervous times" of old, and he found himself unable to deliver his entire Barnwell speech because of internal fretfulness.

On May 6, 1858, South Carolina senator Josiah J. Evans died of a heart condition at age seventy-one. Widely admired for his "fine judgment, great benevolence of character, and . . . urbane and polished demeanor," as the *Mercury* put it, he had never emerged as a particularly influential senator. His death after a five-year Senate tenure occasioned appropriate expressions of regret and sympathy, and the state then moved on to a special legislative election in November to select a successor for the remainder of Evans's current term, set to expire the following March, and for the subsequent six-year term.

Many names were put forward, and fully six serious contenders emerged, including, once again, Barnwell Rhett, as well as former governor James Adams, described by one newspaper as a "slave trade zealot," and longtime legislator and president of the state senate James Chesnut Jr., generally a moderate but a man of indistinct opinions.

On the tenth ballot the seat went to Chesnut. Though a solid states' rights man, the forty-three-year-old Chesnut was no fire-eater. He strongly opposed reopening the slave trade and called for dealing with intersectional tensions within the country's constitutional system. In the battle between South Carolina secessionists and cooperationists in the 1850s, he had been a cooperationist. But he embraced the traditional view that South Carolina should stay away from national political parties and their nominating conventions.

James Hammond considered Chesnut "an amiable, modest gentleman of decent parts." When Hammond encountered the young legislator at the 1850 Nashville convention, he found him to be a "very quiet and apparently unpretending man, but I thought nevertheless quick and keen." The sole surviving son of one of South Carolina's richest planters and married to the intellectually vivacious Mary Boykin Miller, he had stood out for years as a comer. Wrote Hammond to his diary, "I have thought ever since . . . Nashville that he would yet play an important part in public affairs."

Hammond spread the word that he liked the outcome, particularly as it included the defeat of James Adams. The temperamental senator had told friends before the election that he would consider Adams's victory a personal repudiation necessitating his Senate resignation. Instead, South Carolina now would have two men of relatively moderate views representing it in the U.S. Senate.

21

LINCOLN MAKES HIS MOVE

||||||||||||||||||||||||||||||||||||||||||||||||||||||||||||||||||||||||||||||

"A HOUSE DIVIDED AGAINST ITSELF CANNOT STAND"

Back in the fall of 1854, after Stephen Douglas had shepherded the fateful Kansas-Nebraska Act through Congress, the Little Giant returned to Illinois to defend his legislative handiwork against its many detractors. He arrived at the state capital of Springfield on October 3 for an outdoor speech at the Illinois State Fair. A rainstorm forced the event into the capitol building, and at its conclusion, as townsfolk rose to depart, a tall, dark-haired man stood up on the structure's steps and began shouting.

Senator Douglas's arguments, the man announced, would be rebutted the next afternoon at the outdoor venue, either by himself or his friend, the anti–Kansas-Nebraska Democratic politician Lyman Trumbull. Douglas, he added, would be granted time to respond.

Many of those present recognized the man as the Springfield trial lawyer and former one-term congressman, Abraham Lincoln. Douglas knew the interloper well. The two men, representing opposing parties, had served at the same time in the Illinois house of representatives in the mid-1830s and had been in the Illinois congressional delegation together a decade later (though Douglas was in the Senate by then). Lincoln actively opposed Douglas's unsuccessful bid for a congressional seat back in 1838. Two years later the two men sparred in numerous public debates when Lincoln supported the Whigs' presidential candidate, William Henry Harrison, while Douglas promoted Democrat Martin Van Buren.

During their legislative days, both were seen as impressive young men destined for political distinction. But only one had achieved such distinction. While Douglas had operated at the highest levels of national politics since 1850, Lincoln, though eventually a successful and prosperous lawyer, had languished in the political arena. No one felt this disparity more keenly than Lincoln himself, perhaps all the more so because he never much liked Douglas. He viewed the Little Giant as a slippery showman whose brilliance couldn't shroud his political mendacity. He was the kind of man, in Lincoln's view, who "will tell a lie to ten thousand people one day, even though he knows he may have to deny it to five thousand the next." In a sly reference to Douglas's stubby physique, Lincoln called him "the least man I ever saw."

Still, Douglas's high-wire act could not be ignored. "Time was when I was in his way some," Lincoln once recalled, a bit wistfully, "but he has outgrown me . . . & such small men as I am, can hardly be considered worthy of his notice." Some Lincoln friends detected traces of envy in his attitude toward Douglas. His good friend Ward Hill Lamon recalled that Lincoln seemed "intensely jealous" of Douglas and "longed to pull him down, or outstrip him in the race for popular favor."

But despite Lincoln's frustration or perhaps because of it, he was not a man to be dismissed. In preparation for the polemical showdown he forced upon Douglas (who had spurned a previous formal request that they engage in debate), the Springfield lawyer had buried himself in the state library for days, poring over documents and congressional debate transcripts. He arrived at the outdoor event on October 4 fully prepared for a lively joust.

Douglas positioned himself in a chair on the speaking platform in front of Lincoln and, as the local man delivered his three-hour address, the combative senator sought to unnerve him with gibes and refutations.

But Lincoln parried the interruptions adroitly and stayed on script with a legislative critique that was both searing and compelling. He called slavery "a great moral wrong," recognized as such by most people around the world. This attitude, declared Lincoln, "lies at the very foundation of their sense of justice, and it cannot be trifled with." Of course, the Democratic press in the state derided the upstart challenger as something of a bumpkin, but Douglas knew better. Privately he described Lincoln as "the most difficult and dangerous opponent that I have ever met."

Douglas was smart to acknowledge Lincoln's hidden attributes. Emboldened by his success in confronting the Little Giant in Springfield and outraged by Douglas's Kansas-Nebraska legislation, Lincoln spent the next four years pursuing a driving political ambition: the capture of a U.S. Senate seat from Illinois, perhaps even the one held by Douglas, who would be up for reelection in 1859.

Lincoln's inability to keep up with Douglas in the political sphere during the 1840s and '50s can be attributed in part to Democratic dominance of Illinois politics during that period. Aside from a small Whig enclave surrounding Springfield, dubbed by Democrats as "the foul 'spot' upon the state," Democrats consistently controlled the governorship and other statewide offices, the legislature, and the state's congressional districts except the Springfield-based Seventh, which served as Lincoln's bailiwick. To become the state's leading Democrat, as Douglas had done, immediately conferred substantial influence and an avenue to national prominence. To be its leading Whig, as Lincoln had become during his legislative days, offered no such stature or promise.

But other explanations for the man's lack of political success lay in the vagaries of fate and his complex personal story. The remarkable thing about that story is that, despite his disappointments and stark sense of realism, Lincoln never fully relinquished the notion of himself as a man of destiny. "His ambition," said his friend and law partner William Herndon, "was a little engine that knew no rest."

The details of his early life would become well known to history: born into poverty in Kentucky in 1809, the son of a sluggish-minded farmer who barely eked out a subsistence output; moved with his family to Indiana at age seven; hardly any formal schooling but displayed a voracious appetite for reading and study; hired out to neighboring farmers and others by the father to augment his income, a practice the son equated to slavery in that he wasn't allowed to enjoy the fruits of his own labor; devoted his youth to such jobs as woodchopper, riverboat steersman, butcher, and store clerk; settled in New Salem, Illinois, at twenty-one; took up positions as store owner (a flop), postmaster, and surveyor while initiating his eight-year legislative career by getting elected to the state house in 1834; admitted to the bar following legal studies and apprenticeships; moved to Springfield to practice law; married a lively young woman, Mary Todd, from a prominent Kentucky plantation family; a strapping young man of six feet, four inches, weighing 180 pounds, with a pleasant, open-faced demeanor and a penchant for waggish humor, but subject to occasional bouts of melancholia.

Lincoln arrived in Springfield in April 1837 without the means to purchase even a seventeen-dollar bed. He couldn't pay till Christmas, he told the store owner, Joshua Speed, adding, "If I fail in this [legal pursuit], I do not know that I can ever pay you." Speed recalled, "I never saw a sadder face."

But he didn't fail. Speed invited the engaging young man to room with him in a large chamber above his store, and Lincoln soon proved to be a highly effective litigator—clearheaded, quick-minded, with a sympathetic persona and an ability to captivate judges and juries with syllogistic discipline mixed with occasional homespun whimsy. Soon he was viewed as one of the leading lawyers in the sprawling Eighth Judicial Circuit and a welcome presence wherever he appeared. A Boston journalist, traveling with him through the judicial territory, reported that he "knew, or appeared to know, everybody we met, the name of the tenant of every farm-house and the owner of every plat of ground." He added, "Such a shaking of hands—such a how-d'ye do—such a greeting of different kinds."

During his travels on the court circuit, he enjoyed the camaraderie of other lawyers and traveling judges and was known widely for his ability to enlighten and amuse compatriots in casual conversation. But frequently he could be seen off by himself, his face in a book of poetry, history, or philosophy. He sought to master every subject he encountered, to hold it up to the light and examine it from every angle before drawing conclusions as to its essence or its relationship to other things. He devoured and mastered all of Euclid's complex geometric propositions, reflecting his passion for intellectual riddles and hunger for knowledge, as well as his search for order. For Lincoln, said his friend and fellow lawyer Leonard Swett, "life was a school."

He brought to this quest a remarkable ability to remain free of dogma and to synthesize seemingly divergent concepts into a coherent whole. An example was his view of his own ancestry—New England Puritan on his father's side; southern Cavalier on his mother's. The two cultures were so disparate that the *New York Herald* observed that there was "nothing in common between them but hate." Yet Lincoln sought to puzzle out the conflicting elements of the two sensibilities so they could be forged into a logical amalgam. The aim was to find a vision of national unity.

A leading recurrent challenge embraced by Lincoln, writes historian David Reynolds, was to find a "balance between reason and passion." This nearly always led him to a solid middle ground. It particularly guided his struggles with the wicked institution of southern bondage, which he loathed from adolescence and longed to see terminated. In his effort to examine all aspects of the issue, he subscribed to both Garrison's *Liberator* and the *Charleston Mercury*, though he disagreed with much of what was written in both publications.

Recoiling at the fulminations against the U.S. Constitution issued by Garrison and other New England abolitionists, he placed the sanctity of the Union above their passion for immediate emancipation. "In the West," he said, "we consider the Union our ALL." Thus he accepted that the Constitution sanctioned slavery in the original thirteen states and felt compelled to support, however reluctantly, the Fugitive Slave Act.

Further, he expressed deep skepticism about the higher law concept that was proving so nettlesome in the 1850s (though Lincoln was quick to note that many proslavery southerners also invoked the will of God, as they defined it, to justify their attitudes). The problem with the higher law, he felt, was that it could be invoked by anyone to justify just about anything. Regarding the concept, Lincoln declared that "in so far as it may attempt to foment a disobedience of the Constitution, or of the constitutional laws of the country, it has my unqualified condemnation."

Lincoln's search for middle-ground solutions led him to the doctrine eventually embraced by the fledgling Republican Party: leaving slavery alone where it existed, while employing federal power to prohibit it from spreading into new territories. The idea was that, under such a policy, the institution would be squeezed into eventual extinction. This was in direct conflict, of course, with Douglas's cherished doctrine of popular sovereignty, which denied that Congress had any legitimate power to interfere with the right of territorial folks to decide the matter for themselves. It conflicted also with the views of many abolitionists. As Lincoln gained political stature, the antislavery Bostonian Wendell Phillips dismissed him as "that slave hound from Illinois."

Before all this turmoil stormed the body politic, however, Lincoln earned an opportunity to place his political career on a new and promising course. He muffed it. In 1846, after he dutifully had supported two successive Whig candidates to represent Illinois's Seventh Congressional District, party officials turned to Lincoln for the next nomination. He won the seat and moved his family to Washington for the 30th Congress, which extended from March 1847 to March 1849. Largely avoiding the slavery topic (although David Wilmot's proviso was generating plenty of heat on the issue), Lincoln put forth a series of stinging rebukes to President Polk for maneuvering America into the Mexican War. The president "talks like an insane man," said Lincoln. "His mind, taxed beyond its power, is running hither and thither, like an ant on a hot stove."

Many in Washington and back home in Illinois considered the attacks unseemly coming from an obscure freshman while the president struggled with the vagaries and difficulties of war. Though Lincoln had promised, upon getting the nomination, to serve only one term, he hoped that his performance might induce Seventh District Whig leaders to grant him a second nomination. This wouldn't happen after the controversy he had kicked up. And his bid for a coveted federal job in Zachary Taylor's new Whig administration crumbled when numerous political figures in Illinois opposed the appointment based largely on his congressional performance. On top of that, the Democrats captured the Seventh District seat at the next election, following Whig dominance of it for more than a decade. Disheartened and depressed, Lincoln returned to Springfield, turned away from politics, and devoted himself to building up his law practice. It seemed that, in a Democratic state like Illinois, his political career was over.

Lincoln's hiatus from politics lasted nearly five years, until the 1854 Kansas-Nebraska provocation rekindled his political passion and spurred his senatorial ambition. It also inspired his clever ambush of Douglas during that rainy night in October. That episode was followed by a burst of Lincoln speechmaking in opposition to incumbent Democratic senator James Shields, up for reelection before the Illinois legislature in January 1855. Seeing an opportunity, Lincoln set his sights on cadging the Shields seat for himself.

Of course, the ambitious lawyer fully understood that his Whig Party was dying in Illinois, as in the country, and that the Democrats remained dominant in the state. But Kansas-Nebraska had unleashed new currents of civic passion and scrambled up the old partisan fault lines, and Lincoln perceived prospects for a successful fusion between restive anti-Nebraska Democrats and old-line antislavery Whigs. "It might come round that a whig may, by possibility, be elected to the U.S. Senate," he wrote to a newly installed Illinois house member, "and I want the chance of being the man."

But the ever-alert Douglas quickly scuttled Shields as the Democratic standard-bearer and replaced him with a more formidable candidate. As the balloting unfolded, it appeared that Douglas's gambit would yield another victory for the Little Giant. That's when Lincoln released his supporters to vote for the anti-Nebraska Democrat Lyman

Trumbull, who emerged victorious. Thus did the fusion concept prevail, though not with Lincoln or his party heading the ticket. But Lincoln gained notice as a selfless figure willing to place principle above his own ambition.

He fashioned for himself three goals: to help usher in the new Republican Party in Illinois and become its premier leader; to enhance his public profile through widespread speechmaking during the 1856 elections; and to unseat Stephen Douglas by helping elect a pro-fusion legislature in 1858 and getting the senatorial nod from lawmakers the following January. He pursued these goals with increasing ardor as the country struggled through Bleeding Kansas, the grim Six Days in May, the *Dred Scott* controversy, the Buchanan-Douglas clash, and the ominous rise in venomous rhetoric over slavery.

In 1856 Lincoln participated in two momentous Illinois conferences designed to fashion a state Republican affiliate centered on steadfast opposition to slavery expansion, while accepting the Fugitive Slave Act's constitutionality and embracing noninterference in states where slavery already existed. At a Decatur gathering in February, one delegate toasted Lincoln as "our next candidate for the U.S. Senate." Three months later, when he was selected to give what was essentially a keynote address at a party-organizing conference in Bloomington, he pronounced himself "ready to fuse with anyone who would unite . . . to oppose slave power."

Later, during John C. Frémont's presidential quest, the Springfield lawyer delivered some fifty speeches for the adventurer in an effort to unify the state against James Buchanan. When Buchanan captured Illinois in his White House bid, Lincoln promptly turned his attention to his plan to unseat Douglas.

Two years later, when Stephen Douglas returned to Illinois following Congress's 1858 adjournment, he had reason to be buoyant over his recent marriage to the lovely Adele Cutts, twenty-two years younger than he. She had a marked influence on her husband, who celebrated his good fortune by curtailing what had become troublesome drinking habits and improving his wardrobe appearance.

But Douglas had reason to be worried over the powerful political crosscurrents buffeting his reelection campaign and his planned pursuit of the presidency two years hence. The South despised him now for his opposition to the Lecompton constitution and his role in destroying prospects for a slave-state Kansas. But if he softened his adherence to popular sovereignty to placate the South and nurture his presidential hopes, northern Democrats—including Illinois Democrats, crucial to his reelection effort—would defect in droves to the Republicans.

Meanwhile, President Buchanan and his top officials, still smarting from the Little Giant's defiance in the turbulent Lecompton battle, were determined to destroy his career by thwarting his senatorial quest. They couldn't abide the thought of Douglas winning reelection, gaining party dominance, and capturing the White House. The Buchanan men employed two powerful stratagems to bring down Douglas. One was patronage. No Douglas men were being hired for federal jobs in Illinois, particularly postal jobs, and any Douglas men working there were fired unless they joined the anti-Douglas forces. The other stratagem was to split the party by building up an anti-Douglas faction within the ranks.

The ploy seemed quixotic when the state Democratic convention met on April 21 and quickly demonstrated its enthusiasm for Douglas. It awarded him the party nomination in a frenzy of excitement and embraced by acclamation the 1856 Cincinnati platform with its pro–Kansas-Nebraska plank. But a contingent of Buchanan men shunned the convention and convened their own gathering nearby, where they declared themselves to be the real Democratic Party and issued a statement equating support for Douglas to party "treason." They then adjourned with a plan to reconvene in June.

Buchanan's approval of all this became apparent when Washington's *Daily Union*, always closely aligned with any Democratic administration, printed an editorial essentially reading Douglas out of the party. "Democratic candidates, or democratic conventions, that array themselves against the policy supported by the democratic organization of the Union," declared the paper, "cannot claim with any color of right, the support of faithful members of the party."

When the rump group of pro-Buchanan Democrats reconvened in

Springfield on June 9, the attacks on Douglas intensified. One participant predicted the senator would be "crushed and ground to powder."
To help bring about that outcome, the anti-Douglas gathering nominated former U.S. senator Sidney Breese as its candidate for Douglas's seat. But the delegates represented fewer than 50 percent of Illinois
counties, and Douglas remained optimistic that he could overcome intraparty frictions by Election Day.

Still, he took the unusual step of airing his complaints against the
Buchanan forces in a Senate speech on June 14, the last day of the session, though he carefully avoided any suggestion that Buchanan himself
had sanctioned the attacks on him. Attributing the controversy to lingering anger over the Lecompton outcome, he defiantly declared, "If . . .
the great principle of self-government upon which all our institutions
rest . . . is to be the issue, my position is taken, and I am ready to maintain it."

Still, the Douglas predicament gave rise to intriguing rumors that he
might pursue some kind of fusion with Illinois Republicans impressed
with his adherence to principle during the Lecompton battle and looking for ways to siphon off Democratic votes in the 1860 presidential
election. It was never very practical, and Douglas soon dismissed any
thought of it by informing Lincoln's friend William Herndon that he
had crossed the river and burned his boat behind him. He would pursue
his political survival within the Democratic fold.

On June 16 the Illinois Republican Party convened in Springfield
and, with great fanfare and intense fervor, unanimously anointed
Abraham Lincoln as its standard-bearer for the coming senatorial election. At eight o'clock that evening, he rose before the delegates and
guests to deliver his acceptance speech. He began:

> If we could first know *where* we are, and *whither* we are
> tending, we could then better judge *what* to do, and
> *how* to do it.
> We are now far into the *fifth* year, since a policy was

initiated, with the *avowed* object and *confident* promise, of putting an end to slavery agitation.

Under the operation of that policy, that agitation has not only, *not ceased*, but has *constantly augmented*.

In *my* opinion, it w*ill* not cease, until a *crisis* shall have been reached, and passed.

"A house divided against itself cannot stand."

This was breathtaking, not only for its invocation of Scripture but also for its stark realism. Every compromise effort over forty years to subdue the slavery agitation had been an effort to prop up a divided house. All had been based on an acceptance of slavery as an ongoing institution. Lincoln now was explaining why none of it had worked or could work. This was not entirely a novel observation. Others had said as much in different words. And southerners particularly had expressed a similar sense of determinism, usually prefatory to secession talk. Lincoln emphasized, though, that he wasn't advocating any outcome, but merely making a prediction. He continued:

I believe this government cannot endure, permanently half *slave* and half *free*.

I do not expect the Union to be *dissolved*—I do not expect the house to *fall*—but I *do* expect it will cease to be divided.

It will become *all* one thing or *all* the other.

Lincoln argued that either the opponents of slavery would put the institution in a place where all would know its extinction had become inevitable; or its advocates would successfully render it "alike lawful in *all* the States, *old* as well as *new*—*North* as well as *South*."

That latter prospect, slavery lawful in all the states, said Lincoln, might seem impossible to the North's slavery opponents. But, at the beginning of 1854, he noted, slavery was prohibited in half the states by state constitutions and in most of the national territory by the Missouri Compromise prohibition. Four days later, a political struggle commenced that ended in repealing the Missouri Compromise and opening the national territory to slavery through the concept of popular sovereignty, which Lincoln defined as: "[I]f any one man chooses to enslave another, no third man shall be allowed to object."

Then came the *Dred Scott* decision declaring that, under the Constitution, neither Congress nor any territorial legislature could exclude slavery from U.S. territories. Lincoln saw here "another nice little niche" to be filled in by a future Supreme Court decision, prohibiting states from excluding slavery within their limits. "Such a decision," said Lincoln, "is all that slavery now lacks of being alike lawful in all the States."

Although Lincoln carefully avoided any direct attack on Taney's *Scott* ruling or the court itself, he suggested slyly that they had been part of a "common plan" by "the present political dynasty" of Douglas, Pierce, Taney, and Buchanan to set America upon a course toward a nationwide slave culture. "To meet and overthrow the power of that dynasty," said Lincoln, "is the work now before all those who would prevent that consummation."

Twenty-three days later, Douglas returned to Illinois after an extended tour through New York, Ohio, Indiana, and Michigan. Arriving at Chicago's Tremont House hotel for the inaugural speech of his reelection campaign, he was greeted by some thirty thousand enthusiasts. Seeing Lincoln in the crowd, Douglas invited his adversary to the Tremont balcony, from which he was to address the throng below. He made an elaborate show of political magnanimity by calling Lincoln a "worthy gentleman" who was "kind, amiable, and intelligent . . . an honorable opponent."

Douglas made clear that he harbored no plans to swerve from the path he had chosen for himself in attacking and eventually killing the "Lecompton monstrosity," as he called it. There would be no flirtation with Republicans nor any concessions to his Buchananite enemies. "I regard the great principle of popular sovereignty," he said, "as having been vindicated and made triumphant in this land."

But now, he emphasized, he must direct his firepower against his friend Abe Lincoln, who had "totally misapprehended the great principles upon which our government rests." The idea that the American house could not stand as a divided entity, argued the senator, assaulted the very principles of states' rights and federalism. A vast democratic nation such as America, he continued, certainly could thrive with different states embracing different local laws and domestic institutions. In fact, he averred, Lincoln's notion of uniformity represented a threat to America, in that it was an invitation for sectional strife over divergent visions of what the nation should be.

No, he said, let the various states and regions decide for themselves how they want to conduct their domestic affairs, to fashion life in the granite hills of New Hampshire differently from life on the rice plantations of South Carolina or in the farm districts of Pennsylvania or the lumber regions of Maine. "I am driven irresistibly to the conclusion," said Douglas, "that diversity, dissimilarity, variety in all our local and domestic institutions, is the great safeguard of our liberties."

This certainly applied also, in the senator's view, to matters of race. Illinois, for example, was a free state, but free blacks there could not vote, serve on juries, or enjoy political privileges. "I am content with that system," the senator declared, ". . . [and] deny the right of any other State to complain of our policy." If those other states wished to give blacks a right to vote, as Maine had done, or to exclude blacks altogether from their confines, as Indiana had done, that was fine with him.

Here's where Douglas's views diverged most starkly from Lincoln's. As Douglas characterized Lincoln's views, he opposed *Dred Scott* because it barred blacks from enjoying U.S. citizenship and hence the rights bestowed upon white citizens, including the right of freedom. He considered this disparity, as he had said many times, a great moral wrong. Douglas, on the other hand, argued that the U.S. government was, as he said at the Tremont House, "founded on the white basis. It was made by the white man, for the benefit of the white man, to be administered by white men, in such manner as they should determine." Blacks, in his view, should not be treated cruelly by governments or citizens, but needn't be treated equally. Morality didn't come into it.

The combatants' initial campaign speeches—Lincoln's House Divided address and Douglas's Tremont House presentation—set the tone for what was to become a two-month political spectacle that riveted

Illinois and much of the nation. In mid-July the two men agreed to engage in seven debates between August 21 and October 15—one in each congressional district except those in the Chicago and Springfield areas, where the candidates already had campaigned. The formula was simple: the first man would speak for an hour; his opponent for an hour and a half; then the first man would have a half hour for a final response. Douglas, as the challenged party, insisted on getting the favorable opening-and-closing position in four of the seven debates.

The events drew large audiences—probably exceeding fifteen thousand at Ottawa and Galesburg, perhaps reaching thirteen thousand at Charleston and Quincy. Attendance for the seven debates certainly exceeded seventy-five thousand. Newspapers throughout the country covered the confrontations extensively, and soon the exchanges captured national attention. Journalists and politicians naturally provided plenty of stump-performance assessments, mostly colored by partisan sentiments.

Henry Villard, a brilliant journalist who later became a financier and railroad entrepreneur, covered the debates for New York newspapers and rendered a trenchant portrait of the two adversaries at the first exchange. Douglas, he wrote, displayed "a strong, sonorous voice, a rapid, vigorous utterance, a telling play of countenance, impressive gestures, and all the other arts of the practiced speaker." In terms of outward appearance and performance, "there was nothing in favor of Lincoln," said Villard, adding the challenger cut an "indescribably gawky figure" and used "singularly awkward, almost absurd, up-and-down and sidewise movements of his body to give emphasis to his arguments." Further, Lincoln's voice, while robust enough, sometimes soared to an "unnatural pitch."

But, continued Villard, Douglas's talents couldn't match Lincoln's sincerity and soundness of thought. "There was nothing in all Douglas' powerful effort that appealed to the higher instincts of human nature, while Lincoln always touched sympathetic chords." Others noted a significant distinction between Douglas's fist-pounding intensity and Lincoln's more conversational and easygoing style, with gentle jabs and playful humor.

The scene at Ottawa on debate day resembled the scenes that would follow at the subsequent locations. People poured in, braving the extreme heat of the day, on foot and horseback and buckboards, in carriages and aboard canal boats. A privileged few set out in Chicago aboard a special fourteen-car train, with other cars added along the way. Though the debate was set to begin at two o'clock, the start time had to be delayed a half hour so the candidates could get through the throng to the platform.

Douglas spoke first, displaying his polemical pugnacity, though he offered some introductory words of esteem for the Lincoln he had known and liked during their days together as young legislative strivers. But he quickly went on the attack, saying Lincoln had distinguished himself as a congressman "by his opposition to the Mexican war, taking the side of the common enemy . . . against his own country." He accused Lincoln of initiating a plan to "abolitionize" both the old Whig Party and the northern Democratic entity and embracing an early Republican resolution calling for repeal of the Fugitive Slave Act, abolition of slavery in the District of Columbia, and the prohibition of any more slave states emanating from current or prospective territories.

In reply Lincoln scored Douglas for misrepresenting his position on the Fugitive Slave Act and other elements of the early Republican resolution, with which, he said, he had had no involvement. He repeated his warning of a second *Dred Scott*–type decision designed to nationalize slavery and closed by placing slavery once again into the kind of moral framework that seemed to leave Douglas cold. In the final debate, at Alton, he crystallized slavery's moral dimension while advocating "the mildest policy" in thwarting its spread and placing it on a path to extinction. He said:

> The sentiment that contemplates the institution of slavery as being wrong, is the sentiment of the Republican party. . . . They look upon slavery as a moral, social, and political wrong, and while they contemplate it as being such, they nevertheless have due regard for its actual existence among us and the difficulties of getting rid of it . . . and for all the constitutional obligations thrown

around it; nevertheless, they do desire to see a policy instituted that looks to the thing not growing any larger.

But Lincoln emphasized at this final debate, as he had at others, that he didn't advocate "a perfect social and political equality" between whites and blacks. "These are false issues," he said, "that Judge Douglas has all the while tried to force this controversy upon without foundation." Indeed, Lincoln's view of equality between the races seemed to take on a minimalist aspect, designed in part to distinguish himself from the full-equality sentiments of a Garrison or even a Seward. In this he seemed in harmony with the prevailing sentiment of his state, which wanted an end to slavery but didn't want full equality for blacks or intermingling of the races. This ambiguity complicated Lincoln's effort to place himself upon a moral high ground.

But ambiguity was an inevitable element of the complex and emotional slavery debate. This was reflected also in a noteworthy exchange in the Lincoln-Douglas debates during the second session, at Freeport, where Lincoln posed to his opponent a provocative question. It was whether, in the face of *Dred Scott*, a territory could exclude slavery prior to the formation of a state constitution. In other words, how could Douglas reconcile the *Scott* ruling, which declared slavery exclusion unconstitutional in the territories, with his cherished popular sovereignty, designed to allow territorial residents to decide that matter for themselves?

Douglas had devised an answer that he had tested on numerous occasions, but many political observers weren't yet aware of his approach to the question. The *New York Herald*, no friend of Douglas since his break with Buchanan, phrased the Douglas predicament with a certain wicked malice, noting with apparent pleasure the political peril it posed to the senator. "Is Mr. Douglas," asked the paper, "riding two horses— Dred Scott [the southern horse] and Uncle Tom [the northern one]—at the same time?" In other words, was Douglas trying to hold two irreconcilable convictions?

Douglas sought to meet that acrobatic challenge by arguing that, irrespective of Supreme Court rulings, the people of a territory could preclude slavery simply by enacting "local police regulations" and various laws "unfriendly" to the institution. Thus did Douglas proclaim his continuing fealty to the Supreme Court while adhering to his particular interpretation of popular sovereignty. In the South, however, this artful construction seemed to negate *Dred Scott*, widely viewed in the region as its only true victory of the entire decade. The *Charleston Mercury* said Douglas's contorted logic demonstrated "the utter unsoundness and trickery of the man." But in the proudly free state of Illinois, where Douglas's political imperatives were more immediate, his political prospects brightened.

The debates represented only a part of the campaign as both candidates crisscrossed the state in pursuit of votes. Lincoln delivered some sixty-three speeches during the canvass, while Douglas pegged his appearances at 130. When the ballots were counted on November 2, Republican legislative candidates narrowly outpolled Democratic contenders, 125,000 votes to 121,000, with candidates committed to Sidney Breese, Buchanan's spoiler, getting 5,000. But, based on unequal district populations, the popular-vote outcome would place forty-six Democrats in the legislature to just forty-one Republicans. That guaranteed a Douglas victory when the legislature convened in January.

Stephen Douglas, employing his famous political wiles and combativeness, had survived the Buchanan onslaught and the Republicans' statewide rise to remain his state's premier political leader and become a contender for Democratic supremacy throughout the country. But he found himself in a precarious situation. The *Charleston Mercury*'s New York correspondent filed a perceptive postelection analysis saying that "Seward abolitionists" within the Republican Party couldn't decide whether to laugh or cry at the Douglas victory.

On one hand, they had no reason to cheer the defeat of their "peculiar pet and fellow nigger-worshipper, Abe Lincoln," at the hands of "Squatter Sovereignty Douglas." On the other hand, there was no need for chagrin at a result that was "a slap in the face for the President" and likely to hasten "the demoralization and defeat of the democratic party" in the 1860 presidential election. Besides, wrote the correspondent, Douglas had campaigned rather like a Black Republican himself, with his ironclad fealty to popular sovereignty and his Freeport argument that artful legislative maneuvers in the territories could negate the thrust of Roger Taney's *Dred Scott* ruling. "[I]t would be difficult," said the correspondent, "to determine on what ground Douglas can claim the slightest sympathy or support of the Southern States." Reclaiming his southern standing while mollifying northern Democrats would remain, for the next two years, a fearsome challenge for the Little Giant.

As for Lincoln, the exposure afforded him by the lively Illinois debate and his distinctive antislavery dialectic placed him within the leading circle of Republican spokesmen, along with Seward, Chase, Wilson, and Sumner. He had tasted once again the bitterness of defeat, an all-too-familiar flavor, and it wasn't clear what avenues of political ambition would be open to him. But he was nationally known now, as he always had wished to be, and neither Stephen Douglas nor anyone else could consider him unworthy of notice.

22

REALIGNMENT

|||||||||||||||||||||||||||||||||||||||||||||||||||||||||||||||||||||||||||||||||||

THE ONRUSH OF NEW POLITICAL REALITIES

In March 1858 an unannounced visitor appeared at Lloyd Garrison's *Liberator* offices on Boston's Cornhill Street. It was William Herndon, Abe Lincoln's law partner and a man of mark in his own right: Springfield mayor; member of his state's Republican central committee; presidential elector; even a possible gubernatorial candidate. He had traveled east to check out those disturbing rumors of an incipient alliance between major Republican figures and Douglas Democrats in the wake of the Lecompton uproar and the subsequent Democratic Party split. Whatever merit there was in such an alliance, it would devastate Lincoln's cherished senatorial hopes, and Illinois party leaders wished to know precisely what was going on.

It turned out, of course, that not much was going on, and Lincoln found himself with a clear shot at upending Douglas (which proved, however, an impossible task). But, after conversations with Douglas in Chicago and Horace Greeley in New York, Herndon traveled on to Boston to seek out the men he considered to be "the three *living* institutions" of that city—Theodore Parker, Wendell Phillips, and Garrison. The first two snubbed the hinterland figure with snobbish disregard,

but the always genial Garrison gave the impromptu visitor a hearty welcome and engaged him in a discursive conversation, vividly captured by
Henry Mayer in his consummate Garrison biography.

Herndon was a jaunty fellow, full of good cheer and bursts of chatty
animation, with a penchant for splashy clothes and high-flying philosophical musings. He engaged the editor for some time on the "animat-
ing purposes of the universe," as Mayer put it, "with the snap and pep of
a railroad promoter." But the men soon turned to the more immediate
topics of politics and slavery. Given that Greeley, in his conversation
with Herndon, had evinced a lingering enthusiasm for a Republican
alliance with Douglas, Herndon took pains to emphasize that the idea
could never work, in large measure because Douglas was "the greatest
demagogue in America."

Herndon revealed to his host that he shared elements of the editor's
radicalism, embraced more fervently than ever after the Kansas agonies
and Taney's abhorrent *Scott* ruling. But he certainly wasn't interested in
recruiting Garrison to his Republican Party, whose moderate ethos the
unyielding editor consistently denounced. Indeed, the Springfield lawyer suggested that Garrison, in his current mode of contention, played
a valuable role in nudging the party toward more emphatic action than
it might otherwise pursue. But he urged the editor to consider the dual
reality that the Republicans just might win the presidency in 1860 and
that they represented the best hope available for an eventual emancipation.

Garrison replied that he couldn't abide the Republicans' preoccupation with ancillary issues such as Kansas and their acceptance of slavery
where it already existed. His aim was to strike at the heart of the odious
institution with fatal blows, or at least with unadulterated, uncompromising boldness of expression.

Herndon cheerfully brushed aside the disagreement. "We are as we
are," he said. "You hate Republicanism, but never mind *that*: it is a
midlink"—in other words, part of a process bending events inexorably
toward the hallowed goal of slavery extinction. "Republicanism," said
Herndon, "is a condition—absolute and unannihilable to your march."

The exchange, writes Mayer, "epitomized the political problem facing Garrison's leadership in the aftermath of *Dred Scott* and the growing influence of both a moderate [antislavery] party and a belligerent sectionalism." For nearly three decades Garrison had cast lightning-bolt aspersions upon all who didn't share his stark radicalism and ideological purity. Don't abate the radical sensibility or debase that purity, Herndon was saying, but step away from the outsider defiance and become, as Mayer later expressed it, "an independent participant, rather than an alien fanatic."

It wasn't clear, as Herndon tipped his silk hat toward Garrison upon departing, if the Springfield lawyer had had much impact on the editor's thinking. But political developments were pushing Garrison toward a personal reckoning on the tone and tactics of his commentary. Would he continue to regard as enemies those who didn't embrace his views in their entirety and with equal passion? Could he pull back from his assaults on the Constitution and his call for disunion? Those questions would take on greater immediacy and force with unfolding events.

Down in South Carolina, Barnwell Rhett faced a different dilemma. He knew what he wanted: the dissolution of the United States and the creation of a new southern nation based on slave labor and dominated by a well-born (or, in some instances, well-wedded) planter class. But it wasn't clear how best to pursue that goal, though he certainly knew how not to pursue it: by any kind of frontal attack on the Union or his state's unionist political leaders. Had he learned that lesson as a U.S. senator back in 1852, he might still be a senator. He was far more attuned now to the currents of political sentiment, and he knew that, while South Carolina might be open to secession theoretically, it wasn't ready for any overt action, certainly no separate action. Hammond's new moderate outlook and Chesnut's election constituted a warning about getting ahead of popular thinking.

Rhett also worried about his newspaper. The *Mercury*'s financial footing was precarious, and Rhett couldn't afford to sustain its losses indefinitely. He needed to expand its readership, and that argued for eschewing the kind of disunionist bellicosity that once defined the paper, as well as Rhett. Thus the Rhetts studiously avoided attacks on Hammond or Chesnut under the *Mercury*'s imprimatur (though they published letters from readers criticizing the senators) and fashioned a recurrent theme of regional harmony—"a united state in a united South," as one biographer put it—in order to ensure the region's capacity to protect itself from the North's growing power.

In July 1858 the Rhetts improved their newspaper's finances by purchasing Leonidas Spratt's *Charleston Southern Standard* and its twelve hundred subscribers for $800. The transaction tripled the *Mercury*'s circulation overnight and augmented its annual revenue by $17,000. "It shall be the object of the *Mercury*," said the paper in announcing the purchase, ". . . to bury the past political differences in the State, and to draw together all in the South who are really desirous to defend her interests and honor." In a follow-up piece the paper emphasized that it had long abandoned any interest in "separate action of the State."

But Rhett wouldn't need to worry about getting ahead of southern opinion if southern opinion moved his way. And that could happen, he surmised, if the country elected a Republican president in 1860, particularly if he turned out to be William Seward. The New Yorker for years had outraged the South with his stark pronouncements about the rise of the antislavery movement and its threat to what Charles Sumner called "the house of bondage." The pronouncements were all the more jarring to southerners because they seemed to be coming true. And so Rhett abjured any secession talk and undertook instead to advocate southern preparation for the coming crisis, which he anticipated as a secession crisis. And, if he could quietly hasten the arrival of that crisis, all the better.

He was joined in this thinking by William Lowndes Yancey of Montgomery, Alabama, known throughout the South as "the prince of the fire-eaters." A lawyer, planter, former newspaper publisher, and former U.S. congressman, Yancey had been brought up in Troy, New York, after his widowed mother married a Presbyterian minister from that town. There he encountered a strong abolitionist sensibility intertwined with his stepfather's professed religion. It didn't take. As a young man, Yancey moved back to the South, entered the planter class through marriage, and embraced the southern cause.

He didn't look like a revolutionary. One northern newspaperman described him as a "mild and gentlemanly man, always wearing a genuinely good-humored smile and looking as if nothing in the world could disturb the equanimity of his spirits." But that facade was deceptive. He once had entered into a brutal fight with a man that ended with the man's death. Though sentenced to a year in prison, he shortly was pardoned.

A compact figure "with a square built head and face, and an eye full of expression," Yancey was said to have tucked away in his brain a three-day speech, full of fire and eloquence, on the imperative of secession and the glory of the coming slave empire.

Rhett and Yancey came together in May 1858 when Rhett traveled to Montgomery to attend a "southern commercial convention" organized by Yancey to discuss the southern fate. Some two thousand delegates from eleven slave states (excluding Maryland, Delaware, Missouri, and Kentucky, where slavery was not a dominant political factor) met in a large building that had served as a railroad storehouse. The tone of the gathering was "extreme Southern," reported the *Mercury* correspondent on the scene, who added that he had "not met a single man, except the Virginians, who approves of the late compromise in Kansas."

Thus it wasn't surprising that the convention quickly took up resolutions extolling the proposed resumption of the African slave trade as "expedient and proper" and saying the convention should "lend its influence in every legitimate way to that end." Yancey endorsed the idea while expressing skepticism about its political prospects.

But Rhett persuaded the Alabamian to soften his approval and acknowledge that the slave-trade resumption was "utterly impracticable." Meanwhile, the *Mercury* correspondent covering the proceedings left no doubt about his paper's position or Rhett's. "I am sorry to say," he wrote, "that the agitation of this question here is breeding great dissension." Since Congress would never approve any slave-trade renewal, he added, it was folly to press such a contentious issue, which was certain to "divide and paralyze the South, and thus tend to keep her in the present Union." In the end, the convention declined to approve the slave-trade resolutions.

But Rhett had successfully separated himself from southern fire-eaters, who felt compelled to push for slavery expansion in all manifestations and at all costs, including through the slave trade, the acquisition of Cuba, forays into Central America, or anything else that would bring more slaves to America or take America to more slaves. To Rhett this was madness. He kept his eye on the target, which was secession. The imperative now was to ensure that the South was prepared for it, which in turn meant unifying the region and suppressing unnecessary contentions.

The congressional election results of autumn 1858 reinforced Rhett's strategy, just as they accentuated Garrison's dilemma. Stephen Douglas's success in fending off Lincoln's Republican challenge represented an aberration in that campaign year, in which Republicans scored big victories nationwide. As the fall election results filtered out, it became clear that the American people had had enough of Buchanan's Lecompton outrage and his party's inability to manage the slavery discord. Voters particularly went after members of Congress who had supported the proslavery Lecompton constitution or William English's later effort to finesse the issue in Congress.

Indiana, for years a Democratic stronghold, sent seven Republicans to the U.S. House of Representatives, along with two Douglas Democrats and only two Buchanan loyalists. Republicans also captured both houses of the legislature. Ohio's twenty-two-member House delegation now would include only four Democrats, three of them Douglas men. Republicans nearly swept the New England states and took the two Senate seats in both Minnesota and Iowa. New Jersey's five-member House delegation would comprise three Republicans and two anti-Lecompton Democrats.

Only four of New York's thirty-two House members would be Democrats in the new Congress after the tone for the state's election season was established by William Seward. On October 25 he delivered a speech at Rochester that set the South ablaze. Echoing Abraham Lincoln's "House Divided" warning of four months earlier, but employing far more stark and challenging language, Seward declared that the free-labor system generated "strength, wealth, greatness, intelligence, and freedom," while the slave system bred "poverty, imbecility, and anarchy," as seen in the nations of Spanish and Portuguese America. The two systems, he said, were incompatible.

The New Yorker then uttered two words that would attach to him throughout his life and beyond. The Union, he said, was engaged in an "irrepressible conflict" between "opposing and enduring forces," and one or the other of those forces would prevail. Like Lincoln, he predicted that the nation would go all one way or all the other. In casting their votes that fall, New Yorkers clearly embraced the Seward thesis.

Buchanan's Pennsylvania, meanwhile, spurned its leading politician by sending only two Lecompton Democrats to the next Congress and voting against Buchanan candidates in state, county, and town elections. As Pennsylvania returns hit the telegraph wires and reached Washington on the evening of October 14, the president was enjoying a gourmet repast with three friends at the White House, with fine wine in abundance. As aides interrupted intermittently with dreadful new reports, the assembled cronies succumbed to a bit of mirth at the sheer magnitude of the rebuff. "Yesterday . . . we had a merry time of it," wrote Buchanan to his niece, Harriet Lane, "laughing among other things over our crushing defeat. It is so great that it is almost absurd."

When the balloting finally closed in November, Buchanan's party lost thirty seats in the U.S. House, while Republicans picked up twenty-one. That gave Republicans 113 seats to 101 for Democrats. But the balance of power rested with twenty-three members from other parties, mostly die-hard Whigs and southern American Party adherents. Thus Republicans could dominate the chamber if they could command six votes from the splinter groups, while Democrats were clearly eclipsed. The turnaround stemmed largely from a massive migration of northern Douglas Democrats to the Republican Party.

The outcome quickly intensified North-South tensions. Greeley's *Tribune* gleefully declared that slavery expansion was now dead, as the country would "in future belong . . . to that portion of the population which entertains anti-Lecompton views." The *Mercury*, quoting that passage, replied that if anti-Lecompton forces had indeed captured the Union, "it is a question for the people of the South to consider how long shall they remain a component part of it."

Massachusetts, as usual, placed itself at the vanguard of the Republican movement with a party sweep of House seats, dominance of the legislature, and the reelection of Nathaniel Banks as governor. In addition, the Bay State's Third Congressional District finally sent to Congress that son and grandson of presidents, Charles Francis Adams, who was so shocked to hear he was being considered for the nomination that he refused to put any credence in the reports. He had been passed over two years before, to his great consternation, and didn't want to suffer another disappointment.

But the man and the hour converged nicely in 1858. Upon getting the nomination at the state party convention, Adams received offers of campaign help from Sumner, Wilson, and even William Seward, but there was no need. He waltzed to victory with a vote total twice as large as his nearest competitor.

He was fifty-one now, his white hair receding and thinning, but his azure-eyed gaze as steely as ever and his convictions as sturdy. For years he had been touted for his intellectual depth and studied rectitude but dogged also by questions of whether he possessed the fire needed for the raucous realities of politics. But the political environment was less raucous now, with the state dominated by Republicans. Thus the Massachusetts party didn't need another battler like Sumner or inside maneuverer like Wilson; it needed a touchstone figure personifying the old civic verities of John and John Quincy Adams. Charles Francis fit the role nicely.

When the lame-duck second session of the 35th Congress convened on December 6, President Buchanan sent to lawmakers his Second Annual Message, as notable for what it didn't say as for what it did. There was no mention of the heavy blow delivered to the president's Democratic Party in the late elections, no hint of any lessons to be learned from it, and certainly no acknowledgment of his own contribution through his Lecompton embrace. The men around the president seemed to attribute the drubbing to transitory factors such as the 1857 financial panic that lingered into the following campaign year and overblown reports of the Kansas chaos. Buchanan himself told Harriet Lane that he planned to present to Congress a glowing report of the nation's civic health under his leadership.

In a bland narrative of Kansas events, Buchanan hailed the *Dred Scott* decision and the popular sovereignty doctrine as having pacified the slavery issue and pulled the country into a new era of tranquility. "The just equality of all the states," he declared, "has thus been vindicated and a fruitful source of dangerous dissension among them has been removed." He ignored Stephen Douglas's artful suggestion, anathema in the South, on how territorial residents could nullify the Taney ruling by enacting "police power" legislation unfriendly to slavery.

With the troublesome slavery issue finally subdued, in the president's view, he turned his attention to a series of expansionist foreign policy ideas. In doing so he generated an appearance of wanting to mollify the South by expanding U.S. territory as a means of expanding slavery. He reiterated his desire to acquire Cuba and suggested a possible need for America to intervene in a civil war then raging in Mexico, which was interfering, he said, with U.S. transit rights in that country. Issues involving transit rights also stirred expressions of presidential bellicosity toward Nicaragua. Congress essentially brushed aside the president's call for a bold foreign adventurism.

On domestic policy, he embraced congressional action to raise certain tariff rates, foster construction of a Pacific railroad, and enact a national bankruptcy law. Congress, though still under Democratic dominance until the 36th Congress convened in December 1859, thwarted most of Buchanan's domestic agenda—in part, perhaps, because the president didn't fight for it. In putting forth his tariff measure, he placidly said he had "thrown out these suggestions as the fruit of my own observations, to which Congress, in their better judgment, will give such weight as they may justly deserve."

In an interview with a reporter for the *Sun* of Worcester, Massachusetts, the president attributed his troubles to the fractious nature of his party: "split up into all sorts of factions," as the reporter put it, quoting the president indirectly, "incapable of adhesion, or of carrying any measure as a party." Thus, the president lamented, his "recommendations pass for nothing." But he predicted that history would judge his administration as "not only a successful but a popular one." This at a time when his popular support clearly was dissolving.

Buchanan's greatest folly, though, was in flattering himself with the notion that he had tamed the slavery issue. That notion disintegrated beginning on February 23, 1859, when New Hampshire Republican John Hale, with his usual conviction and bluster, rose in the Senate to offer an appropriations amendment dealing with the one subject certain to unleash a torrent of political emotion: Kansas. Hale's measure would repeal the restrictive clause in the previous year's English bill whereby Kansas was to be barred from statehood until it had reached a territorial population of some ninety-three thousand. Like other antislavery congressional members, Hale wanted Kansas brought into the Union as a free state as soon as possible.

The wily Republican also may have intended to execute a subtle ploy to drive a wedge through the opposition party. If so, it worked. Taking the floor to oppose the amendment, Mississippi senator Albert Brown attacked not just Hale's measure but the state of slave relations in the country as a whole. He demanded legislation to codify the constitutional property rights of territorial slaveholders, as interpreted by Taney's *Dred Scott* ruling. "Mr. President," intoned Brown, "the Supreme Court of the United States decided . . . that slaves were property, and that slaveholders had the same right to carry their slave property to the Territories that any other citizen from any other State, had to carry any other kind of property." That meant, he added, that slave property in the territories must be protected by the federal government. "Now, sir, by protection, if the word be not a cheat and delusion, we understand *adequate* protection, *sufficient* protection."

He was calling for a federal slave code that would, if enacted, destroy Charles Sumner's "freedom national" concept embraced since 1852 by many of the great antislavery figures who also were pro-Constitution—Seward, Chase, Hale, Wilson, Lincoln. It was based on the conviction that the Founders had disdained slavery as immoral, but had accepted it as a state institution because there was no other way to pull the states together into a constitutional structure.

Now Brown was demanding that Congress stitch that institution into the national fabric by proclaiming a federal responsibility for protecting it. Further, Brown invoked the authority of the Supreme Court in doing so. Suppose, said the Mississippian, he went into Kansas with his slaves in expectation of his ownership being protected by authorities there. But suppose those authorities refused or enacted Douglas's "police power" laws discouraging him from going there in the first place. "Am I . . . to abandon my constitutional rights?" asked Brown, then answered, "No, sir."

As the Senate debate raged over several days with increasing intensity, Stephen Douglas entered the chamber with the same air of self-assurance he had displayed throughout his conspicuous Senate tenure. There was no hint of the political blow administered to him at the beginning of the session by Buchanan's Senate allies. Having failed in their effort to destroy Douglas's career in the 1858 Illinois balloting, they now sought to diminish it. While the senator was away visiting Cuba at the start of the congressional session, the Senate Republican caucus voted to bounce him from his chairmanship of the Committee on Territories, which he had led since 1847.

Even some of Douglas's most ardent political foes expressed outrage at the action, while southerners basked in glee. The *Mercury* expressed pleasure that "punishment is rapidly following upon the heels of a great political traitor." Republicans, while enjoying the spectacle of intraparty strife across the aisle, warily viewed it as a sign of just how obdurate the proslavery forces had become in exacting revenge against Douglas and pushing outlandish measures such as Brown's slave code.

Douglas thrust himself into the debate by pushing back on Brown's effort to give slave property a special status. This, he said, was politically untenable as well as undemocratic. "How many votes," Douglas asked Alabama's senator Clement Clay Jr., a slave-code advocate, "do you think Mr. Buchanan would have obtained in Pennsylvania if he had then said that the Constitution . . . plants slavery in all the Territories and makes it the duty of the Federal Government to keep it there and maintain it at the point of the bayonet?"

The question crystallized a fundamental new reality of American politics as the 1860 presidential election approached. The Democratic Party as a national party had split into two regional factions that were incompatible. The northern party was the Douglas party, wending its way through the thicket of slavery emotion under the ensign of popular sovereignty and Douglas's corollary Freeport doctrine on the use of local police powers to thwart the institution's expansion. But more and more southerners opposed the concept with unsparing vehemence. As Senator Brown expressed it, "I utterly, totally, entirely, persistently, and consistently, repudiate the whole doctrine of squatter sovereignty."

The demands of southern Democrats, meanwhile, were becoming increasingly problematic for northerners. They could swat down easily enough the radical notions about acquiring Cuba or building a slave empire in Central America or reinstituting the African slave trade. Those were minority ideas never destined to sweep the South. But the slave-code concept, bolstered by *Dred Scott*, was not so easily dismissed. It threatened to spread through the South like unruly kudzu vines.

The political journey of Jefferson Davis represented a case in point. The Mississippian, back in the Senate now after his stint as Franklin Pierce's war secretary, delivered a speech in Maine in which he disavowed any notion of the South demanding congressional protection for slavery in the territories or of spreading the institution into the free states. "So much for the oft-repeated fallacy of forcing slavery upon any community," he said. Back in his home state, however, he swiftly swung around to Albert Brown's slave-code demand with the zeal of a convert. He called the nonintervention doctrine "a delusive gauze thrown over the public mind . . . withholding from an American citizen the protection he has a right to claim."

But such views would never gain traction in the North. Douglas put it starkly in declaring, "I never would vote for a slave code in the Territories by Congress; and I have yet to learn that there is a man in a free State of this Union, of any party, who would."

Thus it was clear now that the country had moved into a new political system, with three parties vying for political dominance: the northern Democrats, beset by ongoing frictions between the Buchanan and Douglas factions; the southern Democrats, struggling with swirls of political sentiment represented by James Orr unionists, Barnwell Rhett secessionists, and the new slave-code advocates; and the Republicans, an exclusively northern entity with promising prospects in the nation's Electoral College.

The slave-code provocation had injected a disruptive new dynamic into the mix. With its spreading resonance in the South and almost universal rejection in the North, it posed a question of how the ongoing slavery confrontation could be adjudicated through normal political processes; how the nation could withstand the civic shocks that just kept coming.

23

HARPERS FERRY

||||||||||||||||||||||||||||||||||||||||||||||||||||||||||||||||||||||||||||||||

"WE MUST SEE MUCH DARKER HOURS BEFORE IT IS DAYLIGHT"

I n the early-morning darkness of Monday, October 17, 1859, Colonel Lewis Washington was roused from slumber by four armed men who had breached the security of his spacious manor house near the Virginia town of Harpers Ferry. They entered his bedroom and surrounded him. One of the intruders asked another, who had known Washington, if this was indeed the man who owned the surrounding farmland. Upon getting confirmation, he turned to Washington and announced: "You are our prisoner." The same words were uttered some three hours earlier in the nearby kidnapping of a night watchman guarding the bridge connecting Virginia and Maryland over the Potomac River.

Those words touched off John Brown's quixotic plan to spark an armed slave rebellion in Virginia and mount a guerrilla offensive against southern bondage from rugged Allegheny hideaways. When the audacious adventure was over, just thirty-six hours after it began, ten of Brown's twenty-one recruits lay dead or dying in a field, while six civilians and two U.S. Marines also died. Six Brown men survived the bloodshed and were soon hanged along with their leader. Five escaped.

It was a pathetic initiative—ill-conceived, ill-executed, and ill-fated. Frederick Douglass, the free black intellectual, warned Brown beforehand that his plan would snare him in "a perfect steel-trap," and that's what happened. Given the magnitude of the debacle, Brown could easily have been dismissed as the charlatan that he always had been in just about every walk of life that he had pursued, except on a far larger scale this time and with more woeful results. But the collective psychology of the nation in those turbulent times rendered impossible such a commonplace evaluation on either side of the sectional divide. Instead, the man immediately took on a mythic symbolism, with many in the North hailing him as a paragon of higher law purity, while southerners conjured up visions of a gigantic threat to life and livelihood germinating in the land of the enemy.

When John Brown returned to Kansas for the last time in June 1858, after he and the Secret Six had agreed to postpone his Harpers Ferry mission, he encountered a territory much subdued from earlier times. The evenhanded leadership of back-to-back governors Robert Walker and James Denver, coupled with the rejection of the Lecompton constitution by the U.S. Congress and Kansas voters, had largely settled the slavery question there. There wasn't much point in continued fighting.

But before Brown's arrival, a fanatical Georgian named Charles Hamilton, with a group of proslavery followers, defied the free-state victories by rounding up eleven antislavery settlers, herding them into a ravine, and riddling them with bullets. Five died outright, while five more were wounded and one escaped unharmed. The episode shocked the nation as one more Kansas outrage in the name of slavery.

No one was more outraged than John Brown. On December 20 he led a raiding party of vengeance into Missouri that plundered the homes of two slaveholders, shot one of them dead, and made off with livestock, wagons, weapons, and a hundred dollars in cash. The party also liberated eleven slaves and, in a remarkable thousand-mile trek through winter hardships, spirited them to freedom in Canada. Historian David

Potter called this feat "perhaps the most successful operation Brown ever engaged in."

The episode brought further attention to the bold antislavery warrior, now known widely to his admirers as Osawatomie Brown and sometimes just Old Brown. But many territorial free-staters expressed fear that it might reignite the fires of Bleeding Kansas. Old Brown didn't care. When President Buchanan ostentatiously offered a $250 reward for capture of the brazen fighter, the fighter in turn offered to pay $2.50 to anyone who would capture Buchanan.

Upon completion of his Canada trek, Brown turned his attention to preparations for his grand Harpers Ferry scheme. In May 1859 he sent to the area a recruit named John Cook as a kind of advance agent, charged with collecting information on terrain, people, customs, and the like. As part of his mission, he approached the prosperous farmer Lewis Washington, great-grand-nephew of the nation's first president, and asked whether he might be permitted to inspect some of Washington's striking heirlooms, including a sword given to his ancestor by Prussia's Frederick the Great and a pistol bestowed by General Lafayette. Lewis Washington, accustomed to such entreaties, assented, and the two men struck up a casual friendship. It was Cook who identified Washington as the farm owner when Brown's men kidnapped him in the middle of the night of October 16–17.

Brown, meanwhile, arrived near Harpers Ferry in June under the name of Isaac Smith. He rented a farm about five miles from the town, on the Maryland side of the Potomac, and transported to the farm multiple boxes filled with guns and ammunition, as well as nearly a thousand deadly pikes that had been specially made for use by slaves, to compensate for their presumed lack of familiarity with firearms. To quash curiosity about the boxes and the men who shortly arrived at the farm, he passed himself off as a miner bent on finding precious metals in the nearby mountains.

Based on the plan, at around ten thirty on Sunday evening, October 16, telegraph lines connecting the town with the outside world were severed. Around the same time, Brown and several of his men overwhelmed the lone armory guard and took possession of the federal facility, with its several million dollars' worth of weapons. The Virginia-Maryland bridge was seized and its sentinel taken to the armory, where employees also were commandeered as they showed up for work on Monday. These hostages, eventually numbering nearly thirty, were held under arms in the armory engine house. They included Lewis Washington and a prominent neighbor named John Allstadt, both slaveholders and both transported to the armory in Washington's carriage. Their slaves were freed.

Several Brown men were dispatched to transport Brown's cache of weapons from the rented farm to a schoolhouse, about a mile from the armory. There they would be distributed to slaves, who, it was assumed, would flock to the schoolhouse as soon as they learned that their savior, Brown, had arrived to extricate them from bondage. Brown would be waiting at the armory, with the hostages as protection from menace by townsfolk. He would lead the newly freed slaves into military action against slaveholders or send them north to freedom.

But how would area slaves learn about those weapons and the freedom opportunity created by Brown? And would they flee their masters, in any event, to become insurrectionary combatants? That was a large gap in the plan, rendered all the more problematic by the fact that there weren't many slaves anyway in that part of Virginia. Another gap was Brown's misperception of how local folks would react when an armed group of alien malefactors sought to spread racial havoc through their sleepy town.

Things began to go awry for the Brown forces almost immediately as townspeople woke up to discover that their village was under armed occupation. First, few blacks showed up at the schoolhouse and most of those who did hurriedly returned to their masters when they heard gunfire in the town. The gunfire came mostly from local men, who quickly grabbed whatever weapons they possessed and set out to crush the invasion. Soon they were joined by militia groups from nearby villages. Meanwhile, Brown's men detained for several hours a Baltimore and Ohio train passing through town, but eventually allowed it to proceed. That was a big mistake, ensuring that Washington officials got word via telegraph that Harpers Ferry was under assault.

When President Buchanan got the news late on Monday morning, he dispatched to the area a contingent of marines, with ample artillery, under the command of Colonel Robert E. Lee. The troops, traveling by train through the night, arrived early Tuesday morning. In the meantime, the armory and its surrounding area had become the scene of much bloodshed beginning late Monday morning and extending until dark. Brown and a contingent of his men now were pinned down in the armory engine house, as Frederick Douglass had predicted, surrounded by several hundred armed locals and militiamen, many of them boosting their outrage and fortitude with alcohol.

Town defenders quickly went after two sentinels at the bridge, a free mixed-race blacksmith from Ohio named Dangerfield Newby and Brown's son Oliver. Oliver managed to scamper back to the armory engine room unhurt, but Newby was killed with a bullet to the throat. Another early casualty was Heyward Shepherd, a free black baggage handler at the train station, reportedly shot by one of Brown's men for refusing to heed commands that he freeze in place as he walked to his location of work.

But soon the center of action became the armory, beset by highly inflamed locals bent on killing any raiders who posed an inviting target. It was a scene of boisterous, almost celebratory excitement. A chant of "*Kill them! Kill them!*" arose from the throng. Osborne Anderson, a free black from Canada and a Brown loyalist, reported after his successful escape from Harpers Ferry that his leader seemed "puzzled" at the scene of whites reveling in ways he had hoped to see among throngs of blacks after their liberation.

Seeing the helplessness of his situation, Brown sent out longtime associate Will Thompson under a white flag to negotiate a truce. The throng promptly arrested him. Brown later tried again, sending out his son Watson with Aaron Stevens, a Brown loyalist with an impressive record of military derring-do in the Mexican War and later in Kansas. This time the crowd shot the emissaries, wounding both and taking Stevens captive with four bullets in his body. Watson managed to scramble back to the protected armory grounds, where he whimpered in agony until his father blurted out in disgust, "If you must die, die like a man."

Shortly thereafter William Leeman from Maine, a twenty-year-old Brown acolyte, fled the armory and scampered down to the Potomac in a desperate escape attempt. He was promptly pursued and killed, his body left in the river as a warning to others and as an object of intermittent target practice by wrathful locals. A subsequent escape attempt by three Brown followers led to a similar outcome: two more deaths and another captive. When the Brown forces opened fire on the surrounding townsfolk, killing a prominent local farmer and the town mayor, an enraged mob led by a relative of the mayor dragged Will Thompson down to the river, shot him in the head, and left him there as another object lesson.

With Lee's appearance early Tuesday, order was restored. The colonel positioned nearly a hundred troops and multiple cannons at strategic locations around the armory, with the local militias arrayed behind. He then dispatched lieutenant J. E. B. ("Jeb") Stuart to parlay with Brown through the slightly opened door of the engine house. Stuart handed Brown a note from Lee ensuring the safety of Brown and his men if they would surrender without condition. Brown refused, then slammed the door shut as Lee issued an attack order. The marines smashed down the door and rushed into the cramped space with fixed bayonets as the besieged Brown partisans fired their weapons. It was over in a few minutes, with two marines dead and two Brown men fatally wounded. Brown, slightly injured by a sword thrust, was beaten unconscious by one of Lee's lieutenants.

The insurrectionists—dead, wounded, and unhurt—were plopped down in a row upon a lawn outside the engine house. Several, including Watson Brown (soon to die, along with one of his brothers), continued to cry out in pain as townsfolk hovered nearby, some shouting, "Hang them, hang them." Brown, roused from unconsciousness, faced swift justice as he entered the final phase of his checkered life. He was indicted on October 25, stood trial beginning on October 27, was convicted on October 30, and hanged on December 2. His co-conspirators, tried separately, were rushed to justice in similar fashion.

For Brown, the forty-five days between capture and execution constituted a final opportunity to shape his historical identity by, first, showcasing what he considered his defining attribute, his implacable opposition to the scourge of slavery; and, second, by obscuring the true intent of his insurrection plan. With heroic self-possession, he projected himself as a martyr in the cause of freedom, remaining calm throughout and presenting a matter-of-fact, even friendly demeanor without a hint of concern about his worldly fate.

He conveyed this image through two widely distributed documents: the transcript of an interview of sorts conducted with a number of officials, journalists, and private citizens; and his brief address to the court on November 2, just before sentencing. Both reflected Brown's eloquence, conviction, and courage—as well as a willingness to lie for the cause. Present at the interview were Virginia's senator Mason, Ohio's congressman Clement Vallandigham, Jeb Stuart, a few reporters, and a number of citizens. Throughout the session, the antislavery combatant remained polite but firm in his convictions. Some excerpts:

Sen. MASON: How do you justify your acts?

BROWN: I think, my friend, that you are guilty of a great wrong against God and humanity. . . . It would be perfectly right for any one to interfere with you, so far as to free those you wilfully and wickedly hold in bondage. I do not say this insultingly. . . .

Mr. M: You consider yourself the commander-in-chief of this provisional military force?

BROWN: I was chosen agreeably to the ordinance of a certain document, commander-in-chief of that force. [The document was a "constitution" promulgated in Canada by Brown for his organization.]

Mr. M: What wages did you offer?

BROWN: None.

Lieut. STUART: The wages of sin is death.

BROWN: I would not have made such a remark to you if you had been a prisoner and wounded, in my hands. . . .

Mr. MASON: Does this talking annoy you at all?
BROWN: Not in the least. . . .

Asked by a citizen interviewer to identify the principle that guided him, he replied, "By the golden rule . . . that is why I am here; it is not to gratify any personal animosity, or feeling of revenge. . . . It is my sympathy with the oppressed . . . [who are] as good as you and as precious in the sight of God." Another local asked if he had killed a man named Sherrod in Kansas. "I killed no man except in fair fight," he said. "I fought at Black Jack and at Osawatomie, and if I killed anybody, it was at one of these places."

But, of course, he had led the 1856 killing spree at Pottawatomie Creek that could hardly be called a fair fight to those five helpless men dragged from their beds and hacked to death. Also, those killings certainly had no strategic significance to the free-state cause in Kansas.

The court speech was a masterpiece of political exhortation, rendered all the more powerful by the circumstances of its delivery. He acted upon what he considered to be God's instruction, insisted Brown, adding: "I believe that to have interfered as I have done—as I have always freely admitted I have done—in behalf of His deposed poor was not wrong, but right. Now, if it is deemed necessary that I should forfeit my life for the furtherance of the ends of justice, and mingle my blood further with the blood of my children and with the blood of millions in this slave country whose rights are disregarded by wicked, cruel, and unjust enactments—I submit, so let it be done!"

Such pronouncements from the condemned man generated waves of sympathy and support in the North and an inclination of many to hail the rough-hewn warrior as a kind of secular saint destined to die for America's sins. Throughout the region, bells tolled at the hour of execution, cannon fire erupted, prayer gatherings and polemical forums commenced, and newspaper special editions appeared. At a gathering of civic mourning at Boston's Tremont Temple on the day of Brown's execution, a large likeness of the bold combatant was hung from the ceiling, with nearby quotes from the insurrectionist, including: "I don't know as I can better serve the cause I love so well than to die for it."

The outpouring was particularly effusive in and around Boston. Emerson predicted that Old Brown would "make the gallows as glorious as the cross," while Thoreau described the rustic warrior as "an angel of light." Wendell Phillips castigated Virginia as a "pirate ship" and sanctified Brown as "a Lord High Admiral of the Almighty" who had "twice as much right to hang Governor Wise [of Virginia] as Governor Wise has to hang him."

Such threatening rhetoric became increasingly commonplace. The Reverend George Cheever of New York said that, compared to slavery, it would be "infinitely better that three hundred thousand slaveholders were abolished, struck out of existence." Another pastor hailed Brown's "sacred and radiant treason," while still another pronounced treason a "holy" word.

Even in the North, though, sharp disagreements ensued. The *Boston Post*, a feisty Democratic paper, accused leading Republicans of instigating and abetting Brown's deadly radicalism. It demanded, "Does not Brown profess the same principles that Seward and Chase and Wilson . . . profess? Is not his state of mind the direct fruit of their appeals?" New York's *Journal of Commerce* added, "The leader of this diabolical attempt to array the slaves against their masters, and . . . imbrue their hands in the blood of the whole white population, is the pet and paid employee of the Republicans of Massachusetts."

That was too much for Henry Wilson, who assailed the "poor, miserable, futile effort" of the slave power and Democrats to charge "the responsibility of an insane man's acts, at Harpers Ferry, on the Republican party." No, said the senator, it was proslavery Democrats themselves who were mostly responsible. "The slave power has seized the Democratic party in this country," he said, "and has used it for the extension of slavery." It was the specter of slavery expansion, insisted Wilson, that fueled the North-South conflict and radicalized men such as John Brown.

Many northerners bolstered their defense of Brown by embracing his most blatant and consequential lie: that he never intended to unleash a servile revolution throughout the South and thus never meant to harm anyone in the region. He just wanted to free slaves, he asserted, and lead them north to freedom. "I deny," he declared in his court address, "everything but what I have all along admitted. . . . I never did intend murder, or treason, or the destruction of property, or to excite or incite slaves to rebellion, or to make insurrection."

Of course, as much of the northern commentary demonstrated, some abolitionists avidly embraced what Brown now abjured, including treason, insurrection, and slave rebellion, as necessary elements of any antislavery movement. But, although much of Brown's declaration was refuted by fact, it eased the way for even nonviolent antislavery north-erners to praise him and his actions without violating, in their minds, their nonresistance principles.

This was precisely the dilemma faced by Lloyd Garrison over on Cornhill Street, as reflected in his first *Liberator* commentary on the Harpers Ferry episode. He described the rebellion itself (not its leader) as "wild, misguided, and apparently insane" and noted that his views on "war and bloodshed, even in the best of causes, are too well known to need repeating." But he hedged by characterizing the action also as "well-intended" and adding that anyone who appreciated the American Revolution would respect "the right of the slaves to imitate the example of our fathers." As Garrison biographer Henry Mayer writes, the editor "was foundering on the shoals of a radical adventurism he had so long tried to avoid."

The problem was that, in the context of the Brown raid, he couldn't reconcile his abolitionist passion with his nonresistance convictions without swallowing Brown's transparent lie. And, in the milieu of antislavery fervor stirred by Brown, any dilution of Garrison's own fervor likely would be met with considerable opprobrium from allies in the abolition cause. In the end he swallowed the lie and hailed Brown as a transcendent figure.

"The man who brands him as a traitor is a calumniator. (Applause)," declared the editor at the Tremont Temple rally. "The man who says that his object was to promote murder, or insurrection, or rebellion, is . . . 'a liar, and the truth is not in him.' (Loud applause.)" No, said Garrison, Brown meant merely "to effect, if possible, a peaceful exodus from Virginia." In a contortion of logic mixed with a flight of naivete, he added that, had Brown not been so concerned about the safety of his engine-room hostages, "he would in all probability have succeeded, and not a drop of blood would have been shed."

But, he asked, what about those Sharps rifles and deadly pikes? What did they signify? "Nothing offensive, nothing aggressive," replied Garrison. "Only this:—he designed getting as many slaves as he could to join him, and then putting into their hands those instruments for self-defense. But, mark you! Self-defense."

Garrison's resolution of the Harpers Ferry dilemma reflected a new political reality. John Brown had swept aside many of the old centrist sensibilities of the slavery issue—the earnest attempts at compromise going back to 1850; the efforts to place radical abolitionists and implacable southern fire-eaters at the fringes of discourse; Stephen Douglas's embrace of popular sovereignty as a means of bridging the sectional divide; even the Republicans' professed acceptance of slavery where it already existed. For more and more Americans in the wake of Brown's desperate insurgency and its brutal execution, those efforts of past intellectualism were giving way more and more now to sentiments of a burgeoning emotionalism on both sides, far more difficult to counter or adjudicate than intellectual arguments.

In the South this new reality gained added force from an emotion not evident in the North: fear. It was induced by that ever-present unmentionable, the ominous specter of slave uprisings, captured by Mississippi's senator Jefferson Davis in referring to "the spectacle of those who come to incite slaves to murder helpless women and children."

In South Carolina, slave relations had been relatively placid for several decades, but folks there still shuddered when contemplating the 1739 Stono River episode or Denmark Vesey's foiled 1821 plot. Nat Turner's more recent bloody rebellion in Virginia also haunted the southern consciousness. Rhett's *Mercury*, while assuring readers that the pitiful Brown uprising wasn't particularly alarming in itself, added that it likely was "a prelude to what must and will recur again and again as the progress of sectional hate and Black Republican success advance to their consummation."

The problem, as many southerners saw it, was that more and more northerners now seemed comfortable with Brown's justification of violence based on slavery's evil and the sanctity of higher law. As the *Mercury*'s Washington correspondent put it, "Thus they tell us that if the Declaration of American Independence is not a lie, a general rising among the slaves is quite proper at any time." That was not a comforting thought for southerners.

Not surprisingly, the *Mercury* viewed secession as the only solution to the John Brown problem. "The great source of the evil is, that we are one government with these people," said the paper, adding that Seward's "irrepressible conflict" was "destined to go on . . . until one of two things shall take place: the Union shall be dissolved or slavery shall be abolished." The paper concluded, "The South must control her own destinies or perish."

The violent rebellion at Harpers Ferry agitated South Carolina politics like a boulder tossed atop an anthill. It immediately boosted secessionist sentiment in the state and thrust unionists onto the defensive. But it wasn't immediately apparent how far the state would be willing to go even now on the weighty question of secession or what impact it would have on the careers of anti-secessionists such as James Orr and James Henry Hammond. The always apprehensive Hammond perhaps demonstrated his alarm, though, by delaying his departure for the new congressional session as long as he could and, when finally setting out, said he did so "more reluctantly than John Brown did to the gallows."

It didn't take long for the Secret Six to lose their cloak of secrecy following the Harpers Ferry raid. Among Old Brown's many lapses when he set out on his mission was leaving behind at the Maryland farmhouse a passel of letters to and from followers and supporters, including the Six. Up around Boston and at Peterboro, New York, the reaction was panic. There was no doubt that the Six were complicit in Brown's crimes, which included, according to the charges against him, treason, murder, and seeking to incite a slave rebellion.

As early as October 19, newspapers reported the discovery of a letter from Gerrit Smith, along with two checks totaling $300. "You live in our hearts," wrote Smith to Brown, "and our prayer to God is that you may have strength to continue in your Kansas work." Fortunately for Smith, he referenced only Brown's "Kansas work" without mentioning Harpers Ferry. But the letter represented a lead for investigators that eventually would ensnare the other five.

So distraught was Smith at his likely arrest that he seemed to suffer a mental breakdown. A *New York Herald* reporter, visiting Peterboro, found Smith in a state of extreme agitation. "I'm going to be indicted, sir, indicted!" exclaimed Smith in an interview. The reporter described the philanthropist's bloodshot and restless eyes, his flush face, and "his excitable and illy-balanced mind." The *Utica Herald* reported in early November that Smith had been admitted to the nearby New York State Lunatic Asylum with "marks of insanity. No one is allowed to see him, but it is understood that he refers in his ravings to the Harpers Ferry matter and supposes himself arrested."

In the meantime, the schoolmaster Franklin Sanborn traveled to Boston from Concord to consult a prominent lawyer named John Albion Andrew, who counseled him to leave the country immediately while Andrew studied the circumstances. Sanborn promptly informed the clergyman Thomas Higginson by letter that he planned to flee to Canada. He signed off with the words "Burn this."

Samuel Gridley Howe, hearing of Sanborn's exit, rode off into the night to consult with George Stearns. The former combat physician and fighter in foreign wars showed up at the Stearns home, as Mary Stearns later recalled, "with a dread that threatened to overwhelm his reason." When Howe suggested the two men should follow Sanborn to Canada, Stearns proposed that they wait for a definitive legal opinion from Andrew. The next day Andrew suggested that the Six could fight successfully any extradition effort and thus avoid trial. Relieved, Sanborn returned to Massachusetts, and the Six resumed their daily routines, though Theodore Parker was in Rome, where it was expected that he would soon die from tuberculosis.

Then, in mid-November, about two weeks before Brown's scheduled execution, John Andrew delivered bad news: he had discovered an obscure 1846 statute under which the Six likely could be extradited after all. They needed to gird themselves for a protracted legal fight—or else flee the country. Howe and Stearns shipped out to Montreal and, en route, Howe penned a letter to the *New York Tribune* in which he distanced himself from Brown and lied about his prior knowledge of the raid (though he had never known where specifically it would take place). "That event was unforeseen and unexpected by me," he wrote.

That's when the solidarity of the Secret Six began to unravel. Howe's letter enraged Higginson, who already had been unhappy with Howe and Stearns because of their flight to Canada. He felt that they should stay in Massachusetts and fight extradition in a display of defiance. Parker, informed of the tensions by letter, offered a partial defense of Howe, while Sanborn argued that members of the group should feel free to divulge their own connections with Brown, so long as they didn't implicate the others. Sanborn, it appears, feared that Higginson's sense of guilt over Brown's fate might induce him to violate the interests of his colleagues. No, said Higginson, he would never do that, to which Sanborn expressed relief.

And so it went as the Secret Six grappled with the psychological burden of waiting for their fate to unfold through forces beyond their control. On December 5, Senator Mason offered a Senate resolution for the creation of a special committee to investigate the Harpers Ferry revolt, with particular attention to "whether any citizens of the United States not present were implicated therein, or accessory thereto, by contributions of money, arms, munitions or otherwise." The Senate voted to form the committee on December 14, with Mason as chairman and three of its five members in the proslavery camp.

The men of the Secret Six then faced the decision whether to testify before the committee if called. Howe and Stearns ultimately did, both perjuring themselves when asked if they had had any intimation of John Brown's plot. "Never," said Howe. Stearns replied, "No, sir; I never supposed that he contemplated anything like what occurred at Harpers Ferry."

As for Gerrit Smith, the *New York Tribune* reported in late November that his doctor at Utica expected "the afflicted gentleman will be entirely restored to mental health." The doctor added that Smith's physical condition also would be "re-established." It was a remarkable recovery given his state when admitted to the Utica institution. "So prostrated was he when he arrived at Utica," said the *Tribune*, "that it was the opinion of his physician that he would not have survived forty-eight hours longer, had he remained at his home." And yet, interestingly, Smith had had the presence of mind, just before being admitted to the asylum, to dispatch his brother to Boston and Ohio with instructions to destroy any incriminating letters he might find there.

Whatever Smith's true condition, he managed to avoid compliance with the panel's summons to testify. Higginson never received a summons, which irritated him because it deprived him of the chance to praise Brown in a high-profile public setting. Sanborn, meanwhile, ignored his summons. When U.S. marshals appeared to forcibly restrain him and take him to Washington, the arrest was quashed on a technicality, the handcuffs were removed, and the young schoolmaster avoided testimony.

The Sanborn episode reflected a growing perception about Mason's committee: that it was incompetently run and not likely to break open the case. It failed, in fact, to implicate a single person not present at Harpers Ferry at the time of the raid. Some historians later developed a theory that Mason, certainly no incompetent, opted to get the country past the incendiary Harpers Ferry issue as smoothly as possible, without further inflaming the already inflamed nation. There was indeed reason for concern. Tensions were so high now that more and more members of Congress had taken to carrying small weapons. One congressman inadvertently let a pistol drop from his pocket to the floor, causing great alarm among members. "The only persons who don't have a revolver and a knife," said Senator Hammond, "are those who have two revolvers."

John Brown's success in heightening the emotionalism of the slavery issue could be seen now throughout the country. Even Theodore Parker could see it from his sickbed in Rome. In a letter to Gerrit Smith, he said he felt "great anxiety about the immediate future of America. . . . We must see much darker hours before it is daylight, darker and also bloody, I think."

A TIME OF FOREBODING

||||||||||||||||||||||||||||||||||||||||||||||||||||||||||||||||||||||||||||||||||||||

**"WOULD TO GOD I WERE ABLE TO
GIVE A SATISFACTORY ANSWER"**

Charles Sumner returned to the Senate in December 1859 after three and a half years of fluctuating health, multiple diagnoses and treatments, two extended European trips, widespread ridicule from skeptics, and deep ambivalence about whether he should resign his Senate seat or hang on in hopes of a thorough recovery. "Never before," he complained to a friend, "was I so uncertain what to do or where to go."

Back in Washington after his first European sojourn from March to November 1857, he received an unfriendly reception from old enemies and a letter from a self-described "South Carolina Plug Uglie" warning him to stay away from the Senate "if you value your life." He wrote to his friend Thomas Higginson, "I suppose I shall be shot. I don't see what else is left for them to do."

He found himself frequently exhausted and unmoved by congressional debates. "I cannot work with the mind, except in very narrow limits," he complained to a friend. He left Washington for five months, returning only for important floor votes. With every return his bouts of exhaustion and mental anxiety intensified. His doctors issued various diagnoses and warnings, one urging him to refrain from all serious activity for at least several months.

In late May 1858, he departed once again for Europe, where he hoped to keep at bay the anxieties that arose whenever he got near the scene of his beating. In Paris he sought out an internationally renowned neurologist named Charles Edward Brown-Séquard, who identified what he considered two areas of spinal injury. He prescribed the application of hot irons to the flesh of Sumner's back to absorb excess fluid around the brain and diminish membrane congestion. Though the treatments produced excruciating pain, Sumner bore up bravely through six of them, until an unrelated attack of angina pectoris occasioned a cessation of the unpleasant treatments, which the medical profession later dismissed as quackery.

According to Sumner biographer David Donald, several physicians who later studied the voluminous records of the senator's symptoms and treatments concluded that he suffered from what would become known as "post-traumatic syndrome," a largely "psychogenic" condition stirring mental reenactments of his trauma long after his physical wounds had healed. But Donald speculated that the Brown-Séquard treatments may have helped Sumner mentally by easing his guilt from the long Senate absence and by fortifying his self-image as a worthy figure of martyrdom. Writes Donald, "Secure in his faith that his and the Almighty's ways were identical, Sumner began to mend."

His political standing back home in Massachusetts also needed mending. Nathaniel Banks, who had parlayed his House Speakership into a one-year gubernatorial term, began eyeing Sumner's six-year Senate seat as a considerably more secure political perch. At the Republicans' state convention, Banks's allies put forth a resolution, written secretly by Banks, declaring that the first duty of every legislative representative was "to attend the sessions of the body of which he is a member." The aim was to force Sumner's resignation and clear the way for Banks. Sumner's legislative friends quashed the maneuver by promulgating their own resolution, extending to the senator the party's "undivided affection, our high regard and our constant prayer."

But the episode demonstrated that the wayward legislator needed to get back to Washington relatively soon if he wanted to retain his political standing. He bought some time by issuing a statement from three of his most noted physicians saying it remained "unadvisable" for him to resume his senatorial duties during the 1858–59 winter, but that he would "surely recover" with time. He spent the winter in southern France, then traveled through Italy in the spring. After he visited Theodore Parker in Rome, the dying abolitionist noted, "He walks on those great long legs of his at the rate of four or five miles an hour. . . . [A]ll the trouble has vanished from his brain."

Soon Sumner made plans for a Washington return for the next congressional session in December. He got there seething once again with antislavery emotion. "This is a barbarous place," he wrote to a friend. "The slave-masters seem to me more than ever barbarians—in manner, conversation, speeches, conduct, principles, life. All things indicate a crisis." Though he insisted his feelings were purely political and not personal, he had indicated otherwise during his dark times in Europe by declaring, "If health ever returns I will repay to slavery and the whole crew of its supporters, every wound, burn, . . . ache, pain, trouble, grief which I have suffered."

Sumner was not alone in perceiving a gathering crisis. A confluence of events and developments had spread a deep sense of foreboding across the country. The House of Representatives found itself once again unable to elect a Speaker. John Brown's raid had pushed the North and South further apart than ever. Prominent southerners were pushing for the inflammatory notion of a national slave code for the territories. The Democratic Party seemed on the verge of a blowup. And President Buchanan appeared strangely aloof from his nation's perilous condition.

When the House convened on December 5, Republicans, with their 113 votes in the chamber, figured they could corral the six splinter-party ballots needed to reach a 119-vote majority and elect a Speaker. They chose as their nominee Ohio's John Sherman, a lanky, rustic-looking figure with a meticulously cropped beard and fiery pale-blue eyes. He hailed from a family of prominent Connecticut and Ohio landowners and jurists, but he left home as a rebellious teenager after being expelled from school for punching a teacher. He entered the law at twenty-one and excelled.

But he had a problem. It related to publication of a book digest that enraged the South. The book itself, titled *The Impending Crisis of the South: How to Meet It*, was written by a provocateur named Hinton R. Helper and published in 1857. It castigated the southern aristocracy for maintaining the backward and inefficient slave-labor system that, as Helper saw it, relegated southern whites more and more to a permanent poverty status. He cared hardly at all about the plight of chattel blacks, whom he disdained. His aim was to spread class frictions between rich and poor whites throughout the South, a particularly incendiary attitude for southern aristocrats, who viewed white solidarity as crucial for civic stability and personal security.

Now the plans for a digest version and Republican intentions to distribute some one hundred thousand copies of it stirred anger among southerners. Though Helper was attacked as "dishonest, degraded, and disgraced," some sixty Republican members of Congress signed a letter endorsing the book-distillation plan. One of them was John Sherman.

A crafty Missouri congressman named John B. Clark put forth a House resolution declaring that the "doctrines and sentiments" of Helper's book were "insurrectionary and hostile to the domestic peace . . . of the country" and that "no member of this House who has induced and recommended it, or the compend from it, is fit to be Speaker of this House." The controversy generated by Clark's language precluded any prospect for Republicans to collect the extra six votes needed to secure a Sherman victory.

It took eight weeks, though, for Republicans to finally accept his defeat. Meanwhile, House Democrats, splintered along sectional lines, couldn't coalesce behind anyone with enough votes to reach the required 119. Republicans finally turned to a New Jersey moderate named William Pennington, a bland former governor who pulled to his side enough Douglas Democrats to capture the speakership on the forty-fourth ballot.

Hovering over the speakership drama was John Brown's ghost. It was clear that Harpers Ferry radicalized many southern moderates, but not because he had perpetrated a potentially serious threat to life and property. He was widely viewed as too incompetent for that. The true threat, in the view of many southerners, was the widespread canonization of the man among many northerners. Southern editors filled their newspapers with quotations from northern clergymen and intellectuals, whose violent language, said the *New York Express*, was "fully up to the Harpers Ferry standard." At a Chicago convention of clergymen, reported the paper, one cleric declared himself in favor of "having the slaves rise up against their masters, and, if necessary, 'wading' their way to freedom, through the blood of their oppressors, knee deep."

Such expressions stirred one *Mercury* letter writer to identify himself as a former "co-operationist," but now "perfectly fanatical for secession." The reasons for his conversion, he said slyly, were "founded on my 'higher law.'"

A more serious southern response came on February 2, when Mississippi's Jefferson Davis introduced in the Senate a series of resolutions protecting slavery in all U.S. territories. Neither Congress nor any territorial legislature, asserted one resolution, "possesses the power to annul or impair the constitutional right of any citizen . . . to take his slave property into the common Territories." The resolution asserted the federal government's "duty" to provide "the needful protection; and if experience should at any time prove that the judiciary does not possess power to insure adequate protection, it will then become the duty of Congress to supply such deficiency."

Davis didn't ask for a floor debate on his resolutions. Instead he placed them before the Senate Democratic caucus, which embraced the language after minor tinkering. The aim wasn't to push for slave-code legislation, which had no chance of passage, but rather to get the language onto the Democratic platform at the party's forthcoming national convention and deliver a crushing blow to Douglas and popular sovereignty. This fit nicely into the convention-showdown strategy crafted by Barnwell Rhett and Alabama's Yancey. Indeed, under Yancey's sway, his state's Democratic leaders had instructed their convention delegates to demand slave-code language for the platform and, failing to get it, to bolt the convention.

Even some prominent southern lawmakers recoiled at the anti-Douglas maneuver as they clung to hopes for a Democratic presidential victory in 1860 against the rising Republicans. But for some Democratic fire-eaters, certainly including Rhett and Yancey, the objective was to tear their party asunder, thus causing a Democratic defeat and a likely southern rebellion.

Many Americans, viewing these intertwined developments, feared a dark future. But James Buchanan didn't seem to harbor any such anxiety. He began his Annual Message with the words "Our deep and heartfelt gratitude is due to that Almighty Power which has bestowed upon us such varied and numerous blessings throughout the past year."

Once again he attributed the nation's sectional tensions largely to the antislavery agitations of the North and hailed the *Dred Scott* decision as "the final settlement" on territorial slavery. The right had been established, said Buchanan, "of every citizen to take his property of any kind, including slaves, into the common Territories . . . and to have it protected there under the Federal Constitution."

On February 27, 1860, Abraham Lincoln delivered a speech in New York City, at the new Cooper Union in lower Manhattan. Though snow was falling, some 1,500 persons showed up to hear this political newcomer, known for his awkward appearance but often awesome delivery. His topic was the state of American politics and the imperative of thwarting any slavery expansion into the territories. Two days later, in the U.S. Senate, William Seward delivered a speech covering much of the same ground. Both addresses were salients of political ambition, designed to help secure the Republican presidential nomination at Chicago less than three months away.

There were other candidates as well, notably Salmon Chase, Simon Cameron, Francis Blair, and Edward Bates. But Seward clearly was the front-runner, while Lincoln was only beginning to be seen by a few national players as a viable challenger. But the two speeches together constituted a window on the state of the nomination battle at that point. Seward also wished to address what he considered a campaign weakness: his reputation as a sometimes harsh-voiced polemicist whose blunt expressions occasionally struck some as jarring. In this speech he notably softened his rhetoric. But he demonstrated less success in curbing his occasional tendency to talk down to audiences, employing fancy words and pretentious phrases seemingly designed to demonstrate his complex intellect.

By contrast Lincoln spoke in a conversational and sometimes amusing style, bringing his audience up to his level of thinking with simplicity and logical precision. In rebutting Stephen Douglas's contention that Congress lacked the constitutional authority to interfere with slavery in the territories, he cited a simple Douglas sentence: "Our fathers, when they framed the Government under which we live, understood this question just as well, and even better than we do now." Then he gave the sentence an elaborate dissection, separating out the various questions at issue, the identity of the fathers who framed the government, and what they did and what they thought in framing it. When he was finished, it could be seen that twenty-one of the thirty-nine signers of the Constitution had demonstrated their conviction, in various votes, that the division of local from federal authority did not forbid the federal government from addressing slavery policies in the territories.

"As those fathers marked it," said Lincoln, "so let it be again marked as an evil not to be extended." But regarding slavery's current status, Lincoln added, "Let all the guarantees those fathers gave it be, not grudgingly, but fully and fairly maintained. For this Republicans contend, and with this, so far as I know or believe, they will be content."

Addressing the South (though hardly expecting to be heeded), he gently but effectively picked apart many of the region's arguments. "[Y]ou will break up the Union rather than submit to a denial of your Constitutional rights," he said. "That has a somewhat reckless sound; but it would be palliated, if not fully justified, were we proposing by the mere force of numbers, to deprive you of some right, plainly written down in the Constitution. But we are proposing no such thing."

In addressing Republicans, he asked what could be done to satisfy anti-Republican southerners of Republican good intentions. His answer: "Simply this: We must not only let them alone, but we must somehow, convince them that we do let them alone. This, we know by experience, is no easy task." In fact, he added, the only way to do it would be to cease to call slavery wrong and to join them in calling it right. "The whole atmosphere," he said, "must be disinfected from all taint of opposition to slavery, before they will cease to believe that all their troubles proceed from us." But that wasn't going to happen, which crystallized the magnitude of the crisis. "Their thinking it right and our thinking it wrong," said Lincoln, "is the precise fact upon which depends the whole controversy."

Like Lincoln, Seward contended that the Founders never intended to deny Congress the right to regulate slavery in the territories, and he rose to flights of eloquence in extolling the "wonderful machine" of the Union that was pulled together by "millions of fibers of millions of contented, happy human hearts." Seward sought to portray the great slavery confrontation as a contest between "capital states" (slave) and "labor states" (free), which was an interesting dichotomy that may have shed light on the cultural backgrounds of those engaged in the issue. But in consideration of the pressing and immediate slavery confrontation it seemed a bit esoteric.

Lincoln's speech caused an immediate stir and was published in its entirety in four New York newspapers, including the *Tribune* and the *Evening Post*, and later in papers in Chicago, Detroit, Albany, and elsewhere. In New York, editors William Cullen Bryant of the *Evening Post* and Horace Greeley of the *Tribune*, both instrumental in getting Lincoln to the city, were engaged in a stop-Seward movement and were looking for the right man to overtake him. They were part of a Republican contingent skeptical of Seward's chances of carrying the crucial swing states of Illinois, Pennsylvania, Indiana, and New Jersey.

Both now saw Lincoln as a serious contender for the Republicans' presidential nomination. Bryant called his speech "logically and convincingly stated," while Greeley declared the Illinoisan to be "one of Nature's orators, using his rare powers solely and effectively to elucidate and to convince, though their inevitable effect is to delight and electrify as well." Based on such notices, New England Republicans invited Lincoln to speak also in their region, which led to a twelve-day tour during which he addressed audiences in eleven cities and cemented relationships with men who could advance his as-yet-unannounced presidential candidacy.

With the presidential campaign year looming, South Carolina continued to struggle with the state's persistent sense of drift. Now, in the wake of John Brown and with rising prospects for a Black Republican in the White House, that feeling took on ever greater urgency. But there didn't seem to be much prospect for a consensus on what course to pursue. As the state's governor, William Gist, lamented, "Would to God I were able to give a satisfactory answer to this momentous question . . . ; but I must confess my utter inability to point out the path of honor and safety in the midst of the difficulties which surround us."

Senator Hammond personified his state's struggles. It wasn't clear if he could gain much political purchase now with his expressed confidence in the South's ability to protect slavery from northern attacks, particularly in the wake of the John Brown rebellion. Disunion talk was on the rise, while Hammond seemed boxed in with his optimism and lack of any recommendation if his optimism proved misguided. Hammond faced a risk of being left behind by events.

Barnwell Rhett, on the other hand, believed he had positioned himself in the path of events with his blithe confidence that a new southern nation could emerge and thrive without much pain or suffering. Besides, he had gained stature with his ownership of the *Mercury*, now operating on a more sound financial basis. The *New York Home Journal* praised the paper's "fine original poems, admirable literary articles, and high-toned editorials," while the *New York Herald* called it "the ablest, most consistent and most sagacious of the organs of the southern fire-eaters." This new stature emboldened Rhett to cultivate once again a public persona as the state's foremost disunionist.

On July 4, 1859, he stepped into the breach with a major address at Grahamville, South Carolina. Foreseeing a fracturing of the Democratic Party, he wanted to be the man to pick up the pieces. He declared:

> How long shall we stand the resistless and despised vic-
> tims of northern fanaticism and rapacity? How long
> shall we cry "wait!" whilst the North advances in power
> and insolence and each successive year brings her nearer
> to the consummation of her policy of dominion over
> us, and over this continent? . . . When will [the South's]
> mighty heart beat free in the enjoyment of her rights,
> safe under the shield of her own protection; and, casting
> off the incubus of ignorance, and error, and fear, which
> now like a foul toad sits upon her bosom?

Rhett later augmented his fiery call to action with a six-step practical program designed to guide the South through the current crisis
and toward either full southern security within the Union or full independence outside of it. Published in the *Mercury* in October, just days
before the Harpers Ferry raid, it boiled down to a declaration that, if
the 1860 election didn't produce a strongly pro-southern Democratic
government, then the South must leave the Union.

The *Mercury* headlined its six-item formula "Measures of Southern
Resistance to Northern Rule," and it wasn't difficult to see its intent.
Rhett, perceiving the increasing power in the demographic and economic trends he had been warning about for years, now was placing
himself essentially back where he had been in the battle with the cooperationists. The question was whether the state had caught up with him
or would once again turn on him.

Meanwhile, many South Carolinians turned their attention to James
Chesnut, still disturbingly fuzzy on where he stood on many issues despite having been a senator since December 1858. "Can you tell me why
Col. Chesnut has not yet defined his position?" asked a letter writer to
the *Southern Guardian*, who added he had heard rumors that the senator

"would let us know where to find him; and, what was greatly better, that we would not find him treading zealously in the footsteps of his senior," meaning Hammond.

Finally, on September 28, Chesnut delivered a major address at his hometown of Camden in which he described the dangers he saw facing the South, while also dismissing such radical notions as an African slave-trade revival, Cuban acquisition, or U.S. expansion into Central America to bolster up American slavery.

But he painted a bleak picture of the southern predicament. "I do not believe that we are sailing on a summer's sea," he said, adding that he perceived "the portents of a coming storm . . . whose raging power may prove sufficient to crack every rib in the good old ship." He traced the ship's journey from the early years of the Constitution, when (he said) Calhoun's view of state equality seemed to prevail; to the South's Missouri Compromise defeat, when Congress prohibited slavery (unconstitutionally, he said) north of the 36°30' latitude; to the prospect now that free-state expansion would leave the South in a state of relative impotence. "In such event," he asked, "what have we to expect? We must have 'the irrepressible conflict' waged in hot earnest."

Chesnut decried the notion that Congress could deprive a citizen of his property "merely because he takes it with him to any particular territory," and declared that the only constitutional power conferred on Congress over the subject of slavery was the power needed to guard and protect the rights of slave owners. But those rights were now threatened, he argued, and would become even more threatened if Republicans won the coming presidential election. In that event, "such will be the 'bill of fare' of that feast to which you will be invited," he said. "Go to it with what appetite you may, for myself I would none of it."

It was a cleverly crafted speech, describing in stark language the southern predicament, while maintaining a measured tone and avoiding rash secession talk. Further, in declaring himself "not without hope," the senator cloaked himself in just enough ambiguity to avoid becoming a target of attacks from possible foes. Did the senator advocate disunion in the event of a Republican presidential victory? "We are somewhat at a loss" on that question, said the *Edgefield Advertiser*, citing seemingly contradictory expressions on the matter. But the paper endorsed the address nonetheless.

For all of its ambiguity, though, the speech captured the intertwined elements of South Carolina sentiment as the campaign year approached: a sense of danger should the Republicans capture the White House; confidence that the Supreme Court would protect southern interests in the territories, as it had in the *Dred Scott* ruling; a reluctance to threaten secession impetuously; a need for southern solidarity to face contingencies as they arose; and ultimately a willingness to entertain the treacherous specter of disunion.

This matrix stirred some discomfort among the state's staunchest unionists, most notably Benjamin Perry and James Orr. In December, Perry announced his retirement from public life after three decades as legislator and newspaper editor. The announcement contained a statement suggesting he had perhaps become a bit world-weary: "Thirty years' active experience in public affairs and political excitements has taught me its folly and bitterness." As for Orr, the former U.S. representative and House Speaker planned to continue political activity as a delegate to the Democrats' Charleston convention, where he would present his unionist convictions in an elaborate and heartfelt speech. As a southerner with high standing in the North, he harbored hopes for the party's vice presidential nod if Douglas were to capture the ticket's top spot.

Another ardent unionist was Christopher Memminger, German-born, brought to America as a small boy and orphaned at age four. Growing up, he impressed all who encountered him, including a prominent businessman named Thomas Bennett. Bennett guided young Memminger along a trajectory of education and personal development that led to a highly lucrative Charleston law practice and a prominent civic leadership role. He was a political moderate who supported the free-black community and promoted civic development causes such as railroad construction and public school excellence.

In late 1859, Governor Gist commissioned Memminger as a state emissary to travel to Richmond and urge Virginia leaders to enter into a compact with South Carolina and, it was hoped, other southern states to explore ways of protecting the South from slave rebellions and northern agitations. Memminger and his fifteen-year-old daughter, Lucy, arrived in Richmond on January 12 and were given a rousing welcome by a delegation of legislators who pronounced him a "guest of the state."

For nearly a month Memminger attended dinners, receptions, discussion groups, and private interviews as part of his diplomatic portfolio. But it soon became clear that Virginia could not forge a consensus for any kind of southern compact. Memminger and Lucy left Richmond on February 7, and a month later came the official reply confirming Memminger's perception.

Barnwell Rhett was unfazed, however, as he looked farther south to the cotton states of Alabama and Mississippi and the rice state of Louisiana. Even if just five states were to secede, his *Mercury* declared on March 10, they would be "perfectly safe from northern hostility or attack," while the remaining states would be "at the mercy of a hostile, malignant, and remorseless majority of their enemies." That would induce those "middle-ground states," added the paper, to "unite with their more Southern sister States in their common cause and political connection." Rhett clearly saw on the horizon the southern independence movement of his dreams.

25

PRESIDENTIAL SCRAMBLE

||||||||||||||||||||||||||||||||||||||||||||||||||||||||||||||||||||||||||||||||||||||||||||

THE OLD PARTY SYSTEM FALLS APART

In April 1860 America riveted its attention on Charleston, South Carolina, where the Democratic National Convention would commence on the month's twenty-third day and where events likely would determine the future of the Democratic Party and perhaps even the country. As the *Mercury* declared on the eve of the gathering, "[N]ever have the premonitions of change and revolution been as plainly visible . . . as now." The paper added, "Antagonisms rage in the bosom of the Convention."

Among the reporters on the scene was the *Cincinnati Commercial*'s young Murat Halstead, a tireless, sharp-eyed newshound with a gift for incisive analytical prose. With President Buchanan declining to run again and probably facing a political humiliation if he did, Halstead quickly perceived that the "pivot individual" at Charleston was Stephen Douglas, whose magnetic persona and record of achievement rendered him the party's top presidential contender. Yet he struggled with heavy political baggage: despised throughout the South for his popular sovereignty apostasy and a bête noire to Buchanan and his followers.

For days Douglas's political destiny dominated the conversations of convention-bound railroad travelers. "The questions in every car and at every station," wrote Halstead, "were: Would he be? could he be? should he be nominated? Could he get a majority of the Convention? Could he get two-thirds? Would the South support him if he should be nominated? Would the Administration acquiesce?"

Of course, other candidates also wanted the nod, including Virginia senator Robert M. T. Hunter and two Kentuckians, James Guthrie, a noted businessman and former U.S. Treasury secretary, and Vice President John C. Breckinridge. But their chances seemed slight, as Douglas had amassed the most votes by far, probably even a majority. Still, the Democrats' two-thirds rule for presidential nominations posed a fearsome challenge for anyone vying for the prize.

Then there was the platform issue, which crystallized the party's predicament as it sought to remain a national institution even as sectional tensions welled up within its councils. If the Douglas forces could muster a convention majority to control the platform language, they could thwart southern calls for a national slave code for the territories. That was crucial for northern solidarity, particularly in the major swing states of the old Northwest, where antislavery sentiment ran high. Convention delegate Henry B. Payne of Ohio told Douglas that, with a slave-code plank in the platform, the Ohio delegation would likely "retire from the convention." He added that seven other northwestern states likely would follow.

And yet southerners issued even more emphatic threats if the convention spurned their slave-code insistence or if Stephen Douglas should be nominated. Alabama's Yancey had generated considerable interest among southerners with his state-convention resolution earlier in the year instructing Alabama's national convention delegates to insist on a slave-code plank and, if rebuffed, to bolt the convention. Now, in Charleston, six other southern states—Georgia, Florida, Louisiana, Texas, Arkansas, and Mississippi—met in caucus and agreed to follow Alabama's lead. That gave Yancey considerable sway over seven delegations.

Halstead observed that the Douglas men were "not so stiff in their backs nor as strong in the faith" as these agitated southerners. He suggested to one Alabama delegate that the South might have to accept a vaguely worded platform in order to assuage both sections. No, said the southerner, the 1860 campaign would be the "test campaign" and its issues must be "fought on principle." There could be, he added, "no Douglas dodges—no double constructions—no janus-faced lying resolutions—no double-tongued and doubly damned trifling with the people." He declared that, if the Democratic Party was merely a spoils party preoccupied with winning elections, then it should simply be destroyed.

Halstead wandered down to the Charleston Hotel, where the Alabama delegation was housed, to get a firsthand look at the man they called the prince of the fire-eaters. And there was Yancey, as anticipated, holding court among leading disunionists and predicting, with a certain felicity, that a convention breakup would likely spawn a Union breakup. Halstead, like many before him, discovered the South's leading radical to be surprisingly congenial, but relentless in his passion and sharp as a stiletto in his tactical thinking. The reporter surmised that, while the North might enjoy a preponderance of convention votes, "the south will have the intellect and pluck to make its points."

The symbolism of the convention location was not lost on Americans. Of all the southern cities raising alarms about the North's rise in population, wealth, and power, Charleston was the most defiant and the most likely to take desperate action. Of course, the city and surrounding state had recoiled from any go-it-alone Union withdrawal early in the decade and since then had heeded the warnings of sure-footed unionist statesmen such as James Orr and B. F. Perry. But secessionist sentiment percolated just beneath the surface, perhaps more intensely now than ever following John Brown's raid. Notably, of the state's six U.S. congressmen, four were outspoken secessionists in the mold of Barnwell Rhett.

Further, as the *New York Tribune* noted in a preconvention dispatch, "Charleston is perhaps the most aristocratic city in the country." If there was one thing the city and its surrounding low-country aristocracy most vehemently opposed, it was any change that could upend their stratified political system and slave culture. Clinging tenaciously to both, South Carolinians rejected any hint of political or social equality.

All this contributed to a slightly exotic aspect of the place, accentuated by such elements of natural beauty as the live oaks, draped in Spanish moss, that dotted the expansive and flower-filled Battery Park; the towering palmetto trees with their fan-shaped leaves; and the water views that captured the eye from just about every direction. Charming narrow streets seemed reminiscent of European cities, and stately urban mansions reflected the state's wealth-generating preoccupation, often pursued, though, with a certain languid demeanor.

Some northern delegates, seeking to view firsthand the haunting institution of slavery, visited plantations and concluded that "[t]he yoke seemed to be rather light in these parts," as historian Bruce Catton wrote. An Iowa newspaperman reported that the slaves he saw appeared "happy and contented," with their wants "well supplied and their labors not onerous." But, of course, slave masters took extra pains to present as favorable a picture as possible for these outsiders bent on absorbing, as Catton put it, "such impressions as twenty minutes would give them of the peculiar institution on its own ground." The historian added that most northern Democrats already had formed their opinions about the system and wished now to modulate the slavery issue in order to head off a cataclysmic party rupture.

The convention opened at Institute Hall, on Meeting Street. It was a huge structure capable of containing some three thousand people and displaying, for this occasion, "a good deal of gaudy and uncouth ornamentation," as Halstead captiously observed. Charleston hoteliers, reported the *New York Tribune*, had expanded their capacity to accommodate up to ten thousand visitors, although the paper also noted that, with "a proper appreciation for the habits of their Democratic patrons, they have discreetly removed all the best furniture." With 303 convention delegates, a majority vote would require at least 152 ballots, while a two-thirds nomination victory would necessitate a vote of 202.

On the convention's second day, delegates elected as their president the square-jawed, thin-lipped Caleb Cushing of Massachusetts, former congressman, U.S. envoy to China, and attorney general under Franklin Pierce. A rebellious sort, he was considered by many northerners to be a southern-sympathizing "doughface" in the vein of President Buchanan, whom he admired. He harbored no admiration for Stephen Douglas.

After a series of early procedural votes and credential fights that demonstrated Douglas's majority support, but also his challenge in surmounting the two-thirds hurdle, the convention turned to the platform. By this time some Douglas men had developed a view that a walkout of "ultra-southern" delegates might actually be a blessing if confined to just thirty or forty dissidents. With those anti-Douglas votes gone, they reasoned, the Little Giant would be better positioned to reach the two-thirds threshold.

On April 27 the platform committee presented to the floor two competing documents. A majority report, favored by southerners, declared that neither Congress nor any territorial legislature had the power "to abolish slavery in the territories . . . nor to prohibit the introduction of slavery therein, nor to exclude slaves from the territory, nor any power to destroy or impair the right of property in slaves by any legislation whatever." Jefferson Davis had done his work well when he introduced in the Senate his slave-code language with the aim of getting it embraced officially by the Democratic Party.

The minority report, by contrast, skirted the superheated territorial issue by declaring property rights in states and territories to be "judicial in their character" and hence best left to the Supreme Court, whose rulings the Democratic Party "is pledged to abide by and faithfully carry out." Adherents of this approach hoped that, with a southern majority at the Supreme Court under Chief Justice Taney, enough southern delegates would accept the finesse to yield a Douglas victory.

In the ensuing debate, Yancey thrilled his followers with a ninety-minute philippic castigating northern Democrats for refusing to defend southern rights under the principle that constitutions "are made solely for the protection of the minorities in government." He denied that he and his southern allies were "disunionists, per se," but merely patriotic

Americans seeking to redress long-standing grievances. The aim, he declared, was simply to save the country by getting the Democratic Party to save the South.

Yancey declared, "Ours is the property invaded; ours are the institutions which are at stake; ours is the peace that is to be destroyed . . . ours is the honor at stake." While he may not have been a disunionist per se, he certainly seemed prepared to become one if the South didn't get its way. Slave-code approval, he said, was "the only basis upon which Alabama can associate with the National Democracy" (meaning the national party).

Yancey met his match, though, in Ohio senator George Pugh. While lacking Yancey's electrifying eloquence, Pugh delivered a "keen, shrewd and telling" rebuttal that scored southern Democrats for undermining the party at the North with incessant and increasingly outlandish demands and then taunting the northern party for losing political influence as a result of its acquiescence. Now, he said, the South was demanding that northern Democrats prostrate themselves with their mouths in the dust. "Gentlemen of the South," intoned Pugh, "you mistake us—you mistake us. We will not do it." If the South's party loyalty required such a northern debasement, added the senator, then the southern dissidents should just go.

Such exchanges generated torrents of emotion as delegates lept upon chairs, "screaming like panthers, and gesticulating like monkeys," as Halstead wrote, to get recognition to speak. Cushing lost control of the proceedings until he finally managed to acknowledge a well-timed motion for adjournment. It carried, extricating Cushing and the convention from a donnybrook of ominous proportions.

But everyone knew a party reckoning had only been delayed, not averted. "The Crisis Reached; a Split Predicted," declared the next day's headline in the *Boston Evening Transcript*. Dispatches from Charleston predicted that at least five southern states would bolt the convention if the Douglas-backed platform prevailed, as expected. The *Mercury* captured the emerging southern sentiment by declaring, "If the National Democratic party cannot stand the test of principle on matters on which the destiny of the South depends, let us have a sectional party that can."

The next day, following hours of parliamentary maneuvering during which Cushing revealed his partiality toward the South, the convention finally proceeded to a series of votes on the platform. In the crucial one, the minority report won approval, 165 to 138, with the party's growing divide reflected in the sectional breakdown: free-state delegates, 154 to 30; slave states, 11 to 108.

Shortly thereafter came the long-anticipated southern walkout. It began with the tall, smooth figure of Alabama delegate LeRoy Walker, who informed the convention that his delegation was withdrawing based on state-party instructions, to be activated if Alabama didn't get justice at Charleston, which, declared Walker, it didn't. Mississippi was next, followed by Louisiana, South Carolina (except for B. F. Perry and one other delegate), Florida, Texas, a third of Delaware's delegation, and a smattering of those from Arkansas. The next day, Georgia and the remaining Arkansans bolted. The string of speeches by departing delegation leaders generated thunderous applause in the hall, while throngs of local ladies in the galleries registered their assent, reported Halstead, with smiles, nods of approval, and "delighted fluttering of fans and parasols."

With fifty largely anti-Douglas delegates now gone, the Douglas men continued to hope that the walkout would not spread and therefore would enhance their man's chance of reaching the two-thirds goal (or 169 votes now out of 253 attendees). But then Cushing delivered a devastating blow. He ruled that the required nomination vote would remain at two-thirds of the original number (202 votes) and not the lower number based on the walkout. This precluded any prospect of Douglas or anyone else reaching the nomination threshold. A motion to overturn the chairman's decision failed.

Hoping against hope, the Douglas men spent the next three days and fifty-seven ballots trying to generate a breakthrough stampede. But, with a high mark of just 152½ votes, the Little Giant remained far short of the required 202 and even 16½ votes shy of what he would have needed based on the reduced delegate count. But no other candidate mounted a serious bid, and the result was deadlock. On the convention's tenth day, the delegates adjourned with a stipulation that they would reconvene in Baltimore on June 18 to resume the candidate-selection effort.

Meanwhile, on the day of the walkout the dissident southerners sent out word of a meeting that night at seven o'clock at St. Andrew's Hall, where the rebels developed plans for a June 11 convention at Richmond to establish a new Democratic Party—or rather, as some insisted, to declare themselves the *true* Democratic Party. Yancey set the tone at an outdoor rally at Charleston on April 30, shortly after the walkout, when he derisively labeled the remaining Charleston gathering a "rump convention."

Whichever was the true Democratic Party or whatever gathering deserved the rump designation, the fact remained that there were now two Democratic parties. "The last party, pretending to be a National party, is broken up," crowed Rhett's *Mercury*, "and the antagonism of the two sections . . . has nothing to arrest its fierce collisions." There was also nothing, in the wake of the Democratic debacle, to arrest the rise of the Republican opposition, soon to draft its own platform and select its own standard-bearer at Chicago. As Halstead reported amid the Charleston chaos, a common refrain heard in the city's bars and meeting rooms was "The [next] president will be nominated at Chicago."

Chicago was a boisterous, ungainly adolescent of a town in 1860, with 109,000 residents and ambitions to someday rival the grand eastern cities of New York, Boston, and Philadelphia and reign as the urban fulcrum of the burgeoning Northwest. Here was a fitting place for the national convention of the Republican Party, which matched the city in freshness, energy, and ambition. The party constructed for the occasion a massive temporary wood structure called the Wigwam, built in a month at a cost of $7,000 and designed to hold ten thousand persons. City officials predicted that some twenty-five thousand visitors would descend on the city for the May 16 to 18 gathering.

William Seward was the convention's pivot figure, the man with the most delegates (though nobody knew precisely how many) and with the greatest presumed capacity for building a winning electoral coalition without southern support. Other candidates—Cameron, Chase, Bates, Banks, Ben Wade of Ohio—had seen their movements fizzle. And now Seward's only viable challenger seemed to be Abraham Lincoln.

Few political experts considered Lincoln a match for Seward. *Harper's* magazine, in a special convention issue, signaled the New Yorker's front-runner status by displaying his portrait and profile more prominently than those of his rivals. The *Providence Daily Post* stated flatly that "the nomination belongs to him." Even during the convention, Horace Greeley predicted in print that Seward's opponents "cannot concentrate on any [one] candidate, and . . . he will be nominated."

But Seward labored under some political weaknesses, while Lincoln had positioned himself more adroitly than most people realized. The key was a collection of four northern states that had gone for Buchanan in the 1856 Electoral College count but were crucial for any Republican hoping to win the 1860 general election. That was because no Republican could expect any southern support. The crucial states were Illinois, Indiana, Pennsylvania, and New Jersey, and strains of political discomfort with Seward could be detected in their Chicago delegations. The Republican gubernatorial candidates in Indiana and Pennsylvania publicly warned party leaders that, with Seward at the top of the ticket in November, their campaigns would be hopeless. The Indiana man, Henry Lane, even threatened to abandon his candidacy for governor if Seward became the party's presidential nominee.

Seward's problem was that his blunt-toned rhetoric over the years and his embrace of higher law had stamped him as a bit radical, whereas Lincoln, more obscure and hence more able to fashion his own image, studiously positioned himself as a party moderate always in search of the reasonable middle ground. As he wrote to the editor of the *Illinois State Journal*, "I agree with Seward in his 'Irrepressible Conflict,' but I do not endorse his 'Higher Law' doctrine." Further, Seward, as a longtime scourge of the Know-Nothing movement, suffered from lingering hostility from that quarter, whereas Lincoln, though opposed to Know-Nothingism, had never singled out the movement as a conspicuous target.

Lincoln and his highly effective corps of political operatives also enjoyed a home-state advantage. With their local influence and power they packed the Wigwam with full-throated loyalists to overwhelm the Seward men in the decibel competitions and scattered the floor seating of Seward-supporting delegations to prevent them from conferring with each other effectively at crucial roll call moments. They printed up counterfeit admission tickets to supplant Seward adherents with Lincoln men who could further electrify the hall with powerful signs of growing enthusiasm for the Illinoisan.

Lincoln's campaign leader, David Davis, even ignored the candidate's admonition that there must be *"no contracts that will bind me."* Davis reportedly dangled before leaders of the Pennsylvania delegation a cabinet post for Simon Cameron if that delegation would swing to Lincoln on the second ballot.

On the night of May 17, as the Seward men celebrated their looming victory with champagne dinners, Lincoln's team initiated an all-night frenzy of political entreaty and cajolery designed to augment Lincoln's Illinois base of twenty-two votes. They worked the Indiana delegation with arguments that a Lincoln nomination would assuage Henry Lane's campaign concerns. The result was a first-ballot commitment of twenty-six votes. They set to work on Vermont, New Hampshire, Maine, and Virginia to demonstrate unexpected New England and border strength. It worked. Vermont committed to a second-ballot swing to Lincoln of ten votes, while Maine and New Hampshire promised six and seven first-ballot votes, respectively. Virginia promised Lincoln fourteen first-ballot votes to Seward's eight.

All this was designed to jolt convention delegates into recognizing Lincoln's underlying popularity. Davis wished to procure at least a hundred first-ballot votes, with support building in subsequent tallies. To further that effort he also wanted Lincoln partisans in the Wigwam to outshout and outscream the Seward followers when Lincoln's name came up in the nomination process. Lincoln's men won the first round with a "prodigious" cheer, as Halstead described it, compared to the Seward contingent's mere "enthusiastic" showing.

The Seward men rallied during the seconding speeches with a shouting performance that was "absolutely frantic, shrill and wild." It seemed
like victory until the Lincoln boys responded with a thunderous scream
that struck Halstead as resembling "all the hogs ever slaughtered in Cincinnati giving their death squeals together." Indiana's Henry Lane, now
a fervent Lincoln man, leapt atop a table, swinging his hat and cane in
a wild display of acrobatic bravura.

Then came the balloting, which demonstrated that David Davis
had done his work well. Seward led on the first ballot as expected with
173½ votes out of 233 necessary for victory. But Lincoln scored 102
with strong showings in Illinois, Indiana, Virginia, and New England.
On the second ballot Seward picked up eleven votes while Lincoln
added seventy-nine, including forty-eight from Pennsylvania and fourteen from Ohio. Lincoln now trailed Seward by just three and a half
votes. On the third ballot, as delegates gravitated to Lincoln, the challenger surpassed Seward handily and reached 231½ votes, just one and
a half short of victory.

Then Ohio's former congressman David Cartter rose to transfer
four of his state's Chase votes to Lincoln, thus awarding the nomination
to the Springfield lawyer. The vice presidential slot went to Maine's senator Hannibal Hamlin as the convention and surrounding city prepared
for a frenzy of wild overnight celebration.

Meanwhile, a collection of old-line politicians, dismayed by the
acidic effect of the slavery strife, gathered at Baltimore on May
9 to 10 to establish a new party aimed at leading the nation out of
that destructive contention. They called their organization the Constitutional Union Party, and its members included traditional southern
Whigs clinging to their unionist sensibilities; lingering Know-Nothing
adherents, mostly from the South; and slavery-issue moderates from
around the country.

The party selected as its presidential standard-bearer John Bell of
Tennessee, a colorless Whig and unionist who had served the nation as
congressman, senator, and war secretary. The vice presidential nod went

to the venerable Edward Everett, who personified the genteel politics of Boston's old Cotton Whigs and who was now thoroughly out of favor in the Bay State. The Constitutional Unionists hoped to move the nation beyond the slavery tumult by essentially ignoring it. The party platform didn't mention the issue at all.

The Democratic Party, now divided into two angry contingents, moved north for further efforts in June to find a way out of the morass created at Charleston. The walkout delegates congregated at Richmond on June 11 and quickly decided to withhold any action until after the official party had met in Baltimore beginning on June 18 to finally select a presidential candidate. Meanwhile, the dissident faction struggled with some big questions: Would they be allowed to reclaim the convention seats they had abandoned at Charleston? If so, could they force a reconsideration of the platform language and a rejection of the Douglas nomination?

Whatever the answers, the men at Richmond didn't seem in any mood for compromise. "[W]e must yield nothing," demanded Alabama's John Erwin as he assumed the convention chairmanship. "The serpent of 'Squatter Sovereignty' must be strangled."

When the mainline Democrats reconvened at Baltimore's Front Street Theatre, with Caleb Cushing once again in the chair, tensions ran high. Immediately the delegates confronted the question of whether to seat the Charleston walkout figures or to seat instead replacement delegates chosen by party officials in several states, including Louisiana, Alabama, and Georgia. Seating the walkout men would destroy the Douglas candidacy; seating the replacement men would likely destroy the party. Cushing ducked the controversy by ruling that he had no authority as chairman to settle it. He sent the issue to the Credentials Committee, which struggled for three days before finally crafting two competing reports.

The majority report favored seating the replacement delegates from Alabama and Louisiana, as well as half of those from Georgia and two from Arkansas. That approach would ensure a Douglas nomination, and the convention embraced it. The anti-Douglas forces failed to undo the decision through parliamentary maneuvering.

Then Cushing recognized Virginia delegate Charles W. Russell for an announcement. It had become his duty, said Russell, "by the direction of a large majority of the delegation from Virginia, respectfully to inform this body that it is inconsistent with their convictions of duty to participate longer in its deliberations." This signaled a second party rupture. The Virginia delegates, save just a few, rose from their seats, entered the aisles, and walked out. Then eight of ten North Carolina delegates also departed, along with half of the Maryland delegation. The galleries, which seemed particularly hostile to Douglas on this day, cheered uproariously.

In the end, the two walkouts involved a majority of delegates from Virginia, North Carolina, Tennessee, Maryland, Kentucky, Missouri, Arkansas, California, and Oregon, as well as anti-Douglas delegates from Massachusetts. This amounted to a full or partial withdrawal of a majority of states. The once-proud Democratic Party was now a mere fragment of a party.

But the remaining delegates were there to place Stephen Douglas into nomination, and they proceeded to do so. On the first ballot, Douglas garnered 173 votes out of 190½ cast, while on the second he received 181½ out of 194½. That precipitated the unanimous adoption of a motion declaring Douglas the winner, bypassing Cushing's full-convention voting baseline. The convention later selected Herschel Johnson of Georgia as its vice presidential candidate and then adjourned.

The anti-Douglas faction, seeing no possibility of the Little Giant being abandoned by northern Democrats, proceeded with their own gathering at Baltimore's Maryland Institute Hall. Cushing, who had resigned his presidency of the traditional party, was quickly installed as chairman of a gathering that was now devoid of contention or anger. Yancey "glowed with satisfaction," and the Baltimore Sun reported that "the most cordial unanimity and harmony characterized every man and every feature."

A smattering of delegates could be seen from New York, Vermont, Iowa, and Massachusetts, along with California and Oregon. And the border states sent full delegations. Otherwise, this was an entirely southern gathering operating under an entirely southern outlook. Its platform contained the slave-code advocacy that had been rejected at Charleston and called for the acquisition of Cuba and construction of a Pacific railroad. For president it nominated Vice President John C. Breckinridge, just thirty-nine, a former state legislator and two-term U.S. House member. For vice president the convention nominated Joseph Lane of Oregon.

The political forces that upended the American party system in 1860 represented merely a part of the broader tempest roiling the nation. Sectionalism born of slavery, having destroyed the Whig Party earlier in the decade, now sliced the Democratic Party in two. It produced a strictly sectional Republican Party in the North and a vehemently southern entity in the slave states. It even spawned a charmingly naive new party driven by hopes that the slavery issue would fade simply through the unspoken wishes of the populace.

The emergence of four political parties that campaign year wasn't a sustainable development in a country whose stability seemed tied to a two-party tradition. That unsustainability foreshadowed further frustration, further dissension, and further civic chaos. The political system that had served the nation well for more than seven decades was breaking up, as reflected in the breakup of the Whigs and the Democrats and the general political oscillations of the time. It was getting increasingly difficult to see where all this political belligerence would lead the nation and how it could ever be resolved.

26

LINCOLN VICTORIOUS

||||||||||||||||||||||||||||||||||||||||||||||||||||||||||||||||||||||||||||||||

"I FELT AS NEVER BEFORE THE RESPONSIBILITY UPON ME"

The rap on Barnwell Rhett was that his political passions too often distorted his perception of reality. This view was well documented in his biography, stretching back to his stunning miscalculation during the secessionist-cooperationist struggles. But now many were beginning to think that Rhett's perception of reality perhaps wasn't wrong but merely premature. This was based on the dual perception that Lincoln would be elected president and his election would splinter the country.

That was Rhett's view, as reflected in his desire now to get back into the political arena. "About eight years ago," he told an audience on July 9, "I addressed the people of Charleston" on the "great question" of the right of southerners to take their slaves into newly acquired U.S. territories. And now, he continued, "I again stand before you, pleading the same great cause. . . . The peace—the security anticipated from the Compromise measures of 1851—have not been realized."

The *Mercury* rounded out the concept on July 20 with a prediction that the election would become more and more distilled into a "sectional antagonism," with Douglas and Bell fading away and the battle narrowing down to Lincoln and Breckinridge, the North against the South. "The South will be defeated," predicted the paper, "and then the grave responsibility for future events will fall on the State Legislatures of the South."

Rhett and his newspaper were not alone in this perception. "It would be idle," declared the *New York Herald*, "to deny that . . . the dissolution of the confederacy is more than probable." Southerners, meanwhile, issued secession warnings with more abandon than ever. Buchanan's treasury secretary, Howell Cobb of Georgia, considered a southern moderate, stated flatly that his state would leave the Union upon a Lincoln election. And the always measured *Charleston Courier*, for years a consistent counterweight to the *Mercury*'s radicalism, warned that a Lincoln victory would precipitate an abrupt change of attitude at the paper: "We prefer the alternative of disunion, however sad, to any further submission to Northern aggression."

Nearly a thousand miles to the north, a similar call for a Union dissolution mixed with similar attacks on the Constitution rang out from Lloyd Garrison, now operating from spacious new offices on Boston's Washington Street. In its columns, the *Liberator* displayed no particular enthusiasm at Lincoln's nomination and in fact barely took notice of it, beyond a complaint that he was running on a platform that declined to attack the Supreme Court's *Dred Scott* decision, the Fugitive Slave Act, and slavery in the District of Columbia.

In a later speech before the American Anti-Slavery Society, printed in his newspaper, Garrison ventilated his feelings more aggressively. "It is by a stern logical and moral necessity," he declared, "that we have been driven to demand the dissolution of the Union." He had had his fill, he said, of shouting, "The Union forever!" and "of glorying in the star-spangled banner and the American Constitution." Now, he said, "we abhor the Constitution," and he would not let that banner, "clotted with human blood," fly above his head.

As for the Republican Party, he posed a number of provocative

questions, then supplied answers: Does the party oppose the slaveholding guarantees embedded in the Constitution? No. Does it accept the
despised fugitive slave language of the Constitution? Yes. Does it accept
the added political power bestowed on the South by the three-fifths
method of counting slaves for representation? Yes. Does it place the federal government at the ready to put down slave insurrections? Yes. He
concluded, "Then, how can I, claiming to be a friend . . . of the slave,
on the day of election, march up to the ballot-box, and give my vote for
such a party, and say that I have done a deed for freedom?"

Garrison's friend Wendell Phillips, in a speech two days earlier before another antislavery organization (also printed in the *Liberator*),
dismissed the Republicans as feckless, with leaders who lacked the courage to advocate the eradication of slavery in the southern states and
who didn't even participate in such antislavery meetings as the one he
was addressing. Take, for example, he said, Henry Wilson and Charles
Sumner—"the very best specimens, perhaps, of the Republican mind.
Do you ever see one of them here?"

Phillips's passion blinded him to a significant distinction between
activists such as himself and politicians such as Wilson or Sumner. The
activist's job is to employ stark moral exhortation to crystallize issues,
stir up emotions, and generate agitations, with the hope that those emotions and agitations would congeal slowly into a civic consensus. No
one exemplified this calling with greater aplomb than Lloyd Garrison,
with Wendell Phillips not far behind.

But the politician's job is to accumulate and wield political power
through coalition building, inside maneuvering, deft compromising,
and carefully crafted rhetoric designed to pull voters together under the
banner of a compelling civic message. This requires a certain flexibility
of thought, action, and rhetoric, a willingness to take what is available
in the political arena when it *is* available and accept politics as the art of
the possible.

No one in America personified these traits and talents more clearly
than Henry Wilson. No one could question his contribution to the rise
of the Republican Party from its first stirrings in 1848 as the fledgling
Free Soil initiative to its current status as a party with serious prospects

of capturing the U.S. presidency. That emergence was a remarkable political achievement, and it never could have happened had the party embraced a Garrison-like dialectic proclaiming the American republic and its governing document to be inherently foul. Wilson didn't embrace such a dialectic because he didn't believe it.

As for Sumner, despite his often stark and aggressive rhetoric, he had taken great pains to place his antislavery passion into the context of the popular American narrative and the Constitution. Never would there be in Sumner's discourse a call for disunion or a retreat from his resolve to press his antislavery crusade within the framework of the Founders.

Further, it was a bit rich for Phillips to question Sumner's commitment to the cause simply because he didn't attend antislavery rallies of the kind that consumed so much time and energy of voluble New England abolitionists. Certainly the price Sumner paid for his convictions deserved recognition, particularly since he continued to receive menacing threats. But the senator wouldn't blunt his lacerating rhetoric, as he demonstrated on June 4 with a Senate speech entitled "The Barbarism of Slavery." Many friends urged him to rise above his reputation for polemical harshness and strike a tone of "benevolence and charity," as Samuel Gridley Howe put it.

Sumner rejected the counsel. Announcing at the beginning of his oration that he was about to critique not just the character of slavery but also the character of slaveholders, he unfurled four hours of antislavery invective mixed with an extensive historical analysis of the institution. He intoned:

> Barbarous in origin; barbarous in the law; barbarous in all its pretensions; barbarous in the instruments it employs; barbarous in its consequences; barbarous in its spirit; barbarous wherever it shows itself, Slavery must breed Barbarians, while it develops everywhere, alike in the individual and the society in which it belongs, the essential elements of barbarism. . . . There is nothing in its character, its manifold wrong, its wretched results, and especially in the influence on the class who claim

to be "ennobled" by it, that will not fall naturally under consideration [of his speech].

Citing extensive statistics, Sumner demonstrated that the South, despite its advantages in climate, navigable rivers, and harbors, had been far outstripped by the North in population, property value, the number of farms and plantations in operation, the number of acres under improvement, the number of railroad miles, the number of college graduates produced, the number of newspapers, the number of patents acquired, and much more. The South's lagging performance in all these areas of endeavor, he said, stemmed from the blight of southern slavery.

Sumner conceded that many southern slaveholders demonstrated individual virtue, but "it is not reasonable or logical to infer that the masses of Slave-masters are better than the Law of Slavery." That law, he continued, "degrades the slave to be a chattel, and submits claim to [the slaveholder's] irresponsible control, with power to bind and to scourge; to usurp the fruits of another's labor; to pollute the body; and to outrage all ties of family, making marriage impossible." All these elements of slavery, said Sumner, degrade the slaveholder just as they do the slave.

"Tell me not," demanded the senator, "of the sympathy which overflows from the mansion of the master to the cabin of the slave. . . . In vain you assert that there are individuals who do not exert the wickedness of the law. The Barbarism still endures, solemnly, legislatively, judicially attested in the very Slave Code, and proclaims constantly the character of its authors."

The speech signaled to the nation that Sumner was back, fully recovered physically and psychologically, and anxious to take up where he left off with his fateful "Crime against Kansas" speech of 1856. The *Mercury* said the speech presaged the fate of the South under a rising North. Warned the paper: "It will be . . . like the embrace of the slimy, remorseless anaconda." Senator Chesnut lamented slyly that, "[a]fter ranging over Europe, sneaking through the back doors of English aristocracy, and fawning at their feet, this slanderer of States and men has reappeared in the Senate."

Sumner still stirred emotion, and some of it could be menacing. On the evening of June 8 a stranger appeared at his Washington residence with a request to discuss his speech. The senator invited the man into his drawing room, whereupon the stranger turned nasty. He said he was a southern slaveholder, hence a victim of Sumner's slander, and he was there to hold Sumner responsible for it. Feeling uneasy, the senator ordered the man out of his house and summoned a servant to show him out. He left, but only after issuing threats. He said he was one of four men who had traveled to Washington from Virginia with the purpose of holding Sumner accountable. The four soon would appear, he said, and demand a private interview.

Sumner promptly summoned Henry Wilson, who arrived in time for two more episodes that occurred that night involving strangers wishing to see Sumner but insisting that he be alone during their visits. This being refused, they left, but one issued a threat that if they couldn't see Sumner alone by the next night, they would "cut his d—d throat." The next morning, with several Sumner friends now present for protection, yet another man appeared at the senator's door.

"My name is Darien," said the man, "and I wish to see you privately."

"You can see me here, and now," replied Sumner. "I do not know you."

The stranger refused to enter, then backed out and fled. The *Liberator* reported that the senator's friends were "determined that Mr. Sumner shall not be taken unawares or alone again." Several walked him to the Senate chamber that morning to thwart any attack.

On May 31, Charles Francis Adams delivered his maiden House speech and acquired a new level of political stature. Not surprisingly, he chose as his subject the issue of slavery and displayed his notable talent for sound reasoning packaged in lucid, analytical prose. Responding to southern arguments that slavery represented a natural state in the relationship of the races, Adams cautioned that this posed a direct challenge to Thomas Jefferson's iconic contention in the Declaration of Independence that all men are created equal and born alike with certain inalienable rights.

A view had emerged in the South, said Adams, that Jefferson didn't really mean it, that when he said all men were created equal he really meant just white men. Thus, under this view, "the rights which he pronounces inalienable in all, are in fact alienable in a great majority of the human race." But if that was what Jefferson meant, asked Adams, why did he not say so? "Surely," he continued, "it is pretty hard to believe that so lucid a writer could, with his eyes open, have fallen into such a delusion as to mean, in a public paper which he regarded as the crowning merit of his life, the precise reverse of what he actually said."

Still more difficult, added Adams, was explaining why Jefferson would never clarify his meaning during the fifty years of his life after writing that "immortal paper," given that his dictum was construed widely as applying to all humankind. "He well knew the sense which his contemporaries universally attached to his words," said Adams. "If he had had any other in his mind, why did he not disclose it?"

Thus did Adams join Sumner, Lincoln, and others in maintaining that the Founders never wanted slavery to become embedded on the continent into permanence. No, he argued, the framers wanted it constricted and placed upon a path of eventual extinction. That was the Republican perception and the Republican policy, as articulated by Adams.

Northern newspapers hailed the speech as a throwback to Adams's legendary father, often remembered as "Old Man Eloquent." One letter writer to the *Boston Journal* said that Adams's facial features, "usually cold and passionless, glowed with excitement" during his delivery. And the *Liberator* published a letter from Washington describing the speech as "able, polished, scholarly, but scathing." Even the *Charleston Mercury* saw fit to describe Adams as "one of the shining lights of the Black Republicans." After years of fits and starts in the political arena, Charles Adams was emerging now as a serious figure on the American scene.

As the November 6 election approached, with the fate of the country in the balance, Americans became increasingly fixated on the four-man presidential campaign. The Republicans' commanding position in the North gave Lincoln a shot at scoring an Electoral College victory, while no other candidate seemed positioned for such a triumph. But with the vote split four ways, it was possible that no candidate could capture an Electoral College win. In that event the election would go to the House of Representatives, where the top three vote-getters would vie for the prize and each state delegation would cast one vote.

An analysis by the *Boston Evening Transcript* identified fifteen states with "undoubted Republican majorities," and fourteen others clearly controlled by Democrats. But the American Party, the lingering remnant of the Know-Nothing movement, dominated the Tennessee delegation and shared an equal division with Democrats in three other slave states: Kentucky, Maryland, and North Carolina. That suggested that American Party members likely would join with Democrats to decide the election should the House become the arbiter.

Then there was New York with its thirty-five electoral votes. As a Republican stronghold it was certain to go for Lincoln—unless, as calculated by some New York politicians, the three opposition parties could "fuse" together and pull the anti-Lincoln votes under one banner. As the *Mercury*'s New York correspondent reported in late August, "There is now no doubt that the Breckinridge men of New York will unite with the Douglas and Bell-Everett parties, in an attempt to defeat Lincoln." A meeting was called for September 9 at New York's Academy of Music to forge the party amalgam, with particular emphasis on the need to pool financial resources as part of the effort. The Republicans, it was reported, were poised to spend a million dollars to ensure a New York victory.

By September 15, though, the fusion effort had collapsed under the weight of partisan pride and animosity, with the Breckinridge men refusing to accept the Douglas faction's insistence that the fusion ticket must run on the popular sovereignty credo. "We suppose," said the *Mercury* in reporting the breakdown, "it may now be conceded that Mr. Lincoln will be elected by the Electoral College."

Already the nation's attention had descended upon the fresh face of Lincoln, whose national profile remained ill-defined. Boston's *Evening Transcript* wrote that there were "no prejudices against him in his own party" and hence he would have no difficulty in uniting Republicans.

The paper praised his "instinctive perception of popular feelings and modes of thinking" and his "insinuating way of proving to the people that he 'is one of them.'"

But southerners perceived a dark and sinister figure little different from the abolitionist agitators they had railed against for years. The *Mercury* complained that the *New York Times* "and other kindred presses" persisted in portraying Lincoln as a "harmless conservative man" whose election would not threaten the South's slavery institution. But, even if that were true, said the paper, he is the "exponent of his party," which was "sufficient to justify the inference that he must carry out their policy."

The *New York Herald*, tilting as always toward the South, echoed the *Mercury* but added a telling insight. Whatever Lincoln's true convictions or aims, said the *Herald*, "he would necessarily have to act on the one great idea which underlies the whole structure of the Black Republican party. . . . That idea is that 'slavery is an evil and a crime.'"

Just so. Lincoln himself expressed it best in his Cooper Union speech when he said that the South's perception of slavery as right and the North's view of it as wrong "is the precise fact upon which depends the whole controversy." Lincoln had sought to mollify the South with his convictions that the Constitution sanctioned slavery where it already existed and Congress couldn't interfere; that fugitive slave laws, however distasteful, were a constitutional mandate; that the prohibition of slavery in the District of Columbia could be justified only if embraced by the residents there; and that he didn't place blacks on an equal social footing with whites. None of it worked. Southerners couldn't get beyond his view of slavery as a moral wrong and thus couldn't draw a distinction between Lincoln and, say, a Garrison or a Phillips.

This southern perception of Lincoln now colored the South's view of its predicament as it faced the specter of that dangerous anaconda described by the *Mercury*. "If Lincoln be elected," said South Carolina representative William Boyce, echoing the words of many southern contemporaries, "I think the Southern States should withdraw from the Union, all; if not all, then as many as will; and if no other, South Carolina alone, in the promptest manner and by the most direct means."

Threats of secession were one thing; northerners had been dismissing those dramatic taunts for years. But now the language of southern defiance was becoming far more bellicose and raw. Former U.S. representative John Crozier of Tennessee said he would consider Lincoln a "perjured traitor" from the moment he took the presidential oath, and he never would submit—"*never—never—never.*" He would "*mount the scaffold* in such a cause."

Representative Roger Pryor of Virginia weighed in with even more obloquy. Casting aside his oath of fealty to the Constitution, he declared that if any president of the United States should employ force to prevent the secession of a southern state, he "*would be the Brutus to plant a dagger in his heart.*" Such quotes were duly reported in the *Mercury* without any hint of discomfort.

But they raised a question: What in fact would the U.S. government do, in the face of Lincoln's election and southern secession, to preserve, protect, and defend the constitutional order, as the Constitution enjoins the president to do? The *Mercury* explored this question in late September in a piece stirred by a previous editorial in the *Washington Constitution*, the official Buchanan newspaper. The *Constitution* piece, titled "The North the Aggressor—the South on the Defensive," implied that the president would not be inclined to pursue a policy of "coercion" in response to secession. That was certainly the right answer, as far as the *Mercury* was concerned, and the newspaper argued further that, in the event of secession, Buchanan must set the government's course during the four months between the election and the inauguration.

"If he attempts coercion," predicted the *Mercury*, "every Southern man in his cabinet, and in the army and navy, will doubtless leave." The president, added the paper, must "enforce his own conscientious conceptions of the rights of the States, under the Constitution." Using the *Mercury* as their bullhorn, the Rhetts expressed confidence that Buchanan and his cabinet would never align themselves with the Black Republican or Squatter Sovereignty factions or ever "shed the blood of a wronged and inoffensive people, who seek their safety by a separation from their aggressors and persecutors." Clearly, the Rhetts wanted secession to be peaceably accomplished and well established by the time Lincoln became president.

Was this yet another instance of Barnwell Rhett's political passion undermining his perception of reality? It could seem that way to anyone who absorbed Stephen A. Douglas's rhetoric and convictions on the subject. The Little Giant had not enjoyed much good fortune in 1860. After nearly a decade of hungering for just the right avenue of opportunity for reaching the White House, he had seized upon 1860 as his best bet. But now he was leading a mere fragment of a party that was likely to be shut out in the South on Election Day and superseded by the upstart Republicans in the North. Worse, his looming career implosion had come about through the likes of the despised William Yancey and his old rival from the low-stakes legislative days, Abe Lincoln, whom he had bested in nearly all contests until now.

But for all of his faults, including the lack of a moral sensibility on the slavery issue, Douglas was a man of conviction on issues dear to his heart, particularly popular sovereignty. He had demonstrated as much on the treacherous Lecompton tangle by taking on the powerful sitting president from his own party in an action that now contributed significantly to his political troubles. In August, traveling through the South to tout the popular sovereignty doctrine, Douglas found himself in Norfolk, Virginia, delivering a two-hour address. When a note was handed up to him in the middle of the speech, he interrupted himself to answer two questions posed in the note. He said:

> The first question is, if Abraham Lincoln be elected President of the United States, will the Southern States be justified in seceding from the Union? To this I emphatically answer no. [Great applause.] The election of a man to the Presidency by the American people, in conformity with the Constitution of the United States, would not justify any attempt at dissolving this glorious confederacy. [Applause.] Now I will read to you the next question, and then answer it.
>
> Question.—If they, the Southern States, secede from the Union upon the inauguration of Abraham Lincoln,

before he commits an overt act against their constitutional rights, will you advise or vindicate resistance by force to their secession?

Voices—"No, no!"

Mr. Douglas.—I answer emphatically that it is the duty of the President of the United States, and all others in authority under him, to enforce the laws of the United States as passed by Congress and as the courts expound them. [Cheers.] And I, as in duty bound by my oath of fidelity to the Constitution, would do all in my power to aid the government of the United States in maintaining the supremacy of the laws against all resistance to them, come from what quarter it may.

Douglas declared his opposition to both northern abolitionists and southern secessionists, and for the same reason: both advocated federal intrusion into territorial slavery policy in opposition to his cherished credo of popular sovereignty. But it was difficult to see how popular sovereignty could survive the election, as the two leading candidates, Lincoln and Breckinridge, both opposed it. As a governing philosophy for the territories, it was finished, as were, it seemed, the presidential hopes of Stephen Douglas.

On Election Day, November 6, in Springfield, Illinois, Abraham Lincoln tore off the top of his election ballot so he wouldn't be tempted to vote for himself, which he felt would be unseemly. Then he voted for the other offices on the ballot and headed over to the capitol building to monitor the returns, relayed from the nearby telegraph office. Early reports gave the Republican candidate Illinois and Indiana as well as other western states. That was good news, but returns from the crucial East were slow in coming, and the Pennsylvania report didn't arrive until after ten o'clock. Lincoln joined friends for dinner at nearby Watson's Saloon, with the crucial New York results still hanging in the balance. Then he waited at the telegraph office until two in the morning, when the New York victory finally came in. Abe Lincoln would be the next president. "I went home, but not to get much sleep," he later recalled, "for I then felt as I never had before the responsibility that was upon me."

In Charleston, large crowds congregated for news at the *Mercury* and telegraph offices. The first dispatch reported that Connecticut had gone for Lincoln, then North Carolina for Breckinridge. Anxieties swelled throughout the crowd as further reports filtered in without confirming an Electoral College winner. Then the Associated Press agent telegraphed that Lincoln had won New York and the election. The crowd, reported the *Mercury*, "gave expression to their feelings by long and continued cheering for a Southern Confederacy."

Four years earlier, in 1856, Republican John Frémont had swept the upper North but lost the election by losing to Buchanan in the crucial northern and western states of Pennsylvania, New Jersey, Illinois, and Indiana. Lincoln, without a single slave state in his column, captured three of those four crucial states along with four of New Jersey's seven electoral votes (the other three going to Douglas). That, along with a sweep of the North and West, gave Lincoln an Electoral College harvest of 180 votes from eighteen states, 28 more electoral votes than he needed for victory. Breckinridge swept eleven slave states for an electoral vote of 72, with Bell and Douglas far behind.

In the popular vote, Lincoln collected only 39.9 percent, compared to 29.5 percent for Douglas, 18 percent for Breckinridge, and 12.6 for Bell. Thus would the new chief executive be a minority president in a profoundly splintered country. The vote totals in Massachusetts and South Carolina reflected the chasm separating those two states stretching back to the early decades of the English colonial experience. Massachusetts Republicans captured nearly 63 percent of the popular vote, while South Carolina demonstrated its contempt for the election by not holding a popular vote at all. The legislature selected the state's eight electoral delegates, who voted in a bloc, as instructed, for Breckinridge.

The results didn't yield any discernible guidance as to what the nation wanted from its new leader or how to forge a governing coalition.

Given that, Lincoln was wise in his postelection reaction when peppered with questions about what he planned to do when inaugurated. He simply asked in reply, "Have you read my speeches?" When pressed further, reported the *Boston Evening Transcript*, "he quietly hands over one of the pamphlet publications of his speeches in the late controversy with Mr. Douglas."

27

DISSOLUTION

||||||||||||||||||||||||||||||||||||||||||||||||||||||||||||||||||||||||||||||||||||||

SOUTH CAROLINA LEADS THE WAY

O n November 7, 1860, with news of Lincoln's triumph hardly a few hours old, U.S. district judge Andrew G. Magrath closed the latest term of the U.S. District Court for South Carolina with a startling announcement. Secession was now inevitable, he said, and he was resigning his judgeship. "Feeling an assurance of what will be the action of the State," said the judge, "I consider it my duty, without delay, to prepare to obey its wishes."

Those who knew Magrath hadn't pegged him as the likely first South Carolinian to plunge into the revolution that many now anticipated. Certainly he was no fire-eater and in fact had been a Barnwell Rhett antagonist for years, stretching back beyond the fateful 1856 duel in which the judge's brother Edward had killed Rhett's nephew William Taber. Magrath and Rhett had been on opposite sides of the earlier struggle between secessionists and cooperationists, and Rhett had viewed Magrath as one of the "wretched self-seekers and charlatans" who disdained his secessionist zeal.

But now Magrath heralded South Carolina's coming secession by severing his own ties to the national government through an action of self-sacrifice. He announced defiantly that "the Temple of Justice, raised under the Constitution of the United States, is now closed," and he thanked God "that its doors have been closed before its altar has been desecrated with sacrifices to tyranny." Then he stood up and "divested himself of the Judicial Robe," as the *Charleston Courier* reported, adding that "there were few dry eyes among the spectators and auditors."

More significant than Magrath's action was the popular response. He was hailed as a hero—"rich in the approving admiration of his fellow-citizens," declared the *Courier.* That evening, when several thousand expectant residents of Charleston organized a procession to celebrate the coming disunion, the throng serenaded the Magrath home.

This lionization represented merely a small part of a broader political phenomenon. Lincoln's election had shifted South Carolina sentiment strongly in favor of immediate dissolution, with or without other states. The shift could be seen in palmetto flags flying everywhere; in nightly rallies and parades, with cannon blasts and fireworks; in the mustering of military units; and in further resignations of federal officials operating in South Carolina. The *Courier* wrote that "the spirits of our people [are] now roused to the highest pitch."

In Massachusetts, Lloyd Garrison and his friends watched all this with skepticism mixed with amusement. Such familiar threats were usually followed by the spectacle of southern firebrands pulling back for lack of sufficient popular support. Besides, as Garrison's *Liberator* pointedly noted, Lincoln advocated "but one point of antagonism to slavery—to wit, no more territorial expansion." On the other big issues that abolitionists cared about, the president-elect sided with southerners. "Will they secede from the Union?" asked Garrison's paper in a jocular vein. "Will they jump into the Atlantic? Will they conflagrate their own dwellings, cut their own throats, and enable their slaves to rise in successful insurrection? Perhaps they will—probably they will not! By their bullying and raving they have many times frightened the North into a base submission to their demands—and they expect to do it again!"

Garrison was wrong this time. South Carolina had placed itself upon a path to secession from which it would not retreat, and the nation was entering an even more ferocious phase in its decade-long crisis of increasing sectional hostility. The pace of events was accelerating, and many of the most powerful events were happening in South Carolina. On November 9, just three days after the election, the state senate approved legislation calling for a January 8 election of delegates to a state convention that would convene a week later to consider secession.

But that would never do, insisted Barnwell Rhett. Legislators, he demanded, must act much more quickly to prevent any hesitancy from spreading and to ensure that South Carolina would lead the nation in secession so that it could lead the South thereafter in governing. He asked, "Will not delay cool the ardor of our people, who incensed now would resist promptly?" Legislators, responding to such arguments from Rhett and other low-country oligarchs, moved up the delegate election to December 6, with the convention to begin eleven days later.

Two days later James Chesnut resigned his Senate seat and informed James Hammond of his action. Within twenty minutes of getting the news, Hammond also resigned. He was never quite sure why he did it so impulsively—perhaps to show unity with his colleague, he later mused. To his friend Simms he likened the action to the ancient Japanese custom of "ripping up their own bowels to revenge an insult." Soon, embracing reality, he announced he would support his state's actions "with all the strength I have." But he was finished now politically. Having embraced the losing side in his state's civic divide, he would be cast aside by events.

Barnwell Rhett, on the other hand, stood tall, referred to widely now as "the father of secession." As the *New York Evening Post* wrote, "This is his hour of triumph, and the triumph is more properly and peculiarly his than that of any other man now living." Rhett moved quickly to secure for himself a commanding position in his state's swirling politics. On November 12 he delivered a fiery address to a packed audience at Charleston's Institute Hall.

He recited the usual litany of southern complaints—including, most recently, the Republicans' push for a homestead law to practically give away western lands to migrants "to strengthen the power of the North in Congress, and aid in the subjugation of the South." He decried the North's "naked sectional despotism [that] is organized over the

South—as hating as it is hated—with all the fury of fanaticism, and all the lust of avarice and ambition." This was what South Carolinians now wanted to hear.

Their secession fever soon spread to other states. By December, Mississippi, Alabama, Georgia, and Florida had joined South Carolina in establishing dates for conventions to consider secession. Texas would soon follow, and few expected any of them to resist the lure of disunion. That was reflected in a torrent of pamphlet literature unleashed by southern leaders and distributed to citizens throughout the South. The writers dutifully explored the region's situation from all angles but ultimately ended up tilting heavily toward the necessity of secession based on the perceived threat to the southern way of life and fears of servile insurrections. The Georgia legislature accentuated the South's seriousness by authorizing a million-dollar expenditure for the purchase of military weapons.

As America stared into the abyss of the unknown, James Buchanan became the man in the middle, caught between those bent on saving the nation and those intent on breaking it apart. He quickly perceived that there was little prospect of preventing South Carolina's secession. But as a lifelong friend of the South, he hoped initially to employ friendly persuasion in heading off further disunion initiatives, at least for the duration of his waning presidency. His vehicle of expression would be his Fourth Annual Message, to be delivered to Congress on December 3.

In preparation Buchanan instructed Attorney General Jeremiah Black to explore the legal ramifications of secession and various federal responses to it. Black concluded that secession was unconstitutional and that the president must protect federal property anywhere in the Union. Further, he could call up militias when, in his judgment, U.S. laws were actively opposed "by any State [or] by combinations too powerful to be suppressed by the ordinary course of judicial proceedings."

But the attorney general also emphasized that the president lacked authority to suppress mere verbal attacks upon the federal government or even the embrace of secession resolutions absent "a direct and positive aggression" upon federal property or personnel. If South Carolina delegates met in convention and voted to recall their congressional representatives and renounce their Union participation, Buchanan lacked the power to prevent it.

The president interpreted Black's report as saying the states possessed no constitutional right of secession but that he possessed no legitimate power to do much about it. That served as the foundation of his message to Congress on December 3.

As usual, Buchanan attributed the nation's sectional crisis to the "incessant and violent agitation of the slavery question throughout the North." Still, he added, northern slavery agitation didn't constitute a rationale for secession, and neither did Lincoln's election. "Reason, justice, a regard for the Constitution," said the president, "all require that we shall wait for some overt and dangerous act on the part of the President elect before resorting to such a remedy." Even in the face of such an act, however, the South should realize that secession was revolution. "It may or may not be justifiable revolution," said the president, "but still it is revolution."

And yet, in Buchanan's view, the government lacked not only the constitutional justification but also the practical means for putting down such a revolution. Military action against an errant state would simply bring about precisely the rupture that coercion was designed to forestall. More states would secede, and the crisis would grow. The president emphasized that "our Union rests upon public opinion, and can never be cemented by the blood of its citizens. . . . If it can not live in the affections of the people, it must one day perish." But the *Cincinnati Enquirer*, a Democratic paper, said it didn't make sense to argue against secession while renouncing coercive actions to fight it. "Seldom have we known so strong an argument come to so lame and impotent a conclusion," said the paper.

Instead of coercion, the president urged Congress to foster creation of a constitutional convention to produce an "explanatory amendment" to the nation's governing document that would do three things: recognize the right of slavery in states where it already existed (supported even

by Lincoln and other antislavery Republicans); codify the national government's duty to protect slaveholder rights in the territories up to the
point of statehood (a slave code); and recognize the right of slaveholders
to have fugitive slaves returned without interference. Buchanan's compromise recommendations, tilted as always toward the South, didn't get
much traction.

But the *Charleston Mercury* hailed the concept that the president couldn't legitimately put down a treasonous insurrection. "We
infer . . . from these positions," said the paper, "that the military power
of the United States will not be used by Mr. Buchanan to coerce South
Carolina. . . . This bugbear is, therefore, at an end."

It wasn't, though, because Buchanan couldn't avoid responsibility
for the security of U.S. military forts, including installations in Charleston Harbor over which South Carolina would soon claim jurisdiction.
Everyone knew these constituted the most likely flash point in the brewing confrontation between the seceding state and the national government. The harbor's central command resided at Fort Moultrie, about
two miles from the Charleston Battery, located on a thin peninsula on
Sullivan's Island. It commanded the northeast side of the three-mile-
wide harbor entrance. Though it could thwart a harbor attack from
the sea, it was vulnerable to land assault from the east. Major Robert
Anderson, a Kentuckian, commanded Moultrie and the other harbor
installations, with nine officers and just seventy or so men, "including
the band," as the *Mercury* wryly noted.

Well inside the harbor, near the Charleston docks, lay a small island
with an installation called Castle Pinckney, unoccupied save for an el-
derly ordnance sergeant and his family. Across the harbor entrance, on
the southeastern side, lay Fort Johnson, hardly more than an abandoned
barracks and hospital area. Between them, some three and a half miles
from the city, stood Fort Sumter, located on an artificial, two-and-a-
half-acre island developed from a sandbar strategically located at the
center of the harbor passageway. The formidable five-sided fortress atop
the island was designed to accommodate a thousand personnel and 140
cannon. But neither men nor guns had yet arrived in any significant
numbers, as the fortress remained under construction.

On December 8 a delegation of South Carolina congressmen met with Buchanan to warn against any attempt to reinforce the forts, which they said would be an act of coercion and war. Two days later they returned with a written promise that South Carolina wouldn't attack the forts as long as there was no reinforcement. The idea was to maintain the status quo as events unfolded. Buchanan seemed to accept that trade-off.

I n Congress, meanwhile, leaders initiated a last-ditch compromise effort. In December both houses established special committees charged with crafting detailed plans of bisectional accord. The Senate panel, called the Committee of Thirteen, seized upon a proposal by Kentucky's venerable John J. Crittenden, the central provision of which was a constitutional amendment restoring the Missouri Compromise line of latitude 36°30', with slavery allowed below that line and prohibited above it. But Crittenden's full handiwork tilted heavily toward the South and assaulted the Republican principle of no slavery extension. On December 31 the Committee of Thirteen reported to the Senate that it couldn't reach consensus on "any general plan of adjustment." Two weeks later the Senate officially rejected the Crittenden compromise.

The Crittenden plan's fate reflected an underlying reality: the time for compromise had passed. The South's demand for a territorial slave code couldn't be meshed with the Republicans' ironclad opposition to slavery extension. As historian David Potter wrote, "As an *exclusive* alternative to separation or war, 'compromise' simply did not exist in the winter of 1860–61."

This seemed to be well understood by some on the House side, notably Charles Francis Adams, who represented Massachusetts on the lower chamber's so-called Committee of Thirty-Three. He emerged as a committee leader, reflecting that his political asceticism of previous years had given way to a more pragmatic sensibility. He knew that the House committee, dominated by Republicans, was viewed with suspicion by most southerners and hence wasn't any more likely to reach a detailed compromise than its Senate counterpart.

But Adams perceived that the committee's deliberations could influence public opinion in the crucial border states, where voters struggled with the question of whether to join the seceding cotton states or remain in the Union. The answer to that question could affect the precise nature of the crisis Lincoln would inherit on Inauguration Day, March 4. Thus Adams vigorously supported three concessions to the South as a way of inducing border states to choose the Union over secession. The measures would facilitate the immediate admission of New Mexico as a slave state (though few expected slavery to prosper there); protect slavery where it existed through a constitutional amendment; and dismantle personal liberty laws in the North designed to thwart the return of fugitive slaves. He further expanded the split between border and cotton states by getting four border-state members to support a resolution declaring that "every good citizen" had a solemn duty to accept presidential election results.

Of course, Adams opposed any language that negated the premier Republican principle of non-extension, and he displayed his antislavery passion forcefully in a well-timed speech before the committee. Also, his resolve waned a bit in the face of criticism from Republican colleagues and as committee deliberations degenerated into an ineffectual political sputter. But Adams's flexibility demonstrated a new political sophistication and leadership skill.

Further, his focus on non-extension aligned with the private views of Abe Lincoln, who continued his refusal to discuss his presidential intentions. "It would make me appear as if I repented for the crime of having been elected," he said, adding that whatever he might say in such a heated political environment would likely be distorted and misinterpreted.

But Lincoln made clear in several letters to well-placed allies that he remained adamant on one fundamental imperative. "Let there be no compromise," he wrote to Illinois senator Lyman Trumbull on December 10, "on the question of extending slavery. If there be, all our labor is lost, and ere long, must be done again." He elaborated: "The tug has to come, and better now than at any time hereafter."

Historian Allan Nevins connects this Lincoln firmness to his earlier

pronouncement that "a crisis must be reached and passed." He fully understood, writes Nevins, that his election had brought on the crisis, and
if he were to shrink from it the country might never get past it. Non-
extension seemed to be the only path through it. On December 22 the
New York Tribune announced in an authorized statement that Lincoln
was "utterly opposed" to any concession that would yield "one iota" of
the Republican position. As leader of the party soon to dominate the
nation's politics, Lincoln was setting the terms of debate for the nation's
new postelection period.

And the southern secession movement helped him do it by adding a
new dimension to the North's political consciousness: a powerful unity
on the imperative of saving the Union. Though Lincoln's election signified the North's growing opposition to slavery, the region remained
divided on numerous aspects of the question, particularly over Douglas's popular sovereignty vs. Lincoln's non-extension. But secession gave
the Republicans what historian Potter called "a second noble cause" of
greater adhesive power than the often divisive slavery issue. Thus did
the North's reverence for America's grand constitutional design bolster
the Republican resolve to reject compromise on the fundamental non-
extension principle.

It also undermined the standing of Lloyd Garrison and his friends
up in Boston, who continued to belittle the importance of Lincoln's
victory and to cry out for the demise of the perfidious Union. Now,
with the country actually facing demise, to the great consternation of
most northerners, vehement abolitionism took on a more unsavory aspect. The *Boston Evening Transcript* responded to one Wendell Phillips
address, filled with his usual cuttingly amusing invective against those
he considered less pure than himself, by declaring that "[n]o eloquence,
and no devotion to a principle, can justify such gross violations of good
taste and good feeling."

Henry Wilson, vehement unionist as well as staunch antislavery warrior, spoke with more political savvy on November 9, with South Carolina's secessionist movement aborning, when he declared, "We have . . .
appealed to the heart and conscience of the nation, and to-night . . .
we stand here with the Slave Power of America beneath our feet."

[Enthusiastic applause, and cries of "Good."] Separating himself implicitly from the Garrison set, he hailed the Republican triumph as "a glorious and brilliant victory" and declared his "most undoubting confidence in the capacity, honor, integrity and devotion of Abraham Lincoln."

Similarly, Charles Sumner praised Lincoln as "prudent, wise, discreet, and also brave" and said his triumph yielded a number of distinct political outcroppings, including a recognition that slavery must derive its existence strictly from local laws and not the Constitution. "Surely," said Sumner, "this is a great action for our country, and forms a landmark in its history."

On December 15 Barnwell Rhett met with the British consul, Robert Bunch, in Charleston. Though the South Carolinian had been elected a delegate to the forthcoming state convention to consider the matter of secession, he had no portfolio for speaking with a foreign diplomat in a way suggesting any official capacity. But such niceties of protocol didn't inhibit Barnwell Rhett. South Carolina, he informed Bunch, would be a new nation by February 15, and he wanted it to establish a strong relationship with Britain based on extensive trade ties. He hinted at nominal tariffs. And don't worry about Buchanan, he added, as the president wouldn't defend the forts in Charleston Harbor or elsewhere (contrary to what Buchanan had said in his Annual Message). He assured the British official that secession would go smoothly.

When Bunch mentioned British discomfort with southern slavery, Rhett waved aside the concern. But Bunch wouldn't let it go. He said Britain certainly wouldn't trade with a country pushing for resumption of the African slave trade, whereupon Rhett turned argumentative. Prohibition of the slave trade, he contended, was tantamount to saying slavery was inherently evil, when in fact it was a foundation of southern civilization. He warned that southern cotton states would simply trade with France and Germany, leaving Britain out. Bunch countered that France and Germany also opposed a slave-trade resumption and even favored suppression measures. Rhett suggested that perhaps the issue could be compromised in some way.

Barnwell Rhett didn't impress Robert Bunch. The diplomat reported to London that the man "indulges in an abundance of utterly absurd invective against all who differ from him." Many South Carolinians agreed. Disappointment greeted those who had hoped that nearly a decade in the political wilderness had taught Rhett the importance of tact, modesty, and good-faith dealing. Those who had considered him incorrigible could see that he remained so. Most could discern that he harbored ambitions far more grandiose than he would ever realize.

Indeed, in mid-December the South Carolina legislature spurned his nomination for governor in favor of former U.S. representative and minister to Russia Francis Pickens. A few days later, at the opening of the secession convention that convened at Columbia on December 17, Rhett was nominated for convention president but received just five votes on the first ballot and none thereafter. It was now clear that, while he would be accepted as a prominent voice in the coming secession deliberations, he would not be looked to for leadership.

After a single day of deliberations at Columbia, the secession convention moved to St. Andrew's Hall in Charleston due to a smallpox outbreak in Columbia. There Rhett helped draft the "Ordinance of Secession," insisting that it be brief and direct to discourage extended debates that could delay the secession action he so ardently favored.

Just before one o'clock in the afternoon of December 20, the South Carolina secession convention received from its ordinance-drafting committee a document declaring that "the union now subsisting between South Carolina and other States, under the name of 'The United States of America,' is hereby dissolved." At precisely seven minutes after one, the convention began voting on the ordinance, and eight minutes later the process was complete. It was unanimous. South Carolina was now, in its own eyes, an independent nation.

"Inscribed among the calends of the world," declared the *Mercury*, "—memorable in time to come—the 20th day of December in the year of our Lord 1860, has become an epoch in the history of the human race." When word spread through the city, businesses suspended operations, church bells rang out, artillery salutes thundered through the

no

air, and newly crafted flags fluttered everywhere. "Never yet," said the *Mercury*, "has the public enthusiasm risen to such a height."

At six thirty that evening, the convention delegates assembled at St. Andrew's for a winding procession through downtown to Institute Hall, where they were greeted by state legislators. The two groups filed into the huge building, with delegates taking seats before an elevated stage and lawmakers lining up along the side walls as some three thousand jubilant townsfolk yelled, cheered, and waved white handkerchiefs. They basked in a civic unanimity that would have seemed impossible just a few weeks before.

On the stage, with the "consecrated parchment" on a table before him, convention president David Jamison read aloud the declaration. Upon the final word of "dissolved," the throng exploded into a tumult of rejoicing that fairly shook the structure. Then came the signing, with every member of the convention stepping up to affix his name upon the document. That ritual consumed two hours, and then there was another spree of fireworks, cannon blasts, martial music, church bells, and bonfires.

The imperative now was for South Carolinians to explain and justify their action to the world, and to that end the convention assigned Rhett and Christopher Memminger, as committee heads, to produce two separate documents. Memminger, the longtime cooperationist and strong unionist, personified the profound shift in outlook that had swept through South Carolina since Lincoln's election. Now he was a secessionist.

His "declaration" focused primarily on the recent tensions between the sections on the slavery issue, while Rhett's more sweeping and forceful document traced northern "despotism" to nearly the beginning of the republic and attributed it to a host of fundamental differences in mores, folkways, and attitudes between the two peoples. "All fraternity of feeling between the North and the South is lost, or has been converted into hate," said the document. British consul Bunch, no more impressed with Rhett's manifesto than he had been with Rhett, termed the document "weakly reasoned and, in some respects, offensive."

On December 26 Major Anderson surreptitiously and skillfully transferred his command and his troops from Fort Moultrie to Fort Sumter. He bundled up all the equipment and provisions he could take, then spiked the Moultrie guns and set fire to what he couldn't remove. It was a smart maneuver. Moultrie was neither easily defended nor well situated for military utility, whereas Sumter was well positioned on both counts.

But the action set off firestorms of emotion in Charleston and Washington. The *Mercury* reported that Charleston was "thrown into a state of the wildest excitement." Rhett, who had been warning about such an event for weeks, was particularly outraged. Now Union troops dominated the harbor entrance; the enemy command would be more difficult to overwhelm; and the city was within range of Anderson's guns. Rhett privately blasted Pickens for his "lamentable incompetency."

In Washington, the news rocked the Buchanan administration, already reeling from cabinet disruptions born of the secession crisis. During December three cabinet members resigned, including two southerners responding to the call of regional solidarity and a northerner who considered the president too soft on South Carolina. Though his new advisers bolstered his resolution in positive ways, the weight of events bore down heavily upon him. He decided to support Anderson's decision as a prudent move and within the spirit of his orders, but he received a torrent of abuse in doing so.

The abuse took a toll. Guests at an early January reception observed that the president looked worn and haggard. "I have never seen him more solemn," said one White House visitor. The president voiced his world-weariness to Alabama's senator Benjamin Fitzpatrick, a former governor, when he said: "Governor, the current of events warns me that we shall never meet again on this side of the grave. I have tried to do my duty to both sections, and have displeased both. I feel isolated in the world."

T he president's predicament tightened in the new year. Between January 9 and February 1, six southern states followed South Carolina into secession: Mississippi, Florida, Alabama, Georgia, Louisiana, and Texas. Further, in the wake of Major Anderson's transfer of troops to Fort Sumter, South Carolina officials seized Fort Moultrie and Castle Pinckney, along with Charleston's U.S. arsenal, customhouse, and post office. Enraged by these seizures and fearful of an attack on Sumter, Buchanan decided to reinforce Anderson's force with supplies and troops.

He hated to make that decision because he feared it could lead to war. From the beginning of South Carolina's secession activity in November to the end of December, the president had maintained an accommodative approach to the errant state and the three commissioners it had dispatched to Washington to negotiate a disposition of the Charleston forts. But he was pressured into the decision by his new pro-Union cabinet, led by his old friend Jeremiah Black, former attorney general and now secretary of state. Ill-kempt and physically unprepossessing but brilliant, Black had threatened to resign if Buchanan wouldn't stand firm against the South Carolina rebellion.

In a searing report to the president, Black argued that Buchanan couldn't constitutionally relinquish federal control of Sumter; that he must reinforce federal troops under his command whenever they were threatened; and that his duties as commander in chief required him to acknowledge as wise and proper Anderson's bold transfer of troops on December 26 to avoid being overrun by hostile forces. Recognizing that if Black resigned, his cabinet would largely disperse and his remaining political support would collapse, Buchanan finally became a unionist president, though hardly a steadfast one.

He mustered enough resolve to order that the military send to Charleston Harbor a load of supplies and some 250 fighting men aboard the USS *Brooklyn*, a twenty-five-gun sloop of war at Fort Monroe, near Hampton, Virginia. But then the army's commanding general, Winfield Scott, never known for decisiveness in political decision-making, buckled. He warned that the *Brooklyn*, a deep-draft vessel, couldn't get into Charleston Harbor except during high tides and, besides, he couldn't justify the transfer of troops from Fort Monroe. Better, he said, to surreptitiously send a couple hundred troops from New York aboard an unarmed merchant steamer to avoid the suggestion of coercion. The president reluctantly agreed, delaying his action and diminishing its symbolic effect.

As it happened, the replacement ship, a chartered side-wheeler called *Star of the West*, soon was identified by southern spies as Buchanan's vessel for the Charleston mission. Thus when she steamed into Charleston Harbor on January 9, local officials were ready. They ordered shore batteries to fire upon the hapless vessel, and the *Star of the West* quickly retreated back to New York without delivering either men or supplies. Meanwhile, the major kept his own guns silent, since he had received no instruction on how to respond to such a situation, nor had he been informed of the *Star*'s impending arrival. Anderson entered into an agreement with South Carolina governor Pickens that stabilized the situation at least while the governor's new emissary to Washington, Isaac Hayne, could get clarification from Buchanan on his actions and aims.

Hayne, who didn't get what he was looking for from Buchanan, left abruptly at the end of January with parting insults aimed at the president. But Buchanan got what he wanted: a standoff that seemed unlikely to ignite into war at least until he was safely back in Pennsylvania. The *Star of the West* caper wasn't without its political price, however, as many northerners felt humiliated by its failure and by the president's seeming listlessness in the face of the southern defiance.

The rebel states now turned their attention away from Charleston Harbor and toward the challenge of southern governance. Back on December 31, the South Carolina constitutional convention had called for a conference of all seceding states to convene on February 4 at Montgomery, Alabama. The aim was to forge a new nation of southern slave states. Rhett, elected to head South Carolina's delegation, anticipated a powerful role for himself in guiding convention deliberations.

His vision encompassed a number of distinct elements: There must be a permanent separation from the American North and the creation of a new confederation of independent and equal states—in other words, no further compromise discussions and no temporary provisional government in the South pending a permanent constitution. The new nation must be built upon a cultural and civilizational foundation of slavery. It must be a nation made up exclusively of slave states—no commingling of slave and free states as in the old, lamented U.S. structure. The new nation must be dominated politically by slave interests; hence, no three-fifths rule for counting slaves for political representation. There would be no curtailment of the African slave trade. Economic and foreign policy would be based on the principle of free trade, and fiscal policy would preclude appropriations for internal improvements such as roads, bridges, and canals; those would be viewed as strictly state and local projects.

As convention deliberations proceeded through February, it became clear that Rhett's vision was not widely shared by his fellow delegates. They voted to create a provisional government based on the U.S. constitutional system, pending a final Confederate constitution to be written with appropriate deliberation. They refused to ban free states from joining the new confederation and retained the three-fifths policy for census tallies. They outlawed Confederate participation in the African slave trade. Rhett's influence extended only to the free-trade and internal-improvement issues.

Worse for Rhett, the convention seemed bent on elevating Mississippi's Jefferson Davis to the presidency of the provisional government. Rhett felt that he himself deserved consideration for the job, since he was, after all, the father of secession. But, barring that, he preferred one of the prominent Georgians, Howell Cobb or Robert Toombs. He never much liked Davis, whom he considered wishy-washy and prone to dismiss disunionists as misguided. He also seemed partial to federal-level internal improvements of the kind that Rhett despised. But Davis captured the position unanimously on February 9, with Rhett actually voting for him out of political expediency.

Rhett's vote didn't help him, though, when Davis undertook to build his cabinet. The father of secession, hoping for the London diplomatic portfolio or perhaps even the State Department, got nothing. No doubt he was shut out in part because he had fed Rhett Jr. inside information about convention deliberations for use in the *Mercury*'s criticisms. As Christopher Memminger put it, "We are annoyed by the chief of our Delegation being the correspondent of the *Mercury* and undertaking through that paper to lecture the rest and the Congress."

But Rhett, as obtuse as ever about his own shortcomings, attributed the rebuff to his demure temperament. "I have never been wise in pushing myself forward to office or power," he said to Rhett Jr. He was particularly disappointed when Jefferson Davis tapped Rhett's arch-adversary Memminger for treasury secretary.

And so the father of secession found himself sidelined as the drama of secession unfolded. For years he had been a man ahead of events, and when events finally caught up with him, so did his reputation as a figure of defective judgment, too often out of control. He was, it could be said, a man of vision, but his vision seemed to many as simply too outlandish to be useful in the crucible of building a nation governed by consensus and based on a system of labor that the world increasingly considered abhorrent and immoral.

Throughout February, as the new Confederate states continued to organize themselves into a government and Buchanan struggled with how to handle or even define the crisis, America seemed precariously positioned at the edge of a precipice. It was widely believed that a northern policy of coercion would expand the secession movement and precipitate war, and yet it seemed almost inevitable that the Sumter issue would precipitate coercion. With Buchanan pursuing a policy that was largely one of drift, eyes turned to Abraham Lincoln, who on February 11 had set out from Springfield on his way to Washington.

In dozens of speeches along the way, he selected his words carefully and chose what he wouldn't say even more carefully. He suggested that the crisis gripping the nation was to some degree "artificial" in that nobody seemed able to define precisely the grievances that were driving the southern states to secession. But never did he hint at any willingness to acquiesce in a union breakup or relinquish federal property or compromise his duty to uphold the Constitution and enforce the laws.

At Indianapolis he posed a rhetorical question to those who perceived "coercion" in a president's resolve to honor his sworn duties. Would it be coercion, he asked, if the government "simply insists upon holding its own forts, or retaking those forts which belong to it, . . . or . . . the collection of duties upon foreign importations . . . or even the withdrawal of the mails from those portions of the country where the mails themselves are habitually violated?" He quickly sought to soften the impact of his words by adding, "Now, I ask the question—I am not deciding anything."

But Barnwell Rhett and his newspaper viewed that expression as a highly provocative manifesto from a formidable figure, all the more reason to leave the Union. Said the paper: "Lincoln is a cool man; an able man; a determined man; a man . . . of action, who says what he means, and means what he says; an earnest man withal, and no politician." But when Lincoln slipped into Washington from Baltimore in disguise to elude a reported assassination attempt, the *Mercury* changed its tune. "Everybody here is disgusted," said the *Mercury*, "at this cowardly and undignified entry."

Which was it? A cool, able, determined Abe Lincoln? Or a cowardly and undignified pretender? The *Mercury* didn't know, and neither did the nation.

28

CIVIL WAR

||||||||||||||||||||||||||||||||||||||||||||||||||||||||||||||||||||||||||||||

THE END AND BEGINNING
OF TORMENTED TIMES

The morning of March 4, 1861, began inauspiciously in Washington, D.C. A charcoal sky threatened rain, while persistent winds kicked up nettlesome swirls of sand and dust. But the clouds soon dissipated, the wind lulled, and a brief drizzle cleansed the air. It turned out to be a fine day for a presidential inauguration. Precisely at noon, President Buchanan and president-elect Lincoln emerged arm in arm from the prestigious Willard's Hotel, at Fourteenth Street and Pennsylvania Avenue, and climbed aboard an open carriage for the ceremonial procession to the Capitol via Pennsylvania Avenue.

Masses of citizens jammed the parade route, and Washington's *Evening Star* speculated that the city had never before seen "so immense a crowd of spectators" on the boulevard. Buchanan, reported the paper, looked "dignified and at his ease," while Lincoln "seemed to bear his honors meekly, and to be not at all excited by the surging, swaying crowd." The throng, added the paper, "seemed to be in a very good humor." But Winfield Scott, responsible for security and concerned about desperado violence in times of high civic tension, wasn't taking

any chances. He had placed armed soldiers and sharpshooters conspicu-
ously along the route and atop nearby buildings to thwart any malefactors who might emerge. None did.

Meanwhile, ceremonial events began unfolding at the Capitol,
where at noon Vice President Breckinridge and former Mississippi
governor Henry Foote escorted into the Senate chamber the vice president–elect, Hannibal Hamlin of Maine. Breckinridge administered the
oath of office to his successor before an august assemblage that included
members of Congress, Supreme Court justices, cabinet officials, governors and ex-governors, and nearly fifty members of the diplomatic corps
in their colorful regalia.

At fifteen minutes past one, the inauguration's marshal in chief, B. B.
French, ushered Buchanan and Lincoln into the chamber and escorted
them to their seats as those assembled began positioning themselves for
the short walk to the temporary inauguration platform outside, at the
east side of the building. With Lincoln's appearance on the platform, a
roar of applause and cheers arose from the estimated thirty thousand
spectators.

On the platform, Lincoln sat in the front row, along with Buchanan,
Chief Justice Taney, and Senator Douglas, all Lincoln adversaries at
one time or another. Behind the president-elect sat Mary Lincoln and
the couple's three sons. Nearby was Edward Baker, a longtime Lincoln
friend who had migrated to Oregon and become a U.S. senator. He
would introduce the president-elect.

Upon being introduced, Lincoln stepped up to a small table that
served as the podium, removed his stovepipe hat, and cast his clear, crisp
voice across the vast assemblage. In some thirty-six hundred words, he
laid out his interpretation of the national crisis and his own awesome
responsibilities in confronting it. He then recited the presidential oath
of office, administered by the eighty-three-year-old Taney, whose hands,
said the *Boston Evening Transcript*, "shook very perceptibly with emotion." Lincoln, with his family, next was escorted to the White House to
begin presiding over a fractured nation.

Lincoln's original inaugural speech draft, written at Springfield before his Washington journey, took on a harsh, even bellicose tone. The president-elect stated in unadorned language the full implications of his constitutional duty to uphold the country's governing document and enforce its laws. "All the power at my disposal," said the early draft, "will be used to reclaim the public property and places which have fallen, to hold, occupy and possess these, and all other property and places belonging to the government, and to collect the duties on imports." Other passages evinced a similar toughness.

Upon his Washington arrival, Lincoln wisely sought guidance on the speech language from men he trusted, most notably the man he had defeated for the Republican nomination and who now was about to become his secretary of state, William Seward. The New Yorker cautioned that the warlike tone could backfire, inducing secession actions by border states, most notably the influential commonwealth of Virginia and perhaps even Maryland, in which case the U.S. capital city would be locked in hostile territory. That would pose a military challenge of a most desperate nature.

More generally, said Seward, the speech needed a more balanced and conciliatory tone, while also emphasizing, as Lincoln had intended, the onus placed upon the South by its own actions and the unacceptability of state seizure of federal property. Combing carefully through the draft, Seward deleted unnecessarily provocative phrases and replaced them with more measured and neutral language. He also urged Lincoln to fashion a concluding passage containing "words of affection . . . of calm and cheerful confidence," designed to inspire an appreciation for the hallowed Union. To illustrate, he crafted his own version of what he had in mind.

Lincoln heeded the advice and in the process connected with his constituency with nuanced and placatory language that also, however, showed firmness and a cold eye of realism regarding the crisis at hand. The result was an address far more appropriate to the occasion, and more stirring, than his initial Springfield draft.

He began by acknowledging the apprehensions felt by many southerners about the perceived threat that Republican governance posed to their property and personal security. But he added, "There has never been any reasonable cause for such apprehension." After all, he said, he and his party had declared repeatedly that they had no intention of interfering with slavery where it existed. He also reiterated his conviction that the Constitution mandated that the states assist in returning fugitive slaves to their owners; "the intention of the lawgiver," he said, "is the law."

In his final draft, Lincoln excised the stark language declaring his intention to use all the power at his disposal to reclaim and hold federal property. But he implied as much, and he dismissed the very notion of secession. "I hold that in contemplation of universal law and of the Constitution the Union of these States is perpetual," declared Lincoln. Perpetuity, he elaborated, is implied in the fundamental law of all governments. Even if the Union were merely an association of states in the nature of a contract, as many southerners maintained, "can it be peaceably unmade by less than all the parties who made it?" No, he answered. A party to a contract may violate it or break it, but it can't be lawfully rescinded without the agreement of all parties.

Lincoln minced no words in expounding the implications of this. "It follows . . . ," he said, "that no State upon its own mere motion can lawfully get out of the Union; that resolves and ordinances to that effect are legally void and that acts of violence within any State or States against the authority of the United States are insurrectionary or revolutionary, according to circumstances." Thus he considered the country and its laws to be unbroken and his own duty, as prescribed by the Constitution, to be the faithful execution of all federal laws in all the states. He could not allow southern states to seize or hold property belonging to the national government.

Turning philosophical, Lincoln posited that secession "does of necessity fly to anarchy or despotism." That's because, he explained, a "majority held in restraint by constitutional checks and limitations, and always changing easily with deliberate changes of popular opinions and sentiments, is the only true sovereign of a free people." Given that unanimity in any polity is impossible and rule by a minority is unacceptable, it follows that if a polity rejects the principle of majority rule, "anarchy or despotism in some form is all that is left."

Softening a point he had expressed more starkly in his original draft, the incoming president said, "In your hands, my dissatisfied fellow-countrymen, and not in mine, is the momentous issue of civil war. The Government will not assail you. You can have no conflict without being yourselves the aggressors. You have no oath registered in heaven to destroy the Government, while I shall have the most solemn one to 'preserve, protect, and defend it.'"

He concluded by taking Seward's suggested valedictory, well conceived and nicely rendered but lacking a full richness of style, and giving it the lilt and cadence of poetry. He said:

> I am loth to close. We are not enemies, but friends. We must not be enemies. . . . The mystic chords of memory, stretching from every battlefield, and patriot grave, to every living heart and hearthstone, all over this broad land, will yet swell the chorus of the Union, when again touched, as surely they will be, by the better angels of our nature.

Not surprisingly, reaction was divided along sectional and partisan lines. The *Boston Evening Transcript* liked the "tone of hope, faith, and brave reliance upon truth," and the *Boston Herald*, a Douglas paper, predicted that, while the extremes of both parties would denounce the speech, the president would be "sustained by the great mass of the people whose sentiments he has so truly reflected."

Of course, the southern papers assaulted it in unsparing terms. "If ignorance could add anything to folly, or insolence to brutality," said the *Mercury*, "the President of the Northern States of America has . . . achieved it." The paper dismissed Lincoln as a "preposterous buffoon" and his constituency as "fanatical, ignorant, presumptuous and vulgar."

Beyond the predictable reactions, however, the speech more fundamentally reflected a haunting reality: the same political vise that had entrapped James Buchanan now had Lincoln in its grip. The new president, like his predecessor, promised that he would not resort to force against the Confederacy unless the Confederacy did so first. But he further vowed, also like his predecessor, that he would honor his constitutional duty to protect and preserve the Constitution and ensure the enforcement of federal laws. These two commitments could not be maintained for long as intertwined policies.

Indeed, the Confederacy already had taken possession of numerous forts and installations throughout the secessionist states, as well as numerous customs buildings, post offices, and more. In its usual stark manner, Rhett's *Mercury* captured the reality in an editorial written just before Inauguration Day. The president, said the paper, "must proclaim peace or declare war"—in other words, "recognize the independence of the Confederate States, or encounter them in a conflict of arms."

The only way out of the vise—the third option—was through some kind of negotiated settlement by which the United States would give the South sufficient concessions to effect what was called "reconstruction," meaning a reunified country with the slavery issue subdued. But leading politicians had been working on that third option unsuccessfully since the election, as reflected in the sputtering efforts of the Senate's Committee of Thirteen, the House's Committee of Thirty-Three, and a subsequent "Peace Commission" of some 131 prominent politicians proposed by former president John Tyler and sponsored by Virginia governor John Letcher. They all failed because none could bridge the gap between southern demands and Republican principles.

But hopes for some kind of breakthrough persisted into Lincoln's presidency, with various "conciliation" proposals emerging and then fading. The issue generated plenty of northern emotion, though, between those desperate to avoid war, and hence willing to pursue conciliation, and those who viewed secession as an insurrection requiring a firm response, perhaps even a military one. The emotion flared with particular intensity in the longtime friendship of Charles Sumner and Charles Francis Adams. So close were the two Bostonians that Sumner dined at the Adams home every Sunday evening in what became a ritual of friendship.

Sumner, still savoring both the praise and the fury generated by his "Barbarism of Slavery" speech, argued that the best way to retain the border states in the Union was through firmness: no compromise with slaveholders that would violate Republican principles and undermine the political standing of antislavery northerners. "The enmity of Slavery might be dangerous," he said, "but its friendship is fatal."

The underpinning of this outlook was a belief that the cotton states would fail miserably as an independent nation and would eventually, of necessity, slink back into the federal fold, while northern firmness in the meantime would keep the border states in place. When a friend suggested such an approach could lead the cotton states to take up arms, Sumner exploded, "Never! They are too crafty! Bullies! Braggarts! They would be assassins some of them if they dared—but fair fight, never!"

Adams, on the other hand, viewed the Sumner formula as a recipe for war. He believed his friend completely misread border-state sentiment, which could quickly become secession sentiment whenever the border regions saw bellicosity coming from Washington. No, he said, the only way to prevent border-state secession was to bolster and sustain those timid but honest unionist citizens of the South. And that would require a certain degree of conciliation.

The arguments between the two men became so heated that soon the Sunday dinners descended into "violent political wrangling," as Sumner biographer David Donald described them. "Sumner," declared Adams at one point, "you don't know what you are talking about. Yours is the very kind of stiff-necked obstinacy that will break you down."

The secession crisis wasn't the only thing coming between the old friends. Adams found Sumner more and more insufferable with the increasing intensity of his least admirable traits: the orotundity of expression, studied pomposity, and thinly veiled supposition that his "superiority in education, his oratorical power . . . [and] his knowledge of the world, made him the most important member of the Senate," as Henry Adams, Charles Francis's son, put it. For his part, Sumner seemed disturbed by Adams's growing stature in the Massachusetts delegation and the fawning attention he received from the press, something never accorded to Sumner. Whatever the underlying causes for the tensions between the two men, the friendship didn't survive.

Thus it was probably fortunate that Adams received a prestigious position in the new administration that would keep the two men far apart for several years. Within days of his inauguration Lincoln designated the congressman as his choice for minister to London, and on March 20 the Senate voted confirmation. A position previously held by both his father and grandfather, it signified to many, even including Adams himself, that he was unquestionably worthy of his ancestral heritage.

Though Sumner continued to recoil at Adams's apostasy on the secession issue, he became even more disturbed at the similar position embraced by William Seward, who surprised many with a passionate call for Union solidarity through concessions to the South. Sumner and Seward had never been particularly close. In fact, Henry Adams wrote that the "two men would have disliked each other by instinct had they lived in different planets." Now, as Sumner saw it, Seward was undermining the antislavery cause with his irresolute attitude and misplaced certitude. But Sumner harbored a similar certitude. As he complained to Massachusetts governor John Andrew, "I am certain—I see my way so clearly; such a glorious victory was before us; right was with us, God was with us—our success was sure did we only hold firmly to our principles."

The dispute crystallized the broader disagreement throughout the North over how best to retain the border states in the Union: through austerity and firmness, even if it meant war; or conciliation, signaling that the border states needn't fear any northern wrath.

Seward went a step beyond this dichotomy in conceiving a fallback idea if his conciliatory approach failed to foster the climate of national unity he desired: America, he said, should gin up a crisis and maybe even a war with a European power such as Britain, France, or Spain, as a way of binding the country back together. In December he had publicly suggested that, if one of those countries could be induced to attack, say, New York, "all the hills of South Carolina would pour forth their population for the rescue."

Such a wild fancy suggested there was more going on in Seward's mind than mere national unity through inducements to border states. The New Yorker revealed his underlying sentiment when a congressman warned that a mutual friend might be disappointed if passed over for a coveted patronage job. "Disappointment!" retorted the senator. "You speak to me of disappointment. To me, who was justly entitled to the Republican nomination for the presidency and who had to stand aside and see it given to a little Illinois lawyer!"

In fact, Seward harbored hopes of essentially taking command of the government from a president he considered callow and inadequate, at the acquiescence, he envisioned, of the president himself. As the preeminent politician of his day, as he saw himself, he could perceive no reason why that reality shouldn't be codified in a special status within the government. Then, once his efforts in behalf of national unity had proved successful, as he knew they would, he would be hailed as the man who saved the Union. Perhaps another shot at the presidency could even be in the offing.

"I will try to save freedom and my country," Seward wrote to his wife shortly after accepting the State Department portfolio. He later elaborated, "It seems to me that if I am absent only three days, this Administration, the Congress and the District would fall into consternation and despair. I am the only hopeful, calm, conciliatory person here." Others shared the sentiment. The *New York Herald* suggested that Seward held the nation's destiny in his hands, and young Henry Adams, from his vantage site at his father's side, believed Seward had become "the virtual ruler of this country."

Meanwhile, the actual ruler received disturbing news just a day after his inauguration. Major Anderson sent word from Fort Sumter that his situation was becoming hopeless. The Confederates had fortified Charleston Harbor to such an extent that a resupply party could succeed only if the new president backed it up with at least twenty thousand troops—a number impossible to muster in the time remaining before Anderson ran out of provisions and before any new conciliation effort could possibly bear fruit. Lincoln faced the reality that Rhett's *Mercury* had so starkly identified: proclaim peace or declare war.

The new president could see that his options seemed to be narrowing down to one: "to the mere matter," as he put it, "of getting the garrison safely out of the fort." General Scott concurred, telling the president, "Evacuation seems almost inevitable." This would fit nicely into Seward's game plan, but Lincoln couldn't accept the humiliation. With Anderson running out of provisions in about a month, he would use the time to search for a more feasible and less extravagant means of resupplying the garrison.

In the meantime, his secretary of state entered into a stealthy project designed to force Lincoln's hand in favor of giving up Sumter and forswearing any action against the upstart confederacy. On March 8 three commissioners from the Confederate convention arrived in Washington to negotiate a transfer of Fort Sumter and other installations situated in the South but still in federal hands. These included Fort Pickens, near Pensacola, Florida, where local officials had struck an informal arrangement with the fort's command whereby the locals wouldn't attack the fort so long as there would be no military reinforcement. Sumter and Pickens had emerged in the national consciousness as points of the highest symbolic significance in the standoff between the secessionist South and the federal government.

On March 13, Lincoln told Seward that he must not meet with the Confederate commissioners as such a parlay would constitute U.S. recognition of the southern government. The secretary complied but communicated with them anyway through the intermediation of U.S. Supreme Court justice John Campbell, expected to resign his court seat soon and return to his native Alabama. On March 15, Seward told the commissioners, through Campbell, that Lincoln would order the evacuation of Sumter in a matter of days. The news elated the commissioners, who decided to wait in Washington for the grand event.

But it didn't materialize, which led to a March 21 follow-up meeting between Seward and Campbell, during which the secretary reaffirmed his earlier prediction but asked for patience. He based his confidence in part on a cabinet poll of March 15 in which only Postmaster General Montgomery Blair argued strenuously for a resupply mission. His cabinet colleagues generally viewed the situation as hopeless. Also, Lincoln himself seemed reluctant to initiate such a dangerous and provocative operation.

Rumors soon spread through the nation that the president planned to abandon Sumter and perhaps Fort Pickens as well. The reaction in the North was quick and harsh. "The surrender of a post by the new Administration before it has been a fortnight in power, which the outgoing administration, with all its imbecility and pusillanimity, persisted in holding. . . ," said Greeley's *Tribune*, "is an acknowledgment that *the Union is utterly dissolved past all possibility of reconstruction.*"

The *Tribune* added a few days later that a decision based merely on the avoidance of war would be "another way of saying that the Secessionists are to have their own way in everything." But an army officer at Sumter, writing to a friend in Northampton, Massachusetts, emphasized the danger of any resupply initiative. "Could you stand upon these walls and look down upon the formidable preparations made to keep out such a force," wrote the officer in a letter published widely in northern newspapers, "some doubt might arise as to the practicability of sending a mere handful of men for such a purpose." A small force, he added, would be defeated, while a sufficient force couldn't be assembled in time.

Such were the crosscurrents buffeting the president as April approached and a sense emerged in the national consciousness that the status quo couldn't hold for long. For one thing, Fort Sumter would run out of provisions by mid-April, and then Major Anderson would be forced to surrender amid great dishonor for the U.S. government. For another, Lincoln had been talking with a compelling former naval officer named Gustavus V. Fox, who argued buoyantly that Sumter could in fact be supplied with a relatively small force if the right tactical concept were employed. Finally, an extended cabinet meeting on March 29 revealed that a remarkable turnabout had occurred among the members. Now, instead of Montgomery Blair being alone in urging action to resupply the fort, it was Seward who was nearly alone in arguing against it.

Though the new president struggled for a time with the dangerous conundrum facing him, ultimately he came down upon the point of view reflected in the strong language of his first-draft inaugural speech. Recognizing that he must act immediately in order to keep his options open while Anderson could still feed his troops, Lincoln set in motion plans for a resupply mission by sea, prepared to sail by April 6. The president knew that, whether it succeeded or not, the action almost inevitably would lead to war. His guiding principle now was the conviction that he must defend and protect the Constitution.

This posed a huge problem for Seward, whose representations to the Confederate commissioners, through intermediaries, would now be exposed as a sham. His confidence in his ability to control the president and administration policy had induced him to allow a mere prediction to be interpreted by the southerners as a pledge. The result was an appearance of bad faith on his part and perhaps on the president's. But Seward was not one to give up easily. He now argued strenuously for fortifying the more easily defended Fort Pickens in Florida as a demonstration of Union resolve, while accepting the abandonment of the more precarious fort at Charleston.

Responding to entreaties from Seward, Lincoln initiated plans for a second mission to reinforce Pickens simultaneously with the Sumter action. Seward could see that both Lincoln and the cabinet majority were moving toward the Charleston action, but he hoped the Pickens plan might negate the need for it, thus protecting him from exposure of his virtual and inappropriate promise to the southerners. Just in case, though, he executed a remarkable initiative designed to transfer to himself, from the elected president, a large segment of presidential authority.

During Easter Sunday, March 31, Seward produced a memorandum for the president titled "Some thoughts for the President's consideration," which he sent to Lincoln the next day. It amounted to a reproach of the president's performance in office thus far and a call for Lincoln to step back from day-to-day leadership and designate a cabinet official to assume that role. "We are at the end of a month's administration," complained the memo, "and yet without a policy either domestic or foreign." While Seward acknowledged that it was natural for the administration to be preoccupied with patronage matters during its first weeks, he declared that it was time now for an intense concentration on the truly pressing matters facing the nation.

On domestic policy, Seward somewhat patronizingly said Lincoln should transfer his attention from the slavery issue to the fate of the Union (which Lincoln had already done). Fort Sumter, said Seward, should be viewed as a political issue and surrendered—thus, incidentally, getting Seward off the hook for his misrepresentations to the Confederates. But he called for energetic actions to protect all other forts in the Gulf of Mexico, including Pickens, and prepare the navy for a possible blockade.

In a puzzling foreign-policy flight of fancy, Seward recommended that the United States demand explanations from France, Spain, Russia, and Great Britain regarding unspecified complaints; and, should the replies prove inadequate, the country ought to entertain hostilities against one or more of these miscreant nations. Historians have speculated that Seward's complaints centered on Spain's military meddling in Santo Domingo in the Caribbean; France's meddling in Mexican affairs; and prospects that Britain and Russia would recognize the Confederacy. But none of it constituted a legitimate casus belli, particularly given the magnitude of America's internal crisis.

Seward closed with his power-transfer proposal:

> Whatever policy we adopt there must be an energetic prosecution of it. For this purpose it must be somebody's business to pursue and direct it incessantly. Either the President must do it himself and be all the while active in it, or devolve it on some member of his cabinet. Once adopted, debates on it must end, and all agree and abide. It is not in my especial province. But I neither seek to evade nor assume responsibility.

Lincoln responded with remarkable forbearance, though he clearly took umbrage at the suggestion that he had no policy, which was particularly nettlesome, since that had been a common criticism of the president from his adversaries. In a reply memo, the president retorted that he did indeed have a clear policy, which he had elucidated in his inaugural address. It was to hold, occupy, and possess the forts and other property belonging to the government.

Lincoln, of course, had begun the drafting of his inaugural address with precisely that resolve, and he was now moving inexorably to the implication of it, which was that he must endeavor to resupply Major

Anderson and his men at Fort Sumter. But in between he had struggled with the binary decision matrix outlined by the *Mercury* of abandoning his sworn commitment to preserve and protect the Constitution or suppressing his desire to avoid war. In the end, the constitutional commitment prevailed.

As for the proposed delegation of presidential power, Lincoln said simply that his presidential responsibilities would always attach to him irrespective of what he said or did. The president kept his response memo for the record but wisely replied to Seward in a face-to-face conversation. The president didn't alter his approach to dealing with his unpredictable secretary and continued to accept his counsel when he considered it sound.

On April 5, war secretary Gideon Welles ordered four U.S. military vessels and a revenue cutter to Charleston to resupply and perhaps reinforce Major Anderson's beleaguered troops. But the president didn't want to be the one to initiate war, so the next day he sent two emissaries to Charleston to inform Governor Pickens that he intended to resupply Fort Sumter in an effort to maintain the uneasy status quo. If Pickens would allow the resupply effort to proceed, he said, there would be no move to reinforce Sumter with troops. But if the resupply forces met with hostile fire, U.S. troops would return fire and send in reinforcements. Thus did Lincoln engineer a binary choice for Charleston officials: the status quo or war. In doing so, the president preserved his promise that the U.S. government wouldn't initiate hostilities against the errant states unless attacked first.

Down in Montgomery, meanwhile, the southern convention, as expected, elected Jefferson Davis president of the Confederacy on April 10, with Georgia's Alexander Stephens selected as vice president. Already by April 9, however, Davis had made a decision to prevent Fort Sumter from being resupplied or reinforced, come what may. He issued a standing order to the Confederacy's commanding general at Charleston, Pierre Beauregard, to repel any resupply or reinforcement endeavor by Washington. In the meantime, Beauregard was to demand that Anderson surrender the fort or face a devastating artillery barrage. If Lincoln's last communication to Pickens was designed to ensure that the South fired the first shot in the coming war, it worked.

In part that was because Davis didn't trust Washington. For weeks he had been hearing from the highest levels of the U.S. government, in the person of William Seward, that Fort Sumter would be relinquished. All the while, it now seemed, the Washington government had been preparing for an operation to fortify Sumter against a Confederate assault. That suggested a deliberate deception, wrote historian David Potter, who added, "Seward's jugglery and Lincoln's vacillation had utterly destroyed the administration's credibility in Montgomery."

On April 11, Confederate colonel James Chesnut, the former U.S. senator, rowed over to Sumter with two other southern emissaries to confer with Anderson under a white flag of truce. They handed him a dispatch from Beauregard demanding, in courteous but firm language, evacuation of the fort. "The flag which you have upheld so long and with so much fortitude, under the most trying circumstances," said the dispatch, "may be saluted by you on taking it down."

Anderson retreated to a conference room to consult with his officers. They concluded that they would not accept the dishonor of a surrender. Besides, Gustavus Fox's flotilla of warships was heading to Charleston, and, although delayed by stormy seas, it might be arriving at any time. Indeed, the timing of Beauregard's ultimatum had been influenced by southern desires to settle the Sumter problem before those ships arrived and heightened the military challenge for southern forces. Thus did military considerations now impinge upon diplomatic action.

Anderson told Chesnut that his "sense of honor" and "obligations to my Government" precluded compliance. But he mentioned in passing, as the emissaries were about to depart, that he would be starved out anyway in a few days.

On April 12, at 12:45 a.m., the southern emissaries returned for further discussions, motivated by Anderson's remark about being starved out soon. That had led General Beauregard and Confederate war secretary LeRoy Walker to consider withholding any attack pending the anticipated forced surrender due to lack of food. They asked Anderson to state a time for his voluntary surrender and to promise that he would withhold any bombardment unless fired upon. Again the major consulted with his officers and then replied that he would surrender on the fifteenth, but could not promise to keep his guns silent in the meantime if a Union rescue mission should arrive or if he received instructions to the contrary from his government.

That, said Chesnut, was unacceptable. He quickly wrote an official reply: "Sir: By authority of Brigadier General Beauregard, commanding the provisional forces of the Confederate States, we have the honor to notify you that he will open the fire of his batteries on Fort Sumter in one hour from this time." It was 3:30 a.m. Chesnut and his colleagues then rowed across to Fort Johnson, where they ordered the commander of the mortar battery there to open fire at 4:30 with a single shot signaling to the crews of some forty-seven other gun batteries surrounding Sumter that the artillery attack on the famous fort was to commence. Precisely at the designated time the fearsome bombardment began, as did the military conflagration unleashed by that bombardment. The Decade of Disunion had finally come to an end, reaching its culmination only with the far greater torment of a war that would last four years and consume the lives of 750,000 Americans, while freeing nearly 4 million African Americans from human bondage.

Epilogue

CIVIL WAR AND BEYOND

||||||||||||||||||||||||||||||||||||||||||||||||||||||||||||||||||||||||||||||||

WHAT HAPPENED TO THE MAJOR PLAYERS?

The Civil War and its aftermath shook America to its foundations, transformed the nation, and altered the lives of the major players of Massachusetts and South Carolina, as well as those of the nation at large. Following is a summary of what happened to those whose lives and deeds during the Decade of Disunion are chronicled most extensively in this narrative:

Massachusetts

Charles Francis Adams: He resigned his House seat on May 1, 1861, after President Lincoln named him ambassador to Great Britain. His central task in that role was to persuade Britain to maintain neutrality toward the Civil War belligerents, which he largely accomplished (despite some nettlesome British transgressions). Then on January 1, 1863, Lincoln's Emancipation Proclamation removed the danger of Britain recognizing the Confederacy. Adams retained the prestigious diplomatic post until May 13, 1868, when he resigned and returned to Boston. He declined the presidency of Harvard but ran unsuccessfully for Massachusetts governor in 1876. He led the American side in the arbitration of a postwar dispute with Britain involving that country's wartime construction of warships used by Confederate and privateer naval forces against the United States. He died at age seventy-nine on November 21, 1886.

William Lloyd Garrison: The great abolitionist faced a dilemma with the outbreak of war: Would he support the northern war effort or oppose it in fealty to his pacifist convictions? He opted to support the war and embrace the leadership of President Lincoln. At war's end he sought to disband the American Anti-Slavery Society, of which he was president. When the organization resisted, he resigned and turned his attention to other reformist causes, including temperance, women's rights, pacifism, and free trade. Saying that his "vocation as an abolitionist is ended," he published the last issue of his cherished *Liberator* in December 1865. Though he retained his reformist zeal throughout the remainder of his life, he never embraced radical egalitarianism aimed at significant re-distribution of wealth or income. When pressed on the matter, he said, "It is enough for me that every yoke is broken, and every bondman set free." He died on May 24, 1879, at age seventy-three.

Charles Sumner: When James Mason left the U.S. Senate with the Vir-ginia secession in 1861, Sumner became chairman of the Senate Foreign Relations Committee and held the post for ten years. In that role he met frequently with President Lincoln during the war and urged him to in-voke martial law in conquered southern states to free the slaves of those areas. Lincoln did that in issuing his January 1863 Emancipation Proc-lamation. As a so-called Radical Republican, Sumner initially called for harsh treatment of the conquered South during and after the war, but later he favored more lenient policies in the interest of reconciliation. But he never wavered in his support of full civil rights for freed blacks. He took an aggressive stand against Great Britain in seeking indem-nity payments in recompense for Britain's neutrality violations during the war. He even advocated a payment demand so steep that Britain would have had to cede Canada to the United States in order to comply. Though embraced by some northerners, the concept never gained traction. He was designated "dean of the Senate" in 1869 and retained that status until his death from a heart attack on March 11, 1874. He was sixty-three and had served twenty-three years in the Senate.

Henry Wilson: The senator from Natick emerged as a pivotal congressional leader on military and racial issues during the Civil War. As chairman of the Military Affairs Committee (earlier called the Committee on Military Affairs and the Militia), he worked closely with the administration's military figures, including Lincoln. Also, during a forty-day period in 1861 he established the 22nd Massachusetts Volunteer Infantry and then recruited and equipped 2,300 officers and men for the regiment. He successfully sponsored wartime legislation to abolish slavery in Washington, D.C.; to authorize the president to enlist African Americans for military-related manual labor (forerunner to subsequent legislation authorizing freed blacks to serve as soldiers); and to authorize federal funding for elementary education for African American youngsters. He also worked to eliminate pay disparities between black and white military personnel. In addition he sponsored legislation to create the National Academy of Sciences. After the war he stood with the so-called Radical Republicans in advocating relatively austere Reconstruction measures in the South and civil rights protections for freed blacks. He became a leading opponent of the more lenient and less protective measures advocated by Lincoln's successor, Andrew Johnson of Tennessee. After Ulysses Grant was elected president in 1868, the general offered Wilson the post of secretary of war, but the senator declined in order to tend to the needs of his infirm wife. Four years later, when Grant ran for reelection, he selected Wilson as his running mate, and the former shoemaker served as vice president from March 4, 1873, until his death from a stroke on November 22, 1875. By then he also had distinguished himself as a serious historian, marked particularly by his three-volume work entitled *History of the Rise and Fall of the Slave Power in America.*

The Secret Six

Thomas Wentworth Higginson: Higginson fought in the Civil War as a captain in the 51st Massachusetts Infantry from November 1862 to October 1864. He also was a colonel of the First South Carolina Volunteers, the first authorized regiment of freedmen recruited for combat service in the Union army. His service ended with a wound suffered in August 1864. He wrote about his war experiences in a book entitled *Army Life in a Black Regiment*, published in 1870. After the war he became active in various religious organizations and was one of the founders, along with Jack London, Clarence Darrow, and Upton Sinclair, of the Intercollegiate Socialist Society. He died on May 9, 1911, at age eighty-seven.

Samuel Gridley Howe: During the war Howe served in various humanitarian capacities, including as a member of the American Freedmen's Inquiry Commission, charged with investigating the status of freed blacks in the South and Canada. Traveling widely, he learned that life for free blacks in Canada was far superior to that for U.S. freedmen. In 1864 he published a book on the subject entitled *The Refugees from Slavery in Canada West*, which helped pave the way for creation of the federal Freedmen's Bureau, designed to assist free southern blacks after the war. Howe later became active in Freedmen's Bureau activity. He also was a director of the federal Sanitary Commission, raising money for better hygiene practices at military camps to stem the spread of diseases that bred in unsanitary conditions. After the war he continued his work in behalf of blind and deaf persons and also the mentally impaired. He became a vocal advocate for progressive tax policies and served on a presidential commission to study the feasibility of U.S. annexation of Santo Domingo (later the Dominican Republic). He opposed it, apparently at the urging of his close friend Charles Sumner. Howe died on January 9, 1876, at age seventy-four.

The Reverend Theodore Parker: Died, May 10, 1860, in Florence, Italy.

Franklin Benjamin Sanborn: Throughout his career as teacher, writer, thinker, and commentator, the Concord intellectual wrote extensively for the *Boston Commonwealth* and the *Springfield Republican*. Shortly after the Harpers Ferry episode he published an ardent biography of John Brown that glossed over or excused the many transgressions and character flaws of the fiery abolitionist. He later wrote numerous biographies of New England figures he admired, including Emerson, Thoreau, and Nathaniel Hawthorne. He expended much time and energy in his later years in efforts to raise money for the Brown family. While traveling to New Jersey in 1917, he suffered a broken leg that didn't heal properly and became infected. He died as a result on February 24, 1917, at age eighty-five. The Massachusetts house of representatives honored him with a resolution citing his role as "confidential adviser to John Brown of Harpers Ferry, for whose sake he was ostracized, maltreated and subjected to the indignity of false arrest, having been saved from deportation from Massachusetts by only mob violence."

Gerrit Smith: During the war and after, Smith continued his philanthropic endeavors, donating an estimated $8 million in nineteenth-century currency throughout his life to various charities, including antislavery causes, educational institutions, temperance organizations, political causes, churches, and the poor. He gave away some two hundred thousand acres to destitute persons, and some 650 poor women received money from him for home purchases. In 1867 he joined Horace Greeley, Cornelius Vanderbilt, and others in underwriting a $100,000 bond for Jefferson Davis, who had been incarcerated for almost two years on unspecified charges of treason. The action proved to be highly controversial throughout the North. He died on December 28, 1874, at age seventy-seven.

George Luther Stearns: Like Higginson, Stearns spent much of the war recruiting and training black troops for military service. At the request of Massachusetts governor John Andrew, he played a key role in the creation of the state's 54th and 55th regiments and the 5th cavalry. Later, as a U.S. army major, he helped enlist African American soldiers for military units in Pennsylvania, Maryland, and Tennessee. Altogether, he helped usher some thirteen thousand black Americans into the military. Later he was instrumental in the founding of the federal Freedmen's Bureau and in the creation of the *Nation* magazine, the left-leaning political and cultural journal that began in 1865 and survives to today. The idea behind the magazine was that it would help fill the gap left by the termination of Lloyd Garrison's *Liberator*. Stearns died of pneumonia in New York City on April 9, 1867.

South Carolina

James Henry Hammond: With the secession of South Carolina and the other cotton states, Hammond embraced the cause of southern independence with an intensity suggesting that this had been his true sentiment all along. It was, he said, "the cherished dream and hope of my life." He quickly envisioned a major role for himself in the new nation, particularly in the realm of governmental finance. When war broke out, he traveled to Richmond to place himself and his elaborate financial schemes before the new southern leaders. But President Davis ignored him, and he soon realized that "there was no special need of me" in the government. He returned to Redcliffe and established himself as a leading critic of what he considered governmental incompetence at the capital city of Richmond and throughout the war effort. He prepared for the challenges of war by laying in massive amounts of critical supplies, some of which he later sold to less resourceful neighbors at huge markups. His fealty to the southern cause proved limited when Richmond officials, under pressure from invading northern troops, demanded the impressment of farm animals and, later, of slave labor for the war effort. He complained bitterly of the imposed sacrifice, particularly when northern victories after Gettysburg in July 1863 intensified the governmental demands. Meanwhile, Hammond detected in his slaves a new sense of expectation about their lot and an ominous new reserve toward him. He could see a looming military disaster on the horizon, which seemed to correspond with his own waning health. Hammond biographer Drew Gilpin Faust speculates that he succumbed to mercury poisoning after ingesting the substance for years as a treatment for constipation. Whatever the cause, he lived to see much of the awesome destruction of his native state and region but not to witness the end of the war. He died on November 13, 1864, five days after Lincoln's reelection and two days shy of his fifty-seventh birthday.

Christopher Memminger: He served throughout the war as treasury secretary of the Confederacy, in which capacity his primary responsibility was to finance the southern war effort. It was an almost impossible task, and ultimately he proved unsuccessful. He appropriated significant stores of gold from the U.S. Mint in New Orleans, but sought to raise revenue primarily through bond sales and the imposition of tariffs. In the end he resorted to an income tax and the desperate printing of currency, which unleashed a debilitating round of inflation. The government's paper money was devalued throughout the war until it held hardly any value at all in relation to gold. Memminger resigned his government post on July 1, 1864, and settled at his summer residence in North Carolina. After President Andrew Johnson pardoned him in 1866, he returned to Charleston, resumed his law practice, and pursued business and political interests. He won a seat in the state legislature in 1877 and died eleven years later at age eighty-five.

James L. Orr: The prominent unionist Democrat of the pre-secession years remained with his state when it seceded and continued his political career in the Confederate States of America. Becoming a senator from South Carolina in the CSA senate, he served from February 1862 to May 1865. After that he was South Carolina governor, as a Republican, in the immediate postwar years from November 1865 to July 1868. He relinquished the position after the ratification of a new state constitution that established a new governmental structure. He served as a judge for the Eighth Judicial Circuit from 1868 to 1870 and attended the National Republican Convention in 1872. In the spring of 1873 he arrived in St. Petersburg, Russia, as U.S. ambassador there, selected for the position by President Grant. Shortly after arriving, on May 5, 1873, he died. His standing in history remained relatively favorable for decades based on his moderate views in the prewar period, his embrace of the Republican Party after the war, and Grant's selection of him for a major diplomatic post as a gesture of sectional conciliation. His portrait, rendered by the noted painter Esther Edmonds, hung for decades in the U.S. Capitol, just outside the House chamber, as part of a display of House Speakers. But in 2020, House Speaker Nancy Pelosi ordered that portrait, along with three others of Speakers who later served the Confederacy, removed from public display.

Benjamin F. Perry: Though he opposed secession to the very end, Perry remained loyal to his state afterward without illusion. "You are all now going to the devil," he said to secession enthusiasts, "and I will go with you." He held various posts in the Confederate government, including district attorney, assessment commissioner of impressed produce, and a judgeship. After the war, President Andrew Johnson appointed him governor of South Carolina's provisional government. He held the post from June 30 to December 21, 1865, and oversaw the drafting of a new state constitution that established popular elections for governor and a more balanced system of representation in the legislature. Thus did the new governing document clip the power of the conservative low-country oligarchs, whom Perry had opposed for years. But in the postwar period he also opposed black suffrage and ratification of the Fourteenth Amendment, designed to ensure equal protection of the law. On October 30, 1865, he was elected U.S. senator for South Carolina, but the Senate blocked him from serving. He ran unsuccessfully for Congress in 1872. Perry died on December 3, 1886, at age eighty-one.

Robert Barnwell Rhett: His last official position was delegate to the Confederate Provisional Congress in 1861–62, a far cry from the prominent role he envisioned for himself when his dream of South Carolina secession came true. In February 1862 he returned to private life and his role as *Mercury* publisher and spent the war years excoriating Jefferson Davis for what Rhett considered the president's abject incompetence. In 1863 he campaigned for a seat in the Confederate Congress from the Third District, but he was repudiated by his own neighbors there. Biographer Laura White writes, "No more tragic or ironical an anticlimax could have put the period to a career punctuated from the beginning by disappointment and defeat." So wracked with debt was Rhett at the start of the war that he sold thirty-one slaves to escape insolvency, but the war ravaged his finances thoroughly, while his crops had all been burned by the advancing Union army. Further, the *Mercury* ceased publication when its presses were destroyed. Rhett Jr. revived it after the war, but it failed for good in 1868. Meanwhile, Rhett moved to a manor house he called "Castle Dismal," on a rented plantation near Eufaula, Alabama. In 1872 he moved to New Orleans, where the younger Rhett was editing the *Picayune*, and he later moved in with a son-in-law at St. James Parish in Louisiana. An unsightly pimple that had persisted on his face for years became cancerous, and he underwent four surgeries to remove it, all unsuccessful. In 1875 he wrote that he had become "too hideous a spectacle to be seen by any but those whose love and affection can overlook my diseased deformities." He died on September 14, 1876, at age seventy-five.

National Figures

James Buchanan: Upon relinquishing the presidency, the fifteenth president returned to his estate, "Wheatland," in Lancaster, Pennsylvania, and didn't leave often. He liked to say that "age loves home." He spent considerable time attempting to rehabilitate his historical reputation in the knowledge that his performance in office was viewed widely as a failure. He recruited his longtime friend and former secretary of state, Jeremiah Black, to assist him in writing an autobiography. But Black abandoned the project over disagreements with Buchanan regarding details of his narrative. Buchanan remained loyal to his successor throughout the war and refrained from criticizing his war policies, even when he thought that Lincoln had overstepped the Constitution in prosecuting the war. His three-hundred-page autobiography, *Mr. Buchanan's Administration on the Eve of the Rebellion*, appeared in 1866. He pronounced himself "completely satisfied" with his presidential performance and blamed the setbacks he experienced on others, particularly antislavery northerners and Congress. He died at home on June 1, 1868, at age seventy-seven.

Stephen A. Douglas: The Little Giant played a prominent role following the 1860 election in seeking a slavery compromise that could help the country avert secession and civil war. He participated in the failed efforts of both the Senate's Committee of Thirteen and the 1861 Peace Conference. He urged Lincoln to embrace the Peace Conference effort (which Lincoln declined to do, as it would have required an abandonment of his non-extension doctrine). He also suggested to Alexander H. Stephens of Georgia that he would support a movement to annex Mexico as a slave state if such an action could avert war. In political discourse he advocated the abandonment of Fort Sumter. But once the fort was lost, he swung around to full support for the president and the Union. After a two-hour meeting with Lincoln at the White House on April 15, he issued a statement saying that, while he disagreed with Lincoln on just about every domestic political issue, he was "prepared to sustain the President in the exercise of all his constitutional functions to preserve the Union, and maintain the government, and defend the Federal Capital." He told a friend, "We must fight for our country and forget all differences." He didn't get much time to fight. He contracted an illness the next month, was confined to his bed, developed typhoid fever, and died on June 3, 1861, at age forty-eight.

Abraham Lincoln: The story of Lincoln's leadership from the firing on Fort Sumter to his assassination is well known. He won the war (though there were plenty of early miscues), ended slavery, began the process of stitching the country back together following the carnage, and established the Republicans as the nation's premier governing party for the next seventy-four years. In the periodic academic surveys of historians seeking to rank the presidents' performances, following Arthur Schlesinger Sr.'s pioneering poll in 1948, Lincoln has consistently ranked as the greatest president.

Franklin Pierce: With the firing on Fort Sumter the former president became a staunch unionist, although he blamed the Republican Party for initiating the war and quietly disdained some of Lincoln's harsher actions in suppressing war opposition, particularly his suspension of habeas corpus and prosecution of Ohio Democrat Clement Vallandigham. He caused a stir in criticizing the war effort as "fearful, fruitless, [and] fateful" and suggesting that the president should initiate efforts to settle the conflict through negotiation. The former president purchased an eighty-acre plot of seaside land in North Hampton, New Hampshire, and cultivated a large portion of it, stirring him to call himself an "old farmer." He bestirred himself from rustic cares when he became incensed at federal authorities bent on prosecuting Confederate president Jefferson Davis for treason. He traveled to Baltimore, met with Davis for most of a day, and offered to help with his defense. He later offered to let Davis and his wife stay at his seaside cottage for as long as they wished. But no such visit occurred, as Pierce succumbed to complications from his increasingly persistent drinking. He died on October 8, 1869, at age sixty-four.

William Seward: The brilliant but occasionally erratic New Yorker revised his view of Lincoln shortly after his inappropriate power grab in April 1861 and came to view the president as a sage political analyst, astute judge of people, and adroit national leader. The two men formed a professional and personal bond that served themselves and the nation well throughout the war. Seward worked effectively with his old friend Charles Francis Adams in discouraging the British from recognizing the errant Confederate states as a new nation. Seward was the victim of a brutal assassination attempt on the night of Lincoln's killing, April 15, 1861. Though stabbed in the face and neck five times, Seward survived and served nearly four years more as secretary of state under Andrew Johnson. The secretary sought to position himself between President

Johnson's relatively lax policies and the so-called Radical Republicans' stern approach on matters related to Reconstruction of the nation and federal treatment of the South. But Johnson frequently ignored his advice, and the congressional Republicans eventually amassed enough power to essentially run the government. Seward proved a visionary in advocating the U.S. purchase of Alaska from Russia, initially dismissed as "Seward's Folly" but subsequently viewed as a highly strategic possession for an America bent on expanding its global reach and trade relations into Asia. He retired when Johnson's inherited term ended in March 1868 and returned to Auburn, New York. He traveled widely in Europe and Asia and died on October 10, 1872, at age seventy-one.

Acknowledgments

This book began with an offhand observation embedded deep in the late Paul Johnson's magisterial *A History of the American People*, published in 1997. In discussing events leading to the American Civil War, Johnson wrote: "Only two states wanted a civil war—Massachusetts and South Carolina." That turned out to be not precisely correct, as this volume attests. But it reflected the reality that those two states led their respective regions as they struggled with the awesome issue of slavery. In pondering that reality, I concluded that it could provide a clarifying foundation for a narrative history of those turbulent years of the 1850s, culminating in that bloody conflagration.

I'm pleased that the concept found resonance with people in a position to turn that thought into this volume, beginning with my agent, Philippa ("Flip") Brophy, of Sterling Lord Literistic Inc., who took the idea to Bob Bender, vice president and executive editor of Simon & Schuster. The idea clicked, and both agent and editor have been encouraging my efforts since then, along with Johanna Li, an associate editor at Simon & Schuster. For all that I am grateful.

I am grateful also for the excellent and helpful suggestions extended along the way by five friends willing to read the manuscript as it emerged. They are James Dickenson, Mort Kondracke, Stephanie Merry (my daughter, who is a book editor at the *Washington Post*), Thomas Malone, and Professor Jon Wakelyn. Jon brought a special expertise to the project, as he spent decades teaching history and specializing in the Civil War era at the Catholic University of America and Kent State.

The good folks at the Library of Congress's Newspaper and Current Periodical Room and its Manuscript Reading Room offered efficient and pleasant assistance, as they have through five previous projects dating back some three decades. I should like to acknowledge also the newspaper web archive GenealogyBank, an invaluable source for ancestry probes or historical research.

As always I feel a deep sentiment of appreciation for the encouragement and family spirit extended by children Rob Merry, Johanna Derlega, and Stephanie Merry; their spouses, Kristin Merry, John Derlega, and Matt McFarland; and grandchildren Maisie, Elliott, Genevieve, Colton, Penn, and Orla.

Finally, once again a special thank you to Susan Pennington Merry, wife and cherished compatriot through life's joys and sorrows over the past fifty-four years. This book would not be in your hands but for her steady support, wise counsel, and cheerful willingness to pick up household slack created by my literary preoccupations. I'll make it up to her somehow.

Notes

ABBREVIATIONS AND SHORT CITES

AL—Abraham Lincoln
APB—Andrew Pickens Butler
CFA—Charles Francis Adams
CM—Charleston Mercury
CS—Charles Sumner
HW—Henry Wilson
JB—John Brown
JHH—James Henry Hammond
RBR—Robert Barnwell Rhett
SAD—Stephen A. Douglas
TL—The Liberator
WLG—William Lloyd Garrison
WS—William Seward

INTRODUCTION: TWO FUNERALS

1 *"I won't be told"*: Quoted in Coit, 508.
1 *"subject I've thought about"*: Ibid.
2 *"I have but little concern"*: Quoted in Abraham Venable, House speech, April 1, 1850, reprinted in *The Death and Funeral Ceremonies of John Caldwell Calhoun*, 33.
2 *"with fervent interest"*: Coit, 509.
2 *"feeble"*: Quoted in ibid.
2 *"Very well"*: Ibid.
2 *"John, come to me"*: Quoted in Ibid.
2 *"I have never had such facility"*: Ibid.
2 *"You are overtaxing your mind"*: Ibid.
2 *"I cannot help from thinking"*: Ibid.
3 *"long continued agitation"*: Quoted in Remini, *At the Edge of the Precipice*, 92.
3 *"encroachment and oppression"*: Ibid.

3 *"I did not suit the times"*: Quoted in Coit, 351.

3 *"the great 'I am'"*: Quoted in Merry, *A Country of Vast Designs*, 51.

3 *"believed firmly in himself"*: Quoted in Coit, 108.

3 *"I am perfectly comfortable"*: Quoted in ibid., 510.

4 *"in a very tremulous"*: "Proceedings in Congress," *CM*, April 2, 1850, reprinted in the *Charleston Courier*, April 3, 1850.

4 *"affection of the heart"*: APB, Senate speech, April 1, 1850, reprinted in *The Death and Funeral Ceremonies of John Caldwell Calhoun*, 8.

4 *"pulmonary complaint"*: Quoted in ibid., 7.

4 *"His private character"*: Ibid.

4 *"No more"*: Henry Clay, Senate speech, April 1, 1850, reprinted in *The Death and Funeral Ceremonies of John Caldwell Calhoun*, 13.

4 *"love of ease and luxury"*: Martineau, *Retrospect of Western Travel*, 172.

4 *"If it had been otherwise"*: Ibid.

5 *"genius and character"*: Daniel Webster, Senate speech, April 1, 1850, reprinted in *The Death and Funeral Ceremonies of John Caldwell Calhoun*, 15.

5 *"we ourselves shall go"*: Ibid.

5 *"great pain"*: Quoted in Remini, *Daniel Webster*, 754.

5 *"the aspect of a very sick man"*: Quoted in ibid.

5 *"I am in the hands of God"*: Quoted in ibid., 756.

5 *"My light shall burn"*: Quoted in ibid.

5 *"See how the thread"*: Quoted in ibid., 757.

5 *"My heart is full"*: Ibid.

5 *"I will be brave"*: Ibid.

6 *"Now raise me up"*: Quoted in ibid., 759.

6 *"Thank God, for strength"*: Ibid.

6 *"Oh God! I thank Thee"*: Ibid.

6 *"Have I, on this occasion"*: Ibid.

6 *"On the 24th of October"*: Quoted in "Last Hours and Death of Daniel Webster," *Weekly National Intelligencer*, October 30, 1852.

6 *"Poet, poetry"*: Quoted in "Mr. Webster's Last Moments," *Weekly National Intelligencer*, October 30, 1852, reprinted from the *Boston Courier*.

6 *"The curfew tolls the knell"*: Thomas Gray, "Elegy Written in a Country Churchyard," Poetry Foundation, https://www.poetryfoundation.org/poems/44299/elegy-written-in-a-country-churchyard.

6 *"That's it, that's it"*: Quoted in "Mr. Webster's Last Moments," op.cit.

6 *"Yes! . . . Thy rod, thy staff"*: Quoted in Bartlett, *Daniel Webster*, 292.

6 *"I still live!"*: Quoted in "The Death of Daniel Webster," *Boston Evening Transcript*, October 25, 1852.

7 *"filled with ladies"*: "Funeral of Mr. Calhoun," *Weekly Union*, April 6, 1850.

7   *"brief and impressive"*: "Mr. Calhoun's Funeral," *Charleston Courier*, April 3, 1850.

7   *"never-to-be-forgotten moral"*: "Funeral of Mr. Calhoun," *Weekly Union*, April 6, 1850.

7   *"appropriate insignia"*: "Report of the Committee of Twenty-Five," May 24, 1850, reprinted in *The Death and Funeral Ceremonies of John Caldwell Calhoun*, 35.

8   *"Virginia will mingle freely"*: John Floyd, remarks to the Committee of Twenty-Five, April 23, 1850, reprinted in *The Death and Funeral Ceremonies of John Caldwell Calhoun*, 40–41.

8   *"clad in habiliments of woe"*: "South Carolina Mourns for Her Dead," *Charleston Courier*, April 27, 1850.

8   *"the largest of the kind"*: Ibid.

8   *"with the deepest emotions"*: Whitemarsh Seabrook, ceremonial remarks, Charleston, South Carolina, April 25, 1850, reprinted in *The Death and Funeral Ceremonies of John Caldwell Calhoun*, 64.

8   *"incessant stream of visitors"*: "Report of the Committee of Twenty-Five," reprinted in *The Death and Funeral Ceremonies of John Caldwell Calhoun*, 69.

8   *"young and old"*: "South Carolina Mourns for Her Dead."

9   *"greatest moment must be found"*: Edward Everett, Faneuil Hall speech, October 27, 1852, reprinted in "Proposed Monument to Mr. Webster," *National Intelligencer*, October 30, 1852.

9   *some ten thousand mourners*: Untitled article, *Boston Evening Transcript*, October 30, 1852.

9   *"as if Nature herself"*: Ibid.

9   *"at slow and solemn pace"*: Ibid.

10 *"The last scene concluded"*: Ibid.

1. NEW WORLD BEGINNINGS

12 *a thousand or so men*: Brown and Tager, 27.

12 *Nearly two hundred*: Ibid.

12 *transporting some twenty-one thousand*: Fischer, 16.

13 *"dour, stubborn, fond of argument"*: Quoted in ibid., 49.

13 *"throbbing heart of heresy"*: Quoted indirectly in ibid., 47.

13 *"weary of her Inhabitants"*: Quoted in ibid., 16.

13 *"Citty upon a Hill"*: Quoted in Brown and Tager, 22.

13 *"religion was mentioned"*: Fischer, 18.

14 *three hundred university-trained clergymen*: Brown and Tager, 29.

14 *population was doubling*: Fischer, 17.

14 *reached one hundred thousand*: Ibid.

14 *"became the breeding stock"*: Ibid.

14 *ninety-two English emigrants*: Fraser, 2.

15 *promised 150 acres*: Ibid., 3.

15 *two hundred slaves on Barbados*: Edgar, 38.

16 *Rice production shot up*: Ibid., 154.

16 *In one three-year period*: Ibid.

16 *In six years*: Ibid.

16 *"in as thriving circumstances"*: Quoted in Fraser, 25.

17 *More than eighty commercial ships*: Ibid.

17 *nearly five hundred adult males*: Ibid., 26.

17 *"were shaping in the hearts"*: Ibid., 45.

17 *"unashamed pursuit of wealth"*: Edgar, 202.

18 *"The spiritual purposes"*: Fischer, 22.

18 *"city of churches"*: Quoted in Edgar, 292.

18 *"dominant middle way"*: Ibid., 185.

19 *prohibition on Sunday sex*: Fischer, 163.

19 *"institutional savagery"*: Ibid., 189.

19 *thirteen designated capital crimes*: Ibid., 194.

19 *"aristocratic republic"*: Edgar, 249.

20 *"Carolina is a good country"*: Quoted in Van Ruymbeke, xvii.

20 *"the roundness of their Breasts"*: Quoted in Edgar, 189.

21 *shot up to $345,000*: Brown and Tager, 123.

21 *employed 110,000 workers*: Ibid., 129–30.

22 *"emerged as a nursery"*: Ibid., 144.

22 *"hotbed of abolitionism"*: Ibid., 183.

23 *in four or five years*: Edgar, 80.

23 *white population increased 7 percent*: Ibid., 69.

23 *ten thousand West Africans arrived*: Fraser, 42.

23 *"a wicked and barbarous plott"*: Quoted in Ibid.

24 *some seventy-five South Carolinians*: Edgar, 75.

25 *"[P]lease give my compliments"*: Quoted in Merry, *Where They Stand*, 28–29.

25 *"A people owning slaves"*: Quoted in Edgar, 337.

2. CRISIS IN MINIATURE

26 *"A crisis in our affairs"*: "The Meeting of Congress," *Daily Union*, December 1, 1849.

27 *"Having regarded this topic"*: "The First Day of the First Session of the Thirty-First Congress," *National Intelligencer*, December 3, 1849.

27 *"Slavery here"*: Quoted in Remini, *At the Edge of the Precipice*, 66.

27 *"There is so much excitement"*: Ibid., 63.

28 *"above the tricks of intrigue"*: "Sketches of the Twenty-Eighth Congress," reprinted in Winthrop, 43.

28 *"The nomination is due"*: "Veritas," *New York Courier*, reprinted in "Mr. Winthrop," *Daily Union*, December 1, 1849.

28 *"agitate the subject"*: Quoted in Winthrop, 104.

28 *"lickspittle of slavery"*: Quoted in ibid., 99.

29 *"a general favorite"*: Nevins, *Ordeal of the Union,* vol. 1, 253.

30 *"decidedly the most favorable"*: "Organization of Congress," *Daily Union*, December 4, 1849.

30 *On December 5*: "House of Representatives," *Daily Union*, December 6, 1849.

30 *if the next vote*: Ibid.

30 *"preposterous"*: Abraham Venable, House floor speech, ibid.

30 *"to settle with their constituents"*: Ibid.

30 *"shed light upon the predicament"*: "The Whig Caucus: At the Capitol, in This City, on the Night of Saturday Last," *National Intelligencer*, December 7, 1849.

31 *"an evil omen"*: Untitled article, *New York Express*, reprinted in ibid.

31 *"the stormy petrel"*: Remini, *At the Edge of the Precipice*, 51.

32 *seven thousand troops and weapons*: Merry, *A Country of Vast Designs*, 312.

32 *"The truth is"*: Polk, *Polk Diary*, vol. 2, March 28, 1847, 444.

32 "untrammeled with party obligations": Zachary Taylor to Peter Sken Smith, July 6, 1847, reprinted in "The Taylor Correspondence," *Daily Union*, June 21, 1848.

33 *"Gen'l Taylor is"*: Polk, *Polk Diary*, vol. 4, March 5, 1849, 375–76.

33 *"I have given and will give"*: Quoted in Nevins, *Ordeal of the Union*, vol. 1, 251.

33 *"My course became"*: Quoted in Holt, *The Rise and Fall of the American Whig Party*, 468.

33 *"Resolved, That Congress"*: Robert Toombs, resolution in Whig caucus, December 1, 1849, quoted in "Very Important from Washington," *New York Express*, December 2, 1849, reprinted in "The Whig Caucus," *Daily Union*, December 9, 1849.

33 *"an exclusive slavery test"*: William Duer, caucus speech, ibid.

34 *"not . . . in threat"*: Alexander H. Stephens, caucus speech, ibid.

34 *subsequent votes at 102*: "House of Representatives," *Daily Union*, December 9, 1849.

34 *from 88 to 109*: "Congress," *Daily Union*, December 12, 1849.

34 *"than to feel conscious"*: Robert Winthrop, House floor speech, ibid.

34 *"in great confusion"*: Ibid.

34 *without blushing*: Edward Stanly, House floor speech, ibid.

35 *"that something improper"*: Thomas Bayley, House floor speech, ibid. Subsequent floor remarks from this exchange are from the same source.

35 *"Not only are we without"*: Albert Gallatin Brown, House floor speech, "House of Representatives," *Daily Union*, December 14, 1849.

36 *"We have been acting"*: Richard Meade, House floor speech, ibid. Subsequent speeches in this debate are from the same source.

38 *The previous day's balloting*: "House of Representatives," *Daily Union*, December 23, 1849.

38 *"The long agony is over"*: "Congress. A Speaker at Last," *Daily Union*, December 23, 1849.

3. THE CRUCIBLE OF 1850

39 *Louisiana Avenue home*: Fuess, vol. 2, 153.

39 *for eight years*: Holt, *American Whig Party*, 477.

39 *"the peace, concord, and harmony"*: Henry Clay, Senate speech, January 29, 1850, reprinted in "Slavery—Mr. Clay's Proposition," *National Intelligencer*, February 2, 1850.

41 *"all causes of uneasiness"*: Zachary Taylor, "December 4, 1849: First Annual Message," Miller Center, University of Virginia, https:/millercenter.org/the-presidency/presidential-speeches/december-4-1849-first-annual-message.

41 *"mere personal party"*: Quoted in Holt, *American Whig Party*, 347.

41 *"the ruin of the Whigs"*: Quoted in ibid., 477.

42 *"calm the raging elements"*: Quoted in Remini, *The Edge of the Precipice*, 50.

42 *"Much deference and consideration"*: Quoted in ibid., 49.

42 *"an object of as much attraction"*: Quoted in Holt, *American Whig Party*, 476.

42 *"a relic of a bygone era"*: Remini, *Daniel Webster*, 664.

43 *"All this agitation, I think"*: Quoted in ibid., 663.

43 *"Ah, Mr. Rhett"*: Quoted in Nevins, *Ordeal of the Union*, vol. 2, 280.

43 *"If you become united"*: Library of Congress, https://www.loc.gov/item/08025395/.

44 *"the South is fully resolved"*: Quoted indirectly in "Correspondence of the Courier," *Charleston Courier*, March 2, 1850.

45 *"impossible to save the Union"*: Quoted in ibid.

45 *"We do not intend"*: Quoted in Nevins, *Ordeal of the Union*, vol. 1, 262.

45 *"My soul sickens"*: Quoted in Potter, 89.

45 *"without the adoption of any restriction"*: Henry Clay, Senate speech, January 29, 1850, reprinted in "Slavery—Mr. Clay's Proposition," *Weekly National Intelligencer*, February 2, 1850.

46 *"shall be delivered up"*: U.S. Constitution Article IV, Section 2 (superseded), quoted in ibid.

46 *"more crowded than we ever"*: "Mr. Clay's Speech," *Daily Union*, February 6, 1850.

46 *"quite weak and exhausted"*: Remini, *Henry Clay*, 735.

46 *"I have witnessed many periods"*: Henry Clay, Senate speech, February 5, 1850, reprinted in "The Senate," *Daily Union*, February 6, 1850.

47 *"What is a compromise?"*: Henry Clay, Senate speech, February 6, 1850, reprinted in "The Senate," *Daily Union*, February 7, 1850.

47 *"nothing of the true spirit"*: "Mr. Clay's Speech," *Daily Union*, February 6, 1850.

47 *"stoutly resisted"*: "News from Washington," *New York Herald*, February 7, 1850.

47 *"cannot fail to make"*: "Affairs in Congress," ibid.

47 *"The plan of a withdrawal"*: "Correspondence of the Courier," *Charleston Courier*, February 11, 1850.

48 *Some even dangled*: Remini, *At the Edge of the Precipice*, 97.

48 *"multitudes of both sexes"*: "Washington," *Weekly National Intelligencer*, March 9, 1850.

48 *"And candor obliges me"*: Daniel Webster, Senate speech, March 7, 1850, US History.org, https://www.ushistory.org/documents/seventh_of_march.htm.

49 *"fresh lustre to the fame"*: *National Intelligencer*, excerpt published in "Mr. Webster's Speech," *Boston Evening Transcript*, March 11, 1850.

49 *"marks his way so clearly"*: Quoted in Remini, *Daniel Webster*, 674.

49 *"[U]nequal to the occasion"*: *New York Tribune*, response to Webster speech, excerpted in "Mr. Webster's Speech," *Boston Evening Transcript*, March 11, 1850.

49 *only six New England newspapers*: Remini, *Daniel Webster*, 675.

49 *"Throughout the Northern portion"*: "Editorial Correspondence of the Atlas," *Boston Daily Atlas*, March 13, 1850.

49 *"fallen star"*: Quoted in Remini, *Daniel Webster*, 676.

49 *"quite atrocious"*: Quoted in ibid.

49 *"surrendered to the slave-owners"*: Quoted in ibid.

50 *Taylor defiantly threatened*: Nevins, *Ordeal of the Union*, vol. 1, 331.

51 *"My relations with the new chief"*: Quoted in Remini, *On the Edge of the Precipice*, 134.

51 *"Mr. President"*: Henry Clay, Senate speech, July 22, 1850, reprinted in the *National Intelligencer*, July 26, 1850.

52 *"Pluck, quickness and strength"*: Quoted in Johannsen, 4.

53 *33,333 more square miles*: Potter, 111.

53 *On one momentous night*: Ibid., 114.

53 *"in its character final"*: Millard Fillmore, "December 2, 1850: First Annual Message," Miller Center, University of Virginia, https://millercenter.org/the-presidency/presidentialspeeches/december-2-1850.

53 *"Let us cease agitating"*: Quoted in Potter, 121.

53 *"I think the question is settled"*: Quoted in Ibid., 114.

4. BAY STATE TURMOIL

55 *"in a pitiable state"*: Robert Winthrop to John Clifford, July 14, 1850, excerpted in Winthrop, 130.

56 *As Winthrop later described*: Ibid. Subsequent quotations from this episode come from the same source.

56 *"Now, if there is anything"*: Quoted in ibid., 132.

57 *"extreme pressure"*: Quoted in Remini, *Daniel Webster*, 686.

57 *"scholarly instincts"*: Quoted in Winthrop, 23.

58 *After his Senate arrival*: Anecdote from ibid., 138.

58 *"I am by no means sure"*: Winthrop letter (unidentified recipient), October 18, 1850, excerpted in ibid., 142.

58 *"but then, high-minded men"*: Ibid.

59 *"principal loser"*: Ibid.

59 *"most important person"*: Quoted in Remini, *Daniel Webster*, 298.

59 *"All Webster's political systems"*: Quoted in ibid., 604.

60 *"perverse"*: Quoted in Duberman, 8.

60 *"great concern"*: Quoted in ibid., 17.

61 *"distressing vulgarities"*: Quoted in ibid., 5.

61 *"the most expedient course"*: Quoted in ibid., 69.

61 *"died as the fool dieth"*: Quoted in ibid., 62.

61 *"corrupted heart and soul"*: Quoted in ibid., 63.

62 *"a northern man"*: "Mr. Van Buren," *Daily Union*, June 28, 1848.

62 *"valuable only as it places me"*: Quoted in Duberman, 151.

62 *"aim at the life"*: "The New Party," *TL*, August 18, 1848.

63 *"a covenant with death"*: "No Union with Slaveholders," *TL*, April 25, 1851.

63 *"Boy Wanted"*: Quoted in Mayer, 22.

63 *"especially his own"*: Ibid., 33.

63 *"M' Lord Garrulus"*: Quoted in ibid.

63 *"a woman of sorrowful spirit"*: Quoted in ibid., 17.

63 *"vigorous, lustrous [mind]"*: Quoted in ibid., 13.

64 *"I am willing to be persecuted"*: Quoted in ibid., 94.

64 *"I will be harsh"*: "To the Public," *TL*, January 1, 1831.

64 *"like the oak—like the Alps"*: "My Second Baltimore Trial," ibid.

65 *"stirred up bitter passions"*: Quoted in Nevins, *Ordeal of the Union*, vol. 1, 149.

65 *"vindictive, bitter, and unchristian"*: Quoted in Donald, *Sumner*, 132.

65 *"Chatterbox"*: Quoted in ibid., 17.

66 *"almost impervious to a joke"*: Quoted in ibid., 37.

66 *"is truly prodigious"*: Quoted in ibid., 55.

66 *"the great grindstone"*: Quoted in ibid., 68.

66 *"the good of the whole human family"*: Quoted in ibid., 105.

66 *"The darker his own"*: Ibid., 101.

66 *"master of invective"*: Ibid., 125.

67 *"I shall allow no man"*: Robert Winthrop to CS, August 17, 1846, reprinted in Winthrop, 54.

67 *"equalize political power"*: Quoted in Donald, *Sumner*, 192.

68 *"an equitable division"*: Winthrop, letter (unidentified recipient), excerpted in Winthrop, 142.

69 *"so objectionable a politician"*: Quoted in "Opinions at Home and Abroad," *Boston Statesman*, January 25, 1851.

69 *"a Garrison disunionist"*: "The Free Soil Party and the Union," *Boston Statesman*, February 8, 1851.

69 *"an out-and-out one idea"*: "Should Charles Sumner Be Elected," *Boston Statesman*, February 8, 1851.

69 *"one of the most disgraceful"*: Unidentified newspaper, quoted in "The Non-Election of Mr. Sumner," *Boston Statesman*, January 25, 1851.

70 *"depths of infamy"*: Quoted in Donald, *Sumner*, 188.

70 *"All honor to these noble patriots"*: "The Senatorial Question," *Boston Statesman*, February 8, 1851.

70 *"I confess"*: Winthrop letter (unidentified recipient), January 12, 1851, excerpted in Winthrop, 145.

70 *"The long agony is over"*: "Election of Charles Sumner," *TL*, May 2, 1851.

70 *"with rockets and Benghal lights"*: "Celebration of Mr. Sumner's Election," *Boston Evening Transcript*, April 25, 1851.

70 *"to glorify the election"*: Ibid.

71 *"the downfall of Mr. Webster"*: Quoted in Donald, *Sumner*, 103.

71 *"no charms"*: Robert Winthrop, letter (unidentified recipient), March 24, 1851, excerpted in Winthrop, 147.

5. PALMETTO STATE STRUGGLES

73 *"contending with the blasts of winter"*: Windle, 58.

73 *"[G]ive him the stage"*: JHH, 55.

73 *"honorable and fair judge"*: Quoted in Malavasic, 49.

73 *"common sense"*: JHH, *Secret and Sacred*, 55.

73 *"highminded and honorable"*: Ibid.

73 *"powers of rhetoric"*: Ibid.

74 *"No man but Butler"*: Ibid., 167.

74 *"first allegience"*: APB, Senate speech, February 15, 1850, reprinted in "The Senate," *Daily Union*, February 17, 1850.

75 *"fortunes began to rise"*: McCardell, 62.

76 *"His temperament was nervous"*: Quoted in White, 6.

76 *"all his fire"*: Quoted in ibid., 100.

76 *"that of a howling dog"*: Quoted in Davis, 106.

76 *"vain, self conceited, impracticable"*: Quoted in White, 70.

77 *"Washington was a disunionist"*: Quoted in McCardell, 63.

77 *"proved inadequate to protect"*: Quoted in White, 39.

77 *felt a need to caution*: McCardell, 63.

77 *"[I]n all times past"*: John A. Stuart, "To 'Beaufort' of the Courier of the 15th August," *CM*, September 3, 1844.

78 *"separate state action"*: Quoted in White, 74.

78 *"would serve South Carolina"*: Ibid., 91.

79 *"a 'holy thirst'"*: Quoted in Faust, 8.

79 *"[M]any a sound flogging"*: Quoted in ibid., 9.

79 *"I still fear myself"*: Quoted in ibid.

79 *"I often think I should be better"*: Quoted in ibid.

79 *"The Governor notices him"*: Quoted in ibid., 21.

80 *"We demand an abandonment"*: Quoted in ibid., 46.

80 *"decidedly the ablest journal"*: Quoted in ibid., 56.

80 *"met my full approbation"*: Quoted in ibid.

81 *"[b]roken down at Twenty-Eight"*: Quoted in ibid., 183.

81 *"I can bear no fatigue"*: JHH, *Secret and Sacred*, 58.

82 *"lolling on my lap"*: Ibid., 173.

82 *"every thing short of"*: Quoted in Faust, 242.

82 *"eventually required explanation"*: Ibid., 314.

82 *"I am at this moment"*: JHH, *Secret and Sacred*, 126.

83 *"The event"*: Ibid., 120.

83 *"I am wholly to blame"*: Ibid., 212.

83 *"What a mere shell"*: Ibid., 181.

84 *"so unyielding"*: Ibid., 199.

84 *"It presupposes"*: Ibid, 202.

84 *"South Carolina did not desire"*: Hamer, 59.

84 *"arraigned as criminals"*: "Resolutions, Address, and Journal of Proceedings of the Southern Convention: Held at Nashville, Tennessee, June 3d to 12th, Inclusive, in the Year 1850," Portal to Texas History, https://texashistory.unt.edu/ark:/6753/metaph498594/.

85 *"a bed of hotheads"*: Davis, 276.

85 *"I see but one course left"*: Quoted in ibid., 278.

85 *"so full of the demagogue"*: "Mr. Rhett's Speech," *Daily Union*, July 25, 1850.

85 *"he will be a traitor"*: Quoted in Remini, *Henry Clay*, 755.

86 *"injudicious" but "criminal"*: JHH, *Secret and Sacred*, 203.

86 *"send him to the Senate"*: Ibid.

87 *"The fruit is not ripe"*: Ibid., 205.

87 *"I am here in the very focus"*: Quoted in Hamer, 78.

88 *"My career as a public man"*: JHH, *Secret and Sacred*, 205.

88 "abortive violence": Ibid., 207.

88 *"What Does South Carolina Intend"*: Headline, *Daily Union*, December 17, 1850.

6. RHETT IN WASHINGTON

89 *Rhett didn't know what to suggest*: Davis, 288.

90 *"a holy state of mind"*: Quoted in ibid., 289.

90 *"I intend to assail no one"*: Quoted in ibid.

90 *"I fear they will annoy you"*: Quoted in ibid., 293.

90 *"[T]his government has it not"*: RBR, Senate speech, February 24, 1851, reprinted in *CM*, March 4, 1851.

91 *"Why, Mr. Counsel"*: Quoted in Henry Clay, Senate speech, *Congressional Globe*, Appendix, 31st Congress, 2nd Session, 320.

91 *"It would be a bright idea"*: JHH, *Secret and Sacred*, 230.

92 *"never consent to be dragged"*: Quoted in "Unionism in Georgia," *CM*, March 24, 1851.

92 *"So long as the several states"*: Quoted in Hamer, 88.

93 *"the most aristocratic state"*: Quoted in "South Carolina and Her Position," *National Intelligencer*, January 11, 1851.

93 *"too prevailing an influence"*: Quoted in White, 99n.

94 *"Secession, and the withdrawal"*: *National Intelligencer*, quoted in "The Future," *CM*, February 19, 1851.

94 *"South Carolina"*: "South Carolina, the Hope of the South," *CM*, February 27, 1851.

94 *"This manifested so great an apathy"*: JHH, *Secret and Sacred*, 230.

94 *"South Carolina . . . has claimed"*: "South Carolina, the Hope of the South," *CM*, February 27, 1851.

95 *"It will be a war"*: APB, speech before the Southern Rights Association, reprinted in the *CM*, May 17, 1851.

96 *"If ever men had reason"*: "South Carolina," *Richmond Examiner*, reprinted in *CM*, May 15, 1851.

96 *"in council and action"*: "Resolutions," reprinted in "Great Southern Rights and Southern Co-operation Meeting," *CM*, July 30, 1851.

96 *it wasn't easy to tell*: Hamer, 210.

96 *"My friends"*: RBR, speech before the Southern Rights Association, April 7, 1851, reprinted in "Speech of the Honorable R. B. Rhett," *CM*, April 29, 1851.

96 *"blockade is War"*: Ibid.

97 *At one point he traveled*: Davis, 302.

97   *"South Carolina will not secede"*: "The Bugbear Secession," *New York Tribune*, reprinted in *CM*, October 25, 1851.

97   *"burning words"*: "Our Future," *CM*, October 18, 1851.

98   *"should be acquiesced in"*: Quoted in "Correspondence of the Mercury, Washington, Dec. 5, 1851," *CM*, December 9, 1851.

98   *"high gratification"*: Henry Foote, Senate speech, December 15, 1851, reprinted in the *Daily Union*, December 19, 1851.

98   *"I am bound, as I am sworn"*: RBR, Senate speech, December 15, 1851, reprinted in *CM*, December 29, 1851.

99   *"with something like holy horror"*: "Mr. Rhett's Speech in the Senate," *CM*, December 22, 1851.

99   *"there will be an end"*: Quoted in ibid.

99   *"in doing a good thing"*: *New York Herald*, quoted in "The Herald on Foote," *CM*, December 18, 1851.

99   *"an eloquent man"*: "Correspondence of the Mercury, Washington, March 1," *CM*, March 6, 1852.

99   *"There is a sympathy in treason"*: Jeremiah Clemens, Senate speech, quoted in Clemens-Rhett Senate exchange, February 27 and 28, 1852, Library of Congress, https://tile.loc.gov/storage-services/gdc/dcmsibooks.

100 *"It cannot dissolve the bonds"*: "The Convention—What Can It Do?," *Cheraw Gazette*, reprinted in *CM*, April 22, 1852.

100 *"I hope not"*: Quoted in Davis, 327.

100 *"Thus the party refused"*: Quoted in ibid.

100 *"engrafted, as it were"*: "The Result," *CM*, May 8, 1852.

101 *"In consequence of the proceedings"*: RBR, letter to John Means, reprinted in "Interesting Correspondence," *CM*, May 10, 1852.

7. SUMNER IN THE SENATE

102 the credentials of Charles Sumner: "Congress, Washington, Dec. 1," *Boston Evening Transcript*, December 2, 1851.

102 *"I have been requested"*: Lewis Cass, Senate speech, *Congressional Globe*, 32nd Congress, 1st Session, 2.

103 *"evidently become much enfeebled"*: "Washington, Nov. 27th, 1851," *Boston Evening Transcript*, December 2, 1851.

104 *"Most painfully do I feel"*: Quoted in Donald, *Sumner*, 204.

104 *"For myself, I do not desire"*: Quoted in ibid., 205.

104 *"should go far to destroy"*: Quoted in ibid., 204.

105 *"light waistcoat"*: Quoted in ibid., 214.

106 *"My life seems to me"*: Quoted in Goodwin, *Team of Rivals*, 38.

106 *"I almost despair"*: Quoted in ibid., 40.

106 *"a tower of strength"*: Quoted in ibid., 146.

106 *"would have been a scholar"*: Quoted in Donald, *Sumner*, 209.

107 *"the Indian mutiny, lace"*: Quoted in ibid.

107 *dined with the French minister*: Donald, *Sumner*, 209.

107 *"sublime in simplicity"*: Quoted in St. Leger, 64.

107 *"the dread of Despots"*: CS Senate speech, *Congressional Globe*, 32nd Congress, 1st Session, 50.

108 *"scholarship, good sense"*: Quoted in Donald, *Sumner*, 211.

108 *"highly polished"*: "Debut of Mr. Sumner," *Boston Daily Atlas*, December 13, 1851.

109 *"surprise and regret"*: Untitled item, *TL*, March 19, 1852.

109 *"inexplicable"*: Quoted in Donald, *Sumner*, 221.

109 *"Is not this silence"*: "Inquiry after a Back-Bone," *TL*, April 23, 1852.

110 *"The moral tone of the Free States"*: Quoted in Duberman, 179.

110 *who had defended Sumner*: Theodore Parker speech, July 5, 1852, Abington, Massachusetts, reprinted in *TL*, July 30, 1852.

110 *"imminent deadly peril"*: Quoted in Donald, *Sumner*, 222.

110 *"whining and feeble"*: "Mr. Sumner's Abolition Effort," *Boston Statesman*, July 31, 1852.

110 *"Resolved, That the Committee"*: CS resolution, *Congressional Globe*, 32nd Congress, 1st Session, 1934.

110 *"yield to a brother Senator"*: CS Senate speech, *Congressional Globe*, 32nd Congress, 1st Session, 1950. Subsequent quotes in the following debate are from the same citation.

111 *"You may speak next term"*: Quoted in Donald, *Sumner*, 225.

111 *"Even gristle would be better"*: Untitled item, *TL*, August 6, 1852.

111 *"extraordinary expenses"*: Robert Hunter amendment, *Congressional Globe*, 32nd Congress, 1st Session, 2371.

112 *"not originality . . . but skill"*: Quoted in Donald, *Sumner*, 234.

112 *"a higher law than the Constitution"*: William Seward, Senate speech, March 11, 1850, reprinted in the *Daily Union*, March 13, 1850.

112 *"those of the extreme fanatics"*: Quoted in Goodwin, *Team of Rivals*, 148.

112 *"sent me to bed"*: Quoted in ibid.

112 *"with sorrow and shame"*: Quoted in ibid.

113 *"Institutions are formed"*: Quoted in Donald, *Sumner*, 228.

113 *"[A]ccording to undeniable words"*: CS Senate speech, *Congressional Globe*, Appendix, 32nd Congress, 1st Session, 1102–13.

114 *"the ravings of a maniac"*: Jeremiah Clemens, Senate speech, ibid., 1113.

114 *"shall be delivered up"*: Quoted by Augustus Dodge, Senate speech, ibid., 1118.

114 *"side by side"*: John Hale, Senate speech, ibid., 1119.

115 *"All that is said"*: SAD, Senate speech, ibid., 1120.

115 *"enlarge and consolidate"*: "Speech of Mr. Sumner," *TL*, September 17, 1852.

116 *"big, and pompous"*: Quoted in Donald, *Sumner*, 210.

116 *"more egotistical than ever"*: Quoted in ibid.

8. 1852

117 *"poor, decrepit old man"*: Quoted in Finkelman, 127.

118 *it purged from the legislature*: "Massachusetts Election," *National Intelligencer*, November 29, 1851.

118 *"Belonging to the party"*: "Address to the People of the Union," Daniel Webster campaign statement, reprinted in "The Webster Convention," *Boston Evening Transcript*, November 26, 1851.

118 *"the greatest living soldier"*: Quoted in Merry, *A Country of Vast Designs*, 389.

119 *He placed two large mirrors*: Eisenhower, *Agent of Destiny*, 11.

119 *"The chief ruling passion"*: Quoted in ibid., 143.

119 *As Washington's* Daily Union: "The Whig Party and the Compromise," *Daily Union*, May 7, 1852.

119 *"uncommitted and unpledged"*: "Correspondence of the Mercury, Washington, April 25," *CM*, April 30, 1852.

121 *"He will not do, sir"*: Quoted in Bordewich, 30.

121 *"All is apathy"*: Quoted in Remini, *Daniel Webster*, 732.

121 *"things are not in a good way"*: Ibid.

122 *"Can General Scott"*: "W. H. Seward and His Anti-Slavery League—Danger to the South," *New York Herald*, reprinted in *CM*, April 5, 1852.

122 *"could not place himself"*: Quoted in Eisenhower, *Agent of Destiny*, 325.

122 *"young blood" and "young ideas"*: quoted in Johannsen, p. 360.

122 *"heavy calamity"*: "Nevins, *Ordeal of the Union*, vol. 2, 10.

122 *"more an event than a book"*: Quoted in Reynolds, *Mightier Than the Sword*, xi.

123 *"No book in American history"*: Ibid.

124 *"moved over to the side of evil"*: Quoted in ibid., 119.

125 *"We see nothing to be gained"*: "The Presidential Contest," *CM*, June 1, 1852.

125 *"to their fullest capacity"*: "Correspondence of the Mercury, Baltimore, May 31," *CM*, June 4, 1852.

126 *"will resist all attempts"*: Democratic Party Platform 1852, reprinted in "Baltimore National Democratic Convention," *CM*, June 9, 1852.

127 *"respectable portion"*: "General Pierce at the South," *CM*, reprinted in the *TL*, June 18, 1852.

127 *"are received and acquiesced in"*: Whig Party Platform 1852, reprinted in "The National Whig Convention," *CM*, June 21, 1852.

127 *"My friends will stand firm"*: Quoted in Remini, *Daniel Webster*, 736.

128 *"All I ask"*: Quoted in ibid., 738.

128 *"We accept the candidate"*: Quoted in Eisenhower, *Agent of Destiny*, 328.

128 *"with a padlock on his lips"*: Commentary from the *Savannah Republican*, quoted in "Opinions of the Press on the Nominee," *Charleston Courier*, June 25, 1852.

128 *"We have dirked him!"*: Quoted in Nevins, *Ordeal of the Union*, vol. 2, 29.

128 *"The result has caused me"*: Quoted in "The Great Rejected," *TL*, July 2, 1852.

128 *"Nothing could more plainly evince"*: Ibid.

129 *"inconsistent with all the principles"*: Free Soil Platform 1852, excerpted in Marshall, 154.

130 *"slavery is a sin"*: Ibid.

130 *"Waterloo defeat"*: "Waterloo Defeat of the Whig Party," *Boston Daily Atlas*, November 3, 1852.

130 *"repudiated and abjured"*: "The Triumph and Its Teaching," *Daily Union*, November 4, 1852.

130 *"This is a Whig city"*: *Boston Post* article, excerpted in "Presidential Election," *Boston Evening Transcript*, November 3, 1852.

131 *"the Whig party"*: Quoted in "The Result," *Boston Evening Transcript*, November 4, 1852.

9. PRESIDENT PIERCE

133 *"to shun harsh and personal criticism"*: Quoted in Benson, 33.

133 *"skill and dignity of demeanor"*: "Correspondence of the Mercury, Dec. 17, 1851," *CM*, December 22, 1851.

134 *"the great amiability"*: "Correspondence of the Mercury, Oct. 22, 1852," *CM*, October 27, 1852.

135 *"dexterous blend of fealty"*: Malavasic, 18.

135 *"many influential men"*: Quoted in Donald, *Sumner*, 239.

135 *"was never formed"*: Quoted in ibid., 241.

136 *"Webster's fall was not"*: Quoted in ibid.

136 *"a calamity to the Liberal cause"*: Quoted in Holt, *The Rise and Fall of the American Whig Party*, 787.

138 *"was like a giant lottery"*: Potter, 146.

139 *"the moral duty of the government"*: Quoted in Malavasic, 68.

139 *"entirely too magnificent"*: Quoted in Potter, 150.

140 *"Now, sir,"*... *"I am free to admit"*: Quoted in Nevins, *Ordeal of the Union*, vol. 2, 90.

141 *"pedestrian progress"*: "Inauguration of President Pierce," *Baltimore Sun*, reprinted in *CM*, March 5, 1853.

141 *"in obedience to the unsolicited"*: Franklin Pierce, Inaugural Address, printed in *CM*, March 5, 1853.

142 *"the art of the scholar"*: Quoted in "President Pierce," *CM*, March 8, 1853, reprinted from the *Daily Union*.

142 *"for the most part, neat"*: Ibid.

142 *"has never had a pulsation"*: "The Inaugural Address," *TL*, March 11, 1853.

142 *"an unmitigated disaster"*: Holt, *Franklin Pierce*, 67.

143 *"shivered to atoms"*: Quoted in ibid., 71.

143 *"raise invective"*: Quoted in ibid., 70.

143 *"promptly marks out a line"*: Quoted in ibid.

144 *"solicitous that the Atlantic"*: Franklin Pierce, First Annual Message, American Presidency Project, UC Santa Barbara, https://www.presidency.ucsb.edu/doc uments/first-annual-message-8.

10. KANSAS AND NEBRASKA

147 *"a temporary blight"*: Smith, *Magnificent Missourian*, 112.

147 *"Of all the humbugs"*: Quoted in Nevins, *Ordeal of the Union*, vol. 2, 93.

147 *"we pledge ourselves"*: Ibid.

148 *"when admitted as a State"*: "A Bill to Organize the Territory of Nebraska," reprinted in the *Washington Sentinel*, January 7, 1854.

148 *"in order to avoid all misconstruction"*: S. 21, excerpted in "The Nebraska Bill," *Washington Sentinel*, January 14, 1854.

149 *"intended to place the Territory"*: Ibid.

149 *"cannot be set aside or weakened"*: Ibid.

149 *"no room should be left"*: Ibid.

149 *"no one appeared more startled"*: Quoted in ibid., 93.

150 *"By God, sir"*: Quoted in Potter, 160.

150 *"in any manner they may think"*: Quoted in Malavasic, 95.

151 *"the rights of persons and property"*: Quoted in Johannsen, *Stephen Douglas*, 414.

152 *"cold formality"*: Quoted in Malavasic, 97.

152 *"was superseded by the principles"*: Quoted in Potter, 162.

153 *"a gross violation of a sacred pledge"*: "Appeal of the Independent Democrats in Congress to the People of the United States," reprinted in the *Daily Union*, February 1, 1854.

154 *"declared inoperative"*: Quoted in "The Nebraska Question," *Washington Sentinel*, January 24, 1854.

154 *"the agitation of the question"*: "Correspondence of the *Baltimore Sun*, January 29, 1854," reprinted in *CM*, February 2, 1854.

154 *"a hollow truce, by which the South"*: "The South and the New York Faction," *CM*, January 26, 1854.

155 *"a manifest falsification"*: "Note," reprinted in "Appeal of the Independent Democrats in Congress to the People of the United States," *Daily Union*, February 1, 1854.

155 *"lost his temper before he began"*: Quoted in Johannsen, *Stephen Douglas*, 419.

155 *"defiant tone and pugnacious"*: Quoted in ibid.

155 *"a higher and a more solemn obligation"*: SAD, Senate speech, *Congressional Globe*, 33rd Congress, 1st Session, 275.

156 *"Art, literature, poetry, religion"*: CS, Senate speech, February 21, 1854, Library of Congress, http://loc.gov/resource/rbaapc.28500.

157 *"Is the black man equal"*: APB, Senate speech, February 24–25, 1854, Library of Congress, https://www.loc.gov/item/18005981.

159 *"The Democratic Party has been"*: Quoted in Johannsen, *Stephen Douglas*, 468.

11. THE MASSACHUSETTS SHOEMAKER

161 *"with the unalterable determination"*: Quoted in Nevins, *Ordeal of the Union*, vol. 2, 413.

161 *"aristocratic prejudices"*: Quoted in Duberman, 182.

161 *"tricks of demagogues"*: Quoted in ibid.

163 *"duplicity"*: Quoted in ibid., 176.

163 *"than the mere bargaining"*: Quoted in ibid., 168.

164 *"dead apathy in regard to politics"*: JHH, *Secret and Sacred*, 256.

166 *"My who[le] life"*: Quoted in Davis, 341.

166 *"His admiration and love"*: White, 133.

166 *"the Southern people have but one"*: Quoted in Davis, 341.

166 *"Every hope of life"*: JHH, *Secret and Sacred*, 259.

166 *"Every ideal crushed"*: Ibid.

167 *"The result of my experience"*: Ibid., 264.

167 *"animal propensities"*: Ibid., 265.

167 *"matters of too much delicacy"*: Ibid., 257.

167 *"the vulgar appetites of scandal"*: Ibid.

167 *"He falls and is crushed"*: Ibid.

167 *"want of caution"*: Quoted in Faust, *James Henry Hammond and the Old South*, 314.

167 *"injustice and cruelty to others"*: Quoted in Ibid., 315.

167 *"more solitary than any hermit"*: JHH, *Secret and Sacred*, 259.

167 *"plunged hereafter"*: Ibid., 261.

168 *"I am now too old"*: Ibid., 266.

169 *"The Whig party is . . . completely"*: Quoted in Holt, *The Rise and Fall of the American Whig Party*, 890.

169 *"used up"*: Ibid.

169 *"If we are to have Mr. Wilson"*: Quoted in Duberman, 186.

169 *"dirty, negotiating, trading politics"*: Quoted in ibid.

170 *25 percent of Worcester's*: Donald, *Sumner*, 269.

170 *"of a very repulsive character"*: Quoted in Holt, *The Rise and Fall of the American Whig Party*," 892.

170 *"small traders, mechanics, & artisans"*: Quoted in ibid.

171 *"spawned upon us"*: Quoted in ibid.

171 *"the result of our state election"*: Quoted in ibid., 890.

171 *"Ehew! Ehew!"*: Quoted in Donald, *Sumner*, 249.

171 *"stuff not good enough"*: Quoted in ibid., 257.

171 *"a great moral wrong"*: Quoted in ibid., 259.

172 *"the privileges of an American"*: Quoted in ibid.

172 *"declines in favor of Mr. Gardner"*: Untitled item, *Boston Courier*, November 2, 1854.

173 *"Poor old Massachusetts!"*: Quoted in Holt, *The Rise and Fall of the American Whig Party*, 893.

174 *"the very embodiment"*: "The Senator from Massachusetts," *CM*, February 5, 1855.

12. BOSTON BLOOD

175 *"notorious kidnapper"*: "Great Excitement in Worcester! A Kidnapper Almost Kidnapped," *Worcester Spy*, October 31, 1854, reprinted in *TL*, November 3, 1854. Other quotations from the Asa Butman episode come from the same source, unless otherwise noted.

177 *"expel from our territory"*: Quoted in "Samuel Hoar," Wikipedia, https://en.wikipedia.org/wik/Samuel_Hoar.

179 *"The Dissolution of the Union"*: Headline, *TL*, September 28, 1855.

179 *"Of course, the judgment"*: "A Letter from Senator Sumner," *National Intelligencer*, reprinted in *TL*, November 10, 1854.

181 *"a worthless cheat"*: "What Is to Be Done?," *CM*, July 11, 1855.

182 *"these unexpected and deplorable occurrences"*: Millard Fillmore, "Message Regarding Disturbance in Boston, February 19, 1851," Miller Center, University of Virginia, https://millercenter.org/the-presidency/presidential-speeches/february-19-1851-message-regarding-disturbance-boston.

183 *"at such a price"*: "The Boston Fugitive Case," *CM*, April 21, 1851.

183 *"[O]f what use is such a law"*: Ibid.

183 *"Another Sims Case"*: Headline, *TL*, June 2, 1854.

183 *"consider what steps should be taken"*: "Great Meeting in Faneuil Hall," *TL*, June 2, 1854.

183 *"between four walls"*: Quoted in ibid. All quotations from the Faneuil Hall rally come from the same source.

185 *"hisses, groans, and other marks"*: "Another Sims Case," *TL*, June 2, 1854.

185 *"On the law and facts"*: Ibid.

185 *"Great sensation was manifest"*: "Decision in the Fugitive Slave Case!," *Boston Evening Transcript*, June 2, 1854.

186 *"A grave crisis has arrived"*: "Massachusetts and the Laws of the United States," *Worcester Transcript*, reprinted in the *Daily Union*, June 3, 1854.

186 *"the open rebellion"*: *Springfield Post* article, reprinted in ibid.

186 *"an Irishman"*: "Treason! Treason! Treason!," *TL*, October 20, 1854.

186 *"treason against the laws"*: Quoted in ibid.

187 *"[i]t is the fanaticism"*: CS Senate speech, *Congressional Globe*, 33rd Congress, 1st Session, 1515.

187 *"ought not to exist"*: Ibid.

187 *"a species of rhetoric"*: APB, Senate speech, ibid., 1516.

187 *"Will the honorable Senator"*: CS, ibid., 1517.

187 *"These are the prettiest"*: Ibid.

188 *"The Senator asked me"*: CS, ibid.

188 *"fanatic . . . whose reason is dethroned"*: James Mason, Senate speech, ibid.

188 *"and then boldly proclaim"*: John Pettit, Senate speech, ibid., 1518.

188 *"shunned like a leper"*: Clement Clay, Senate speech, ibid., 1554.

188 *"I swore to support it"*: CS, Senate speech, ibid., appendix, 1011–15.

189 *"You have given the heaviest blow"*: Quoted in Donald, *Sumner*, 266.

189 *"matchless eloquence and power"*: Ibid.

189 *"You have done gallantly"*: Ibid.

189 *"I find myself 'a popular man'"*: Ibid.

189 *"Henceforth Southern senators"*: Ibid., 165.

13. PRAIRIE TENSIONS

190 *"Come on, then, gentlemen"*: Seward Senate speech, *Congressional Globe*, 33rd Congress, 1st Session, Appendix, 759.

191 *"I accept your challenge"*: SAD Senate speech, ibid., 788.

191 *"the tide of population"*: "The People Rapidly Settling the Nebraska Question for Themselves," *Weekly Union*, April 1, 1854.

192 *"This is [as] fine a country as any"*: "The Fertility of Kansas," *Natchez Free Trader*, reprinted in *CM*, January 18, 1856.

193 *"the prosperity or the ruin"*: Quoted in Etcheson, 47.

193 *Indeed, some Atchison friends*: Malavasic, 146.

193 *"If we cannot get Kansas"*: Quoted in Martin, ed., *Transactions of the Kansas State Historical Society*, vol. 10, 127.

194 *"We are too far off"*: Quoted in Nevins, *Ordeal of the Union*, vol. 2, 382.

195 *"free ferry, a dollar a day"*: Quoted in Etcheson, 32.

195 *"Imagine a fine looking man"*: "The Border Ruffian," *Abbeville Banner*, reprinted in *CM*, July 15, 1856.

195 *"pukes"*: Quoted in Etcheson, 31.

196 *"thoroughly identified with the interests"*: "Slavery in Kansas," *Washington Senti-nel*, reprinted in *CM*, January 11, 1855.

196 *"is lost to freedom"*: "The South at Work," *Hartford Republican*, reprinted in *TL*, January 12, 1855.

196 *"There is a good deal of trouble"*: "State of Things in Kansas," *Missouri Demo-crat*, reprinted in *TL*, November 3, 1854.

196 *"which occasions great commotion"*: "Serious Work in Kanzas," *Milwaukee Sen-tinel*, reprinted in *TL*, November 3, 1854. Other details of the episode come from the same source.

196 *"Everything betokens war"*: Ibid.

196 *"armed to the teeth"*: Nevins, *Ordeal of the Union*, vol. 2, 385.

197 *"Kansas has been invaded"*: Quoted in ibid., 386.

198 *"as a master stroke of policy"*: "The Election in Kansas," *CM*, April 4, 1855.

198 *"Such laws will never be enacted!"*: Quoted in "Slavery in Kansas," *TL*, April 13, 1855.

198 *"Violence, outrage, force and fraud"*: "The Invasion of Kansas," *TL*, May 11, 1855.

199 *"without coming in collision"*: Quoted in Potter, 205.

199 *"untimely and inexpedient"*: Quoted in ibid.

199 *"We owe no obedience"*: Quoted in ibid.

200 *"harmonize"*: Quoted in Etcheson, 69.

200 *"the Wakarusa Demonstration"*: Nevins, *Ordeal of the Union*, vol. 2, 408.

201 *"unprincipled Abolitionists"*: "Kansas—the South," *Atlanta Examiner*, reprinted in *CM*, January 12, 1856.

201 *"My deliberate opinion"*: Quoted in Nevins, *Ordeal of the Union*, vol. 2, 410.

202 *"Our fighting spirit is fully up"*: Quoted in ibid.

202 *"I was a peace-maker"*: "Kansas–the South," *CM*, January 12, 1856, from David Atchison letter printed in *Atlanta Examiner*.

203 *"forebodings as to the future"*: Quoted in ibid.

14. SECTIONALISM RISING

204 *"All that is claimed"*: "Death of Honorable Abbott," *TL*, August 24, 1855.

205 *"everyone considered him"*: "The Speakership," *Providence Transcript*, reprinted in *TL*, February 15, 1856.

205 *"Abolitionism, the offspring"*: "The Success of Abolitionism," *Mobile News*, re-printed in *TL*, April 13, 1855.

205 *He was known throughout*: Mayer, 458.

206 *A New York newspaper*: Ibid., 466.

206 *"feeling both prosperous and grateful"*: Ibid., 459.

206 *"moral agency"*: Quoted in ibid., 448.

206 *"Beecher's Bibles"*: Quoted in Nevins, *Ordeal of the Union*, vol. 2, 431.

207 *"As a general rule"*: Quoted in "Meeting of the New England Non-Resistance Society," *TL*, March 24, 1855.

207 *"ought to be put out"*: Quoted in ibid.

207 *"[y]ou say by this act"*: Quoted in ibid.

207 *"God never made these fiends"*: "The Civil War in Kansas," *TL*, January 4, 1856.

207 *"our impulsive friend"*: "Remarks," ibid.

208 *"a terrible paradox"*: Mayer, 450.

208 *"polyglot opposition"*: Holt, 962.

209 *"I have attained the highest"*: Quoted in Nevins, *Ordeal of the Union, Vol. II*, 416.

209 *"unscrupulous, selfish"*: "The Result," *CM*, February 5, 1856.

209 *"changes his politics"*: Untitled article, *CM*, December 19, 1855.

209 *"that Abolition, which has been"*: "Congress," *CM*, December 22, 1855.

210 *"willing to elect a Speaker"*: "House of Representatives," *National Intelligencer*, January 18, 1856.

210 *"The importance of this victory"*: Quoted in Holt, *Rise and Fall of the American Whig Party*, 963.

211 *"It is a matter of congratulation"*: Franklin Pierce, "Third Annual Message, December 31, 1855," American Presidency Project, UC Santa Barbara, https://www.presidency.ucsb.edu/documents/third-annual-message-8.

211 *"its force, its originality"*: "The President's Message," *CM*, January 7, 1856.

211 *"South Carolinian fire-eater"*: "President's Message," *Dedham Gazette*, reprinted in *TL*, January 11, 1856.

211 *"merited the title"*: "The President's Message," *Boston Journal*, reprinted in *TL*, January 11, 1856.

212 *"They murdered me like cowards"*: Quoted in Etcheson, p. 91.

212 *"duly constituted"*: Franklin Pierce, "January 24, 1856: Message Regarding Disturbances in Kansas," Miller Center, University of Virginia, https://millercenter.org/the-presidency/presidential-speeches/january-24-1856.

212 *"firmly withstood"*: Franklin Pierce, "February 11, 1856: Proclamation Addressing Disturbances in Kansas," Miller Center, University of Virginia, https://millercenter.org/the-presidency/presidential-speeches/february-11-1856.

212 *"Pierce says we are traitors"*: Quoted in Etcheson, 92.

213 *"Let what will come"*: Quoted in ibid., 93.

213 *"[Y]ou and your people"*: Quoted in ibid., 94.

214 *"My Dear General"*: Quoted in Malavasic, 148.

214 *"dignity of mind"*: Windle, 60.

214 *"abilities which give him"*: Ibid., 58.

215 *"I do not intend"*: APB, Senate speech, *Congressional Globe*, 34th Congress, 1st Session, 584.

216 *"elaborate speech"*: Quoted in Donald, *Sumner*, 277.

216 *"I shall pronounce"*: Quoted in ibid.

15. SIX DAYS IN MAY

218 *"a man of generous nature"*: Quoted in Mathis, 302.

218 *"Let Free-Soilers come"*: Preston Brooks, House speech, March 15, 1854, reprinted in Benson, 28.

218 *"He seldom looks those"*: Quoted in Tim Rues, "Samuel J. Jones," Historic Lecompton, https://lecomptonkansas.com/learn/samuel-j-jones-by-tim-rues/.

219 *"Continued Resistance"*: Quoted in Etcheson, 101.

219 *"the idea that God had raised him"*: Quoted in Nevins, *Ordeal of the Union*, vol. 2, 474.

220 *"consecrate my life to the destruction"*: Quoted in Reynolds, *John Brown: Abolitionist*, 65.

220 *"He was, in truth, a calvinistic"*: Quoted in ibid., 19.

220 *"[t]here was no middle ground"*: Reynolds, *John Brown: Abolitionist*, 25.

222 *"No such scene has been"*: Quoted in Donald, *Sumner*, 283.

222 *"the rape of a virgin Territory"*: CS, Senate speech, May 19–20, 1856, Digital History, https://www.digitalhistory.uh.edu/disp_textbook.cfm?smtID=38psid=3915.

223 *"That damn fool"*: Quoted in Johannsen, *Stephen A. Douglas*, 503.

223 *"the most un-American"*: Lewis Cass, Senate speech, May 20, 1856, reprinted in Benson, 122.

223 *"the depth of malignity"*: SAD, Senate speech, May 20, 1856, reprinted in ibid., 123.

225 *"constructive treason"*: Quoted in Nevins, *Ordeal of the Union*, vol. 2, 432.

225 *"I expect before you get this"*: Quoted in Etcheson, 104.

225 *"We never have been"*: Quoted in ibid.

225 *"This is the happiest moment"*: Quoted in "Sacking of Lawrence," Wikipedia, https://en.wikipedia.org/wiki/Sacking_of_Lawrence.

226 *"The Law and Order party"*: "Affairs in Kansas," *Independence (Missouri) Messenger*, reprinted in *CM*, June 5, 1856.

226 *"that notorious abolition hole"*: "From the Doniphan Constitutionalist," *Doniphan Constitutionalist*, reprinted in ibid.

226 *"Mr. Sumner"*: Quoted in Preston Brooks, letter to L. H. Brooks, reprinted in Benson, 131.

227 *"almost unconsciously"*: CS, testimony, "Alleged Assault on Senator Sumner," reprinted in ibid., 136.

227 *"bleeding and powerless"*: House of Representatives, 34th Congress, 1st Session, Report No. 132, reprinted in ibid., 2.

227 *"severe and calculated"*: Ibid.

227 *"Let them alone"*: James Simonton, testimony, "Alleged Assault on Senator Sumner," reprinted in ibid., 138.

227 *"Don't kill him"*: Quoted in Donald, *Sumner*, 296.

227 *"I did not intend to kill"*: Quoted in ibid.

227 *"I could not believe"*: Quoted in ibid., 297.

228 *"one of the most enthusiastic"*: "Sumner Indignation Meeting," *TL*, May 30, 1856.

228 *"as citizens of this broad land"*: Quoted in ibid.

228 *"prompt and chivalrous"*: "Brooks Demonstration," *CM*, June 4, 1856.

228 *"chastisement," "castigation"*: Ibid.; "Messrs. Brooks and Sumner," *Richmond Enquirer*, reprinted in *CM*, June 4, 1856.

228 *"perfect old woman"*: Quoted in Etchison, 109.

228 *"broken-down politicians"*: Ibid.

228 *"more talk than cider"*: Ibid.

229 *"wild and frenzied"*: Quoted in Reynolds, *John Bown: Abolitionist*, 158.

229 *"gun-happy nonconformist"*: Quoted in Etcheson, 107.

229 "hurry up the fight": Quoted in Reynolds, *John Brown: Abolitionist*, 154.

230 *"Something is going to be done now"*: Quoted in ibid., 158.

230 *"went crazy—crazy!"*: Quoted in ibid., 159.

230 *"I am eternally tired"*: Ibid.

231 *"an uncalled for, wicked act"*: Quoted in ibid., 174.

231 *"God is my judge"*: Quoted in ibid.

232 *"Nothing remained"*: Quoted in Nevins, *Ordeal of the Union*, vol. 2, 476.

232 *"The war seems to have commenced"*: Quoted in Etcheson, 111.

232 *"WAR! WAR!"*: Quoted in Nevins, *Ordeal of the Union*, vol. 2, 476.

16. CAMPAIGN OF '56

233 *"powerful intellect"*: "Two Portraits of the Democratic Candidate for the Presidency: James Buchanan's Public Career," Potsdam (NY) *Courier and Journal*, reprinted in the *Weekly Union*, July 3, 1856.

234 *"an inept busybody"*: Quoted in Merry, *A Country of Vast Designs*, 135.

234 *"Aunt Nancy"*: Ibid.

235 *"the natural and almost necessary"*: "Federal Politics," *CM*, January 14, 1856.

235 *"Every day, and each new development"*: "Correspondence of the Mercury, Washington, April 24, 1856," *CM*, April 28, 1856.

236 *"fossil remains of too low"*: Quoted in Holt, *The Rise and Fall of the American Whig Party*, 975.

238 *"There is no reason why"*: "The Presidential Convention," *CM*, December 20, 1855.

239 *"a low-reckless debaucher"*: Quoted in Davis, 316.

239 *"should send a full, able"*: Quoted in "Judge Butler and the Convention," *CM*, June 10, 1856.

239 *"These strictures are hard"*: Ibid.

240 *"should be held exclusively"*: APB, Senate speech, June 12, 1856, reprinted in Benson, 141.

240 *"brutal, murderous, and cowardly"*: *Congressional Globe*, 34th Congress, 1st Session, 1306.

240 *"You're a liar!"*: Quoted in untitled item, *TL*, May 30, 1856.

240 *"I have never used an epithet"*: *Congressional Globe*, 34th Congress, 1st Session, 1306.

240 *"I have no qualification whatever"*: Quoted in HW, *Rise and Fall of the Slave Power in America*, vol. 2, 486.

241 *"defend my life, if possible"*: Quoted in ibid., 487.

241 *"scathing even by the paper's"*: Davis, 349.

242 *"very confident"*: "Democratic National Convention," *Baltimore Sun*, reprinted in *CM*, June 6, 1856.

242 *"the only sound and safe"*: Democratic National Platform, 1856, reprinted in the *Weekly Union*, July 17, 1856.

242 *"an embittered state of feeling"*: Quoted in Nevins, *Ordeal of the Union*, vol. 2, 458.

243 *"a constant state of excitement"*: "Telegraphic Intelligence," *CM*, June 9, 1856.

243 *"as acceptable a man"*: "The Nomination of Mr. Buchanan," *CM*, June 7, 1857.

244 *"opposed to the repeal"*: Republican National Platform, 1856, reprinted in "Political Platforms," *Weekly Union*, July 10, 1856.

245 *"mutiny"*: Quoted in Merry, *A Country of Vast Designs*, 422.

245 *"conduct to the prejudice"*: Quoted in ibid., 423.

246 *"An abolitionist cannot lose"*: "Black Republican Balderdash," *New York Herald*, reprinted in *CM*, May 22, 1856.

246 *"their intensity has been increased"*: "The Black Republican Nomination," *CM*, June 20, 1856.

247 *"when compared with the grand"*: Quoted in Klein, 258.

247 *"willing . . . to let the Union slide"*: Quoted in ibid., 257.

247 *"is not worth supporting"*: Quoted in ibid., 258.

247 *"bring the parties of the country"*: Quoted in ibid., 257.

247 *"servile insurrection"*: Ibid.

248 *"arrest . . . the agitation"*: Quoted in ibid., 261.

248 *"victorious defeat"*: Quoted in Nevins, *Ordeal of the Union*, vol. 2, 514.

17. BUCHANAN AT THE HELM

249 *"systematically manufactured"*: "Senator Sumner," *Weekly Union*, June 19, 1856.

249 *"septicemia"*: Donald, *Sumner*, 314.

249 *twenty-two hours a day*: Smith, *The Francis Preston Blair Family in Politics*, vol. 1, 348.

249 *"elasticity and vigor"*: Quoted in ibid.

250 *"From the time of the assault"*: Quoted in Donald, *Sumner*, 317.

250 *"shamming"*: Ibid., 323.

250 *"playing the political possum"*: Quoted in ibid.

250 Boston Post *accused*: Ibid., 323.

250 *"it is this supplementary assault"*: Quoted in ibid.

250 *"Sumner is not merely their champion"*: Quoted in ibid., 303.

250 *"Massachusetts loves and honors"*: Quoted in "Reception of Charles Sumner," *Boston Evening Transcript*, November 3, 1856.

250 *"now, at last, the free States"*: Josiah Quincy speech, reprinted in "Senator Sumner's Welcome Home," *Boston Evening Transcript*, November 4, 1856.

251 *"the suffering which I have undergone"*: CS speech, reprinted in ibid.

251 *"from your field of intellectual victory"*: Henry Gardner speech, reprinted in ibid.

251 *"constrained to confess"*: CS, second speech, reprinted in ibid.

251 *"like an invalid"*: "Senator Sumner's Welcome Home," *Boston Evening Transcript*, November 4, 1856.

251 *"a popular demonstration"*: Ibid.

253 *"unequaled by that conferred"*: "Local News," *Daily Union*, March 5, 1857.

253 Washington's Evening Star *even noted*: "The Inauguration," *Evening Star*, March 4, 1857.

253 *"most auspiciously"*: Ibid.

253 *"mosaic of humanity"*: "Local News," *Daily Union*, March 5, 1857.

253 *"the tempest at once subsided"*: James Buchanan, "March 4, 1857: Inaugural Address," Miller Center, University of Virginia, https://millercenter.org/the-presidency/presidential-speeches/march-4-1857-inaugural-address.

255 *"a dark and fell spirit"*: Quoted in Simon, 102.

256 *"because he is a negro"*: Quoted in ibid., 103.

257 *"galling chain of slavery"*: Quoted in ibid., 12.

257 *"has already earned"*: Quoted in "In Senate: Chief Justice Rutledge," *Daily Globe*, February 7, 1856.

257 *"alacrity and force of mind"*: Quoted in Stampp, 93.

258 *"On conversation with the chief justice"*: Quoted in ibid., 92.

258 *"Thus, three southern justices"*: Ibid., 92.

259 *"were not included"*: "Judgment in the U.S. Supreme Court, Dred Scott versus John F. A. Sandford," National Archives, https://www.archives.gov/mile stone-documents/dred-scott-v-sandford.

260 *"strained reasoning"*: Simon, 125.

261 *"has stripped Congress of a power"*: "The Supreme Court of the United States," *New York Evening Post*, reprinted in *TL*, March 20, 1857.

261 *"carries slavery wherever it waves!"*: Quoted in Stampp, 105.

261 *As historian Simon has written*: Simon, 127.

262 *"wheezy voice"*: Quoted in Merry, 85.

262 *"cordially concurred in the opinion"*: Quoted in Potter, 298.

262 *"submitted to the people"*: Quoted in Stampp, 160.

263 *"In no contingency"*: Quoted in Potter, 299.

18. BUTLER DEPARTS

264 *"so that the rapid and fatal"*: William Boyce, House speech, reprinted in "House of Representatives," *CM*, December 18, 1857.

264 *"It may be truly said"*: James Petigru, speech, printed in "Tribute of Respect," *CM*, May 30, 1857.

265 *"Distrust and suspicion"*: James Mason, Senate speech, printed in "Hon. A. P. Butler," *CM*, December 18, 1857.

265 *"sincerely beloved hero"*: "Death of Preston S. Brooks," *Evening Star* of Washington, January 28, 1857.

265 *"personal friends"*: "Death of Preston Brooks," *TL*, January 30, 1857.

265 *"Who, like a caitiff base and low"*: "Modern Chivalry," *New York Evening Post*, reprinted in *TL*, January 30, 1857.

266 *"explicitly and decidedly"*: JHH, *Secret and Sacred*, 268.

266 *"diversion for himself"*: Faust, 335.

266 *"beautiful situation"*: JHH, *Secret and Sacred*, 266.

267 *"How would my career differed"*: Ibid.

267 *"equal to, if not superior to"*: JHH, *Secret and Sacred*, 269.

267 *According to Walker's analysis*: Potter, 299.

268 *"you resist the authority"*: Robert J. Walker, Inaugural Address, LLMC Digital, https://llmc.com/OpenAccess/docDisplay5.aspx?textid=78302961.

269 *"Governor Walker"* . . . *"can deceive no one"*: "Governor Walker's Address to the People of Kansas," *CM*, June 9, 1857.

270 *"baseless vaporing"*: "Gov. Walker in Kansas," *CM*, June 27, 1857.

270 *"Was there ever such folly"*: Quoted in Harmon, 59.

270 *"On the question of submitting"*: Quoted in ibid., 61.

270 *"We all fear that Governor Walker"*: Quoted in Potter, 305.

271 *"I doubt, now"*: Quoted in Harmon, 64.

271 *"usurpation and outrage"*: "Kansas and the Administration," *CM*, November 9, 1857.

272 *"partial submission"*: Potter, 310.

272 *"constitution with slavery"*: Ibid., 307.

274 *"Mr. Douglas, I desire you to remember"*: Quoted in Johannsen, *Stephen A. Douglas*, 586.

274 *"Mr. President"*: Quoted in ibid.

274 *"go back to the good old days"*: "Ex-Governor Hammond," *CM*, July 14, 1857.

275 *"constitute possibly the ultimate apologia"*: Clyde N. Wilson, Introduction, *Selections from the Letters and Speeches of the Hon. James H. Hammond*, xix.

275 *"one of the most refined"*: "The Senatorial Election," *CM*, December 1, 1857.

275 *"the strangest and most unexpected"*: JHH, *Secret and Sacred*, 270.

276 *"This is a signal triumph"*: Ibid., 271.

276 *"Oh Lord"* . . . *"I have struggled"*: Ibid.

276 *"regulate the affairs of this Country"*: Ibid., 270.

19. RISE OF THE RADICALS

277 *"From the foundation of our Republic"*: "The Edgefield Advertiser," *Edgefield Advertiser*, reprinted in *CM*, November 6, 1857.

278 *"The last cargo heard of"*: Untitled item, *CM*, January 10, 1855.

279 *"an insane experiment"*: Quoted in Stampp, 128.

279 *"[I]n no possible contingency"*: "Speech of Wendell Phillips, Esq," printed in *TL*, January 30, 1857.

280 *"Give me men of good principles"*: Quoted in Ibid., 184.

280 *"hardly looked heroic in flight"*: Reynolds, *John Brown: Abolitionist*, 200.

281 *"He loved the idea"*: Quoted in Renehan, 4.

282 *"a fighter and a purifier"*: Quoted in ibid., 110.

283 *"cannot be successfully palliated"*: Quoted in ibid., 111.

283 *"some inkling that Brown"*: Quoted in ibid., 115.

283 *"I am no adventurer"*: Quoted in Reynolds, *John Brown, Abolitionist*, 211.

284 *"quiet, steadfast earnestness"*: Quoted in Renehan, 109.

284 *"I do not like caution"*: Quoted in ibid., 34.

284 *"terrible faults of character"*: Quoted in ibid.

284 *delivered eighty-four lectures*: Renehan, 44.

285 *"God's fanatic"*: Quoted in ibid., 4.

285 *"Disunion Abolitionist"*: Quoted in ibid., 54.

285 *"the life of a Reformer"*: Quoted in ibid., 53.

285 *"To Disunion I now subscribe"*: Quoted in ibid., 54.

285 *"I would mortgage all I own"*: Quoted in ibid., 59.

286 *"true course now"*: Quoted in ibid., 130.

286 *"misfits, idealists, and charlatans"*: Ibid., 133.

287 *"our dear friend"*: Quoted in ibid., 144.

287 *"I am always ready"*: Quoted in ibid., 142.

288 *"I seldom leave the house"*: Quoted in Davis, 354.

290 *"If we have to turn pirates"*: Quoted in Sinha, 129.

290 *"[u]nity of purpose"*: "The Remedies: To Open the African Slave Trade," *CM*, June 25, 1857.

291 *"justified in wrenching it"*: "Ostend Manifesto," San Diego State University, October 15, 1854, https://loveman.sdsu.edu/docs/1854OstendManifesto.pdf.

20. 35TH CONGRESS

293 *"revolutionary organization"*: James Buchanan, "First Annual Message to Congress on the State of the Union, December 8, 1857," Miller Center, University of Virginia, https://millercenter.org/the-presidency/presidential-speeches/december-8-1857-first-annual-message.

293 *"we heartily support his policy"*: "The President's Message," *CM*, "December 11, 1857.

294 *"I propose to examine this question"*: SAD, Senate speech, *Congressional Globe*, 35th Congress, 1st session, 14.

295 *"the clap-trap of a demagogue"*: "Another Compromise," *CM*, December 25, 1857.

295 *"We have made Kansas this day"*: "Correspondence of the Mercury, Kansas, December 22, 1857," *CM*, January 6, 1858.

296 *"tantamount to a decree"*: "The Impending Political Convulsion on the Slavery Question," *New York Herald*, reprinted in *CM*, January 13, 1858.

297 *"great delusion"*: James Buchanan, Message to Congress, February 2, 1858, Miller Center, University of Virginia, https://millercenter.org/the-presidency/presidential-speeches/february-2-1858-message-congress-transmitting-constitution.

297 *"more weight to our cause"*: Quoted in Potter, 321.

297 *"I but do the senator justice"*: Quoted in "The President's Message," *Daily Union*, December 24, 1857.

299 *"Most of the people of Kansas"*: Nevins, *The Emergence of Lincoln*, vol. 1, 301.

299 *"an assembly of the people"*: JHH, Senate speech, *Congressional Globe*, 35th Congress, 1st Session, 58.

300 *"the battle has been fought and won"*: Quoted in ibid.

300 *"He leaps into the arena"*: "Governor Hammond's Speech," *The South of Richmond*, reprinted in *CM*, March 17, 1858.

300 *"I don't feel at home here yet"*: Quoted in Faust, *James Henry Hammond and the Old South*, 348.

300   *"I have not put myself forward"*: Quoted in ibid.

301   *"a corporal's guard of a few"*: Quoted in "Senator Hammond—A Change of Tone," *CM*, August 2, 1858.

301   *"We should address ourselves"*: Quoted in ibid.

301   *"A dark and portentous cloud"*: Ibid.

301   *"aid and strength"*: Quoted in ibid., 349.

302   *"the North is unanimously against it"*: JHH speech, October 29, 1858, reprinted in Simms, ed., *Selections from the Letters and Speeches of the Hon. James H. Hammond*, 323.

302   *"the whole body of extreme"*: Quoted in Faust, *James Henry Hammond and the Old South*, 352.

303   *"thinking & patriotic men"*: Quoted in ibid., 353.

303   *"I am sorry to say"*: "For the Mercury," *CM*, November 10, 1858.

303   *"those nervous times"*: Quoted in ibid.

303   *"fine judgment, great benevolence"*: "Death of Hon. Josiah J. Evens," *CM*, May 8, 1858.

303   *"slave trade zealot"*: "Correspondent of the News: Columbia, December 4, 1858," *CM*, December 8, 1858.

304   *"an amiable, modest gentleman"*: JHH, *Secret and Sacred*, 214.

304   *"I have thought ever since"*: Ibid.

21. LINCOLN MAKES HIS MOVE

306   *"will tell a lie to ten thousand"*: Quoted in Guelzo, 29.

306   *"the least man I ever saw"*: Ibid.

306   *"Time was when I was in his way"*: Quoted in ibid., 30.

306   *"intensely jealous"*: Ibid.

307   *"a great moral wrong"*: Quoted in Simon, 88.

307   *"the most difficult and dangerous"*: Quoted in ibid., 86.

307   *"the foul 'spot'"*: Quoted in Winkle.

307   *"His ambition"*: Quoted in Reynolds, *Abe*, 65.

308   *"If I fail in this"*: Quoted in ibid., 138.

308   *"I never saw a sadder face"*: Ibid.

308   *"knew, or appeared to know"*: Quoted in Donald, *Lincoln*, 106.

309   *Euclid's complex geometric*: Reynolds, *Abe*, 243.

309   *"life was a school"*: Quoted in ibid., xvi.

309   *"nothing in common"*: Quoted in ibid., 3.

309   *"balance between reason and passion"*: Ibid., 190.

309   *"In the West"*: Quoted in ibid., 312.

310   *"in so far as it may attempt"*: Quoted in ibid., 347.

310 *"that slave hound from Illinois"*: Quoted in Simon, 75.

310 *"talks like an insane man"*: Quoted in Van der Linden, 3.

311 *"It might come round"*: Quoted in Guelzo, 327.

312 *"our next candidate"*: Quoted in Donald, *Lincoln*, 190.

312 *"ready to fuse with anyone"*: Quoted in ibid., 191.

313 *"treason"*: Quoted in Johannsen, *Stephen A. Douglas*, 624.

313 *"Democratic candidates"*: "Democratic Conventions," *Daily Union*, May 27, 1858.

314 *"crushed and ground to powder"*: Quoted in Johannsen, *Stephen A. Douglas*, 627.

314 *"If . . . the great principle"*: *Congressional Globe*, Thirty-Fifth Congress, Fifth Session, 3057.

314 *"If we could first know where"*: AL, "House Divided Speech," Abraham Lincoln Online, June 16, 1858, https://www.abrahamlincolnonline.org/lincoln/speeches/house.htm.

316 *"worthy gentleman"*: SAD, "Speech of Stephen A. Douglas in Chicago, July 9th, 1858," Real Cause of the U.S. Civil War, http://www.civilwarcauses.org/douglas.htm.

318 *"a strong, sonorous voice"*: Quoted in Holzer, 19.

319 *"by his opposition"*: SAD speech, first debate, reprinted in ibid., 51.

319 *"the mildest policy"*: AL speech, seventh debate, ibid., 357.

319 *"The sentiment that contemplates"*: Ibid., 356.

320 *"Is Mr. Douglas"*: "The Illinois Campaign," *New York Herald*, reprinted in *CM*, August 19, 1858.

321 *"local police regulations"*: SAD speech, second debate, reprinted in Holzer, 106.

321 *"the utter unsoundness and trickery"*: "What Douglas Means by 'Popular Sovereignty,'" *CM*, September 8, 1958.

321 *"Seward abolitionists"*: "From Our Own Correspondent, New York, November 7," *CM*, November 12, 1858.

22. REALIGNMENT

323 *"the three living institutions"*: Quoted in Mayer, 485. All quotations from this exchange are from the same source.

326 *"a united state in a united South"*: White, 150.

326 *"It shall be the object"*: Untitled item, *CM*, July 8, 1858.

326 *"separate action of the State"*: "The Mercury and Standard Consolidated," *CM*, July 15, 1858.

326 *"the prince of the fire-eaters"*: Halstead, 5.

327 *"mild and gentlemanly"*: Ibid., 48.

327 *"with a square built head"*: Ibid.

327 *"extreme Southern"*: "Correspondence of the Mercury, Montgomery, May 11, 1858," *CM*, May 14, 1858.

327 *"expedient and proper"*: Quoted in "Southern Commercial Convention," *CM*, May 13, 1858.

327 *soften his approval*: White, 144. White writes: "In the end Yancey seems to have been converted to Rhett's position and thereafter to have joined him in refusing to be distracted from secession as the immediate aim."

327 *"utterly impracticable"*: Quoted indirectly in "Correspondence of the Mercury, Montgomery, May 11, 1858," *CM*, May 14, 1858.

327 *"I am sorry to say"*: Ibid.

329 *"strength, wealth, greatness"*: WS, Rochester speech, October 25, 1858, http://www.myhistory.com/central/conflict.htm.

329 *"Yesterday . . . we had a merry time"*: Quoted in Klein, 330.

329 *"in future belong"*: Quoted in "The Late Elections," *CM*, October 19, 1856.

330 *"it is a question"*: Ibid.

331 *a glowing report*: Taken from Nevins, *The Emergence of Lincoln, Vol. I*, 403.

331 *"The just equality of all the states"*: James Buchanan, "Second Annual Message to Congress on the State of the Union, December 6, 1858," American Presidency Project, UC Santa Barbara, https://www.presidency.ucsb.edu/documents/second-annual-message-congress-the-state-the-union.

332 *"split up into all sorts"*: Quoted indirectly in "Mr. Buchanan and the Democratic Party," *Sun* (Worcester, MA), reprinted in *CM*, March 8, 1859.

332 *"Mr. President"*: Albert Brown, Senate speech, *Congressional Globe*, 35th Congress, 2nd Session, 1242.

333 *"punishment is rapidly following"*: "Correspondence of the Mercury, Washington, December 10, 1858," *CM*, December 10, 1858.

333 *"How many votes"*: SAD, Senate speech, *Congressional Globe*, 35th Congress, 2nd Session, 1246.

334 *"I utterly, totally, entirely"*: Albert Brown, ibid., 1244.

334 *"So much for the oft-repeated"*: Quoted in Nevins, *The Emergence of Lincoln*, vol. 2, 417.

334 *"a delusive gauze"*: Jefferson Davis, Senate speech, *Congressional Globe*, 35th Congress, 2nd Session, 1247.

334 *"I never would vote"*: SAD, Senate speech, ibid., 1244.

23. HARPERS FERRY

336 *"You are our prisoner"*: Quoted in Rehehan, 197.

337 *"a perfect steel-trap"*: Quoted in ibid., 90.

338 *"perhaps the most successful operation"*: Potter, 369.

340 "Kill them! Kill them!": Quoted in Rehehan, 200.

340 *"puzzled"*: Ibid.

340 *"If you must die"*: Ibid., 202.

341 *"Hang them, hang them"*: Ibid., 204.

342 *Sen. Mason—How do you justify*: Interview transcript, "The Virginia Insurrection," *Baltimore American*, reprinted in *CM*, October 25, 1859.

343 *"I believe that to have interfered"*: JB, "His Speech to the Court at His Trial," Bartleby, https://www.bartleby.com/lit-hub/hc/america-ii-1818-1865/his-speech-to-the-court-at-his-trial/.

343 *"I don't know as I can better serve"*: Quoted in "Great Meeting at Boston," *TL*, December 9, 1859.

344 *"make the gallows as glorious"*: Quoted in Potter, 379.

344 *"an angel of light"*: Ibid.

344 *"pirate ship"*: Ibid.

344 *"infinitely better"*: Ibid.

344 *"sacred and radiant treason"*: Ibid.

344 *"holy"*: Ibid.

344 *"Does not Brown profess"*: "The Harpers Ferry Insurrection," *Boston Post*, reprinted in *TL*, November 4, 1859.

344 *"The leader of this diabolical attempt"*: Untitled item, *Journal of Commerce*, reprinted in *TL*, October 28, 1859.

344 *"poor, miserable, futile effort"*: "Senator Wilson on the Harpers Ferry Outbreak," *TL*, November 4, 1859.

345 *"wild, misguided and apparently insane"*: Quoted in Mayer, 494.

345 *"was foundering on the shoals"*: Ibid.

345 *"The man who brands him"*: WLG speech, December 2, 1859, printed under "Speech of Wm. Lloyd Garrison," *TL*, December 16, 1859.

346 *"the spectacle of those who come"*: Jefferson Davis, Senate speech, *Congressional Globe*, 36th Congress, 1st Session, 62.

346 *"a prelude of what must"*: "The Harpers Ferry Insurrection," *CM*, October 20, 1859.

347 *"Thus they tell us"*: "Correspondence of the Mercury, Washington, October 26," *CM*, November 1, 1859.

347 *"The great source of the evil"*: "The Plan of Insurrection," *CM*, November 3, 1859.

347 *"more reluctantly than John Brown"*: Quoted in Faust, *James Henry Hammond and the Old South*, 354.

348 *"You live in our hearts"*: Gerrit Smith, letter to JB, June 4, 1859, published in "Letter from Gerrit Smith to Captain John Brown," *CM*, October 25, 1859.

348 *"I'm going to be indicted"*: Quoted in Rehehan, 222.

348 *"his excitable and illy-balanced mind"*: Ibid.

348 *"marks of insanity"*: "Gerrit Smith's Insanity," *Utica Herald*, reprinted in *CM*, November 15, 1859.

348 *"Burn this"*: Quoted in Renehan, 208.

348 *"with a dread that threatened"*: Quoted in ibid.

349 *"That event was unforeseen"*: Quoted in Reynolds, *John Brown*, 343.

349 *"whether any citizens"*: Quoted in Rehehan, 237.

349 *"Never"*: Quoted in ibid., 249.

349 *"No, sir; I never supposed"*: Quoted in ibid., 250.

349 *"the afflicted gentleman"*: Untitled item, *New York Tribune*, reprinted in *CM*, November 21, 1859.

350 *"The only persons who don't have"*: Quoted in Potter, 389.

350 *"great anxiety"*: Quoted in Rehehan, 224.

24. A TIME OF FOREBODING

351 *"Never before"*: Quoted in Donald, *Sumner*, 333.

351 *"South Carolina Plug Uglie"*: Quoted in ibid., 330.

351 *"I suppose I shall be shot"*: Ibid.

351 *"I cannot work with the mind"*: Ibid., 331.

352 *"post-traumatic syndrome"*: Ibid., 336.

352 *"Secure in his faith"*: Ibid., 341.

352 *"to attend the sessions of the body"*: Quoted in ibid., 343.

352 *"undivided affection"*: Ibid.

353 *"unadvisable"*: Ibid., 344.

353 *"He walks on those great long legs"*: Ibid., 346.

353 *"This is a barbarous place"*: Ibid., 349.

353 *"If health ever returns"*: Ibid., 347.

354 *"dishonest, degraded, and disgraced"*: Quoted in Potter, 387.

354 *"doctrines and sentiments"*: John B. Clark, House speech, *Congressional Globe*, 36th Congress, 1st Session, 3.

355 *"fully up to the Harpers Ferry standard"*: Quoted in "Harper's Ferry in a Tract Society," *CM*, October 29, 1859.

355 *"having the slaves rise up"*: Ibid.

355 *"perfectly fanatical for secession"*: "For the Mercury," *CM*, December 19, 1859.

355 *"possesses the power to annul"*: Jefferson Davis, Senate speech, 36th Congress, 1st Session, *Congressional Globe*, 658.

356 *"Our deep and heartfelt gratitude"*: James Buchanan, "Third Annual Message to Congress on the State of the Union, December 19, 1859," American Presidency Project, UC Santa Barbara, https://www.presidency.ucsb.edu/documents/third-annual-message-congress-the-state-the-union.

357 *"Our fathers, when they framed"*: AL, quoting Stephen Douglas, "Cooper Union Address," Abraham Lincoln Online, February 27, 1860, https://www.abrahamlincolnonline.org/lincoln/speeches/cooper.htm.

357 *"As those fathers marked it"*: AL, "Cooper Union Address."

358 *"wonderful machine"*: WS, Senate speech, 36th Congress, 1st Session, *Congressional Globe*, 910.

358 *"logically and convincingly stated"*: Quoted in Donald, *Lincoln*, 239.

358 *"one of Nature's orators"*: Ibid.

359 *"Would to God I were able"*: Quoted in "The Conservative North," *New York Times*, reprinted in *CM*, December 10, 1859.

359 *"fine original poems"*: "The Charleston Mercury," *New York Home Journal*, reprinted in *CM*, July 1, 1859.

359 *"the ablest, most consistent"*: "Political Signs of the Times," *New York Herald*, reprinted in *CM*, April 28, 1859.

360 *"How long shall we stand the resistless"*: RBR, "Speech of Hon. R. B. Rhett," Grahamville, SC, speech, *Charleston Mercury*, July 7, 1859.

360 *"Can you tell me why"*: Quoted in "Senator Chesnut's Position," *Southern Guardian*, reprinted in *CM*, August 11, 1859.

361 *"I do not believe that we are sailing"*: James Chesnut, Camden speech, reprinted in "Speech of Hon. James Chesnut Jr.," *CM*, September 29, 1859.

361 *"We are somewhat at a loss"*: "The Edgefield Advertiser on Senator Chesnut," *CM*, October 11, 1859, reprinted from the *Edgefield Advertiser*.

362 *"Thirty years' active experience"*: "Major B. F. Perry," *CM*, December 24, 1859.

363 *"guest of the state"*: Quoted in Starobin, 33.

363 *"perfectly safe from northern hostility"*: "Virginia Refused to Confer with her Southern Sister States," *CM*, March 10, 1860.

25. PRESIDENTIAL SCRAMBLE

364 *"[N]ever have the premonitions"*: "The Convention," *CM*, April 21, 1860.

364 *"pivot individual"*: Halstead, 1.

365 *"The question in every car"*: Ibid.

365 *"retire from the convention"*: Quoted in Potter, 408.

365 *"not so stiff in their backs"*: Halstead, 3.

366 *"test campaign"*: Quoted in ibid.

366 *"the south will have the intellect"*: Ibid., 6.

366 *"Charleston is perhaps"*: "Highly Interesting from Charleston," *New York Tribune*, April 23, 1860.

367 *"[t]he yoke seemed to be rather light"*: Catton, 5.

367 *"happy and contented"*: "From Charleston Correspondence," *New Albany Ledger*, reprinted in *Charleston Mercury*, June 11, 1860.

367 *"such impressions as twenty minutes"*: Catton, 5.

367 *"a good deal of gaudy"*: Halstead, 5.

367 *Charleston hoteliers*: "Highly Interesting from Charleston."

368 *"to abolish slavery in the territories"*: Democratic National Platform, majority report, reprinted in the *Boston Evening Transcript*, April 27, 1860.

368 *"judicial in their character"*: Democratic National Platform, minority report, ibid.

368 *"are made solely for the protection"*: William Yancey, Democratic National Convention speech, April 28, 1860, https://www.forgottenbooks.com/en/read book/SpeechoftheHonWilliamLYanceyofAlabama_10545468#0.

369 *"keen, shrewd and telling"*: Halstead, 50.

369 *prostrate themselves*: Indirect quote in Johannsen, *Stephen A. Douglas*, 754.

369 *"Gentlemen of the South"*: Quoted in Catton, 32.

369 *"screaming like panthers"*: Halstead, 50.

369 *"The Crisis Reached"*: "The Charleston Convention," *Boston Evening Transcript*, April 30, 1860.

369 *"If the National Democratic party"*: "The Convention," *CM*, April 30, 1860.

370 *"delighted fluttering of fans"*: Halstead, 73.

371 *"rump convention"*: Quoted in Catton, 38.

371 *"The last party, pretending"*: "The Convention Breaking Up," *CM*, May 1, 1860.

371 *"The [next] president"*: Quoted in Halstead, 61.

372 Harper's *magazine, in a special*: Stahr, *William Seward*, 184.

372 *"the nomination belongs"*: Quoted in ibid., 185.

372 *"cannot concentrate"*: Quoted in Halstead, 142.

372 *"I agree with Seward"*: Quoted in Donald, *Lincoln*, 246.

373 "no contracts that will bind me": Quoted in Goodwin, 247.

373 *"prodigious"* . . . *"enthusiastic"*: Halstead, 144.

374 *"absolutely frantic, shrill and wild"*: Ibid., 145.

374 *"all the hogs ever slaughtered"*: Ibid.

375 *"[W]e must yield nothing"*: Quoted in ibid., 157.

376 *"by the direction of a large majority"*: Quoted in Catton, 73.

376 *"glowed with satisfaction"*: Ibid., 77.

376 *"the most cordial unanimity"*: Quoted in Halstead, 217.

26. LINCOLN VICTORIOUS

378 *"About eight years ago"*: "Speech of the Hon. R. B. Rhett," *CM*, July 13, 1860.

379 *"sectional antagonism"*: "The Southern State Legislatures," *CM*, July 20, 1860.

379 *"It would be idle"*: "The Issue in the Presidential Campaign," *New York Herald*, reprinted in *CM*, July 30, 1860.

379 *Buchanan's treasury secretary*: Untitled item, *CM*, August 20, 1860.

379 *"We prefer the alternative"*: Quoted in "The Position of the Charleston Courier on Disunion," *CM*, August 28, 1860.

379 *"It is by a stern logical and moral necessity"*: "Speech of Wm. Lloyd Garrison," *TL*, June 1, 1860.

380 *"the very best specimens"*: "Speech of Wendell Phillips, Esq.," *TL*, June 8, 1860.

381 *"benevolence and charity"*: Quoted in Donald, *Sumner*, 353.

381 *"Barbarous in origin"*: CS, Senate speech, 36th Congress, 1st Session, *Congressional Globe*, 2591.

382 *"It will be . . . like the embrace"*: "Mr. Sumner's Speech," *CM*, July 3, 1860.

382 *"[a]fter ranging over Europe"*: "Mr. Chesnut's Reply," *TL*, June 8, 1860.

383 *"cut his d—d throat"*: "The Plot against Mr. Sumner," *TL*, June 15, 1860.

383 *"determined that Mr. Sumner"*: "Senator Sumner Threatened with Personal Violence," *TL*, June 15, 1860.

384 *"the rights which he pronounces"*: CFA, House speech, 36th Congress, 1st Session, *Congressional Globe*, 2514.

384 *"usually cold and passionless"*: "Miscellaneous," *Boston Journal*, reprinted in *CM*, June 15, 1860.

384 *"able, polished, scholarly"*: "Letter from Washington," *TL*, June 8, 1860.

384 *"one of the shining lights"*: "Northern Sentiment," *CM*, September 3, 1860.

385 *"undoubted Republican majorities"*: "The Present Aspect of Politics," *Boston Evening Transcript*, May 1, 1860.

385 *"There is now no doubt"*: "Our New York Correspondent," *CM*, August 24, 1860.

385 *"We suppose"*: "No Fusion," *CM*, September 15, 1860.

385 *"no prejudices against him"*: "The Chicago Nominations," *Boston Evening Transcript*, May 19, 1860.

386 *"and other kindred presses"*: "Lincoln an Abolitionist," *CM*, September 12, 1860.

386 *"he would necessarily have to act"*: "Lincoln's Radicalism Proved," *New York Herald*, reprinted in *CM*, September 15, 1860.

386 *"If Lincoln be elected"*: "Letter from Hon. W. W. Boyce," *CM*, August 9, 1860.

387 *"perjured traitor"*: "Col. Crozier on Lincoln's Election," *CM*, September 24, 1860.

387 "would be the Brutus": "Hon. Roger A. Pryor on Coercion of a Seceding State," *CM*, September 24, 1860.

387 *"If he attempts coercion"*: "The North the Aggressor—The South on the Defensive," *CM*, September 24, 1860.

388 *"The first question is"*: Quoted in "Douglas in the South," *CM*, August 30, 1860.

389 *Abraham Lincoln tore off the top*: Donald, *Lincoln*, 255.

390 *"I went home, but not to get much sleep"*: Quoted in ibid.

390 *"gave expression to their feelings"*: "The Presidential Election," *CM*, November 7, 1860.

391 *"Have you read my speeches?"*: "Special Despatch to the N.Y. Times," *Boston Evening Transcript*, November 9, 1860, reprinted from the *New York Times*.

27. DISSOLUTION

392 *"Feeling an assurance"*: "The Last Term," *Charleston Courier*, November 8, 1860.

392 *"wretched self-seekers and charlatans"*: Quoted in Davis, 349.

393 *"the Temple of Justice"*: "The Last Term," *Charleston Courier*.

393 *"rich in the approving admiration"*: "The Late Judge," *Charleston Courier*, November 8, 1860.

393 *"the spirits of our people"*: "Correspondence of the Courier," *Charleston Courier*, November 9, 1860.

393 *"but one point of antagonism"*: "Southern Desperation," *TL*, November 16, 1860.

394 *"Will not delay cool the ardor"*: Quoted in Davis, 398.

394 *"ripping up their own bowels"*: Quoted in Faust, *James Henry Hammond and the Old South*, 358.

394 *"with all the strength I have"*: Ibid.

394 *"the father of secession"*: Quoted in White, 194.

394 *"This is his hour of triumph"*: Quoted in ibid., 181.

394 *"to strengthen the power of the North"*: RBR speech, November 12, 1860, published in *CM*, November 21, 1860.

395 *"by any State [or] by combinations"*: Quoted in Klein, 359.

396 *"incessant and violent agitation"*: James Buchanan, "Fourth Annual Message to Congress on the State of the Union, December 3, 1860," American Presidency Project, UC Santa Barbara, https://www.presidency.ucsb.edu/documents/fourth-annual-message-congress-the-state-the-union.

396 *"Seldom have we known"*: Quoted in Nevins, *Emergence of Lincoln*, vol. 2, 353.

397 *"We infer . . . from these positions"*: "The President's Message," *CM*, December 6, 1860.

397 *"including the band"*: "Our Harbor Defences," *CM*, December 13, 1860.

398 *"any general plan of adjustment"*: Quoted in Potter, 532.

398 *"As an* exclusive *alternative"*: Ibid., 528.

399 *"every good citizen"*: Quoted in ibid., 534.

399 *"It would make me appear"*: Quoted in ibid., 523.

399 *"Let there be no compromise"*: Quoted in Nevins, *Emergence of Lincoln, Vol. II*, 394.

400 *"a crisis must be reached"*: Quoted in ibid.

400 *"utterly opposed"*: Quoted in ibid., 396.

400 *"a second noble cause"*: Potter, 527.

400 *"[n]o eloquence, and no devotion"*: "Wendell Phillips," *Boston Evening Transcript*, November 8, 1860.

400 *"We have . . . appealed to the heart"*: Quoted in "Speech of Hon. Henry Wilson," *TL*, November 23, 1860.

401 *"prudent, wise, discreet"*: Quoted in "Hon. Charles Sumner on the Result of the Election," *Boston Evening Transcript*, November 9, 1860.

402 *"indulges in an abundance"*: Quoted in Davis, 407.

402 *"the union now subsisting"*: "An Ordinance," reprinted in *CM*, December 21, 1860.

402 *"Inscribed among the calends"*: "The 20th Day of December, in the Year of Our Lord, 1860," *CM*, December 21, 1860.

403 *"Never yet"*: "The News in Charleston," *CM*, December 21, 1860.

403 *"consecrated parchment"*: Quoted in Starobin, 207.

403 *"despotism"*: "The Address of the People of South Carolina, Assembled in Convention, to the People of the Slaveholding States of the United States," Real Cause of the U.S. Civil War, https://www.civilwarcauses.org/rhett/htm.

403 *"weakly reasoned"*: Quoted in White, 190n.

404 *"thrown into a state of the wildest"*: "The Events of Yesterday," *CM*, December 28, 1860.

404 *"lamentable incompetency"*: Quoted in Davis, 414.

404 *"I have never seen him more solemn"*: Quoted in Klein, 389.

404 *"Governor, the current of events"*: Quoted in "Affecting," *CM*, January 31, 1861.

405 *In a searing report to the president*: An extensive passage from the report appears in Swanberg, 119.

408 *"We are annoyed by the chief"*: Quoted in Davis, 428.

408 *"I have never been wise"*: Quoted in ibid., 435.

409 *"simply insists upon holding"*: Quoted in Donald, *Lincoln*, 276.

409 *"Lincoln is a cool man"*: "Lincoln Speaks," *CM*, February 15, 1861.

409 *"Everybody here is disgusted"*: "Our Washington Despatches," *CM*, February 25, 1861.

28. CIVIL WAR

410 *"so immense a crowd"*: "The Inauguration of Abraham Lincoln, President of the United States," *Evening Star* of Washington, March 4, 1861.

410 *"seemed to be in a very good humor"*: Ibid.

411 *"shook very perceptibly"*: "The Inauguration of President Lincoln," *Boston Evening Transcript*, March 5, 1861.

412 *"All the power at my disposal"*: Quoted in Donald, *Lincoln*, 283.

412 *"words of affection"*: Quoted in ibid., 284.

412 *"There has never been"*: AL, First Inaugural Address, https://avalon.law.yale
.edu/19th_century/lincoln.asp.

414 *"tone of hope, faith, and brave reliance"*: "The Inaugural of President Lincoln,"
Boston Evening Transcript, March 5, 1861.

414 *"sustained by the great mass"*: Quoted in ibid.

414 *"If ignorance could add anything"*: "The Inaugural Address of President Lincoln," *CM*, March 5, 1861.

415 *"must proclaim peace or declare war"*: "The Fourth of March," *CM*, March 4,
1861.

416 *"The enmity of Slavery"*: Quoted in Donald, *Sumner*, 366.

416 *"Never!"*: Quoted in ibid., 368.

416 *"violent political wrangling"*: Quoted in ibid., 375.

416 *"Sumner," declared Adams*: Quoted in ibid.

416 *"superiority in education"*: Henry Adams, 102.

417 *"two men would have disliked"*: Ibid.

417 *"I am certain--I see my way"*: Quoted in Donald, *Sumner*, 373.

417 *"all the hills of South Carolina"*: Quoted in Potter, 563.

418 *"Disappointment!"*: Quoted in Goodwin, 327.

418 *"I will try to save freedom"*: Quoted in Potter, 562.

418 *"It seems to me"*: Ibid.

418 *"the virtual ruler of this country"*: Ibid.

418 *"to the mere matter"*: Quoted in Swanberg, 225.

418 *"Evacuation seems almost inevitable"*: Ibid.

420 *"The surrender of a post"*: *New York Tribune* editorial, reprinted in "Coercion
Papers," *CM*, March 18, 1861.

420 *"another way of saying"*: "Fort Sumter," *CM*, March 20, 1861.

420 *"Could you stand upon"*: "From Fort Sumter," *Northampton Courier*, reprinted
in *CM*, March 25, 1861.

421 *"Some thoughts for the President's"*: Quoted in Stahr, *Seward*, 269.

424 *"Seward's jugglery"*: Potter, 581.

424 *"The flag which you have upheld"*: Quoted in Swanberg, 291.

424 *"sense of honor"*: Quoted in ibid., 292.

425 *"Sir: By authority of Brigadier General"*: Reprinted in ibid., 296.

EPILOGUE: CIVIL WAR AND BEYOND

428 *"vocation as an abolitionist"*: Quoted in the *Encyclopedia Britannica*, https://
www.britannica.com/summary/-William-Lloyd-Garison.

428 *"It is enough for me"*: Ibid.

431 *"confidential adviser to John Brown"*: Quoted in "Franklin Benjamin Sanborn," Boston Athenaeum, https://bostonathenaeum.org/bio/franklin-benjamin-sanborn.

432 *"the cherished dream and hope"*: Quoted in Faust, *James Henry Hammond and the Old South*, 360.

432 *"there was no special need"*: Quoted in ibid., 364.

434 *"You are all now going to the devil"*: Quoted in South Carolina Encyclopedia, https://www.scencyclopedia.org/sce/entries/perry-benjamin-franklin/.

435 *"No more tragic or ironical"*: White, 234.

435 *"Castle Dismal"*: Quoted in ibid., 240.

435 *"too hideous a spectacle"*: Quoted in ibid., 242.

435 *"age loves home"*: Quoted in Baker, 142.

436 *"completely satisfied"*: Quoted in ibid., 143.

436 *"prepared to sustain the President"*: Quoted in Johannsen, *Stephen A. Douglas*, 860.

436 *"We must fight for our country"*: Ibid.

437 *"fearful, fruitless, [and] fateful"*: Quoted in Holt, *Franklin Pierce*, 125.

437 *"old farmer"*: Quoted in ibid., 128.

Bibliography

BOOKS

Adams, Henry. *The Education of Henry Adams*. 1918; Boston: Houghton, Mifflin, 1974.

Ames, William E. *A History of the National Intelligencer*. Chapel Hill: University of North Carolina Press, 1972.

Baker, Jean H. *James Buchanan*. New York: Holt, 2004.

Barnett, Randy E., ed. *The Life and Writings of Salmon P. Chase*. Washington, DC: Georgetown Center for the Constitution, 2020.

Bartlett, Irving H. *Daniel Webster*. New York: Norton, 1978.

_____. *John C. Calhoun: A Biography*. New York: Norton, 1993.

Bauer, Jack K. *Zachary Taylor: Soldier, Planter, Statesman of the Old Southwest*. Baton Rouge: Louisiana State University Press, 1985.

Benson, T. Lloyd. *The Caning of Senator Sumner*. Belmont, CA: Thomson/Wadsworth, 2004.

Benton, Thomas Hart. *Thirty Years View; or, A History of the Working of the American Government for Thirty Years, from 1820 to 1850*. New York: Appleton, 1856.

Birkner, Michael J., ed. *James Buchanan and the Political Crisis of the 1850s*. Selinsgrove, PA: Susquehanna University Press, 1996.

Blumenthal, Sidney. *The Political Life of Abraham Lincoln: All the Powers of Earth, 1856–1860*. New York, Simon & Schuster, 2019.

_____. *The Political Life of Abraham Lincoln: Wrestling with His Angel, 1849–1856*. New York: Simon & Schuster, 2017.

Bordewich, Fergus M. *America's Great Debate: Henry Clay, Stephen A. Douglas, and the Compromise That Preserved the Union*. New York: Simon & Schuster, 2012.

Brinkley, Alan, and Davis Dyer, ed. *The American Presidency*. Boston: Houghton Mifflin, 2004.

Brodie, Fawn M. *Thaddeus Stevens: Scourge of the South*. New York: Norton, 1959.

Brown, Richard D., and Jack Tager. *Massachusetts: A Concise History*. Amherst: University of Massachusetts Press, 2000.

Carson, Clarence B. *The Sections and the Civil War, 1826–1877*, Wadley, AL: American Textbook Committee, 1985.

Catton, Bruce. *The Coming Fury*. Garden City, NY: Doubleday, 1961.

Channing, Steven A. *Crisis of Fear: Secession in South Carolina*. New York, Simon & Schuster, 1970.

Chesnut, Mary Boykin. *Mary Chesnut's Civil War*. Edited by C. Vann Woodward. New Haven, CT: Yale University Press, 1981.

Cohn, Mary, ed. *Guide to Congress*, 4th ed. Washington, DC: Congressional Quarterly, 1991.

Coit, Margaret L. *John C. Calhoun, American Portrait*. Boston: Houghton Mifflin, 1950.

Cole, Arthur C. *The Irrepressible Conflict*. Chicago: Quadrangle, 1962.

Congressional Quarterly Staff. *National Party Conventions, 1831–2000*. Washington, DC: CQ Press, 2001.

_____. *Presidential Elections, 1789–2000*. Washington, DC: CQ Press, 2002.

Craven, Avery O. *The Growth of Southern Nationalism, 1848–1861*. Baton Rouge: Louisiana State University Press, 1953.

Dalzell, Robert F., Jr. *Daniel Webster and the Trial of American Nationalism, 1843–1852*. Boston: Houghton Mifflin, 1973.

Davis, William C. *Rhett: The Turbulent Life and Times of a Fire-Eater*. Columbia: University of South Carolina Press, 2001.

Dennis, Frank L. *The Lincoln-Douglas Debates*. New York: Mason & Lipscomb, 1974.

Detzer, David. *Allegiance: Fort Sumter, Charleston, and the Beginning of the Civil War*. New York: Harcourt, 2001.

Dew, Charles B. *Apostles of Disunion: Southern Secession Commissioners and the Causes of the Civil War*. Charlottesville: University of Virginia Press, 2001.

Donald, David. *Charles Sumner and the Coming of the Civil War*. New York: Knopf, 1960.

_____. *Lincoln*. New York: Simon & Schuster, 1995.

Duberman, Martin. *Charles Francis Adams, 1807–1886*. Stanford, CA: Stanford University Press, 1960.

Dumond, Dwight Lowell, ed. *Southern Editorials on Secession*. New York: Century, 1931.

Egan, Ferol. *Fremont: Explorer for a Restless Nation*. Garden City, NY: Doubleday, 1977.

Eisenhower, John S. D. *Agent of Destiny: The Life and Times of General Winfield Scott*. New York: Free Press, 1997.

_____. *Zachary Taylor*. New York: Holt, 2008.

Etcheson, Nicole. *Bleeding Kansas: Contested Liberty in the Civil War*. Lawrence: University Press of Kansas, 2004.

Evans, Clement A., ed. *Secession and the Civil War: Confederate Military History*, vol. 1. Secaucus, NJ: Blue & Grey Press, undated.

Faust, Drew Gilpin, ed. *The Creation of Confederate Nationalism: Ideology and Identity in the Civil War South*. Baton Rouge: Louisiana State University Press, 1988.

————, ed. *The Ideology of Slavery: Proslavery Thought in the Antebellum South, 1830–1860*. Baton Rouge: Louisiana State University Press, 1981.

————. *James Henry Hammond and the Old South: A Design for Mastery*. Baton Rouge: Louisiana State University Press, 1982.

Fehrenbacher, Don E. *Prelude to Greatness: Lincoln in the 1850s*. Stanford, CA: Stanford University Press, 1962.

Finkelman, Paul. *Millard Fillmore*. New York: Holt, 2011.

Fischer, David Hackett. *Albion's Seed: Four British Folkways in America*. New York: Oxford University Press, 1989.

Fogel, Robert William, and Stanley L. Engerman. *Time on the Cross, Vol. I: The Economics of American Negro Slavery*. Boston: Little, Brown, 1974.

————. *Time on the Cross, Vol. II: Evidence and Methods—A Supplement*. Boston: Little, Brown, 1974.

Fraser, Walter J., Jr. *Charleston! Charleston! The History of a Southern City*. Columbia: University of South Carolina Press, 1989.

Freehling, William W. *The Road to Disunion, Vol. I: Secessionists at Bay, 1776–1854*. Oxford, UK: Oxford University Press, 1990.

————. *The Road to Disunion, Vol. II: Secessionists Triumphant, 1854–1861*, New York: Oxford University Press, 2007.

Fuess, Claude M. *Daniel Webster, Vol. I, 1782–1830*. 1930; Cambridge, MA: Da Capo, 1968.

————. *Daniel Webster, Vol. II, 1830–1852*. 1930; Cambridge, MA: Da Capo, 1968.

Genovese, Eugene D. *Roll, Jordan, Roll: The World the Slaves Made*. New York: Pantheon, 1974.

————. *The World the Slaveholders Made: Two Essays in Interpretation*. New York: Pantheon, 1969.

Goodwin, Doris Kearns. *Team of Rivals: The Political Genius of Abraham Lincoln*. New York: Simon & Schuster, 2005.

Guelzo, Allen C. *Lincoln and Douglas: The Debates That Defined America*. New York: Simon & Schuster, 2008.

Halstead, Murat. *Caucuses of 1860: A History of the National Political Conventions of the Current Presidential Campaigns*. Cincinnati: Cincinnati Commercial, 1860.

Hamer, Philip May. *The Secession Movement in South Carolina, 1847–1852*. Allentown, PA: Ray Haas, 1918.

Hammond, James Henry. *Secret and Sacred: The Diaries of James Henry Hammond, a Southern Slaveholder*. Edited by Carol Bleser. Columbia: University of South Carolina Press, 1988.

————. *Selections from the Letters and Speeches of the Hon. James H. Hammond.*

Edited by William Gilmore Simms. Introduction by Clyde N. Wilson. New York: John F. Trow, 1866.

Heidler, David S., and Jeanne T. Heidler. *Henry Clay: The Essential American*. New York: Random House, 2010.

Holt, Michael F. *Franklin Pierce*. New York: Holt, 2010.

———. *The Political Crisis of the 1850s*. New York: Norton, 1978.

———. *The Rise and Fall of the American Whig Party: Jacksonian Politics and the Onset of the Civil War*. Oxford, UK: Oxford University Press, 1999.

Holzer, Harold, ed. *The Lincoln-Douglas Debates*. New York: HarperCollins, 1993.

Johannsen, Robert W. *Stephen A. Douglas*. New York: Oxford University Press, 1973.

Johnson Paul. *A History of the American People*. New York: HarperCollins, 1998.

Karp, Matthew. *This Vast Southern Empire: Slaveholders at the Helm of American Foreign Policy*. Cambridge, MA: Harvard University Press, 2016.

Klein, Philip Shriver. *President James Buchanan*. Norwalk, CT: Easton Press, 1962.

Lerner, Gerda. *The Grimke Sisters from South Carolina: Pioneers for Women's Rights and Abolition*. Chapel Hill: University of North Carolina Press, 1962.

Lincoln, Abraham. *Abraham Lincoln Great Speeches*. Edited by John Grafton. New York: Dover, 1991.

Lundberg, James M. *Horace Greeley: Print, Politics, and the Failure of American Nationhood*. Baltimore: Johns Hopkins University Press, 2019.

Malavasic, Alice Elizabeth. *The F Street Mess: How Southern Senators Rewrote the Kansas-Nebraska Act*. Chapel Hill: University of North Carolina Press, 2017.

Martin, George W., ed. *Transactions of the Kansas State Historical Society*, vol. 10. Topeka: Kansas Historical Society, 1908.

Martineau, Harriet. *Retrospect of Western Travel*, vol. 1. New York: Saunders and Otley, 1838.

———. *Society in America*, vols. 1 and 2. New York: Saunders and Otley, 1837.

Mayer, Henry. *All on Fire: William Lloyd Garrison and the Abolition of Slavery*. New York: St. Martin's Press, 1998.

Mayo, Bernard. *Henry Clay: Spokesman of the New West*. Boston: Houghton Mifflin, 1937.

McCardell, John. *The Idea of a Southern Nation: Southern Nationalists and Southern Nationalism, 1830–1860*. New York: Norton, 1979.

Merry, Robert W. *A Country of Vast Designs: James K. Polk, the Mexican War, and the Conquest of the American Continent*. New York: Simon & Schuster, 2009.

———. *Where They Stand: The American Presidents in the Eyes of Voters and Historians*. New York: Simon & Schuster, 2012.

Moore, John L., Jon P. Preimesberger, and David R. Tarr, ed. *Guide to U.S. Elections*, vol. 1, 4th ed. Washington, DC: CQ Press, 2001.

———. *Guide to U.S. Elections*, vol. 2, 4th ed. Washington, DC: CQ Press, 2001.

Nevins, Allan. *Ordeal of the Union, Vol. I: Fruits of Manifest Destiny, 1847–1852.* New York: Scribner, 1947.

_____. *Ordeal of the Union, Vol. II: A House Dividing, 1852–1857.* New York: Scribner, 1947.

_____. *The Emergence of Lincoln, Vol. I: Douglas, Buchanan, and Party Chaos, 1857–1859.* New York: Scribner, 1950.

_____. *The Emergence of Lincoln, Vol. II: Prologue to Civil War, 1859–1861.* New York: Scribner, 1950.

_____. *The War for the Union, Vol. I: The Improvised War, 1861–1862.* New York: Scribner, 1959.

Nichols, Roy F. *The Stakes of Power, 1845–1877.* New York: Hill & Wang, 1961.

Oates, Stephen B. *The Approaching Fury: Voices of the Storm, 1820–1861.* New York: HarperCollins, 1997.

_____. *With Malice toward None: The Life of Abraham Lincoln.* New York: Harper & Row, 1977.

Perry, Benjamin Franklin. *Reminiscences of Public Men, with Speeches and Addresses.* Greenville, SC: Shannon, 1889.

Peterson, Merrill D. *The Great Triumvirate: Webster, Clay, and Calhoun.* New York: Oxford University Press, 1987.

Polk, James K. *The Diary of James K. Polk during His Presidency, 1845–1849*, vol. 2. Edited and annotated by Milo Milton Quaife. Chicago: A. C. McLurg & Co., 1910. Reprinted by the Chicago Historical Society.

_____. *The Diary of James K. Polk during His Presidency, 1845–1849*, vol. 3. Edited and annotated by Milo Milton Quaife. Chicago: A. C. McLurg & Co., 1910. Reprinted by the Chicago Historical Society.

_____. *The Diary of James K. Polk during His Presidency, 1845–1849*, vol. 4. Edited and annotated by Milo Milton Quaife. Chicago: A. C. McLurg & Co., 1910. Reprinted by the Chicago Historical Society.

Potter, David M. *The Impending Crisis, 1848–1861.* Completed and edited by Don E. Fehrenbacher. New York: Harper & Row, 1976.

Rayback, Robert J. *Millard Fillmore: Biography of a President.* Newtown, CT: American Political Biography Press, 1959.

Remini, Robert V. *At the Edge of the Precipice: Henry Clay and the Compromise That Saved the Union.* New York: Basic Books, 2010.

_____. *Daniel Webster: The Man and His Time.* New York: Norton, 1997.

_____. *Henry Clay: Statesman for the Union.* New York: Norton, 1991.

Renehan, Edward J., Jr. *The Secret Six: The True Tale of the Men Who Conspired with John Brown.* Columbia: University of South Carolina Press, 1997.

Reynolds, David S. *Abe: Abraham Lincoln in His Times.* New York: Penguin Press, 2020.

———. *John Brown, Abolitionist: The Man Who Killed Slavery, Sparked the Civil War, and Seeded Civil Rights.* New York: Vintage, 2005.

———. *Mightier than the Sword:* Uncle Tom's Cabin *and the Battle for America.* New York: Norton, 2011.

Rhett, Robert Barnwell. *A Fire-Eater Remembers: The Confederate Memoir of Robert Barnwell Rhett.* Edited by William C. Davis. Columbia: University of South Carolina Press, 2000.

Rusk, Jerrold G. *A Statistical History of the American Electorate.* Washington, DC: CQ Press, 2001.

Schott, Thomas F. *Alexander H. Stephens of Georgia: A Biography.* Baton Rouge: Louisiana State University Press, 1988.

Silbey, Joel H. *Martin Van Buren and the Emergence of American Popular Politics.* Lanham, MD: Rowman & Littlefield, 2002.

Simon, James F. *Lincoln and Chief Justice Taney: Slavery, Secession, and the President's War Powers.* New York: Simon & Schuster, 2006.

Sinha, Manisha. *The Counter-Revolution of Slavery: Politics and Ideology in Antebellum South Carolina.* Chapel Hill: University of North Carolina Press, 2000.

Smith, Elbert B. *Magnificent Missourian: The Life of Thomas Hart Benton.* Philadelphia: Lippincott, 1957.

Smith, William Ernest. *The Francis Preston Blair Family in Politics,* vol. 1. New York: Macmillan, 1933.

South Carolina General Assembly. *The Death and Funeral Ceremonies of John Caldwell Calhoun; Containing the Speeches, Reports, and Other Documents Connected Therewith.* Columbia: South Carolina General Assembly, 1850.

Stahr, Walter. *Salmon P. Chase: Lincoln's Vital Rival.* New York, Simon & Schuster, 2021.

———. *Seward: Lincoln's Indispensable Man.* New York: Simon & Schuster, 2012.

Stampp, Kenneth M. *America in 1857: A Nation on the Brink.* New York: Oxford University Press, 1990.

Starobin, Paul. *Madness Rules the Hour: Charleston, 1860 and the Mania for War.* New York: PublicAffairs, 2017.

Stowe, Harriet Beecher. *Uncle Tom's Cabin.* Boston: John P. Jewett, 1852.

Strozier, Charles B. *Lincoln's Quest for Union: Public and Private Meanings.* New York: Basic Books, 1982.

Swanberg, W. W. *First Blood: The Story of Fort Sumter.* New York: Scribner, 1957.

Thomas, Benjamin P. *Abraham Lincoln: A Biography.* New York: Knopf, 1952.

Treese, Joel D., ed. *Biographical Directory of the American Congress.* Alexandria, VA: CQ Staff Directories, 1997.

Van der Linden, Frank. *Lincoln: The Road to War.* Golden, CO: Fulcrum, 1998.

Van Ruymbeke, Bertrand. *From New Babylon to Eden: The Huguenots and Their*

Migration to Colonial South Carolina. Columbia: University of South Carolina Press, 2006.

Walter, Edgar. *South Carolina: A History*. Columbia: University of South Carolina Press, 1998.

Watson, Ritchie Devon, Jr. *Normans and Saxons: Southern Race Mythology and the Intellectual History of the American Civil War*. Baton Rouge: Louisiana State University Press, 2008.

Weaver, Richard M. *The Southern Tradition at Bay: A History of Postbellum Thought*. New Rochelle, NY: Arlington House, 1968.

Wellman, Paul I. *The House Divides: The Age of Jackson and Lincoln, from the War of 1812 to the Civil War*. Garden City, NY: Doubleday, 1966.

White, Laura A. *Robert Barnwell Rhett: Father of Secession*. 1931; Gloucester, MA: Peter Smith, 1965.

Wilson, Henry. *History of the Rise and Fall of the Slave Power in America*, vol. 2. Boston: James R. Osgood, 1874.

————. *History of the Rise and Fall of the Slave Power in America*, vol. 3. Boston: James R. Osgood, 1877.

Windle, Jane Mary. *Life in Washington and Life Here and There*. Philadelphia: Lippincott, 1859.

Winthrop, Robert Charles. *A Memoir of Robert C. Winthrop*. Boston: Little, Brown, 1897.

NEWSPAPERS

Boston Courier
Boston Daily Atlas
Boston Evening Transcript
Boston Statesman
Charleston Courier
Charleston Mercury
Congressional Globe
Daily Globe
Daily Union (Washington, DC)
Liberator
National Intelligencer (Washington, DC)
New York Herald
New York Times
New York Tribune
South (Richmond, VA)
Evening Star of Washington
Washington Sentinel

Weekly Union
Weekly National Intelligencer
Worcester Spy

ARTICLES AND PAPERS

Douglas, Stephen A. "The Dividing Line between Federal and Local Authority. Popular Sovereignty in the Territories." *Harper's*, September 1859.

Harmon, George D. "President James Buchanan's Betrayal of Governor Robert J. Walker of Kansas." *Pennsylvania Magazine of History and Biography* 53, no. 1 (1929): 51–91.

Johannsen, Robert W. "Stephen A. Douglas, 'Harper's Magazine,' and Popular Sovereignty." *Mississippi Valley Historical Review* 45, no. 4 (March 1959): 606–31.

La Moy, William T., and F. B. Sanborn. "The Secret Six and John Brown's Raid on Harpers Ferry: Two Letters." *New England Quarterly* 88, no. 1 (March 2015): 141–48.

Marshall, Schuyler C. "The Free Democratic Convention of 1852." *Pennsylvania History: A Journal of Mid-Atlantic Studies* 22, no. 2 (April 1955): 146–67.

Mathis, Robert Neil. "Preston Smith Brooks: The Man and His Image." *South Carolina Historical Magazine* 79, no. 4 (October 1978): 296–310.

St. Leger, John Bartholomew. "Louis Kossuth in America, 1851–1852," master's thesis, University of Richmond, 1961. Available through https://scholarship.richmond.edu/masters-thesis.

Takaki, Ronald. "The Movement to Reopen the African Slave Trade in South Carolina." *South Carolina Historical Magazine* 66, no. 1 (January 1965): 38–54.

Winkle, Kenneth J. "The Second Party System in Lincoln's Springfield." *Civil War History* 44, no. 4 (December 1998): 267–84.

WEBSITES

Abraham Lincoln Online. https://www.abrahamlincolnonline.org.

American Presidency Project. University of California, Santa Barbara. http://www.presidency.ucsb.edu.

Avalon Project: Documents in Law, History, and Diplomacy. Lillian Goldman Law Library, Yale School of Law. http://avalon.law.yale.edu.

Bartleby: Great Books Online. http://www.bartleby.com.

Boston Athenaeum. https://bostonathenaeum.org.

Brian Loveman. https://loveman.sdsu.edu.

Civil War Causes. http://civilwarcauses.org.

Dartmouth College. https://dartmouth.edu.

Digital History. https://www.digitalhistory.uh.edu.
Encyclopedia Britannica. https://www.britannica.com.
Forgotten Books. https://www.forgottenbooks.com/en/readbook.
Historic Lecompton. https://lecomptonkansas.com.
JSTOR. https://www/jstor.org.
Kansas Historical Society. https://www.kshs.org/kansaspedia.
Library of Congress. https://tile.loc.gov/storage-services/gdc/dcmsibooks.
———. https://www.loc.gov/item/18005981.
———. https://www.loc.gov/resource/rbaapc.28500.
Miller Center, University of Virginia. http://www.millercenter.org.
National Archives. https://www.archives.gov.
New York History Net. https://www.nyhistory.com/central/conflict.htm.
South Carolina Encyclopedia. https://www.scencyclopedia.org.
University of North Texas. https://texashistory.unt.edu/ark.
Wikipedia. http://en.wikipedia.org.

Illustration Credits

1. Library of Congress
2. Library of Congress
3. Library of Congress
4. Library of Congress
5. Library of Congress
6. Massachusetts Historical Society
7. Library of Congress
8. Library of Congress
9. Library of Congress
10. Yale University Library
11. Library of Congress
12. Library of Congress
13. Library of Congress
14. Library of Congress
15. Library of Congress
16. New York Public Library
17. Library of Congress
18. Francis F. Browne, *Every-Day Life of Abraham Lincoln* (New York, 1886)
19. Library of Congress
20. Library of Congress
21. The Union is Dissolved! (*Charleston Mercury* Extra Ed.) (The Gilder Lehrman Institute of American History, GLC02688).

Index